Neural Connections,
Mental Computation

Computational Models of Cognition and Perception
Editors: Jerome A. Feldman, Patrick J. Hayes, David E. Rumelhart

Parallel Distributed Processing: Explorations in the Microstructure of Cognition. Volume 1: Foundations
David E. Rumelhart, James L. McClelland, and the PDP Research Group

Parallel Distributed Processing: Explorations in the Microstructure of Cognition. Volume 2: Psychological and Biological Models
James L. McClelland, David E. Rumelhart, and the PDP Research Group

Neurophilosophy: Toward a Unified Science of the Mind-Brain
Patricia Smith Churchland

Qualitative Reasoning about Physical Systems
Daniel G. Bobrow, editor

Induction: Processes of Inference, Learning, and Memory
John H. Holland, Keith J. Holyoak, Richard E. Nisbett, and Paul R. Thagard

Production System Models of Learning and Development
David Klahr, Pat Langley, and Robert Neches, editors

Minimal Rationality
Christopher Cherniak

Vision, Brain, and Cooperative Computation
Michael A. Arbib and Allen R. Hanson, editors

Computational Complexity and Natural Language
G. Edward Barton, Jr., Robert C. Berwick, and Eric Sven Ristad

Neural Connections, Mental Computation
Lynn Nadel, Lynn A. Cooper, Peter Culicover, and R. Michael Harnish, editors

Neural Connections,
Mental Computation

Lynn Nadel, Lynn A. Cooper,
Peter Culicover, and
R. Michael Harnish, editors

A Bradford Book
The MIT Press
Cambridge, Massachusetts
London, England

This book was set in Times Roman and was printed and bound by Halliday Lithograph in the United States of America.

Library of Congress Cataloging-in-Publication Data

Neural connections, mental computation.

(Computational models of cognition and perception)
"A Bradford book."
Includes bibliographies and index.
1. Cognition—Mathematical models. 2. Cognition—Computer simulation. 3. Neural circuitry. 4. Neural computers. I. Nadel, Lynn. II. Series.
QP395.N48   1988   153.4   88-8949
ISBN 0-262-14042-X

Contents

Foreword

The problem of understanding behavior is the problem of understanding the total action of the nervous system, and vice versa. (Hebb 1949, p. xiv)

If one hopes to achieve a full understanding of a system as complicated as a nervous system, a developing embryo, a set of metabolic pathways, a bottle of gas, or even a large computer program, then one must be prepared to contemplate different kinds of explanation at different levels of description that are linked, at least in principle, into a cohesive whole, even if linking the levels in complete detail is impractical. (Marr 1982, p. 20)

After decades of productive, essentially reductionist research, neuroscience has begun to focus on the whole organism and its systematic behavior. D. O. Hebb was a pioneer in this effort. Hebb proposed that percepts, concepts, ideas, and images could all be realized in the brain in reentrant ensembles of nerve cells he called *cell assemblies* and *phase sequences*. He pointed to the dense thickets of nerve cells described by Cajal and Lorente de Nó, and to the possibility that these circuits could sustain reverberatory activity. He also suggested that *learning could occur at the synapses between nerve cells in an assembly whenever conditions of sufficient correlated activity existed;* reverberation increased the likelihood that these threshold conditions would be achieved. This learning principle, termed *Hebb's rule,* has been variously interpreted, but it seems to capture a central truth about learning in the brain. Hebb's theory was a resolutely developmental theory—his cell assemblies self-assembled during the maturation of the organism, utilizing the learning rule.

Although Hebb's thinking had a great impact, particularly in stimulating the study of development and of the learning process, his speculations about nerve-cell assemblies were rarely addressed. The techniques needed to study the relation of even a single nerve cell to behaviors that might qualify as "cognitive" have only recently been developed. Computational resources needed to simulate neurobiologically realistic "neural nets" on a reasonable scale are just becoming available. And we are only now gaining access to information about brain structure and function at the quantitative level necessary for accurate simulation of its network structure.

Hebb was concerned not only with the neural realization of cognition, but also with the very nature of cognition itself. He assumed that at a minimum the study of one would help inform our understanding of, if not completely explain, the other. He was a *cognitive neuroscientist* before that ungainly label was invented. Marr carried Hebb's program forward in his influential book on computational models of vision (1982). According to Marr, there are three levels at which any information processing system must be understood: the level of *computational theory,* the level of *representation and algorithm,* and the level of *hardware implementation.* Marr thought that "each of the three levels of description will have its place in the eventual understanding of . . . information processing, and of course they are logically and causally related" (1982, p. 25).

Reflecting both Hebb's and Marr's concern with neural and cognitive functions, cognitive science has in recent years begun to focus on a new breed of computational models. These models typically can be evaluated both in terms of their explanatory power with regard to mental faculties *and* in terms of their biological plausibility. *Connectionism* is a framework for constructing such models. Central among the claims of connectionism is the notion that it comprises a "brain style" of computation and hence is to be preferred to purely abstract computational theories, which do not seek, and could not find, support in the detailed structure of the nervous system. This claim served as the starting point for the present book.

In February of 1986 we held, in Tucson, a conference called Neural Connections and Mental Computation. The conference, which was dedicated to D. O. Hebb, had as its central goal the consideration of "parallel distributed processing" (PDP) or "connectionist" models in terms of their computational sufficiency *and* their neurobiological plausibility. Accordingly, the participants included cognitive scientists and neuroscientists. The former were to consider the nature of the phenomena that *any* theory of cognition must account for, the computational power of PDP networks, and the specific claims of connectionism; the latter were to consider PDP networks from the perspective of the nervous system (Are the assumptions of connectionism neurobiologically meaningful? What do *real* neural networks look like, and how do they function?).

Much has happened since the conference. The field we explored tentatively and very selectively has exploded. Whereas several years ago little published literature existed in this area, now there is a new journal (*Neural Nets*), and there is an active program of empirical research and theoretical development that seeks to apply connectionist principles to a wide range of phenomena (see, for example, Rumelhart, McClelland, et al., 1986). Though the conference was held some time ago, the chapters in the present volume are largely of more recent vintage. Many of the authors took the opportunity to prepare updated manuscripts reflecting their more recent thinking and the discussions that took place at the meeting. In one case, two authors combined forces to prepare a joint chapter. In another, a finished chapter was extensively revised to connect it more directly with the substance of other chapters. In all, this has produced a book that reflects the highly interactive meeting from which it stems.

The meeting was initiated by the Cognitive Sciences Committee at the University of Arizona, and was supported by that committee, by the Committee on Neuroscience, by the Department of Psychology, and, most generously, by the Sloan Foundation. Our interest as organizers reflected our own diverse backgrounds in philosophy, cognitive psychology, linguistics, and brain science—we wanted the conference to capture the interdisciplinary nature and some of the diversity of current research on cognition and its possible neural substrates. We wanted, at the same time, to focus on substantive questions: What range of phenomena must a theory of cognition explain, and what counts as an explanation? Can connectionism address these phenomena in a neurobiologically realistic manner?

In our introductory chapter we consider the various contributions to this volume, and we try to place them in a contemporary context. We briefly consider some features of the current state of connectionist thinking, and what we perceive to be its strengths and weaknesses. Interest in network computations has certainly not diminished since the meeting, and there is every reason to expect that it will continue to grow. We hope that this volume makes a contribution to that growth.

References

Hebb, D. O. 1949. *The Organization of Behavior: A Neuropsychological Theory.* New York: Wiley.

Marr, D. 1982. *Vision.* San Francisco: Freeman.

Rumelhart, D. E., J. L. McClelland, and the PDP Research Group. 1986. *Parallel Distributed Processing: Explorations in the Microstructure of Cognition.* Two volumes. Cambridge, Mass.: MIT Press. Bradford Books.

Neural Connections,
Mental Computation

Introduction: Connections and Computations	L. Nadel, L. A. Cooper, R. M. Harnish, and P. Culicover

Is connectionism a plausible alternative to traditional "symbolic" or "sentence-logic" models of cognitive function? To answer this question one must consider the psychological adequacy and the neurobiological plausibility of connectionist models. The conference from which this book emerged was focused on these two issues. In considering these general points, the participants turned their attention to a variety of quite specific questions. Our purpose in this introductory chapter is to draw out some of the themes motivating these questions and to consider how they are approached in the chapters that follow. It is not our purpose to provide a definition of connectionism (it is still defining itself), nor to portray the current state of the art (it is moving too quickly), nor even to delineate the most crucial areas yet to be resolved (chances are we do not know what they are as yet). We will remain content to let the chapters about connectionism speak for themselves.

Part I of the book is devoted to foundational issues surrounding the psychological adequacy and the computational sufficiency of connectionist models. Part II is concerned with real neural circuits and the constraints they impose on the parallel-distributed-processing theorist who wants to remain true to known brain architecture. In this introduction we try to pick out the central issues that determine the psychological adequacy and the kinds of facts about brain architecture that really do matter to PDP formalisms, and the kinds of processes we should expect to uncover if such notions as activation value, connection strength, the delta rule, and back-propagation are to find neurobiological concomitants.

Foundations

The chapters in part I share these underlying themes: the nature of connectionist models, their contrast with traditional models, and their psychological adequacy. In much of our discussion of these and related issues in this introduction, we contrast the emerging class of connectionist or PDP models with so-called traditional or conventional models. These latter comprise the domain that Dennett (1986) has called High Church Computationalism (HCC), and, as with PDP models, it is overly simple to imply that there is agreement on the details among all, or even most, of its adherents. Such matters of doctrinal debate aside, there are certain features that serve to both define and distinguish conventional and connectionist models.

As Smolensky makes clear in chapter 2, and as Fodor and Pylyshyn (1988) have emphasized, a belief in the very existence of representations is *not* one of the distinctions separating HCC from PDP models. In HCC, the term *representation* has generally been reserved for semantically interpretable symbolic elements—parts of a cognitive system of such elements whose business is to interact with and transform one another. Some of these symbols are *primitive* elements in that they are not further divisible into semantically interpretable parts. In PDP, as Smolensky makes clear, *representations are not the primitive computational elements:* rather, representations involve patterns of activity across many processing elements—the individual elements may not be semantically interpretable at all. Thus, representations are defined at a different level with respect to the primitive computational constituents in models of these two types. The most direct effect of this distinction concerns the *rules* that determine how representations are to be transformed and operated on in cognitive processing. For HCC it is a straightforward matter: In systems whose computations are governed by programs (see Stabler 1983), the rules that control information processing are themselves represented symbolically, and this puts them at the same level as, and in direct contact with, the representations they are meant to operate upon. And, most important, the rules operate on symbol structures in virtue of their form (syntax) alone, not in virtue of their semantics. For PDP, things are quite different.

There is an absence in PDP models of explicitly tokened rules to operate upon representations in virtue of their form. Such rules as there are in PDP systems are stated at the level of individual processing units, in terms of activation thresholds and connection weights; representations are realized only in specific patterns among many such units. Knowledge is embodied in "soft constraints"—excitatory and inhibitory interactions between units—realized in the network in terms of activation values and connection strengths, which yield, or "relax into" stable states of appropriately patterned activity. The principles governing activation passing are in fact principles of statistical inference; the principles governing the modification of connection strength are in fact learning and memory procedures (about which a number of the later chapters speak).

Some PDP units receive input from outside the system, some produce outputs that exit from the system, and (optionally) other *hidden* units receive and produce activation only from units within the system. The addition of these hidden units is one of the innovations that separate modern-day PDP work from the "perceptron" work of the 1950s. Powerful as they were, perceptrons were capable of partitioning only those inputs that were linearly separable; as a consequence, such problems as the "exclusive-or" (XOR) could not be solved by perceptrons. As many authors have recently shown, this is a trivially simple problem for a network with even a single hidden unit. (Actually, there is more that separates modern-day PDP from perceptrons than just this use of hidden units. There are also the techniques of "back-propagation" which have solved the problem of "credit-assignment" for multi-layer networks. This problem is at the heart of PDP models, because it relates to how the error-signal, which is the engine of the convergence process, is applied to preceding layers to reshape the pattern of activity elicited by the same input. But these issues arise only in systems with hidden units.)

Important questions arise concerning PDP-based models. Are they computationally sufficient for the modeling of interesting cognitive capacities? How do they relate to HCC models? How do they relate to brain structure and function in detail? In chapter 2, Smolensky argues that connectionist models offer an intermediate alternative located somewhere between symbolic artificial intelligence (HCC) and real neural modeling; he calls PDP the "subsymbolic paradigm." It is, in his view, more abstract than the neural level, but not as abstract as the symbolic level. The symbolic level is only a convenient approximation to actual cognitive behavior, which is more accurately described by subsymbolic connectionist systems in the same way that Newtonian descriptions are approximations to more accurate quantum-mechanical descriptions. These distinctions have further consequences; for example, the natural formalisms differ (in symbolic systems one uses algorithms; when one is dealing with subsymbols, differential equations are called for). Symbolic systems tend to have hard, not soft, constraints, and so they are said to be *brittle*. That is, they are not very good outside the exact environment for which they were developed. PDP systems, with their plenitude of very simple processing units, can be quite tolerant of faults. Much like what is seen after damage in many areas of the brain, large numbers of processing units can be removed with only gentle and gradual decline; this property is known as *graceful degradation*. Hard constraints of the sort that characterize many symbolic systems do not permit graceful degradation, because they imply that when particular units are lost, specific functions will disappear. Abrupt rather than gradual decline is what symbolic systems seem to predict.

The notion of "rule-governed" takes on rather different meanings under the two approaches. In HCC, rules are explicitly symbolized in the cognitive system (even if they are inaccessible to conscious awareness; see Kihlstrom 1987 for a discussion of "the cognitive unconscious"), and the notion of "rule-governed" is easy to define: It is behavior that occurs as a function of the operation of such an explicit rule. Connectionists eschew the use of explicit rules in explaining intuitive processes, and they generally assert that such processes unfold "as though" they were following a rule, but that this "rule-following" is only an approximation to the underlying probabilistic process. At that underlying level there are no rules, only connections, connection weights, and activation values. Smolensky concludes that the symbolic level lacks formal unity, as one might expect if it were merely an approximation to global configurations of "subsymbolic" processes.

But what may be the most important contrast between the symbolic and the subsymbolic paradigm has already been alluded to above: On the symbolic paradigm the entities that are semantically interpretable are also the entities governed by the formal principles that define the system, but on the subsymbolic paradigm this is not true. The semantically interpretable entities are patterns of activation, but the principles that define the system are stated at a lower level: activation values and connection strengths. To put it another way: On HCC certain states are semantically interpretable and causally efficacious, but in connectionist systems the units are causally efficacious and the patterns are semantically interpretable. How do these kinds of symbols combine? In HCC symbolic representations have the property of *compositionality:* As primitive units, they systematically interact (in rule-governed ways) with one another. Concatenation at the syntactic level signals composition at the semantic level. Fodor and Pylyshyn (1988) suggest that this property is absolutely central to the HCC approach. Furthermore, in connectionist models knowledge is distributed across many processing elements, and it is not clear that such representations can act "as a unit" in anything like the way intended by symbolic approaches (that is, in a way that would permit compositionality), since the rules in the PDP system are defined in terms of individual units, not in terms of the patterns across units where representations reside. Smolensky, for example, indicates that representations in PDP models interact through *superposition,* in the fashion of wave-like structures in physical systems. He is talking about PDP systems with very distributed representations where, at the limit, every unit is involved in each representation. In such cases only superposition would seem possible.

The question of just how distributed a distributed representation should be arises in this context. Feldman, in chapter 3, takes up this issue directly; he seems to suggest that superposition might not work, and that this is one reason to prefer more "compact" distributed representations. The conditions under which one might want a more or less distributed representation remain to be defined, but it seems likely that a range exists in the nervous system. In their discussion of NETtalk, a connectionist program that learns to pronounce words, Churchland and Sejnowski (chapter 1) concern themselves with the difference between local and distributed representations, and with the learning of complex tasks without explicit rule formation. What might information processing be like, they wonder, if one were to give up the "sentence-logic" approach of traditional computational theories? As we have seen, one part of the answer is that representations would be like patterns, and in their description of NETtalk Churchland and Sejnowski show how a patterned code and hidden units can accomplish apparently impressive feats of learning. (Their broader answer is that information processing should be viewed in terms of "the trajectory of a complex nonlinear dynamical system in a very high-dimensional space." It is this kind of view that has attracted scientists from the domains of physics, chemistry, and applied mathematics, where the properties of such complex systems are commanding more and more attention.)

The Treatment of Hard Cases

Although it may be productive to explore general properties of connectionist devices as models of cognition, tests of their adequacy must ultimately take the form of applications to well-understood, readily characterizable cognitive phenomena. Sejnowski and Rosenberg's NETtalk is one such application, but its claims and potential have not yet been carefully evaluated. Let us instead consider, briefly, the past-tense learning model proposed by Rumelhart and McClelland (1986). The authors claim that this PDP model can acquire rule-like behavior in regard to the generation of past-tense forms, right down to the commission of errors during "development" that mimic those seen in children. For example, the model overgeneralizes in certain cases, creating incorrect past-tense forms that nevertheless express the "rule." This model has been questioned at two levels. Pinker and Prince (1988) assert that it fails at the empirical level, making predictions that are not upheld and failing to make predictions that it should make. Lachter and Bever (1988) take a different tack: They assume that PDP models "work," and then ask how they manage to do it. Their answer is that built into the PDP nets used by Rumelhart and McClelland, and into their operations, are factors predisposing the creation of the very "rules" supposedly extracted from the corpus of material to which the network had been exposed. The whole point of the Rumelhart-McClelland model, of course, is to account for past-tense learning *without* resorting to the acquisition of explicit "rules" or the use of innate knowledge. In chapter 6, Finkel, Reeke, and Edelman assert confidently that any theory of brain function *must* account for how networks acquire their initial structure, and how this structure contributes to their specific functions.

There is an important difference between the past-tense model of Rumelhart and McClelland and the NETtalk project. The former uses only a single layer (hence no hidden units), and its limits are well known. The latter uses hidden units and a back-propagation algorithm, and the detailed objections raised against the former might not apply to the latter. Shepard, however, suggests in chapter 4 that the problem is likely to be a general one. He argues that, in the absence of some preexisting constraints, connectionist systems are necessarily limited to trivial forms of learning, and would not be capable, for example, of meaningful acts of generalization. (Much the same point is made by Finkel, Reeke, and Edelman.)

The Problem of Development

Many models work with networks that begin with exhaustive connectivity and either zero or randomly distributed initial connection weights—i.e., no initial structure whatever. This abstraction has been useful in simplifying early modeling efforts and in paving the way for the application of formalisms from physics and chemistry (Hopfield 1982), but it surely cannot be either the biological or the cognitive truth of the matter, as we have just seen. Real biological networks have structure, and this structure determines how they process inputs. Shepard's point is that, without preexisting structure of some sort, inputs would not initially be processed "correctly," and the organism would have to go through an excessively long learning period before its perceptions and cognitions about the world could be correct. In the meantime, such an organism would likely provide a meal for some other animal that came into the world better equipped to understand and make use of the world's physical regularities—an animal in which certain aspects of the spatial, temporal, and causal structure of the physical world have been internalized, permitting efficient and adaptive interactions with the environment. The excessively long developmental period forecast by Shepard is avoided in the past-tense model by implicitly importing structure into a supposedly structureless PDP system. Whether such shortcuts prove necessary in all cases remains to be seen, but the point seems clear: PDP networks have difficulty dealing with the initial development of meaningful structure in a biologically plausible way.

Such considerations have led to the dramatically different approach represented by the work of Finkel, Reeke, and Edelman. Their central theme is that cognitive function can be recast as a variety of *categorization* tasks and that a selectional model of network development is the first step in the realization of a complete theory. Their implicit claim is that *any theoretical framework concerned with cognitive function must address the issue of development before it can be taken seriously.* This is a claim we would dispute, but we needn't accept the claim to appreciate the value of an account of the development of structure in biological networks in the life of an individual organism. The model of Finkel et al. is one in which experience drives the selection of the neuronal ensembles used to code for stimuli; these neural representations are then used as inputs to higher-level ensembles generating more abstract representations. This hierarchical model is quite different from the PDP models under discussion; in general, it sticks a good deal closer to the neurobiological base.

The Case for Neurobiological Plausibility at the General Level

In chapter 5, Braitenberg considers the basic architecture of cerebral neocortex in search of clues to its function. He claims that there is essentially one cell type—the pyramidal cell—which connects to about 5,000 other pyramidal cells at weakly excitatory synapses. Interspersed among these pyramidal cells are a much smaller number of inhibitory interneurones, which exert considerably stronger effects but over a narrower range. An essential question to ask, and one that has critical implications for the actual working of any PDP network, concerns the probability that a given input will contact any particular unit once, twice, or more frequently than that. In addition, one needs to know the reliability and the strength with which an input to a unit will actually act. Such considerations critically determine the reliability and the capacity of the network. There are areas of the brain in which one can find a given input cell making a large number of synaptic contacts with the same target cell. This arrangement is quite useful when what is needed is a high probability that a given stimulus will activate a given output. However, it is definitely not what is needed for PDP networks. Braitenberg argues that in much of the cerebral cortex any given pyramidal cell makes only one contact with any other pyramidal cell, thereby making it highly unlikely that a single input could reliably trigger a specific output. As Hebb pointed out many years ago, one needs considerable convergence of inputs to activate

most cortical pyramidal cells. Although the probability of any input *A* contacting any target cell *X* might be low, these contacts are, crucially, of the
modifiable type. This means that the reliability with which input *A* could
elicit output *X* can increase with appropriate experience. In chapter 7, Lynch,
Granger, Larson, and Baudry argue that one way in which contacts between
input and target cells can be modified involves the growth of an additional
synaptic contact. Though this does not constitute the "instructional" acquisition of a new pathway, it does increase dramatically the probability that input
A will activate target *X,* because of the probabilistic nature of neurotransmitter release at any given synapse.

Braitenberg suggests that this sort of architecture is well suited for Hebbian
cell assemblies. Though the cortex is merely an associative matrix device, it
is far from simple. Most important, neurobiological PDP networks do not
appear to be unstructured matrices with unlimited powers of connectivity. Not
all possible connections within a given network start out equal; thus, certain
kinds of "associations" will be predisposed and others will be literally ruled
out. In ways we can only begin to guess, local variations in network architecture must reflect different structures of knowledge and different transforming
mechanisms; it appears, however, that little can be said about these issues as
yet from the kind of neuroanatomical perspective Braitenberg offers.

There is another issue of general neurobiological organization that bears
heavily on PDP models: the issue of the existence, nature, and function of
back-projections in the nervous system. In simple perceptron models, information about the discrepancy between actual and desired inputs could be used
as an "error signal," permitting certain forms of learning. Single-layer perceptrons had limits, however, and interest in them waned for several decades.
The recent rekindling of interest in PDP models is due in part to new possibilities of dealing with multiple-layer networks, and to the introduction of the
so-called *hidden units.* Most prominent, methods were worked out, and continue to evolve, for *back-propagating* an error signal through successive layers of hidden units. This use of re-entrant signalling confers impressive
powers on what were previously rather limited networks; Feldman expands
on some of these points in chapter 3.

In the idealized PDP networks discussed by Hopfield (1982), the assumption was of a network with complete, symmetrical connectivity and symmetrical weight changes—a set of assumptions that was obviously not chosen
for its biological plausibility. What is now known about local circuitry in
neocortex and in the hippocampal formation (discussed to some extent by
Braitenberg) suggests that matrix-like networks of neurons do exist. Further,
we now know about particular networks within which recurrent collateral

projections could accomplish some of the functions of back-projections required by PDP models. McNaughton discusses some of these possibilities in chapter 9 (see also McNaughton and Morris 1987). However, back-projections by themselves are not enough. The additional problem of *credit assignment* must be solved efficiently. What this refers to is the fact that back-propagation is a method for feeding some function of the error signal (the deviation between actual and "desired" or "teacher-defined" output) back to the units of the previous layer, and having this feedback determine the readjustment of the weights. To which input lines should this readjustment signal be applied, and with what strength? This is the problem of credit assignment—a problem that Feldman thinks Hebb's rule simply ignores. The truth, however, remains to be determined in most cases. The level of back-projections within network circuits is but one level at which back-propagation mechanisms might act. There are also projections to and from entire network systems. Thus, it is an exception when a given cortical area fails to send at least some of its output back to the cortical areas supplying it with inputs. What remains unclear (with a few exceptions) is the specificity of this feedback information, and hence the possibility that it could play some role in credit assignment.

Within the literature of neurobiology, these issues are usually approached at a somewhat different level. For example, several models of hippocampal function suggest that the hippocampus interacts with certain neocortical sites in ways that could resemble back-propagation. That is, these models (see, e.g., Squire, Cohen, and Nadel 1984; Teyler and DiScenna 1984) suggest that hippocampal activity contributes in some direct way to plasticity in neocortical sites, and that it does so over an extended period of time. The specificity of these effects is unclear; recent anatomical data suggest that the feedback from the hippocampal formation to neocortex cannot be very specific because it is "widely broadcast" across the target area (David Amaral, personal communication). This sort of information will be crucial in determining which computational model of the hippocampal formation turns out to be on the right track.

The chapters by McNaughton and O'Keefe provide two current approaches to this brain structure. Both are within the "spatial cognition" tradition; hence, both O'Keefe and McNaughton see the hippocampus as an excellent structure to model when one wishes to study a complex cognitive function in a manageable system. Both make clear that the structure of the hippocampal formation is quite compatible with a "matrix-like" system (a point noticed early on; see Marr 1971). Both also show how spatial information can be stored in a distributed fashion in a real neural system. There are important differences between McNaughton's chapter and O'Keefe's, at least in emphasis, but it will take hard empirical work to decide these issues. What is important is what they share: the demonstration that PDP-like networks may indeed exist in the nervous system, or at least in certain parts of the nervous system.

This fact, if it is a fact, is of considerable importance. The hippocampal formation has been the object of intensive investigation in the past few decades. A great deal is known about its detailed structure, its inputs and outputs, its basic neural elements, and even its dynamic functioning. What is more, extensive studies have been carried out on plasticity mechanisms at synapses in the hippocampus; the phenomenon of *long-term potentiation* (LTP), best demonstrated and most thoroughly studied in the hippocampus, is at present our most plausible candidate for a memory process. Converging evidence suggests that something like LTP is occurring at synapses in the hippocampus during certain forms of learning, possibly creating new functional ensembles to represent some aspect of the organism's experience. Thus, there exists in this neural system a set of mechanisms quite like the changes in connection weights that are so essential to PDP models. The same convergence of matrix-like structure and plasticity at the synapses attracted Lynch and his colleagues to the olfactory system, which shares these attributes with the hippocampal formation. (The latter, by the way, was once thought to be olfactory cortex itself, because of its direct connections with the olfactory system, which differ considerably from the way it receives inputs from the other sensory modalities. That there should be a special connection between the olfactory system and episode memory, which the hippocampus seems to be particularly involved with, would surely not have surprised Marcel Proust.)

Lynch et al. note that PDP models based on abstract rather than real neurons assume that connection strengths can be adjusted both upward and downward. The phenomenon of LTP indicates that upward adjustments can be seen in the brain, but there is as yet little convincing evidence of selective downward adjustments of the kind that most PDP models require. What is perhaps most interesting in the work of Lynch et al. is the fact that utilizing physiological learning rules within a network of relatively plausible neural units gives rise to several novel predictions that can be tested in the laboratory. Their chapter reports on the successful test of one such prediction, providing evidence of the potential fruits of interactions between neural and compuational approaches to mental function.

Conclusions

It seems clear from our brief survey of some of the issues that will be taken up in the book that considerable work remains to be done before there will be a direct translation between PDP models and the neurobiology from which they draw part of their general appeal. Some of this work is going to be very hard—for example, laying out the developmental principles by which PDP networks grow in the maturing organism in such a way that they have the structure required to accomplish the tasks in which they are engaged. Difficulty alone will not deter neuroscientists from exploring this approach; it is the only currently available means by which one can even hope to address the system-level phenomena that are of interest to a cognitive scientist.

On the other hand, the cognitive sufficiency of PDP systems has yet to be fully established. Shepard's claims about the need for preexisting structure pose a serious challenge to current connectionist models, which fail to embody principles sufficient to account for such initial structure. And there are other difficult problems which we have not taken up, primarily because they are not much discussed in the chapters. Perhaps the most central of these is the problem of sequential processes, which characterize much of language function but also such things as reasoning, problem solving, and inferencing. It is not at all clear how to account for such sequential capacities within the continuous, dynamical framework advanced by PDP models. This and other problems guarantee a rich source of phenomena for future researchers.

References

Dennett, D. C. 1986. The logical geography of computational approaches: A view from the East Pole. In M. Brand and R. M. Harnish (eds.), *The Representation of Knowledge and Belief* (Tucson: University of Arizona Press).

Fodor, J. A., and Z. Pylyshyn. 1988. Connectionism and cognitive architecture: a critical analysis. *Cognition* 28: 3–71.

Hopfield, J. 1982. Neural networks and physical systems with emergent collective computational abilities. *Proceedings of the National Academy of Sciences* 79: 2551–2558.

Kihlstrom, J. 1987. The cognitive unconscious. *Science* 237: 1445–1452.

Lachter, J., and T. G. Bever. 1988. The Relation between Linguistic Structure and Theories of Language Learning—A Constructive Critique of Some Connectionist Learning Models. *Cognition* 28: 195–247.

Marr, D. 1971. Simple memory: a theory for archicortex. *Philosophical Transactions of the Royal Society* B 262: 23–81.

McNaughton, B. L., and R. G. M. Morris. 1987. Hippocampal synaptic enhancement within a distributed memory system. *Trends in Neurosciences* 10: 408–415.

Pinker, S., and A. Prince. 1988. On Language and Connectionism: A Parallel Distributed Processing Model of Language Acquisition. *Cognition* 28: 73–193.

Rumelhart, D. E., and J. L. McClelland. 1986. On learning the past tenses of English verbs. In J. L. McClelland, D. E. Rumelhart, and the PDP Research Group (eds.), *Parallel Distributed Processing: Explorations in the Microstructures of Cognition,* volume 2 (Cambridge, Mass.: MIT Press—a Bradford Book).

Squire, L. R., N. J. Cohen, and L. Nadel. 1984. The medial temporal region and memory consolidation: A new hypothesis. In H. Weingartner and E. Parker (eds.), *Memory Consolidation: Towards a Psychobiology of Cognition* (Hillsdale, N.J.: Erlbaum).

Stabler, E. 1983. How are grammars represented? *Behavioral and Brain Sciences* 6: 391–421.

Teyler, T. J., and P. DiScenna. 1984. The hippocampal memory indexing theory. *Behavioral Neuroscience* 100: 147–154.

PART I

Foundations

Chapter 1

Neural Representation and Neural Computation	Patricia Smith Churchland and Terrence J. Sejnowski

The types of representation and the styles of computation in the brain appear to be very different from the symbolic expressions and logical inferences that are used in sentence-logic models of cognition. In this chapter we explore the consequences that brain-style processing may have on theories of cognition. Connectionist models are used as examples to illustrate neural representation and computation in the pronouncing of English text and in the extracting of shape parameters from shaded images. Levels of analysis are not independent in connectionist models, and the dependencies between levels provide an opportunity to co-evolve theories at all levels. This is a radical departure from the *a priori,* introspection-based strategy that has characterized most previous work in epistemology.

1 How Do We Represent the World?

The central epistemological question, from Plato on, is this: *How is representation of a world by a self possible?* So far as we can tell, there is a reality existing external to ourselves, and it appears that we do come to represent that reality, and sometimes even to know how its initial appearance to our senses differs from how it actually is. How is this accomplished, and how is knowledge possible? How is science itself possible?

The dominant philosophical tradition has been to try to resolve the epistemological puzzles by invoking mainly intuition and logic to figure out such things as the organization of knowledge, the nature of the "mirroring" of the outer world by the inner world, and the roles of reason and inference in the generation of internal models of reality. Epistemology thus pursued was the product of "pure reason," not of empirical investigation, and thus epistemological theories were believed to delimit the necessary conditions, the absolute foundations, and the incontrovertible presuppositions of human knowledge. For this *a priori* task—a task of reflective understanding and pure reason—empirical observations by psychologists and neurobiologists are typically considered irrelevant, or at least incapable of effecting any significant correction of the *a priori* conclusions. Plato, Descartes, and Kant are some of the major historical figures in that tradition; some contemporary figures are Chisholm (1966), Strawson (1966), Davidson (1974), and McGinn (1982). It is safe to say that most philosophers still espouse the *a priori* strategy to some nontrivial extent.

In a recent departure from this venerable tradition of *a priori* philosophy, some philosophers have argued that epistemology itself must be informed by the psychological and neurobiological data that bear upon how in fact we represent and model the world. First articulated in a systematic and powerful way by Quine (1960),[1] this new "naturalism" has begun to seem more in keeping with evolutionary and biological science and to promise more testable and less speculative answers.

If, as it seems, acquiring knowledge is an essentially biological phenomenon, in the straightforward sense that it is something our brains do, then there is no reason to expect that brains should have evolved to have *a priori* knowledge of the true nature of things: not of fire, not of light, not of the heart and the blood, and certainly not of knowledge or of its own microstructure and microfunction. There are, undoubtedly, innate dispositions to behave in certain ways, to believe certain things, and to organize data in certain ways, but innateness is no guarantee of truth, and it is the truth that *a priori* reflections are presumed to reveal. Innate beliefs and cognitive structure cannot be assumed to be either optimal or true, because all evolution "cares" about is that the internal models enable the species to survive. Satisficing is good enough. It is left for science to care about the truth (or perhaps empirical adequacy), and the theories science generates may well show the inadequacies of our innately specified models of external reality. Even more dramatically, they may show the inadequacy of our model of our internal reality—of the nature of our selves.

The *a priori* insights of the Great Philosophers should be understood, therefore, not as The Absolute Truth about how the mind-brain must be, but as articulations of the *assumptions* that live deep in our collective *conception* of ourselves. As assumptions, however, they may be misconceived and empirically unsound, or at least they may be open to revision in the light of scientific progress. The possibility of such revision does not entail that the assumptions are ludicrous or useless. On the contrary, they may well be very important elements in the theoretical scaffolding as neurobiology and psychology inch their way toward empirically adequate theories of mind-brain function. The methodological point is that in science we cannot proceed with no theoretical framework, so even intuitive folk theory is better than nothing as the scientific enterprise gets underway.

In addition to asking how the self can know about the external reality, Kant asked: How is representation of a *self* by a knowing self possible? One of his important ideas was that the nature of the internal world of the self is no more unmediated or *given* than is knowledge of the external world of physical objects in space and time. A modern version of this insight says: Just as the inner thoughts and experiences may represent but not *resemble* the outer reality, so the inner thoughts may represent but not resemble the inner reality of which they are the representation. This idea, taken with Quine's naturalism, implies that if we want to know how we represent the world—the external world of colored, moving objects, and the internal world of thoughts, consciousness, motives, and dreams—the scientific approach is likely to be the most rewarding. Inner knowledge, like outer knowledge, is conceptually and theoretically mediated—it is the result of complex information processing. Whether our intuitive understanding of the nature of our inner world is at all adequate is an empirical question, not an *a priori* one.

If empirical results are relevant to our understanding of how the mind-brain represents, it is also entirely possible that scientific progress on this frontier will be as revolutionary as it has been in astronomy, physics, chemistry, biology, and geology. With this observation comes the recognition that it may reconfigure our current assumptions about knowledge, consciousness, representations, and the self at least as much as Copernicus and Darwin reconfigured our dearest assumptions about the nature of the universe and our place in it. Our intuitive assumptions, and even what seems phenomenologically obvious, may be misconceived and may thus undergo reconfiguration as new theory emerges from psychology and neurobiology.

Philosophers—and sometimes psychologists, and occasionally even neuroscientists—generally make one of two responses to the naturalists' conception of the status of our self-understanding:

(1) Philosophy is an *a priori* discipline, and the fundamental conceptual truths about the nature of the mind, of knowledge, of reason, etc. will come only from *a priori* investigations. In this way, philosophy sets the bounds for science—indeed, the bounds of sense, as Strawson (1966) would put it. In a more extreme vein, some existentialist philosophers would claim that the naturalistic approach is itself symptomatic of a civilizational neurosis: the infatuation with science. On this view, the scientific approach to human nature is deeply irrational. Mandt (1986, p. 274) describes the existentialist criticism as follows: "That scientific modes of thought have become para-

digmatic indicates the degree to which traditional modes of human life and experience have disintegrated, plunging civilization into a nihilistic abyss." (2) Even if a naturalistic approach is useful for some aspects of the nature of knowledge and representation, the neurosciences in particular are largely irrelevant to the enterprise. Neuroscience may be fascinating enough in its own right, but for a variety of reasons it is irrelevant to answering the questions we care about concerning cognition, representation, intelligent behavior, learning, consciousness, and so forth. Psychology and linguistics might actually be useful in informing us about such matters, but neurobiology is just off the book.

2 Why Is Neurobiology Dismissed as Irrelevant to Understanding How the Mind Works?

2.1 The Traditional Problem
In its traditional guise, the mind-body problem can be stated thus: Are mental phenomena (experiences, beliefs, desires, etc.) actually phenomena of the physical brain? Dualists have answered No to this question. On the dualist's view, mental phenomena inhere in a special, nonphysical substance: the mind (also referred to as the soul or the spirit). The mind, on the dualist's theory, is the ghost in the machine; it is composed not of physical material obeying physical laws but of soul-stuff, or "spooky" stuff, and it operates according to principles unique to spooky stuff.

The most renowned of the substance dualists are Plato and Descartes, and, more recently, J. C. Eccles (1977) and Richard Swinburne (1986). Because dualists believe the mind to be a wholly separate kind of stuff or entity, they expect that it can be understood only in its own terms. At most, neuroscience can shed light on the *interaction* between mind and body, but not on the nature of the mind itself. Dualists consequently see psychology as essentially independent of neurobiology, which, after all, is devoted to finding out how the *physical* stuff of the nervous system works. It might be thought a bonus of dualism that it implies that to understand the mind we do not have to know much about the brain.

Materialism answers the mind-body question (Are mental states actually states of the physical brain?) in the affirmative. The predominant arguments for materialism draw upon the spectacular failure of dualism to cohere with the rest of ongoing science. And as physics, molecular biology, evolutionary biology, and neuroscience have progressed, this failure has become more rather than less marked. In short, the weight of empirical evidence is against the existence of special soul-stuff (spooky stuff). (For a more thorough dis-

cussion of the failures of substance dualism, see P. S. Churchland 1986.) Proponents of materialism include Hobbes (in the seventeenth century), B. F. Skinner (1957, 1976), J. J. C. Smart (1959), W. V. O. Quine (1960), D. C. Dennett (1978), and P. M. Churchland (1988).

Despite the general commitment to materialism, there are significant differences among materialists in addressing the central question of how best to explain psychological states. Strict behaviorists, such as Skinner, thought that explanations would take the form of stimulus-response profiles *exclusively*. Supporting this empirical hypothesis with a philosophical theory, philosophical behaviorists claimed that the mental terminology itself could be analyzed into sheerly physicalistic language about dispositions to behave. (For discussion, see P. M. Churchland 1988.) Curiously, perhaps, the behaviorists (both empirical and philosophical) share with the dualists the conviction that it is not necessary to understand the workings of the brain in order to explain intelligent behavior. On the behaviorists' research ideology, again we have a bonus: In order to explain behavior, *we do not have to know anything about the brain*.

In contrast to behaviorism, identity theorists (Smart 1959; Enc 1983) claimed that mental states, such as visual perceptions, pains, beliefs, and drives, were in fact identical to states of the brain, though it would of course be up to neuroscience to discover precisely what brain sites were in fact identical to what mental states. On the research ideology advocated by these materialists, explanation of behavior will have to refer to inner representations and hence to what the brain is doing.

2.2 The Contemporary Problem: Theory Dualism

Many philosophers who are materialists to the extent that they doubt the existence of soul-stuff nonetheless believe that psychology ought to be essentially autonomous from neuroscience, and that neuroscience will not contribute significantly to our understanding of perception, language use, thinking, problem solving, and (more generally) cognition. Thus, the mind-body problem in its contemporary guise is this: Can we get a *unified* science of the mind-brain? Will psychological theory reduce to neuroscience?

A widespread view (which we call Theory Dualism) answers No to the above question. Typically, three sorts of reasons are offered:

• *Neuroscience is too hard.* The brain is too complex; there are too many neurons and too many connections, and it is a hopeless task to suppose we can ever understand complex higher functions in terms of the dynamics and organization of neurons.

- *The argument from multiple instantiability.* Psychological states are functional states and, as such, can be implemented (instantiated) in diverse machines (Putnam 1967; Fodor 1975; Pylyshyn 1984). Therefore, no particular psychological state, such as believing that the earth is round or that $2 + 2 = 4$, can be identified with exactly this or that machine state. So no functional (cognitive) process can be reduced to the behavior of particular neuronal systems.
- *Psychological states have intentionality.* That is, they are identified in terms of their semantic content; they are "about" other things; they represent things; they have logical relations to one another. We can think about objects in their absence, and even of nonexistent objects. For example, if someone has the belief that Mars is warmer than Venus, then that psychological state is specified as the state it is in terms of the sentence "Mars is warmer than Venus", which has a specific meaning (its content) and which is logically related to other sentences. It is a belief *about* Mars and Venus, but it is not caused by Mars or Venus. Someone might have this belief because he was told, or because he deduced it from other things he knew. In cognitive generalizations states are related semantically and logically, whereas in neurobiological generalizations states can only be *causally* related. Neurobiological explanations cannot be sensitive to the logical relations between the contents of cognitive states, or to meaning or "aboutness." They respond only to *causal* properties. Neurobiology, therefore, cannot do justice to cognition, and thus no reduction is possible.

2.3   What Is Wrong with Theory Dualism?

In opposition to theory dualists, reductionists think we ought to strive for an integration of psychological and neurobiological theory. Obviously, a crucial element in the discussion concerns what is meant by "reduction"; hence, part of what must first be achieved is a proper account of what sort of business inter-theoretic reduction is.

Roughly, the account is this: Reductions are *explanations* of phenomena described by one theory in terms of the phenomena described by a more basic theory. Reductions typically involve the co-evolution of theories over time, and as they co-evolve one theory is normally revised, corrected, and modified by its co-evolutionary cohort theory at the other level. This revisionary interaction can, and usually does, go both ways: from the more basic to the less basic theory and vice versa. It is important to emphasize the modification to theories as they co-evolve, because sometimes the modification is radical and entails massive reconfiguration of the very categories used to describe the phenomena. In such an event, the very data to be explained may come to be redescribed under pressure from the evolving theories. Examples of categories that have undergone varying degrees of revision, from the minor to the radical, include impetus, caloric, gene, neuron, electricity, instinct, life, and very recently, excitability (in neurons) (Schaffner 1976; P. M. Churchland 1979; Hooker 1981).

Because reductionism is frequently misunderstood, it is necessary to be explicit about what is *not* meant. First, seeking reductions of macro-level theory to micro level does not imply that one must first know everything about the elements of the micro theory before research at the macro level can be usefully undertaken. Quite the reverse is advocated—research should proceed at all levels of the system, and co-evolution of theory may enhance progress at all levels. Data from one level *constrain* theorizing at that level and at other levels. Additionally, the reduction of theories does *not* mean that the reduced phenomena somehow disappear or are discredited. The theory of optics was reduced to the theory of electromagnetic radiation, but light itself did not disappear, nor did it become disreputable to study light at the macro level. Nor was the reduced theory cast out as useless or discredited; on the contrary, it was and continues to be useful for addressing phenomena at a higher level of description. As for the phenomenon, it is what it is, and it continues to be whatever it is as theories are reduced or abandoned. Whether a category is ultimately rejected or revised depends on its scientific integrity, and that is, of course, determined empirically. (For more detail on intertheoretic reduction, see P. S. Churchland 1986.)

Given this brief account of reduction as a backdrop, an outline of how the reductionist answers the theory dualist goes as follows:

• Neuroscience *is* hard, but with many new techniques now available, an impressive body of data is available to constrain our theories, and a lot of data are very suggestive as to how neural networks function. (See Sejnowski and Churchland, in press.) We have begun to see the shape of neurobiological answers to functional questions, such as how information is stored, how networks learn, and how networks of neurons represent.

• High-level states are multiply instantiable. So what? If, in any given species, we can show that particular functional states are identical to specific neuronal configurations (for example, that being in REM sleep is having a specified neuronal state, or that one type of learning involves changing synaptic weights according to a Hebb rule), that will be sufficient to declare a reduction relative to that domain (Richardson 1979; Enc 1983; P. S. Churchland 1986; section 3 below). Very pure philosophers who cannot bring themselves to call these perfectly respectable domain-relative explanations "reductions" are really just digging in on who gets to use the word. Moreover, it should be emphasized that the explanation of high-level cognitive phenomena will not be achieved directly in terms of phenomena at the lowest level of nervous-system organization, such as synapses and individual neurons. Rather, the explanation will refer to properties at higher structural levels, such as networks or systems. Functional properties of networks and systems will be explained by reference to properties at the next level down, and so on. What we envision is a chain of explanations linking higher to next-lower levels, and so on down the ladder of structural levels. (See Sejnowski and Churchland, in press.) Aspects of individual variation at the synaptic and cellular levels are probably invisible at the systems level, where similarity of larger-scale emergent properties, such as position in a high-dimensional parameter space, is critical in identifying similarity of information-processing function (Sejnowski, Koch, and Churchland 1988). A theory of how states in a nervous system represent or model the world will need to be set in the context of the evolution and development of nervous systems, and will try to explain the interactive role of neural states in the ongoing neuro-cognitive economy of the system. Nervous systems do not represent all aspects of the physical environment; they selectively represent information a species needs, given its environmental niche and its way of life. Nervous systems are programmed to respond to certain selected features, and within limits they learn other features through experience by encountering examples and generalizing. Cognitive neuroscience is now beginning to understand how this is done (Livingston 1988; Goldman-Rakic 1988; Kelso, Ganong, and Brown 1986). Although the task is difficult, it now seems reasonable to assume that the "aboutness" or "meaningfulness" of representational states is not a spooky relation but a neurobiological relation. As we come to understand more about the dynamical properties of networks, we may ultimately be able to generate a theory of how human language is learned and represented by our sort of nervous system, and thence to explain language-dependent kinds of meaning.

Because this answer is highly cryptic and because intentionality has often seemed forever beyond the reach of neurobiology, the next section will focus on intentionality: the theory dualist's motivation, and the reductionist's strategy.

3 Levels, Intentionality, and the Sentence-Logic Model of the Mind

3.1 Sentential Attitudes and the Computer Metaphor

Two deep and interrelated assumptions concerning the nature of cognition drive the third anti-reductionist argument:

• Cognition essentially involves representations and computations. Representations are, in general, symbolic structures, and computations are, in general, rules (such as rules of logic) for manipulating those symbolic structures.

• A good model for understanding mind-brain functions is the computer— that is, a machine based on the same logical foundations as a Turing machine and on the von Neumann architecture for a digital computer. Such machines are ideally suited for the manipulation of symbols according to rules. The computer metaphor suggests that the mind-brain, at the information-processing level, can be understood as a kind of digital computer; the problem for cognitive psychology is to determine the program that our brains run.

The motivating vision here is that cognition is to be modeled largely on language and logical reasoning; having a thought is, functionally speaking, having a sentence in the head, and thinking is, functionally speaking, doing logic, or at least running on procedures very like logic. Put this baldly, it may seem faintly ridiculous, but the theory is supported quite plausibly by the observation that beliefs, thoughts, hopes, desires, and so forth are essential in the explanation of cognition, and that such states are irreducibly semantic because they are identified in virtue of their content sentences. That is, such states are always and essentially beliefs that p, thoughts that p, or desires that p, where for p we substitute the appropriate sentence, such as "Nixon was a Russian spy" or "Custard is made with milk". Such cognitive states—the so-called sentential attitudes—are the states they are in virtue of the sentences that specify what they are about. Moreover, a content sentence stands in specific logical and semantic relations to other sentences. The state transitions are determined by semantic and logical relations between the content sentences, not by casual relations among states neurobiologically described. Thus, cognitive states have *meaning* (i.e. content, or intentionality), and it might be argued that it is precisely in virtue of their meaningfulness that they play the role in cognition that they do.

The fundamental conception is, accordingly, well and truly rooted in folk psychology, the body of concepts and everyday lore by means of which we routinely explain one another's behavior by invoking sentential attitudes

(Stich 1983; P. M. Churchland 1988)—e.g., Smith paid for the vase because he believed that his son had dropped it and he feared that the store owner would be angry. In these sorts of intentional explanations, the basic unit of representation is the sentence, and state transitions are accomplished through the following of rules: deductive inference, inductive inference, and assorted other rules.

Extending the framework of folk psychology to get an encompassing account of cognition in general, this approach takes it that thinking, problem solving, language use, perception, and so forth will be understood as we determine the sequence of sentences corresponding to the steps in a given information-processing task; i.e., as we understand the mechanics of sentence crunching. According to this research paradigm, known as sententialism, it is the task of cognitive science to figure out what programs the brain runs, and neuroscience can then check these top-down hypotheses against the wetware to see if they are generally possible. (See especially Fodor 1975, Fodor 1981, and Pylyshyn 1984.)

3.2 Is Cognition Mainly Symbol Manipulation in the Language of Thought?

Although this view concerning the nature of cognition and the research strategy for studying cognition may be appealing (where much of the appeal is derived from the comfortable place found for folk psychology), it suffers from major defects. Many of these defects have been discussed in detail by Anderson and Hinton (1981), by P. S. Churchland (1986), and in various chapters of McClelland and Rumelhart 1986. A summary will call them to mind:

• Many cognitive tasks, such as visual recognition and answering simple true-or-false questions, can be accomplished in about half a second. Given what we know about conduction velocities and synaptic delays in neurons, this allows about 5 milliseconds per computational step, which means that there is time for only about 100 steps. For a sequential program run on a conventional computer, 100 steps is not going to get us remotely close to task completion. Feldman and Ballard (1982) call this the hundred-step rule.
• Anatomically and physiologically, the brain is a parallel system, not a sequential von Neumann machine. The neural architecture is highly interconnected. Neurons such as Purkinje cells may have upwards of 80,000 input connections, and neurons in cerebral cortex can have upwards of 10,000

output connections (Anderson and Hinton 1981; Pellionisz and Llinas 1982, Sejnowski 1986).

• However information is stored in nervous systems, it appears to be radically unlike information storage in a digital computer, where storage and processing are separated and items are stored in memory according to addressable *locations*. In nervous systems, information seems to be stored in the connections between the same neurons that process the information. There does not appear to be a distinct storage location for each piece of stored information, and information is content addressable rather than location addressable. Information storage is probably at least somewhat distributed rather than punctate, since memories tend to be degraded with damage to the system rather than selectively wiped out one by one.

• A task may fall gracefully to one architecture and not to another. Certain kinds of tasks, such as numerical calculation, fall gracefully to a von Neumann architecture, but others, such as learning or associative memory, do not. Things we humans find effortless (such as facial recognition and visual perception) are tasks which artificial intelligence has great difficulty simulating on a von Neumann architecture, whereas things we find "effortful" (such as simple proofs in the propositional calculus or mathematical calculations) are straightforward for a digital computer (Anderson and Hinton 1981; Rumelhart, Hinton, and McClelland 1986). This suggests that the computational style of nervous systems may be very unlike that suited to von Neumann architectures.

• The hardware-software analogy fails for many reasons, the most prominent of which are that nervous systems are plastic and that neurons continually change as we grown and learn. Related, perhaps, is the observation that nervous systems degrade gracefully and are relatively fault tolerant. A von Neumann machine is rigid and fault intolerant, and a breakdown of one tiny component disrupts the machine's performance.

• The analogy between levels of description in a conventional computer (such as the hardware-software distinction) and levels of explanation in nervous systems may well be profoundly misleading. Exactly how many levels of organization we need to postulate in order to understand nervous-system function is an empirical question, and it may turn out that there are many levels between the molecular and the behavioral. In nervous systems we may already discern as distinct descriptive levels the molecule, the membrane, the cell, the circuit, networks, maps, brain systems, and several levels of behavior (from the reflexive to the highest levels of cognition). Other levels may come to be described as more is discovered about the nature of nervous systems. As is discussed below, the properties at one level may constrain the kind of properties realizable at another level.

• Nonverbal animals and infraverbal humans present a major problem for the sentence-logic theory of cognition: How is their cognition accomplished? On the sentence-logic theory of cognition, either their cognition resembles the human variety (and hence involves symbol manipulation according to rules, and a language of thought replete with a substantial conceptual repertoire) or their cognitive processes are entirely different from the usual human ones. Neither alternative is remotely credible. The first lacks any evidence. At best, its defense is circular; it helps to save the theory. The second alternative entails a radical discontinuity in evolution—sufficiently radical that language-of-thought cognition is a bolt from the blue. This implies that evolutionary biology and developmental neurobiology are mistaken in some fundamental respects. Since neither alternative can be taken seriously, the hypothesis itself has diminished credibility.

If cognition, then, is *not,* in general, to be understood on the sentence-logic model, the pressing questions then are these: How *does* the brain represent? How do nervous systems model the external world of objects in motion and the internal world of the nervous system itself? And when representations do stand in semantic and logical relations to one another, how is this achieved by neural networks? How is the semantic and logical structure of language—as we both comprehend and speak—represented in the brain? According to the rejected model, we postulate an internal organization—a language of thought—with the very same structure and organization as language. But if that model is rejected, what do we replace it with?

These are, of course, *the* central questions, and getting answers will not be easy. But the difficulty should not make the language-of-thought hypothesis more appealing. In certain respects, the current scientific state of a general theory of representation is analogous to the science of embryology in the nineteenth century. The development of highly structured, complex, fully formed organisms from eggs and sperm is a profoundly amazing thing. Faced with this mystery, some scientists concluded that the only way to explain the emergence of a fully structured organism at birth was to assume that the structure was already there. Hence the homuncular theory of reproduction, which claimed that a miniature but complete human already exists in the sperm and merely expands during its tenure in the womb.

We now know that there *is* structure in the sperm (and the egg)—not in the form of a miniature, fully structured organism, but mainly in the form of DNA—a molecule that looks not at *all* like a fully formed human. Thus, the structure of the cause does not resemble the structure of the effect. Accordingly, the homuncular theorists were right in supposing that the highly structured neonate does not come from *nothing,* but they were wrong in looking for a structural resemblance between cause and effect. It was, of course, terribly hard to imagine the nature of the structural organization that enables development yet in no way resembles the final product. Only through molecular biology and detailed work in embryology have we begun to understand how one kind of structure can, through intermediate mechanisms, yield another, very different kind of structure.

The parallel with cognitive neurobiology is this: The neuronal processes underlying cognition have a structure of some kind, but almost certainly it will not, in general, look anything like the semantic/logic structure visible in overt language. The organizational principles of nervous systems are what permit highly complex, structured patterns of behavior, for it is certain that the behavioral structure does not emerge magically from neuronal chaos. As things stand, it is very hard to imagine what those organizational principles could look like, and, just as in genetics and embryology, we can find answers only by framing hypotheses and doing experiments.

Instead of starting from the old sentence-logic model, we model information processing in terms of *the trajectory of a complex nonlinear dynamical system in a very high-dimensional space.* This structure does not resemble sentences arrayed in logical sequences, but it is potentially rich enough and complex enough to yield behavior capable of supporting semantic and logical relationships. We shall now explore what representing looks like in a particular class of nonlinear dynamical systems called connectionist models.

4 Representation in Connectionist Models

As the name implies, a connectionist model is characterized by connections and differential strengths of connection between processing units. Processing units are meant to be rather like neurons, and communicate with one another by signals (such as firing rate) that are numerical rather than symbolic. Connectionist models are designed to perform a task by specifying the architecture: the number of units, their arrangement in layers and columns, the patterns of connectivity, and the weight or strength of each connection (figures 1 and 2). These models have close ties with the computational level on which the task is specified, and with the implementation level on which the task is physically instantiated (Marr 1982). This species of network models should properly be considered a class of algorithms specified at various levels of organization—in some cases at the small-circuit level, in other cases at the

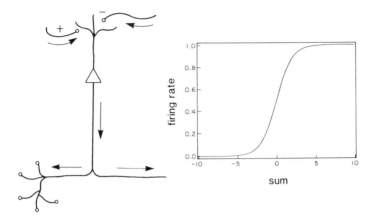

Figure 1

Left: Schematic model of a neuron-like processing unit that receives synapse-like inputs from other processing units. Right: Nonlinear sigmoid-shaped transformation between summed inputs and the output "firing rate" of a processing unit. The output is a continuous value between 0 and 1.

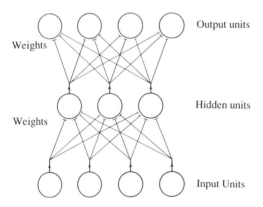

Figure 2

Schematic model of a three-layered network. Each input unit makes connections with each of the hidden units on the middle layer, which in turn projects to each of the output units. This is a feedforward architecture in which information provided as an input vector flows through the network, one layer at a time, to produce an output vector. More complex architectures allow feedback connections from an upper to a lower layer and lateral interactions between units within a layer.

system level. Both the task description and the neural embodiment are, however, crucially important in constraining the class of networks that will be explored. On the one hand the networks have to be powerful enough to match human performance of the computational tasks, and on the other hand they have to be built from the available materials. In the case of the brain, that means neurons and synapses; in the case of network models, that means neuron-like processing units and synapse-like weights.

Digital computers are used to simulate neural networks, and the network models that can be simulated on current machines are tiny in comparison with the number of synapses and neurons in the mammalian brain. The networks that have been constructed should be understood, therefore, as small parts of a more complex processing system whose general configuration has not yet been worked out, rather than as simulations of a whole system. To avoid misunderstanding, it should be emphasized that connectionist models cannot yet support a full cognitive system. To begin to reach that goal will require both a computing technology capable of supporting more detailed simulations and a more complete specification of the nervous system.

Granting these limitations, we may nonetheless be able to catch a glimpse of what representations might look like within the parallel-style architecture of the brain by taking a look inside a connectionist network. The place to look is in the dynamics of the system; that is, in the patterns of activity generated by the system of interconnected units. This approach has its roots in the work of previous generations of researchers—primarily the gestalt school of psychology and D. O. Hebb (1949), who developed many ideas about learning and representation in neural assemblies. Only recently, however, has sufficient computer power been available to explore the consequences of these ideas by direct simulation, since the dynamics of massively parallel nonlinear networks is highly computation intensive. Parallel-network models are now being used to explore many different aspects of perception and cognition (McClelland and Rumelhart 1986; Feldman and Ballard 1982; *Cognitive Science,* volume 9, special issue) but in this chapter we shall focus on two representative examples. The first is NETtalk, perhaps the most complex network model yet constructed, which learns to convert English text to speech sounds (Sejnowski and Rosenberg 1987, 1988). The second is a network model that computes surface curvatures of an object from its gray-level input image. NETtalk will be used primarily to illustrate two things: how a network can learn to perform a very complex task without symbols and without rules to manipulate symbols, and the differences between local and distributed representations.

Connectionist models can be applied on a large scale to model whole brain systems or, on a smaller scale, to model particular brain circuits. NETtalk is on a large scale, since the problem of pronunciation is constrained mainly by the abstract cognitive considerations and since its solution in the brain must involve a number of systems, including the visual system, the motor-articulatory system, and the language areas. The second example is more directly related to smaller brain circuits used in visual processing; the representational organization achieved by the network model can be related to the known representational organization in visual cortex.

In the models reviewed here, the processing units sum the inputs from connections with other processing units, each input weighted by the strength of the connection. The output of each processing unit is a real number that is a nonlinear function of the linearly summed inputs. The output is small when the inputs are below threshold, and it increases rapidly as the total input becomes more positive. Roughly, the activity level can be considered the sum of the postsynaptic potentials in a neuron, and the output can be considered its firing rate (figure 1).

4.1 Speech Processing: Text to Speech

In the simplest NETtalk system[2] there are three layers of processing units. The first level receives as input letters in a word; the final layer yields the elementary sounds, or phonemes (table 1); and an intervening layer of "hidden units," which is fully connected with the input and output layers, performs the transformation of letters to sounds (figure 3). On the input layer, there is *local representation* with respect to letters because single units are used to represent single letters of the alphabet. Notice, however, that the representation could be construed as *distributed* with respect to *words,* inasmuch as each word is represented as a pattern of activity among the input units. Similarly, each phoneme is represented by a pattern of activity among the output units, and phonemic representation is therefore distributed. But each output unit is coded for a particular *distinctive feature* of the speech sound, such as whether the phoneme was voiced, and consequently each unit is local with respect to distinctive features.

NETtalk has 309 processing units and 18,629 connection strengths (weights) that must be specified. The network does not have any initial or built-in organization for processing the input or (more exactly) mapping letters onto sounds. All the structure emerges during the training period. The values of the weights are determined by using the "back-propagation" learning algorithm developed by Rumelhart, Hinton, and Williams (1986). (For a reviews of network learning algorithms, see Hinton 1988 and Sejnowski 1988.) The strategy exploits the calculated error between the *actual* values of

Table 1

Symbols for phonemes used in NETtalk.

Symbol	Phoneme	Symbol	Phoneme
/a/	f*a*ther	/D/	*th*is
/b/	*b*et	/E/	b*e*t
/c/	b*ou*ght	/G/	si*ng*
/d/	*d*ebt	/I/	b*i*t
/e/	b*a*ke	/J/	*g*in
/f/	*f*in	/K/	se*x*ual
/g/	*g*uess	/L/	bott*le*
/h/	*h*ead	/M/	absy*m*
/i/	P*e*te	/N/	butto*n*
/k/	*K*en	/O/	b*oy*
/l/	*l*et	/Q/	*qu*est
/m/	*m*et	/R/	b*ir*d
/n/	*n*et	/S/	*sh*in
/o/	b*oa*t	/T/	*th*in
/p/	*p*et	/U/	b*oo*k
/r/	*r*ed	/W/	b*ou*t
/s/	*s*it	/X/	e*x*cess
/t/	*t*est	/Y/	c*u*te
/u/	l*u*te	/Z/	lei*s*ure
/v/	*v*est	/@/	b*a*t
/w/	*w*et	/!/	*N*azi
/x/	*a*bout	/#/	e*x*amine
/y/	*y*et	/*/	*o*ne
/z/	*z*oo	/|/	log*i*c
/A/	b*i*te	/^/	b*u*t
/C/	*ch*in		

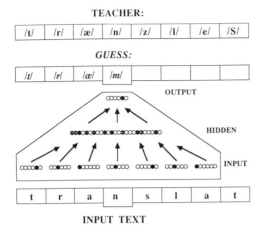

Figure 3
Schematic drawing of the NETtalk network architecture. A window of letters in an
English text is fed to an array of 203 input units arranged in 7 groups of 29 units
each. Information from these units is transformed by an intermediate layer of 80
hidden units to produce a pattern of activity in 26 output units. The connections in
the network are specified by a total of 18,629 weight parameters (including a variable threshold for each unit). During the training, information about the desired output provided by the Teacher is compared with the actual output of the network, and
the weights in the network are changed slightly so as to reduce the error.

the processing units in the output layer and the *desired* values, which is provided by a training signal. The resulting error signal is propagated from the
output layer backward to the input layer and used to adjust each weight in
the network. The network learns, as the weights are changed, to minimize
the mean squared error over the training set of words. Thus, the system can
be characterized as following a path in weight space (the space of all possible
weights) until it finds a minimum (figure 4). The important point to be illustrated, therefore, is this: The network processes information by nonlinear
dynamics, not by manipulating symbols and accessing rules. It learns by
gradient descent in a complex interactive system, not by generating new rules
(Hinton and Sejnowski 1986).

The issue that we want to focus on next is the structural organization that
is "discovered" by the network, in virtue of which it succeeds in converting
letters to phonemes and manages to pronounce, with few errors, the many
irregularities of English. If there are no rules in the network, how is the
transformation accomplished? Since a trained network can generalize quite
well to new words, some knowledge about the pattern of English pronuncia-

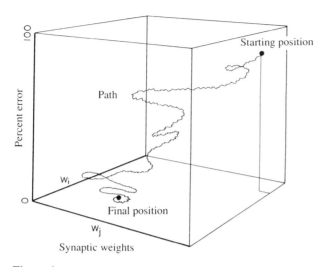

Figure 4
Schematic drawing of a path followed in weight space as the network finds a minimum of the average error over the set of training patterns. Only two weights out of many thousands are shown. The learning algorithm only ensures convergence to a local minimum, which is often a good solution. Typically, many sets of weights are good solutions, so the network is likely to find one of them from a random starting position in weight space. The learning time can be reduced by starting the network near a good solution; for example, the pattern of connections can be limited to a geometry that reduces the number of variable weights that must be searched by gradient descent.

tion must be contained inside the network. Although a representational organization was imposed on the input and output layers, the network had to create new, internal representations in the hidden layer of processing units. How did the network organize its "knowledge"? To be more accurate: How did the equivalence class of networks organize its knowledge? (Each time the network was started from a random set of weights, a different network was generated.)

The answers were not immediately available, because a network does not leave an explanation of its travels through weight space, nor does it provide a decoding scheme when it reaches a resting place. Even so, some progress was made by measuring the activity pattern among the hidden units for specific inputs. In a sense, this test mimics at the modeling level what neurophysiologists do at the cellular level when they record the activity of a single neuron to try to find the effective stimulus that makes it respond. NETtalk is a fortunate "preparation," inasmuch as the number of processing units is relatively small, and it is possible to determine the activity patterns of all the units for all possible input patterns. These measurements, despite the relatively small network, did create a staggering amount of data, and then the puzzle was this: How does one find the order in all this data?

For each set of input letters, there is a pattern of activity among the hidden units (figure 5). The first step in the analysis of the activity of the hidden units was to compute the average level of activity for each letter-to-sound correspondence. For example, all words with the letter c in the middle position yielding the hard-c sound /k/ were presented to the network, and the average level of activity was calculated. Typically, about 15 of the 80 hidden units

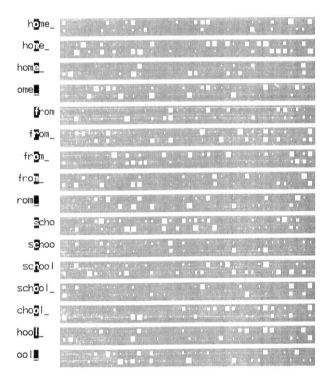

Figure 5
Levels of activation in the layer of hidden units for a variety of words. The input string in the window of seven letters is shown to the left, with the target letter emphasized. The output from the network is the phoneme that corresponds to the target letter. The transformation is accomplished by 80 hidden units, whose activity levels are shown to the right in two rows of 40 units each. The area of each white square is proportional to the activity level. Most units have little or no activity for a given input, but a few are highly activated.

were very highly activated, and the rest of the hidden units had little or no activity. This procedure was repeated for each of the 79 letter-to-sound correspondences. The result was 79 vectors, each vector pointing in a different direction in the 80-dimensional space of average hidden-unit activities. The next step was to explore the relationship among the vectors in this space by cluster analysis. It is useful to conceive of each vector as the internal code that is used to represent a specific letter-to-sound correspondence; consequently, those vectors that clustered close together would have similar codes.

Remarkably, all the vectors for vowel sounds clustered together, indicating that they were represented in the network by patterns of activity in units that were distinct from those representing the consonants (which were themselves clustered together). (See figure 6.) Within the vowels, all the letter-to-sound correspondences that used the letter a were clustered together, as were the vectors of e, i, o, and u and the relevant instances of y. This was a very robust organizational scheme that occurred in all the networks that were analyzed, differences in starting weights notwithstanding. The coding scheme for consonants was more variable from network to network, but as a general rule the clustering was based more on similarities in sounds than on letters. Thus, the labial stops /p/ and /b/ were very close together in the space of hidden-unit activities, as were all the letter-to-sound correspondences that result in the hard-c sound /k/.

Other statistical techniques, such as factor analysis and multidimensional scaling, are also being applied to the network, and activity patterns from individual inputs, rather than averages over classes, are also being studied (Rosenberg 1988). These statistical techniques are providing us with a detailed description of the representation for single inputs as well as classes or input-output pairs.

Several aspects of NETtalk's organization should be emphasized:

• The representational organization visible in the trained-up network is not programmed or coded into the network; it is found by the network. In a sense it "programs" itself, by virtue of being connected in the manner described and having weights changed by experience according to the learning algorithm. The dynamical properties of this sort of system are such that the network will settle into the displayed organization.

• The network's representation for letter-to-sound correspondences is neither local nor completely distributed; it is somewhere in between. The point is, each unit participates in more than one correspondence, and so the representation is not local, but since it does not participate in all correspondences, the representation is not completely distributed either.

Figure 6
Hierarchical clustering of hidden units for letter-to-sound correspondences. The vectors of average hidden unit activity for each correspondence ('1-p' for letter l and phoneme p) were successively merging from right to left in the binary tree. The scale at the top indicates the Euclidean distance between the clusters. (From Sejnowski and Rosenberg 1987.)

• The representation is a property of the collection of hidden units, and does not resemble sentence-logic organization.

• The organization is structured, which suggests that emergent subordinate and superordinate relations might be a general principle of network organization that could be used as input for other networks assigned other tasks if NETtalk were embedded in a larger system of networks.

• General properties of the hierarchical organization of letter-to-sound correspondences emerged only at the level of groups of units. This organization was invariant across all the networks created from the same sample of English words, even where the processing units in distinct networks had specialized for a different aspect of the problem.

• Different networks created by starting from different initial conditions all achieved about the same level of performance, but the detailed response properties of the individual units in the networks differed greatly. Nonetheless, all the networks had similar functional clusterings for letter-to-sound correspondence (figure 1.6). This suggests that single neurons code information relative to other neurons in small groups or assemblies (Hebb 1949).

The representational organization in NETtalk may illustrate important principles concerning network computation and representation, but what do they tell us about neural representations? Some of the principles uncovered might be generally applicable to a wide class of tasks, but it would be surprising if the details of the model bore any significant resemblance to the way reading skills are represented in the human nervous system. NETtalk is more of a demonstration of certain network capacities and properties than a faithful model of some subsystem of the brain, and it may be a long time before data concerning the human neurobiology of reading become available. Nevertheless, the same network techniques that were used to explore the language domain can be applied to problems in other domains, such as vision, where much more is known about the anatomy and the physiology.

4.2 Visual Processing: Computing Surface Curvature from Shaded Images

The general constraints from brain architecture touched on in section 3 should be supplemented, wherever possible, by more detailed constraints from brain physiology and anatomy. Building models of real neural networks is a difficult task, however, because essential knowledge about the style of computation in the brain is not yet available (Sejnowski 1986). Not only is the fine detail (such as the connectivity patterns in neurons in cerebral cortex) not known, but even global-level knowledge specifying the flow of information through different parts of the brain during normal function is limited. Even if more neurophysiological and neuroanatomical detail were available, current computing technology would put rather severe limits on how much detail could be captured in a simulation. Nevertheless, the same type of network model used in NETtalk could be useful in understanding how information is coded within small networks confined to cortical columns. The processing units in this model will be identified with neurons in the visual cortex.

Ever since Hubel and Wiesel (1962) first reported that single neurons in the cat visual cortex respond better to oriented bars of light and to dark/light edges than to spots of light, it has been generally assumed, or at least widely hoped, that the function of these neurons is to detect boundaries of objects in the world. In general, the inference from a cell's response profile to its function in the wider information-processing economy is intuitively very plausible, and if we are to have any hope of understanding neural representations we need to start in an area—such as visual cortex—where it is possible to build on an impressive body of existing data. The trouble is, however, that many functions are consistent with the particular response properties of a neuronal population. That a cell responds optimally to an oriented bar of light is compatible with its having lots of functions other than detecting object boundaries, though the hypothesis that it serves to detect boundaries does tend to remain intuitively compelling. To see that our intuitions might really mislead us as we try to infer function from response profiles, it would be useful if we could demonstrate this point concretely. In what follows we shall show how the same response properties could in fact serve in the processing of visual information about the regions of a surface between boundaries rather than about the boundaries themselves.

Boundaries of objects are relatively rare in images, yet the preponderance of cells in visual cortex respond preferentially to oriented bars and slits. If we assume that all those cells are detecting boundaries, then it is puzzling that there should be so many cells whose sole function is to detect boundaries when there are not many boundaries to detect. It would, therefore, seem wasteful if, of all the neurons with oriented fields, only a small fraction carried useful information about a particular image. Within their boundaries, most objects have shaded or textured surfaces that will partially activate these neurons. The problem, accordingly, is this: Can the information contained in a population of partially activated cortical neurons be used to compute useful information about the three-dimensional surfaces between the boundaries of objects in the image?

One of the primary properties of a surface is its curvature. Some surfaces, such as the top of a table, are flat, and have no intrinsic curvature. Other surfaces, such as cylinders and spheres, are curved, and around each point on a surface the degree of curvature can be characterized by the direction along the surface of maximum and minimum curvature. It can be shown that these directions are always at right angles to each other, and the values are called the *principle curvatures* (Helbert and Cohn-Vossen 1952). The principal curvatures and the orientation of the axes provide a complete description of the local curvature.

One problem with extracting the principal curvatures from an image is that the gray-level shading depends on many factors, such as the direction of illumination, the reflectance of the surface, and the orientation of the surface relative to the viewer. Somehow our visual system is able to separate these variables and to extract information about the shape of an object independent of these other variables. Pentland (1984) has shown that a significant amount of information about the curvature of a surface is available locally. Can a network model be constructed that can extract this information from shaded images?

Until recently it was not obvious how to begin to construct such a network, but network learning algorithms (see above) provide us with a powerful method for creating a network by giving it examples of the task at hand. The learning algorithm is being used in this instance simply as a design tool to see whether some network can be found that performs the task. Many examples of simple surfaces (elliptic paraboloids) were generated and presented to the network. A set of weights was indeed found with this procedure that, independent of the direction of illumination, extracted the principal curvatures of three-dimensional surfaces and the direction of maximum curvature from shaded images (Lehky and Sejnowski 1987).

The input to the network is from an array of on-center and off-center receptive fields similar to those of cells in the lateral geniculate nucleus. The output layer is a population of units that conjointly represent the curvatures and the broadly tuned direction of maximum curvature. The units of the intermediate layer, which are needed to perform the transformation, have oriented receptive fields, similar to those of simple cells in the visual cortex of cats and monkeys that respond optimally to oriented bars and edges (figure 7). It is important to emphasize that these properties of the hidden units were not put into the network directly but emerged during training. The system "chose" these properties because they are useful in performing a particular task. Interestingly, the output units, which were required to code information about the principal curvatures and principal orientations of surfaces, had properties, when probed with bars of light, that were similar to those of a class of complex cells that are end-stopped (Lehky and Sejnowski 1988). The

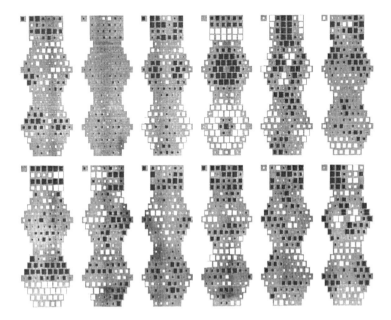

Figure 7
Hinton diagram showing the connection strengths in a network that computes the principal curvatures and direction of minimum curvature from shaded images in a small patch of the visual field corresponding roughly to the area represented in a cortical column. There are 12 hidden units which receive connections from the 122 inputs and project to each of the 23 output units. The diagram shows each of the connection strengths to and from the hidden units. Each weight is represented by one square, the area of which is proportional to the magnitude of the weight. The color is white if the weight is excitatory and black if it is inhibitory. The inputs are two hexagonal arrays of 61 processing units each. Each input unit has a concentric on-center (top) or off-surround (bottom) receptive field similar to those of principal cells in the lateral geniculate nucleus. The output consists of 24 units that conjointly represent the direction of maximum curvature (six columns) and principal curvature (four rows: two for each principal curvature). Each of the 12 hidden units is represented in the diagram in a way that reveals all the connections to and from the unit. Within each of the 12 gray background regions, the weights from the inputs are shown on the bottom and the weights to the output layer are shown above. To the left of each hidden unit, the lone square gives the threshold of the unit, which was also allowed to vary. Note that there emerged two different types of hidden units as revealed by the "projective field." The six units in the botton row and the fourth and fifth from the left in the top row were mainly responsible for providing information about the direction of minimum curvature, while others were responsible for computing the signs and magnitudes of the two principal curvatures. The curvature-selective units could be further classified as convexity detectors (top row, third from left) or elongation filters (top row, second and sixth from left).

surprising thing, given the plausible receptive-field-to-function inference rule, is that the function of the units in the network is not to detect boundary contours, but to extract curvature information from shaded images.

What the shape-from-shading network demonstrates is that we cannot directly infer function from receptive field properties. In the trained-up network, the hidden units represent an intermediate transformation for a computational task quite different from the one that has been customarily ascribed to simple cells in visual cortex—they are used to determine shape from shading, not to detect boundaries. It turns out, however, that the hidden units have *receptive fields similar to those of simple cells in visual cortex.* Therefore, bars and edges as receptive-field properties do not necessarily mean that the cell's function is to detect bars and edges in objects; it might be to detect curvature and shape, as it is in the network model, or perhaps some other surface property such as texture. The general implication is that there is no way of determining the function of each hidden unit in the network simply by "recording" the receptive-field properties of the unit. This, in turn, implies that, despite its intuitive plausibility, the receptive-field-to-function inference rule is untenable.

The function of a unit is revealed only when its *outputs*—its "projective field" (Lehky and Sejnowski 1988)—are also examined. It is the projective field of a unit that provides the additional information needed to interpret the unit's computational role in the network. In the network model the projective field could be examined directly, but in real neural networks it can only be inferred indirectly by examining the next stage of processing. Whether or not curvature is directly represented in visual cortex, for example, can be tested by designing experiments with images of curved surfaces.

4.3   Next-Generation Networks

NETtalk and the shape-from-shading network are important examples because they yield clues to how the nervous system can embody models of various domains of the world. Parallel-network modeling is still in a pioneering stage of development. There are bound to be many snags and hitches, and many problems yet undreamt of will have to be solved. At this stage, the representational structure of networks has not yet been explored in detail, nor is it known how well the performance of network models will scale with the number of neurons and the difficulty of the task. (That is, will representations and computations in a cortical column with 200,000 neurons be similar to those in a model network comprising only a few hundred processing units?)

Moreover, taken literally as a model of functioning neurons, back-propagation is biologically implausible, inasmuch as error signals cannot literally be propagated back down the very same axon the signal came up. Taken as a *systems-level* algorithm, however, back-propagation may have a realization using feedback projections that do map onto neural hardware. Even squarely facing these cautionary considerations, the important thing is that something with this sort of character at least lets us see what representational structure—good, meaty, usable structure—could *look like* in a neuronal network.

Temporal chaining of sequences of representations is probably a prominent feature of many kinds of behavior, and it may turn out to be particularly important for language acquisition and use. It is conceivable that structured sequences—long, temporally extended sequences—are the elements of an abstract sort of neural state space that enable humans to use language. Sereno (1986) has suggested something along these lines, pointing out that DNA, as a spatially extended sequence of nucleotides, allows for encoding; by analogy, one may envision that the development of mechanisms for generating temporally extended sequences of neuronal (abstract) structures may allow for a kind of structured behavior (i.e., language) that short sequences do not allow for. (See also MacKay 1987; Dehaene et al. 1987.)

One promising strategy will be to try first to unscramble the more fundamental kinds of representing accomplished by nervous systems, shelving until later the problem of complex representations such as linguistic representations. To solve such problems, the solutions discovered for simpler representations may be crucial. At the most basic level, there appears to be an isomorphism between cell responses and external events (for example, cells in visual cortex responding to bars of light moving in a specific direction). At higher levels the receptive-field properties change (Allman et al. 1985; Andersen 1987), and it may be that the lower-level isomorphism gives way to more complicated and dynamic network effects. Motivation, planning, and other factors may, at this level, have roles in how a representation is generated. At still higher levels, still other principles may be operative. Once we understand the nature of representing in early sensory processing, as we have indeed begun to do, and go on to address the nature of representations at more and more abstract levels, we may finally be able to address how learning a language yields another kind of representation, and how symbols can be represented in neural networks. Whatever the basic principles of language representation, they are not likely to be utterly unrelated to the way or ways that the nervous system generates visual representations or auditory representations, or represents spatial maps and motor planning. (On semantic relations in connectionist models, see Hinton 1981, 1986.)

5   Dogmas and Dreams: George Boole, Ramon y Cajal, David Marr

The connectionist models discussed are valuable for the glimpse of representational and computational space that they provide, for it is exactly such glimpses that free us from the bonds of the intuitive conceptions of representation as language-like and computation as logic-like. They thus free us from what Hofstadter (1982) called the *Boolean Dream,* where all cognition is symbol-manipulation according to the rules of logic.

Equally important, they also free us from what we call the *Neurobiologists' Dream* (perhaps, with all due respect, it might be called Cajal's Dream), which is really the faith that the answers we seek will be manifest once the fine-grain details of each neuron (its morphology, physiology, and connections) are revealed—these models also teach the tremendously important lesson that *system properties are not accessible at the single-unit level.* In a system, what we need to know is how the elements in large sets of elements interact over time. Until we have new physiological techniques for supplying data of that sort, building network models is a method of first resort.

To be really useful, a model must be biologically constrained. However, exactly which biological properties are crucial to a model's utility and which can be safely ignored until later are matters that can be decided only by hunches until a mature theory is in place. Such "bottom-up" constraints are crucial, since computational space is immensely vast, too vast for us to be lucky enough to light on the correct theory simply from the engineering bench. Moreover, the brain's solutions to the problems of vision, motor control, and so forth may be far more powerful, more beautiful, and even more simple than what we engineer into existence. This is the point of Orgel's Second Rule: Nature is more ingenious than we are. And we stand to miss all that power and ingenuity unless we attend to neurobiological plausibility. The point is, *evolution has already done it,* so why not learn how that stupendous machine, our brain, actually works?

This observation allows us to awake from *Marr's Dream* of three levels of explanation: the computational level of abstract problem analysis, the level of the algorithm, and the level of physical implementation of the computation. In Marr's view, a higher level was independent of the levels below it, and hence computational problems could be analyzed independent of an understanding of the algorithm that executes the computation, and the algorithmic problem could be solved independent of an understanding of the physical implementation. Marr's assessment of the relations between levels has been reevaluated, and the dependence of higher levels on lower levels has come to be recognized.

The matter of the interdependence of levels marks a major conceptual difference between Marr and the current generation of connectionists. Network models are not independent of either the computational level or the implementational level; they depend in important ways on constraints from all levels of analysis. Network models show how knowledge of brain architecture can contribute to the devising of likely and powerful algorithms that can be efficiently implemented in the architecture of the nervous system and may alter even how we construe the computational problems.

On the heels of the insight that the use of constraints from higher up and lower down matters tremendously, the notion that there are basically *three* levels of analysis also begins to look questionable. If we examine more closely how the three levels of analysis are meant to map onto the organization of the nervous system, the answer is far from straightforward.

To begin with, the idea that there is essentially one single implementational level is an oversimplification. Depending on the fineness of grain, research techniques reveal structural organization at many strata: the biochemical level; then the levels of the membrane, the single cell, and the circuit; and perhaps yet other levels, such as brain subsystems, brain systems, brain maps, and the whole central nervous system. But notice that at each structurally specified stratum we can raise the functional question: What does it contribute to the wider, functional business of the brain?

This range of structural organization implies, therefore, that the oversimplification with respect to implementation has a companion oversimplification with respect to computational descriptions. And indeed, on reflection it does seem most unlikely that a single type of computational description can do justice to the computational niche of diverse structural organization. On the contrary, one would expect distinct task descriptions corresponding to distinct structural levels. But if there is a ramifying of task specifications to match the ramified structural organization, this diversity will probably be reflected in the ramification of the *algorithms* that characterize how a task is accomplished. And this, in turn, means that the notion of *the* algorithmic levels is as oversimplified as the notion of *the* implementation level.

Similar algorithms were used to specify the network models in NETtalk and the shape-from-shading network, but they have a quite different status in these two examples. On this perspective of the levels of organization, NETtalk is a network relevant to the *systems* level, whereas the shape-from-shading network is relevant to the *circuit* level. Since the networks are meant to reflect principles at entirely different levels of organization, their implementations will also be at different scales in the nervous system. Other computational principles may be found to apply to the single cell or to neural maps.

Once we look at them closely, Marr's three *levels of analysis* and the brain's *levels of organization* do not appear to mesh in a very useful or satisfying manner. So poor is the fit that it may be doubted whether levels of analysis, *as conceived by Marr,* have much methodological significance. Accordingly, in light of the flaws with the notion of *independence,* and in light of the flaws with the *tripartite* character of the conception of levels, it seems that Marr's dream, inspiring though it was for a time, must be left behind.

The vision that inspires network modeling is essentially and inescapably interdisciplinary. Unless we explicitly theorize above the level of the single cell, we will never find the key to the order and the systematicity hidden in the blinding minutiae of the neuropil. Unless our theorizing is geared to mesh with the neurobiological data, we risk wasting our time exploring some impossibly remote, if temporarily fashionable, corner of computational space. Additionally, without the constraints from psychology, ethology, and linguistics to specify more exactly the parameters of the large-scale capacities of nervous systems, our conception of the functions for which we need explanation will be so woolly and tangled as to effectively smother progress.

Consequently, cross-disciplinary research, combining constraints from psychology, neurology, neurophysiology, linguistics, and computer modeling, is the best hope for the co-evolution that could ultimately yield a unified, integrated science of the mind-brain. It has to be admitted, however, that this vision is itself a dream. From within the dream, we cannot yet reliably discern what are the flaws that will impede progress, what crucial elements are missing, or at which points the vague if tantalizing hunches might be replaced by palpable results.

Notes

1. An earlier exploration of these ideas is to be found in Kenneth Craik's book *The Nature of Explanation* (Cambridge University Press, 1943).

2. NETtalk networks can differ in how input letters and output phonemes are represented, and in the number and arrangement of hidden units.

References

Allman, J., F. Miezin, and E. McGuniness. 1985. "Stimulus specific responses from beyond the classic receptive field." *Annual Review of Neuroscience* 8: 407–430.

Andersen, R. A. 1987. "The role of posterior parietal cortex in spatial perception and visual-motor integration." In *Handbook of Physiology—The Nervous System V,* ed. V. B. Mountcastle, F. Plum, and S. R. Geiger.

Anderson, J. A., and G. E. Hinton. 1981. "Models of information processing in the brain." In Hinton and Anderson 1981.

Chisholm, R. M. 1966. *Theory of Knowledge.* Englewood Cliffs, N.J.: Prentice-Hall.

Churchland, P. M. 1979. *Scientific Realism and the Plasticity of Mind.* Cambridge University Press.

Churchland, P. M. 1988. *Matter and Consciousness* (revised edition). Cambridge, Mass.: MIT Press.

Churchland, P. S. 1986. *Neurophilosophy: Toward a Unified Science of the Mind-Brain.* Cambridge, Mass.: MIT Press.

Davidson, D. (1974). "On the very idea of a conceptual scheme." *Proceedings and Addresses of the American Philosophical Association* 47: 5–20.

Dehaene, S., J.-P. Changeux, and J.-P. Nadal. 1987. "Neural networks that learn temporal sequences by selection." *Proceedings of the National Academy of Sciences* 84: 2727–2731.

Dennett, D. C. 1978. *Brainstorms: Philosophical Essays on Mind and Psychology.* Cambridge, Mass.: MIT Press.

Eccles, J. C. 1977. Part II of K. Popper, *The Self and Its Brain* (Berlin: Springer-Verlag).

Enc, B. 1983. "In defense of the identity theory." *Journal of Philosophy* 80: 279–298.

Feldman, J. A., and F. H. Ballard. 1982. "Connectionist models and their properties." *Cognitive Science* 6: 205–254.

Fodor, J. A. 1975. *The Language of Thought.* New York: Crowell. (Paperback edition: Cambridge, Mass.: MIT Press, 1979.)

Fodor, J. A. 1981. *Representations.* Cambridge, Mass.: MIT Press.

Goldman-Rakic, P. S. 1987. "Circuitry of primate prefrontal cortex and regulation of behavior by representational memory." In *Handbook of Physiology—The Nervous System V,* ed. V. B. Mountcastle, F. Plum, and S. R. Geiger.

Hebb, D. O. 1949. *Organization of Behavior.* New York: Wiley.

Hilbert, J., and S. Cohn-Vossen. 1952. *Geometry and the Imagination.* New York: Chelsea.

Hinton, G. E. 1981. "Implementing semantic networks in parallel hardware." In Hinton and Anderson 1981.

Hinton, G. E. 1986. "Learning distributed representations of concepts." In *Proceedings of the Eight Annual Conference of the Cognitive Science Society.* Hillsdale, N.J.: Erlbaum.

Hinton, G. E. 1988. "Connectionist learning procedures." *Artificial Intelligence,* in press.

Hinton, E. E., and J. A. Anderson, eds. (1981). *Parallel Models of Associative Memory.* Hillsdale, N.J.: Erlbaum.

Hinton, G. E., and T. J. Sejnowski. 1986. "Learning and relearning in Boltzmann machines." In McClelland and Rumelhart 1986.

Hofstadter, D. R. 1982. "Artificial intelligence: Subcognition as computation." *Technical Report No. 132*, Computer Science Department, Indiana University.

Hooker, C. A. 1981. "Toward a general theory of reduction. Part I: Historical and scientific setting. Part II: Identity in reduction. Part III: Cross-categorical reduction." *Dialogue* 20: 38–59, 201–236, 496–529.

Hubel, D. H., and T. N. Wiesel. 1962. "Receptive fields, binocular interaction and functional architecture in cat's visual cortex." *Journal of Physiology* 160: 106–154.

Kelso, S. R., A. H. Ganong, and T. H. Brown. 1986. "Hebbian synapses in hippocampus." *Proceedings of the National Academy of Sciences* 83: 5326–5330.

Lehky, S., and T. J. Sejnowski. 1987. "Extracting 3-D curvatures from images using a neural model." *Society for Neuroscience Abstracts* 13: 1451.

Lehky, S., and T. J. Sejnowski. 1988. "Neural network model for the representation of surface curvature from images of shaded surfaces." In *Organizing Principles of Sensory Processing*, ed. J. Lund (Oxford University Press).

Livingstone, M. S. 1988. "Art, illusion, and the visual system." *Scientific American* 258: 78–85.

McClelland, J. L., and D. E. Rumelhart. 1986. *Parallel Distributed Processing: Explorations in the Microstructure of Cognition*. Cambridge, Mass.: MIT Press.

McGinn, C. 1982. *The Character of Mind*. Oxford University Press.

MacKay, D. 1987. *The Organization and Perception of Action*. Berlin: Springer-Verlag.

Mandt, A. J. 1986. "The triumph of philosophical pluralism? Notes on the transformation of academic philosophy." *Proceedings and Addresses of the American Philosophical Association* 60: 265–277.

Marr, D. 1982. *Vision*. San Francisco: Freeman.

Pellionisz, A., and R. Llinas. 1982. "Space-time representation in the brain. The cerebellum as a predictive space-time metric tensor." *Neuroscience* 7: 2249–2970.

Pentland, A. P. 1984. "Local shading analysis." *IEEE Transactions: Pattern Analysis and Machine Intelligence* 6: 170–187.

Putnam, H. 1967. "The nature of mental states." In *Arts, Mind and Religion*, ed. W. H. Capitan and D. D. Merrill (University of Pittsburgh Press). Reprinted in H. Putnam, *Mind, Language, and Reality: Philosophical Papers*, vol. 2 (Cambridge University Press, 1975).

Pylyshyn, Z. 1984. *Computation and Cognition*. Cambridge. Mass.: MIT Press.

Quine, W. V. O. 1960. *Word and Object*. Cambridge, Mass.: MIT Press.

Richardson, R. 1979. "Functionalism and reductionism." *Philosophy of Science* 46: 533–558.

Rosenberg, C. R. 1988. Ph.D. thesis, Princeton University.

Rumelhart, D. E., G. E. Hinton, and J. L. McClelland. 1986. "A general framework for parallel distributed processing." In Rumelhart and McClelland 1986.

Rumelhart, D. E., G. E. Hinton, and R. J. Williams 1986. "Learning internal representations by error propagation." In McClelland and Rumelhart 1986.

Schaffner, K. F. 1976. "Reductionism in biology: Prospects and problems." In *PSA Proceedings 1974,* ed. R. S. Cohen, C. A. Hooker, A. C. Michalos, and J. W. Van Evra. Dordrecht: Reidel.

Sejnowski, T. J. 1986. "Open questions about computation in cerebral cortex." In McClelland and Rumelhart 1986.

Sejnowski, T. J. 1988. "Neural network learning algorithms." In *Neural Computers,* ed. R. Eckmiller and C. von der Malsberg (Berlin: Springer-Verlag).

Sejnowski, T. J., and P. S. Churchland. In press. "Brain and Cognition." In *Foundations of Cognitive Science,* ed. M. I. Posner (Cambridge, Mass.: MIT Press).

Sejnowski, T. J., and C. R. Rosenberg. 1987. "Parallel networks that learn to pronounce English text." *Complex Systems* 1: 145–168.

Sejnowski, T. J., and C. R. Rosenberg. 1988. "Learning and representation in connectionist models." In *Perspective in Memory Research and Training,* ed. M. Gazzaniga (Cambridge, Mass.: MIT Press).

Sejnowski, T. J., C. Koch, and P. S. Churchland. 1988. "Computational neuroscience." *Science*

Sereno, M. 1986. "A program for the neurobiology of mind." *Inquiry* 29: 217–240.

Skinner, B. F. 1957. *Verbal Behavior.* New York: Appleton-Century-Crofts.

Skinner, B. F. 1976. *About Behaviorism.* New York: Knopf.

Smart, J. J. C. 1959. "Sensations and brain processes." *Philosophical Review* 68: 141–156.

Stich, S. P. 1983. *From Folk Psychology to Cognitive Science: The Case Against Belief.* Cambridge, Mass.: MIT Press.

Strawson, P. F. 1966. *The Bounds of Sense: An Essay on Kant's Critique of Pure Reason.* London: Methuen.

Swinburne, R. 1986. *The Evolution of the Soul.* Oxford University Press.

Chapter 2

Connectionist Modeling: Paul Smolensky
Neural Computation/Mental
Connections

In the past few years the approach to cognitive science and artificial intelligence known as *connectionist modeling* has dramatically increased its influence. Connectionist systems are large networks of extremely simple computational units, massively interconnected and running in parallel. Each unit or processor has a numerical *activation value,* which it communicates to other processors along connections of varying strength; the activation value of each processor constantly changes in response to the activity of the processors to which it is connected. The values of some of the units form the input to the system, and the values of other units form the output; the connections between the units determine how input is transformed to output. In connectionist systems, knowledge is encoded not in symbolic structures but rather in the pattern of numerical strengths of the connections between processors.

The goal of connectionist research is to model both lower-level perceptual processes and such higher-level processes as object recognition, problem solving, planning, and language understanding. The rapidly growing collection of connectionist systems includes models of the following cognitive phenomena:

- speech perception,
- visual recognition of figures in the "origami world,"
- development of specialized feature detectors,
- amnesia,
- language parsing and generation,
- aphasia,
- discovering binary encodings,
- dynamic programming of massively parallel networks,
- acquisition of English past-tense morphophonology from examples,
- tic-tac-toe,

- inference about rooms, and
- qualitative problem solving in simple electric circuits

One crucial question is whether the computational power of connectionist systems is sufficient for the construction of truly intelligent systems. Explorations addressing this question form the bulk of the contributions to the connectionist literature; many can be found in the proceedings of the International Joint Conference on AI and the annual meetings of the American Association for AI and the Cognitive Science Society of the past several years. The connectionist systems referred to in the preceding paragraph can be found in Hinton and Anderson 1981, in *Cognitive Science* 1985, in Rumelhart, McClelland, and PDP Research Group 1986, in McClelland et al. 1986, and in Feldman et al. 1985. In the present chapter I will not address the issue of computational power, except to point out that connectionist research has been strongly encouraged by successful formal models of the details of human cognitive performance and strongly motivated by the conviction that the pursuit of the principles of neural computation will eventually lead to architectures of great computational power.

In addition to the question of whether the connectionist approach to AI *can* work, there is the question: What exactly would it mean if the approach *did* work? There are fundamental questions about the connectionist approach that are not yet clearly understood despite their importance: What is the relation between connectionist systems and the brain? How does the connectionist approach to the modeling of higher-level cognitive processes relate to the symbolic approach that has traditionally *defined* AI and cognitive science? Can connectionist models contribute to our understanding of the nature of the symbol processing that characterizes the mind and its relation to the neural processing that characterizes the brain? In the process of my addressing these questions, it will become clear that the answers are important not only in their own right but also as contributions to the determination of whether the connectionist approach has sufficient power.

1 Levels of Analysis: Neural and Mental Structures

We begin with these questions: How do accounts of intelligence relate to neural and mental structures? What are the roles of the neural and the symbolic levels of analysis? Let us consider the answers first from the traditional symbolic approach to AI, and then from a connectionist alternative.

1.1 The Symbolic Paradigm

We start with the mental structures of "folk psychology": goals, beliefs, concepts, and so forth (figure 1). In the symbolic approach, these mentalist concepts are formalized in terms of a "language of thought," as Fodor (1975) calls it. This language is supposed to provide a literal formalization of folk psychology. The rules for operating on this language are essentially Boole's (1854) "laws of thought." These symbolic structures are supported by a *physical symbol system* (a physical computing device for manipulating symbols), which in turn is supported by lower implementation levels in a computing device. The idea is that eventually, if we were to get low enough down in the human physical symbol system, we would see something like neurons. In other words, on this account we need only figure out how to relate neural structures and mental structures. If it were the case that increasingly lower levels of computers looked more and more like neural systems, this would be a promising approach; unfortunately, insights into the design and implementation of physical symbol systems have so far shed virtually no light on how the brain works.

To more clearly understand the connectionist alternative, it is helpful to articulate a number of the properties of the symbolic approach. Newell (1980, p. 170) formulated this paradigm best in his *physical symbol system hypothesis:*

The necessary and sufficient condition for a physical system to exhibit general intelligent action is that it be a physical symbol system.

"General intelligent action" means rational behavior (ibid., p. 171); "rationality" means that when an agent has a certain goal and the knowledge that a certain action will lead to that goal, the agent selects that action (Newell 1982); and physical symbol systems are physically realized universal computers.

What all this means in the practice of symbolic AI is that goals, beliefs, knowledge, and so on are all formalized as symbolic structures (e.g. Lisp lists) that are built of symbols (e.g. Lisp atoms) that are each semantically interpretable in terms of the ordinary concepts we use to conceptualize the domain. Thus, in a medical expert system we expect to find such structures as (IF FEVER THEN (HYPOTHESIZE INFECTION)). These symbolic structures are operated on by symbol-manipulation procedures composed of primitive operations such as concatenating lists and extracting elements from lists. According to the symbolic paradigm, it is in terms of such operations that we are to understand cognitive processes.

It is important to note that in the symbolic paradigm, levels of cognition

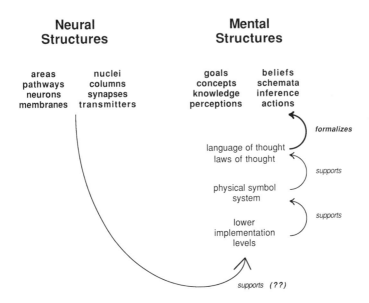

Figure 1
Neural and mental structures in the symbolic paradigm.

are analogized to levels of computer systems. The symbolic level that implements knowledge structures is alleged to be exact and complete. That means that lower levels are *unnecessary* for the accurate description of cognition in terms of the semantically interpretable elements. This relegates the neural question to simply: How does the nervous system happen to physically implement a physical symbol system? The answer to this question does not matter as far as symbol-level AI systems are concerned.

There are a number of inadequacies of this paradigm, which Hofstadter (1985) has called "the Boolean dream." These inadequacies can be perceived from a number of perspectives, which can be caricatured as follows:

• From the perspective of neuroscience, the problem with the symbolic paradigm is quite simply, as I have already indicated, that it has provided precious little insight into the computational organization of the brain.

• From the perspective of modeling human performance, symbolic models, such as Newell and Simon's General Problem Solver (1972), do a good job on a coarse level, but the fine structure of cognition seems to be more naturally described by nonsymbolic models. In word recognition, for example, it is natural to think about activation levels of perceptual units.

• In AI, the trouble with the Boolean dream is that symbolic rules and the logic used to manipulate them tend to produce rigid and brittle systems.

1.2   The Subsymbolic Paradigm

The alternative to the symbolic paradigm that I want to present is what I call the *subsymbolic paradigm* (figure 2). In this paradigm, there is an intermediate level of structure between the neural and symbolic levels. This new *subconceptual level* is supposed to be closer to each of the neural and symbolic levels than they are to one another. When cognition is described at the subsymbolic level, the description is that of a connectionist system.

The subconceptual level is an attempt to formalize, *at some level of abstraction,* the kind of processing that occurs in the nervous system. Many of the details of neural structure and function are absent from the subconceptual level, and the level of description is higher than the neural level. The precise relationship between the neural and subconceptual levels is still a fairly wide-open research question, but it seems quite clear that connectionist systems are much closer to neural systems than are symbolic systems.

The relation between the subsymbolic and symbolic descriptions of cognition is illustrated in figure 2. If we adopt a higher level of description of what is going on in these subsymbolic systems (and that involves, to a significant degree, approximation), then we get descriptions that are approximately like symbolic accounts, like traditional AI constructs. Whereas the subsymbolic paradigm is content to give approximate accounts of things like goals and beliefs, it is not prepared to compromise on actual performance. Behind the accounts of folk psychology and symbolic AI lie real data on

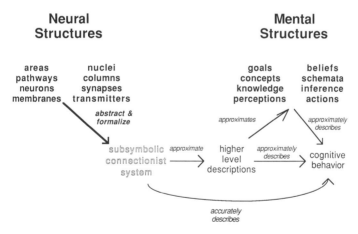

Figure 2
Neural and mental structures in the subsymbolic paradigm.

human intelligent performance, and the claim is that subsymbolic systems can provide accurate accounts of those data.

Note that the subsymbolic paradigm gives an essentially different role to the neural part of the story: Neural structures provide the basis (in some suitably abstract sense) of the formalism that gives the precise description of intelligence, whereas mental structures enter only into approximate descriptions.

In the remainder of the chapter I will elaborate on the nature of the subsymbolic level and on the higher-level descriptions of subsymbolic systems that approximate symbolic accounts. I want to indicate how formalizing cognition by abstracting from neural structures—rather than with symbolic formalizations of mental structures—provides new and exciting views of knowledge, memory, concepts, and learning.

Figure 2 illustrates an important part of the subsymbolic paradigm: that levels of cognition should *not* be thought of by analogy to levels of computer systems, all stacked underneath the "mental" part of the diagram. Just as Newtonian concepts provide approximately valid descriptions of physical phemonena that are more accurately described with quantum concepts, so the symbolic concepts of folk psychology provide approximately valid descriptions of cognitive phenomena that are more accurately described with subsymbolic concepts. Mental structures are like higher-level descriptions of a *physical* system, rather than higher-level descriptions of a *computer* system.

1.3 Semantic Interpretation

Perhaps the most fundamental contrast between the paradigms pertains to semantic interpretation of the formal models. In the symbolic approach, symbols (atoms) are used to denote the semantically interpretable entities (concepts); these same symbols are the objects governed by symbol manipulations in the rules that define the system. The entities that are semantically interpretable are *also* the entities governed by the formal laws that define the system. In the subsymbolic paradigm, this is no longer true. The semantically interpretable entities are *patterns of activation* over large numbers of units in the system, whereas the entities manipulated by formal rules are the individual activations of cells in the network. The rules take the form of activation-passing rules, which are essentially different in character from symbol-manipulation rules.

Now, what I'm talking about here is the particular kind of connectionist system in which what I just said is true: Patterns of activity represent concepts, instead of the activation of individual elements in the network. (In the latter case, we would have a collapsing here of just the same kind that we have in the symbolic paradigm.) So the subsymbolic paradigm involves connectionist systems using so-called *distributed representations,* as opposed to local representations. (The *PDP* books by Rumelhart et al. and McClelland et al. [1986] consider distributed connectionist systems; local connectionist systems are considered in Feldman and Ballard 1982 and in Feldman et al. 1985.)

Thus, in the subsymbolic paradigm the formal system description is at a lower level than the level of semantic interpretation; the level of denotation is higher than the level of manipulation. There is a fundamental two-layer structure to the subsymbolic paradigm, in contrast with the symbolic approach. The higher semantic level is not necessarily precisely formalizable, and the lower level is not "merely implementation" of a complete higher-level formalism. Both levels are essential, the lower level for defining what the system *is* (in terms of activation passing) and the higher level for understanding what the system *means* (in terms of the problem domain).

2   The Subsymbolic Level

I shall now characterize the subconceptual level in more detail. Cognition looks quite different at this level than at the symbolic level. In section 3, where higher-level descriptions of connectionist systems will be considered, we will see some of the characteristics of the symbolic level emerging.

2.1   Subsymbolic Computation

At the fundamental level in subsymbolic systems we have a collection of dynamical variables. There are two kinds of variables: an activation level for each of the units and a connection strength for each of the links. Typically, both kinds of variables are continuous. The rules that define these systems are activation-passing rules and connection-strength-modification rules. Typically, these are differential equations (although they are simulated with finite-difference equations). The differential equations are typically not stochastic, but stochastic versions will enter briefly later.

The computational roles of these two kinds of equations are the following: The activation-passing rules are in fact inference rules—not logical inference rules, but statistical inference rules. The connection-strength-modification rules are memory-storage and learning procedures.

Because the fundamental system is a dynamical system with continuously evolving variables, the subsymbolic paradigm constitutes a radical departure from the symbolic paradigm; the claim, in effect, is that *cognition should be thought of taking place in dynamical systems and not in digital computers.*

This is a natural outcome of the neurally inspired (rather than mentally inspired) conception of computation.

The relation between the subsymbolic formalism and psychological processing is in part determined by the time constants that enter into the differential equations governing activation and connection-strength modification. The time required for significant change in activation levels is of the order of 100 milliseconds; the time it takes for a connection strength to appreciably change is much longer (say, on the order of a minute). Thus, for times less than about 100 msec, what we're talking about is a single equilibration or "settling" of the network; all the knowledge imbedded in the connections is used in parallel. On this time scale, we have parallel computation. When we go beyond this, to cognitive processes that go on for several seconds (such as problem solving and extended reasoning), then we're talking about multiple settlings of the network, and serial computation. This is the part of cognition for which serial symbolic descriptions such as Newell and Simon's (1972) General Problem Solver provide a fairly good description of the coarse structure. The claim of the subsymbolic paradigm is that the symbolic description of such processing is an approximate description of the global behavior of a lot of parallel computation. If we go to still longer time scales, on the order of a minute, then we have adaptation of the network to the situation it finds itself in.

Let me summarize the constrasts between the symbolic and subsymbolic approaches, viewed at the fundamental level. In the subsymbolic paradigm we have fundamental laws that are differential equations, not symbol-manipulation procedures. The systems we are talking about are dynamical systems, not von Neumann machines. The mathematical category in which these formalisms live is the continuous category, not the discrete category, so we have a different kind of mathematics coming into play. The differences are dramatically illustrated in the way memory is modeled in the two formalisms. In the von Neumann machine, memory storage is a primitive operation (you give a location and a content, and it gets stored); memory retrieval is also a primitive operation. In subsymbolic systems, these processes are quite involved; they are not primitive operations at all. When a memory is retrieved, it is a content-addressed memory: Part of a previously instantiated activation pattern is put into one part of the network by another part of the network, and the connections fill out the rest of that previously present pattern. This is a much more involved process than a simple "memory fetch." Memories are stored in subsymbolic systems by adjusting connection strengths so that the retrieval process will actually work (this is no simple matter).

2.2 Subsymbolic Inference and the Statistical Connection

At the fundamental level of subsymbolic formalism, we have moved from thinking about cognition in terms of discrete processes to thinking in terms of continuous processes. This means that different mathematical concepts apply. One manifestation of this, in computational terms, is the claim that inference should be construed not in the logical sense but rather in the statistical sense—at least at the fundamental level of the system. (We will see below that *at higher levels,* certain subsymbolic systems do perform logical inference.)

I have encapsulated this idea in what I have called the Statistical Connection:

The strength of the connection between two units is a measure of the statistical relation between their activities.

The origins of this principle are easily seen. The relationship between statistics and connections was represented in neuroscience by Hebb's (1949) principle that a synapse between two neurons is strengthened when both are active simultaneously. In psychology, this relation appeared in the notion of "strength of association" between concepts, an important precursor of connectionist ideas (although this involved statistical associations between *concepts* and was thus not itself a subsymbolic notion.)

From a physics point of view, the Statistical Connection is basically a tautology, since if two units are strongly connected then when one is active the other is likely to be too. From a computational point of view, however, the Statistical Connection has rather profound implications for AI and for symbolic computation. Activation passing is now to be thought of as statistical inference. Each connection represents a *soft constraint;* and the knowledge contained in the system is the set of all such constraints. If two units have an inhibitory connection, then the network has the knowledge that when one is active the other ought not be; that, however, is a soft constraint that can easily be overridden by countermanding excitatory connections to that same unit (if those excitatory connections come from units that are sufficiently active). The important point is that soft constraints, any one of which can be overridden by the others, *have no implications singly;* only collectively do they have implications. That is why the natural process for using this kind of knowledge is *relaxation,* in which the network uses all the connections at once and tries to settle into a state that balances all the constraints against one another. This is to be contrasted with *hard constraints,* such as rules of the form "If A, then B", which can be used individually, one at a time, to serially make inferences. The claim is that using soft constraints avoids the brittleness that hard constraints tend to produce in AI. (It is interesting to note that advocates of logic in AI have, for some time, been trying to evade the brittleness of hard constraints by developing logics, such as nonmonotonic logics, where all of the rules are essentially used *together* to make inferences, and not separately (see, e.g., *Artificial Intelligence* 1980).

To summarize: In the symbolic paradigm, constraints are typically hard, inference is logical, and processing can therefore be serial. (One can try to parallelize it, but the most natural approach is serial inference.) In the subsymbolic paradigm, constraints are soft, inference is statistical, and therefore it is most natural to use parallel implementations of inference.

3   Higher-Level Descriptions

Having characterized the subsymbolic paradigm at the fundamental, subsymbolic level, I would now like to turn to higher-level descriptions of these connectionist systems. As was stated above, in the subsymbolic paradigm serial, symbolic descriptions of cognitive processing are approximate descriptions of the higher-level properties of connectionist computation. I will only sketch this part of the story; I will point to published work for further details. The main point is that interesting relations *do* exist between the higher-level properties of connectionist systems and mental structures, as they have been formalized symbolically. The view of mental structures that emerges is strikingly different from that of the symbolic paradigm.

3.1   The Best-Fit Principle

That crucial principle of the subsymbolic level, the Statistical Connection, can be reformulated at a higher level as what I call the Best-Fit Principle:

Given an input, a connectionist system outputs a set of inferences that, as a whole, give a best fit to the input, in a statistical sense defined by the statistical knowledge stored in the system's connections.

In this vague form, this principle may be generally true of connectionist systems. But it is exactly true in a precise sense, at least in an idealized limit, for a certain class of systems that I have studied in what I call *harmony theory* (Smolensky 1983, 1984a, 1984b, 1986a, 1986b, 1986c; Riley and Smolensky 1984).

To render the Best-Fit Principle precise, it is necessary to provide precise definitions of "inferences," "best fit," and "statistical knowledge stored in the system's connections." This is done in harmony theory, where the central object is the "harmony function" H, which measures, for any possible set of inferences, the goodness of fit to the input with respect to the soft constraints stored in the connection strengths. The set of inferences with the largest value of H (i.e., the highest harmony) is the best set of inferences, with respect to a well-defined statistical problem.

Harmony theory basically offers three things: a mathematically precise characterization of a very general statistical inference problem that covers a great number of connectionist computations, an indication as to how that problem can be solved using a connectionist network with a certain set of connections, and a procedure by which the network can learn the correct connections with experience. I will comment briefly on each of these three elements, to give the flavor of the form that the Best-Fit Principle takes and to prepare the way for the remaining remarks on higher-level properties of connectionist computation.

Harmony theory analyzes systems that confront the following statistical-inference task: If we give the system some features of an environmental state, it should infer values for unknown features. An example I will consider in the next subsection concerns reasoning about a simple electric circuit: Given the value of some circuit feature (say, that a resistor has increased), what happens to the unknown features (the current and the voltage)? This general task is what I call *the completion task*.

In response to a completion problem, the system is supposed to give the maximum-likelihood set of inferred values with respect to a probability distribution maintained internal to the system as a model of the environment. In other words, the system maintains a probability distribution that represents the likelihood of events' occurring in the environment, and it should give as its output the maximum-likelihood set of values for the unknowns.

What model of the environment—what probability distribution—is the system supposed to use? Here harmony theory adopts a principle commonly used in statistical inference: The system should use the probability distribution with minimal informational content that is consistent with the statistical constraints that the system observes holding in the environment.

Having specified the inference problem in this way, we can now draw some conclusions. The first result says that the minimal information distribution can actually be computed as follows. The probability of a set of inferred values $\mathbf{x}$ is proportional to the exponential of a particular function:

$$\mathrm{prob}(\mathbf{x}) \propto e^{\sum_\alpha \lambda_\alpha f_\alpha(\mathbf{x})}$$

This function has one parameter λ_α for each statistical constraint α observed in the environment. (The function f_α has value 1 when constraint α is satisfied, and 0 otherwise.) It turns out that the maximum-likelihood completions that the system is supposed to give as answers to questions can be computed from a simpler distribution that has a quadratic function in the exponent but uses auxiliary variables to achieve the simplification:

$$\text{prob}(\mathbf{x},\mathbf{y}) \propto e^{H(\mathbf{x},\mathbf{y})}$$

This quadratic function H measures the internal consistency of a set of inferred values with respect to these constraint parameters λ_α; I call it H because it turns out to play the mathematical role of the Hamiltonian of a statistical mechanical system. That is where the name "harmony" comes from: H measures the internal consistency of states of the system.

I call this first result the Competence Theorem because it explicitly characterizes how the system ideally ought to behave. The next result, the Realizability Theorem, describes how to instantiate this competence in a performance system—an actual computing device—the behavior of which obeys the competence theorem in suitably ideal circumstances, but which in real circumstances exhibits performance that deviates from the ideal competence. By creating one computing element for each of the given and to-be-inferred variables in the set $\mathbf{x}$ and one for each of the auxiliary variables in the set $\mathbf{y}$, and using the parameters λ_α to determine connection strengths, a connectionist network can be built that can compute the maximum-likelihood completions by a stochastic relaxation method. The units in this harmony network are stochastic processors—the differential equations defining the system are stochastic. There is a system parameter, called the *computational temperature*, that governs the degree of randomness in the units' behavior; it is high at the beginning of the computation, when there is a lot of randomness in the network, but it is lowered during computation until eventually the system freezes into an answer. In the idealized limit where the system has unlimited relaxation time, the network converges with probability 1 to the correct answer, as characterized by the competence theorem. (The stochastic relaxation process is *simulated annealing,* as in the Boltzmann machine; see Hinton and Sejnowski 1983. For the historical and logical relations between harmony theory and the Boltzmann machine, see Rumelhart, McClelland, and PDP Research Group 1986, p. 148, and Smolensky 1986a.)

The third result is a Learnability Theorem. It says that through statistical sampling of the environment, the values of the parameters λ_α (i.e., the connection strengths) required by the Competence Theorem can be computed by relaxation. That is, the parameters start off with some initial values ("genetically" selected or randomly assigned) which are then gradually tuned through experience to become the correct ones for the given environment.

3.2   Productions, Sequential processing, and Logical Inference

A simple harmony model of expert intuition in qualitative physics has been described in Riley and Smolensky 1984 and in Smolensky 1986a and 1986c. The model answers questions like "What happens to the voltages in this circuit if I increase this resistor?" Higher-level descriptions of this subsymbolic problem-solving illustrate several interesting points.

It is possible to identify *macro-decisions* during the system's solution of a problem; these are each the result of many individual micro-decisions by the units of the system, and each amounts to a large-scale commitment to a portion of the solution. These macro-decisions are approximately like the firing of production rules. In fact, these "productions" "fire" at different times, in essentially the same order as in a symbolic forward-chaining inference system. One can measure the total amount of order in the system and see that there is a qualitative change in the system when the first micro-decisions are made: The system changes from a disordered phase to an ordered one.

A corollary of the way this network embodies the problem-domain constraints, and the general theorems of harmony theory, is that the system, when given a well-posed problem and unlimited relaxation time, will always give the correct answer. Thus, under that idealization, the *competence* of the system is described by *hard* constraints: Ohm's Law, Kirchoff's Law. It is as though the system had those laws written down inside it. However, as in all subsymbolic systems, the *performance* of the system is achieved by satisfying a large set of *soft* constraints. What this means is that if we go outside of the ideal conditions under which hard constraints seem to be obeyed, the illusion that the system has hard constraints inside it is quickly dispelled. The system can violate Ohm's Law if it has to, but if it doesn't have to violate the law it won't. Thus, *outside the idealized domain of well-posed problems and unlimited processing time, the system gives sensible performance.* It isn't brittle the way that symbolic inference systems are. If the system is given an ill-posed problem, it satisfies as many constraints as possible. If it is given inconsistent information, it doesn't fall flat and deduce anything. If it is given insufficient information, it doesn't just sit there and deduce nothing. Given finite processing time, the performance degrades gracefully as well. Thus, the competence/performance distinction can be addressed in a sensible way.

Returning to the theme of physics analogies instead of computer analogies: This "quantum" system appears to be "Newtonian" under the proper conditions. A system that has, at the micro level, soft constraints, satisfied in parallel, *appears* at the macro level, under the right circumstances, to have hard constraints, satisfied serially. But it doesn't *really,* and if you go outside the

"Newtonian" domain you see that it has really been a "quantum" system all along.

3.3 The Dynamics of Activation Patterns

In the subsymbolic paradigm, semantic interpretation occurs at the higher level of patterns of activity, not at the lower level of individual nodes. Thus, an important question about the higher level is: How do the semantically interpretable entities *combine?*

In the symbolic paradigm, the semantically interpretable entities are symbols, which combine by some form of *concatenation.* In the subsymbolic paradigm, the semantically interpretable entities are activation patterns, and these combine by *superposition:* Activation patterns superimpose upon one another, the way that wave-like structures always do in physical systems. This difference is another manifestation of moving the formalization from the discrete to the continuous (indeed the linear) category.

Using the mathematics of the superposition operation, it is possible to describe connectionist systems at the higher, semantic level. If the connectionist system is purely linear (so that the activity of each unit is precisely a weighted sum of the activities of the units giving it input), it can easily be proved that the higher-level description obeys formal laws of just the same sort as the lower level: The subconceptual and symbolic levels are *isomorphic.* Linear connectionist systems are, however, of limited computational power, and most interesting connectionist systems are nonlinear. However, nearly all are *quasi-linear*—that is, each unit *combines* its inputs linearly even though the effects of this combination on the unit's activity is nonlinear. Further, the problem-specific *knowledge* in such systems is in the combination weights (i.e., the *linear part* of the dynamical equations), and in learning systems it is generally only these linear weights that adapt. For these reasons, even though the higher level is not isomorphic to the lower level in nonlinear systems, there are senses in which the higher level *approximately* obeys formal laws similar to the lower level. (For the details, see Smolensky 1986b.)

The conclusion here is rather different from that of the preceding subsection, where we saw how there are senses in which higher-level characterizations of certain subsymbolic systems approximate productions, serial processing, and logical inference. What we see now is that there are also senses in which the laws approximately describing cognition at the semantic level are *activation-passing laws* like those at the subsymbolic level, but operating between "units" with individual semantics. These semantic-level descriptions of mental processing (which include *local* connectionist models) have been of considerable value in cognitive psychology (see, e.g., Mc-

Clelland and Rumelhart 1981; Rumelhart and McClelland 1982; Dell 1985). We can now see how these "spreading activation" accounts of mental processing relate to subsymbolic accounts.

3.4 Schemata

One of the most important symbolic concepts is that of the *schema* (Rumelhart 1980). This concept goes back at least to Kant (1787) as a description of mental concepts and mental categories. Schemata appear in many AI systems in the form of frames, scripts, or similar structures; they are prepackaged bundles of information that support inference in stereotyped situations.

I will very briefly summarize the work on schemata in connectionist systems reported in Rumelhart, Smolensky, McClelland, and Hinton 1986 (see also Feldman 1981 and Smolensky 1986a and 1986c). This work addressed the case of schemata for rooms. Subjects were asked to describe some imagined rooms using a set of 40 features: has-ceiling, has-window, contains-toilet, and so on. Statistics computed from these data were used to construct a network containing one node for each feature and containing connections computed from the statistical data by using a particular form of the Statistical Connection.

The resulting network can do inferences of the kind that can be performed by symbolic systems with schemata for various types of rooms. For example, the network is told that some room contains a ceiling and an oven; the question is, what else is likely to be in the room? The system settles down into a final state, and the inferences contained in that final state are that the room contains a coffee cup but no fireplace, and a coffee pot but no computer.

The inference process in this system is simply one of greedily maximizing harmony. To describe the inference of this system on a higher level, we can examine the global states of the system in terms of their harmony values. How internally consistent are the various states in the space? It is a 40-dimensional state space, but various two-dimensional subspaces can be selected and the harmony values there can be graphically displayed. The harmony landscape has various peaks; looking at the features of the state corresponding to one of the peaks, we find that it corresponds to a prototypical bathroom; others corresond to a prototypical office, and so on for all the kinds of rooms subjects were asked to describe. There are no *units* in this system for bathrooms or offices; there are just lower-level descriptors. The prototypical bathroom is a pattern of activation, and the system's recognition of its prototypicality is reflected in the harmony peak for that pattern. It is a consistent, "harmonious" combination of features—better than neighboring points like one representing a bathroom without a bathtub, which has distinctly lower harmony.

During inference, this system climbs directly uphill on the harmony landscape. When the system state is in the vicinity of the harmony peak representing the prototypical bathroom, the inferences it makes are governed by the shape of the harmony landscape there. This shape is like a "schema" that governs inferences about bathrooms. (In fact, harmony theory was created to give a connectionist formalization of the notion of schema; see Smolensky 1986a and 1986c.) Looking closely at the harmony landscape, we can see that the terrain around the "bathroom" peak has many of the properties of a bathroom schema: variables and constants, default values, schemata imbedded inside of schemata, and even cross-variable dependencies. The system behaves as though it had schemata for bathrooms, offices, etc., even though they are not "really there" at the fundamental level. These schemata are strictly properties of a higher-level description. They are informal, approximate descriptions—one might even say they are merely metaphorical descriptions—of an inference process that is too subtle to admit such high-level descriptions with great precision. Even though these schemata may not be the sort of object on which to base a formal model, nonetheless they *are* useful descriptions—which may, in the end, be all that can really be said about schemata anyway.

Conclusion

The view of symbolic structures that emerges from viewing them as entities of high-level descriptions of dynamical systems is quite different from the view that comes from the symbolic paradigm. "Rules" are not symbolic formulae but the cooperative results of many smaller soft constraints. Macroinference is not a process of firing a symbolic production; rather, it is one of qualitative state change in a dynamical system, such as a phase transition. Schemata are not large symbolic data structures but rather the potentially quite intricate shapes of harmony maxima. Similarly, categories turn out to be attractors in dynamical systems: states that "suck in" to a common place many nearby states, such as peaks of harmony functions. Categorization is not the execution of a symbolic algorithm but the continuous evolution of the dynamical system—the evolution that drives states into the attractors, to maximal harmony. Learning is not the construction and editing of formulas but the gradual adjustment of connection strengths with experience, with the effect of slowly shifting harmony landscapes, adapting old and creating new concepts, categories, schemata.

The heterogeneous assortment of high-level mental structures that have been embraced in this chapter suggests that the symbolic level lacks formal unity. This is just what one expects of approximate higher-level descriptions, which, capturing different aspects of global properties, can have quite different characters. The unity underlying cognition is to be found not at the symbolic level but rather at the subconceptual level, where a few principles in a single formal framework lead to a rich variety of global behaviors.

If connectionist models are interpreted within what I have defined as the subsymbolic paradigm, we can start to see how mental structures can emerge from neural structures. By seeing mental entities as higher-level structures implemented in connectionist systems, we get a new, more complex and subtle view of what these mental structures really are. Perhaps subsymbolic systems can achieve a truly rich mental life.

Acknowledgments

This chapter is a slightly revised version of "Connectionist AI, symbolic AI, and the brain," *Artificial Intelligence Review* 1 (1987): 95–109. A considerably expanded and improved treatment of these issues may be found in "On the proper treatment of connectionism," *Behavioral and Brain Sciences* 11 (1988): 1–74. The research was supported by NSF grants IRI-9609599 and ECE-8617947 to the author, by a grant to the author from the Sloan Foundation's computational neuroscience program, and by the Department of Computer Science and the Institute of Cognitive Science at the University of Colorado at Boulder.

References

Artificial Intelligence. 1980. Special issue on non-monotonic logic: volume 13, number 1–2.

Boole, G. 1854. *An Investigation of the Laws of Thought*. New York: Dover, 1961.

Cognitive Science. 1985. Special issue on connectionist models and their applications: volume 9, number 1.

Dell, G. S. 1985. "Positive feedback in hierarchical connectionist models: Applications to language production." *Cognitive Science* 9:3–23.

Feldman, J. A. 1981. "A connectionist model of visual memory." In *Parallel Models of Associative Memory*, ed. G. E. Hinton and J. A. Anderson. Hillsdale, N.J.: Erlbaum.

Feldman, J. A., and D. H. Ballard. 1982. "Connectionist models and their properties." *Cognitive Science* 6: 205–254.

Feldman, J. A., D. H. Ballard, C. M. Brown, and G. S. Dell. 1985. Rochester Connectionist Papers: 1979–1985. Technical Report 172, Department of Computer Science, University of Rochester.

Fodor, J. A. 1975. *The Language of Thought*. New York: Crowell.

Hebb, D. O. 1949. *The Organization of Behavior*. New York: Wiley.

Hinton, G. E., and J. A. Anderson, eds. 1981. *Parallel Models of Associative Memory*. Hillsdale, N.J.: Erlbaum.

Hinton, G. E., and T. J. Sejnowski. 1983. "Analyzing cooperative computation." In *Proceedings of the Fifth Annual Conference of the Cognitive Science Society*.

Hofstadter, D. R. 1985. "Waking up from the Boolean dream, or, subcognition as computation." In D. R. Hofstadter, *Metamagical Themas* (New York: Basic Books).

Kant, I. 1787. *Critique of Pure Reason*. Second edition, translated by N. Kemp Smith. London: Macmillan, 1963.

McClelland, J. L., and D. E. Rumelhart. 1981. "An interactive activation model of context effects in letter perception: Part 1. An account of the basic findings." *Psychological Review* 88: 375–407.

McClelland, J. L., D. E. Rumelhart, and the PDP Research Group. 1986. *Parallel Distributed Processing: Explorations in the Microstructure of Cognition. Volume 2: Psychological and Biological Models*. Cambridge, Mass.: MIT Press. A Bradford Book.

Newell, A. 1980. "Physical symbol systems." *Cognitive Science* 4: 135–183.

Newell, A. 1982. "The knowledge level." *Artificial Intelligence* 18: 87–127.

Newell, A., and H. A. Simon. 1972. *Human Problem Solving*. Englewood Cliffs, N.J.: Prentice-Hall.

Riley, M. S., and P. Smolensky. 1984. "A parallel model of (sequential) problem solving." In *Proceedings of the Sixth Annual Conference of the Cognitive Science Society*.

Rumelhart, D. E. 1980. "Schemata: The building blocks of cognition." In *Theoretical Issues in Reading Comprehension*, ed. R. Spiro et al. Hillsdale, N.J.: Erlbaum.

Rumelhart, D. E., and J. L. McClelland. 1982. "An interactive activation model of context effects in letter perception: Part 2. The contextual enhancement effect and some tests and extensions of the model." *Psychological Review* 89: 60–94.

Rumelhart, D. E., J. L. McClelland, and the PDP Research Group. 1986. *Parallel Distributed Processing: Explorations in the Microstructure of Cognition. Volume 1: Foundations*. Cambridge, Mass.: MIT Press. A Bradford Book.

Rumelhart, D. E., P. Smolensky, J. L. McClelland, and G. E. Hinton. 1986. "Schemata and sequential thought processes in parallel distributed processing models." In McClelland et al. 1986.

Smolensky, P. 1983. "Schema selection and stochastic inference in modular environments." In *Proceedings of the National Conference on Artificial Intelligence*.

Smolensky, P. 1984a. "Harmony theory: Thermal parallel models in a computational context." In P. Smolensky and M. S. Riley, Harmony Theory: Problem Solving, Parallel Cognitive Models, and Thermal Physics, Technical Report 8404, Institute for Cognitive Science, University of California at San Diego.

Smolensky, P. 1984b. "The mathematical role of self-consistency in parallel computation." In *Proceedings of the Sixth Annual Conference of the Cognitive Science Society.*

Smolensky, P. 1986a. "Information processing in dynamical systems: Foundations of harmony theory." In Rumelhart et al. 1986.

Smolensky, P. 1986b. "Neural and conceptual interpretations of parallel distributed processing models." McClelland et al. 1986.

Smolensky, P. 1986c. "Formal modeling of subsymbolic processes: An introduction to harmony theory." In *Directions in the Science of Cognition,* ed. N. E. Sharkey (Chichester: Ellis Horwood).

Chapter 3

Neural Representation of Conceptual Knowledge

Jerome A. Feldman

How it is that the brain codes, stores and retrieves memories is among the most important and baffling questions in science. (Thompson 1986)

In addition to its compelling scientific interest, the neural substrate of memory is of considerable practical importance. There are obvious applications in neurology, but it goes well beyond that. Our understanding of how human minds incorporate and process information has a profound influence on many aspects of social intercourse, including formal and informal education, psychotherapy, public information, and interpersonal communication (Roediger 1980). Research in the behavioral and brain sciences entails implicit assumptions about neural encoding. Cognitive science is particularly concerned with how conceptual information is treated by human brains.

Recent advances in the behavioral, biological, and computational sciences may yield a major improvement in our understanding of the neural coding of memory. Neurobiology is making remarkable strides in elucidating the structure of the nervous system and the details of its functioning. The behavioral sciences are developing deep structural models of language, vision, etc., and employing increasingly sophisticated experimental and simulation techniques to refine them. Computer science has produced powerful devices and profound theories of representation and computation which are supporting the study of how the complex structural theories of the behavioral scientists could be carried out by the information-processing mechanism revealed by neurobiology. The neural encoding of conceptual knowledge is a central element in this enterprise.

This entire chapter is predicated on the direct neural encoding of conceptual structure—could it be otherwise? In a conventional digital computer, the wiring diagrams tell us virtually nothing about the information structure stored in the system; the computer is a general-purpose interpreter. Almost all its hardware is passive memory, and this memory is idle except when accessed by the interpreter. Many cognitive scientists still like to think of the brain in this way, and for them the study of neural encodings makes no sense. One explores the high-level structure of cognition in a way that is independent of any embodiment. A great deal can be learned in this way, and this chapter relies heavily on the results of such studies. The problem with this stance is that the speed of the system (the brain) relative to that of its elements (the neurons) places very severe constraints on the possible organization of knowledge. Human reactions, over a wide range of tasks, take a few hundred milliseconds—about 100 times the switching time of individual neurons. Thus, for example, an interpreter of the standard kind would be too slow by many orders of magnitude. Though in principle there are a wide range of possible realizations of intelligence, we know that our brains are constrained to use one that is quite direct. This chapter can also be viewed as an exploration of the relationships among three kinds of structure: the structure of the brain, the structural characterization of behavior, and the conceptual structure of knowledge. The questions addressed in this chapter are these: What do we now know about the range of possible encodings of knowledge in the brain? What does this suggest for experimental and theoretical research? All this falls within a research domain characterized by such terms as *connectionist, neural model, massively parallel, cell assembly, pattern of activation,* and *parallel distributed processing.*

I will pursue these questions following what has become the paradigmatic method of cognitive science: converging constraints. Neither behavioral, biological, nor computational results alone greatly restrict theorizing, but taken together these results preclude many models that look plausible from a narrow perspective. The 100-step rule for simple behaviors is an elementary example of how converging constraints can lead to insights.

For concreteness, let us suppose that the problem is to describe how a human brain could represent and exploit the information in a standard encyclopedia. We assume that any representation will employ some notion of "concept" that corresponds roughly to a dictionary word-sense. The only other primitive needed is the "relation." We will assume that all the required knowledge can be captured as a collection of relations among concepts. The encyclopedia contains pictures, so some appearance models are required, but these can also be expressed in terms of concepts and relations. There is no attempt to define formally the notions of concept and relation, because the various representational schemes discussed will entail properties of the primitives. What I will do is show how different models of neural encoding relate to constraints arising from various branches of science. To begin, I will focus only on the representation of concepts, ignoring relations as most of the literature continues to do.

Even leaving relations aside, the literature contains a wide range of notions of what a concept is and how it might be represented neurally. The simplest view restricts consideration to very concrete nouns such as 'horse' or 'chair', ignoring more complex concepts such as 'game', 'yesterday', 'active', and 'love'. Even in this quite restricted context, the representation of concepts has proved to be a deep problem for philosophers, linguists, and psychologists (Smith and Medin 1981). Our point of departure is the computational models of artificial intelligence, which have made explicit many of these issues of conceptual knowledge (Charniak and McDermott 1985). A minimum requirement is that the representation support the answering of questions about concepts (and later about their relations). One particularly simple kind of question concerns the structure of the object itself, e.g., how many legs some chair has. Models that treat concepts as unstructured collections of attributes will need to provide additional mechanisms for answering even these simple questions. Many studies of neural concept representations ignore entirely the issue of how concepts are used. No serious attempt to understand real cognition can afford to do so.

The range of possible representations of concepts in the brain is constrained by a combination of computational considerations and neurobiological findings. The 100-step rule for simple tasks already eliminates any conventional computer model. Other pertinent facts include the relatively small number of neurons (about 10^{11}, or 100 billion), the large number of connections between neurons (about 10^4 per unit), and the low rate of information transfer. It may seem that 10^{11} is not a small number; however, in 10^6 input fibers from each eye a computer scientist immediately detects a major constraint. For example, dedicating one unit to test for a possible line between any pair of points in the retina would take $(10^6)^2$ neurons—more than there are. The information rate between individual neurons at a firing rate of 100 spikes per second is about five bits, enough to encode one letter of the alphabet. (If complex messages are being conveyed, it is not by individual neurons.) Much of the computational power of the brain derives from its great connectivity, and a challenge to theory is to explain how this power is realized. Although this chapter concentrates more on representation than on learning, there are also constraints on plasticity that are pertinent. The major findings are that the growth of new fibers in adults is much too slow and constrained to account for learning and that there is no generation of new neurons. There is sufficient converging evidence (Lynch 1986) to allow us to assume that long-term concept and relation memory comes about through changes in connection strength, although rapid connection change is problematic. There is also reason to believe that skill learning may involve significantly different mechanisms than concept learning (Thompson 1986).

The best way to begin a serious discussion of neural encoding of concepts is to tie down two simple theories that embody the extreme ends of the range of possible answers. The most compact representation possible would have a unique unit dedicated to each concept. If we assume that a unit corresponds to one neuron, then this is the "grandmother cell" or "pontifical cell" theory. The other extreme would have each concept represented as a pattern of activity in all the units in the system. This is well known as the "holographic" model of memory, and it is the most highly distributed theory that we will consider. In addition to the pure theory based on optical holograms, we will call holographic any model that has all the units in a system encoding each concept (Willshaw 1981); most of these are matrix formulations. Nothing much would change in either theory if a "unit" corresponded to a dendritic subtree instead of an entire neuron. The discussion will proceed by moving in from the extremes to examine the range of plausible encoding models and some of their properties. A great deal of excellent work has been done employing the end-case assumptions, but neither of them could actually be right.

The extreme opposing models of neural representation lead to radically different views of many aspects of cognitive science. Table 1 presents a number of contrasting terms that arise, respectively, from the punctate and the fully distributed view of neural coding. Not all these items will be meaningful to every reader, but everyone should recognize some striking contrasts in perspective. All these contrasting notions will find their way into the discussion. One term that may be misleading in table 1 is "distributed repre-

Table 1
Contrasting terms.

punctate	diffuse
local	distributed representation
grandmother neuron	hologram, spin-glass
disjoint codes	homogeneous code
detector	filter
labeled line	pattern of activity
active memory	passive memory
reduction	emergence
hierarchy	complete connectivity
recruiting	adapting
general computation	correlation

sentation." The problem is that people have been using this term to denote everything from a fully holographic model to one where two units help code a concept; thus, the term has lost its usefulness. The various contrasting terms often accompany significant differences in research goals and strategies. One intriguing idea that we will pursue is that many of these apparent conflicts are basically alternative ways of looking at the same set of phenomena; this is vaguely reminiscent of atomic physics and thermodynamics.

We should first dispense with an abstract argument that equates the punctate and hologram models. It is true, in a sense, that an encoding having one active unit per concept is a pattern of activity in the mass. But this identification is too abstract to be meaningful. Another proposed way to identify holographic and punctate representations comes from linear algebra and the idea of alternate coordinate axes for a vector space. If, as in many models, the output of a unit is the (thresholded) linear combination of its inputs, one can view this unit as a (very large) vector, v, whose coordinates are the outputs of each predecessor unit. There is, in principle, another set of bases for the vector space for which this vector, v, is an axis and can therefore be represented by one nonzero coordinate. This argument fails for three reasons. Even for strictly linear input combinations, the output threshold destroys the applicability of linear algebra and there is no biologically plausible way to eliminate nonlinearity. In addition, no single transform would work unless the set of concepts were independent and therefore small (see section 3.2). More important, the computational properties of the two representations are radically different, as in the example just above.

1 Punctate Models

The next step is to show why neither the pure punctate model nor the holographic model is consistent with the facts. We will start with the punctate model because the story here is simpler.

The extreme end of the compact-representation position is to assume that each concept is represented by exactly one neuron. This view received considerable support from single-unit recording research, which found that units in sensory areas responded best to a relatively narrow class of stimuli (Hubel and Wiesel 1979). The punctate encoding is also called "labeled lines", emphasizing the fact that, in this encoding, each axon will be conveying a specific message when it is active. The most influential expression of this position was Horace Barlow's "neuron doctrine," which is worth quoting in its outline form:

The following five brief statements are intended to define which aspect of the brain's activity is important for understanding its main function, to suggest the way that single neurons represent what is going on around us, and to say how this is related to our subjective experience. The statements are dogmatic and incautious because it is important that they should be clear and testable.

First dogma
A description of that activity of a single nerve cell which is transmitted to and influences other nerve cells, and of a nerve cell's response to such influences from other cells, is a complete enough description for functional understanding of the nervous system. There is nothing else 'looking at' or controlling this activity, which must therefore provide a basis for understanding how the brain controls behavior.

Second dogma
At progressively higher levels in sensory pathways information about the physical stimulus is carried by progressively fewer active neurons. The sensory system is organized to achieve as complete a representation as possible with the minimum number of active neurons. [See figure 3.7 of the present chapter.]

Third dogma
Trigger features of neurons are matched to the redundant features of sensory stimulation in order to achieve greater completeness and economy of representation. This selective responsiveness is determined by the sensory stimulation to which neurons have been exposed, as well as by genetic factors operating during development.

Fourth dogma
Just as physical stimuli directly cause receptors to initiate neural activity, so the active high-level neurons directly and simply cause the elements of our perception.

Fifth dogma
The frequency of neural impulses codes subjective certainty: A high impulse frequency in a given neuron corresponds to a high degree of confidence that the cause of the percept is present in the external world. (Barlow 1972)

These five dogmas are much less controversial in their original form than in most of the straw-man characterizations derived from them. Obviously enough, much of their force is in defense of the direct-encoding position shared by all connectionist models. The point most relevant to the present discussion is that individual neurons are the appropriate object for study in determining how the brain does its work. This is commonly identified with the most compact, punctate style of neural model, and it is an appropriate introduction to this end of the spectrum.

Figure 1 presents a vastly oversimplified version of how a punctate system might encode and exploit conceptual knowledge. The memory network is a category-based hierarchy with each concept and each property name represented by a rectangular unit. The triangular nodes stand for intermediate units which become active when two of their three input lines are active. Suppose the system has a routine that retrieves its knowledge of food tastes as an aid

Feldman   74

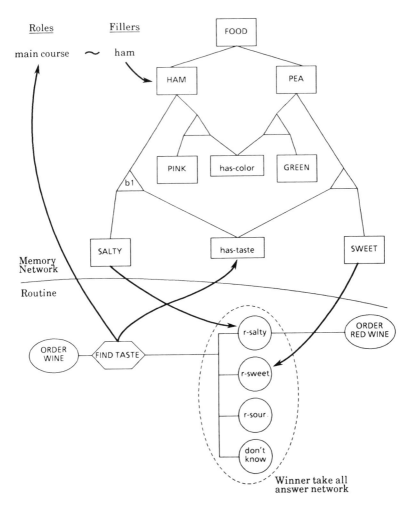

Figure 1
Connectionist retrieval system. After Shastri (1985).

to ordering wine, such as that cartooned in the lower half of the figure. If activation is spread simultaneously to the "main course" of the meal and to the desired property, 'has-taste', exactly one triangular evidence node, b1, will receive two active inputs, and this will lead to the activation of the concept 'salty'. This is the required answer, but for technical reasons an intervening clean-up network is needed where the answer is actually put to use. One interesting feature of Shastri's (1985) model is that the same memory network is able to classify a salty, pink food as ham—the triangular evidence nodes work in both directions.

Though it is oversimplified, figure 1 does convey much of the flavor of punctate (and other compact) connectionist models and their appeal to some scientists and rejection by others. The main point is that everything is quite explicit; the concepts, the properties, and even the rules of operation are simple and direct. This makes it relatively easy to express and test specific models, either at the neural level or more abstractly as in our example. No one believes that the brain uses exactly the structure of figure 1, but any highly compact concept representation could behave in essentially the same way. The very explicitness of all this is what makes many scientists reject punctate models either for abstract study or as a theory of brain structure. Although any particular structure or theory can be encoded (just as in circuit design), nothing may be learned about the general properties of intelligence. Moreover, how could such a hard-wired system develop and adapt in living brains? I will discuss this last issue in section 3; the others are questions of scientific taste and judgment. But the answer to how the brain represents knowledge is not a matter of taste, and we next explore some arguments that it cannot be in the punctate style of figure 1.

The first point is that a large number of neurons ($\sim 10^5$) die each day, and these are distributed throughout the brain. If each concept were represented by a single neuron, one would expect to lose at least some concepts (at random) each day. This argument is often taken to be conclusive evidence against the compact model, but there is a slight variant of the punctate view that is proof against the death of individual units. Suppose that instead of one unit per concept, the system dedicated three or five, distributed somewhat physically. All the theories and experiments would look the same as in the one-unit case, but the redundancy would solve the problem of neuron death. Although the number of neurons dying is large, the fraction is quite small ($\sim 10^{-6}$), so the probability of losing two of the representatives of a concept in a lifetime is quite low ($\sim 10^{-7}$). There is also considerable redundancy at the system level; there are several separate ways to perform a given function.

As we will see, there are other reasons for rejecting the punctate model, but the death of neurons is not critical.

Another, and more telling, argument against a purely punctate model is that there would not be enough units to represent everything. It is fine to envision a unit that is active when you recognize your grandmother's picture in the encyclopedia, but what about all your other memories of her? Is there a separate unit for each age, each outfit, each body position, etc.? There are two aspects to this argument: the sheer number of things to be represented and the relational structure among them. Merely representing all the possible concepts is not a problem if efficient encodings are used. For example, a group of 100 binary units can represent 2^{100} ($\sim 10^{30}$) distinct patterns, which is far more than the number of concepts required. A million such groups is ample memory, and it is a small fraction of the neurons available. (~ 0.1 percent). The most efficient coding of information is not the main design criterion, but there are constraints that preclude some encodings as too wasteful. Supporters of the compact end of the spectrum have conceded this and have developed coding techniques that permit the encoding of significantly more information without a major change in computational architecture.

In parallel with these theoretical developments, experimentalists have been reframing their view of the activity of single units. The idea of a neuron as a "detector" of one kind of event has been declining for some time, but no alternative term has yet evolved. The psychophysicist's idea of a "filter" is the diffuse equivalent (all units filter all signals) and is equally misleading. Although no new word has been established, many experimentalists now (correctly, in my view) view sensory neurons as having responsivity of different fineness to a variety of stimulus dimensions. Single-unit neurophysiology studies are finding effects of stimuli beyond the classical receptive field (Allman et al. 1985) as is inevitable in an interacting system of units. And, of course, any idea that all of intelligence could be understood simply by finding the neuron for each concept was always silly. It is clear that Barlow's dogmas could use some revision, and the appendix to the present chapter suggests a variant that seems reasonable. For example, the fifth dogma should reflect the fact that firing frequency encodes some information about stimulus features as well as some about confidence. Figure 2 shows the firing rate of a visual-system neuron as a function of binocular temporal and spatial offset of a target, and is typical. When one includes the firing rate (instead of just on/off) as part of the information code, the range of the distinct entities that are representable goes up significantly (Ballard 1986b). For example, the relative activity rate of three color "channels" is enough to specify a wide range of

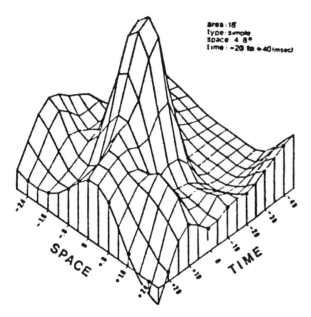

area : 18
type : simple
space : 4 8°
time : -20 to +40 (msec)

SPACE   TIME

Figure 2
Response of a cat visual (area 18) cell to a binocular stimulus as a function of temporal and spatial offset. Spatial offset is from −2.4° to 2.4°; temporal offset is from −20 to 40 msec. Source: Gardner et al. 1985.

hue and intensity combinations. Summarizing the discussion to this point: Whereas the purely punctate view is unsupportable, there is no numerical problem with a theory that has each concept represented by the activity of a few units. Such an encoding shares many of the properties of the punctate model and is consistent with single-unit experiments in a wide range of brain structures.

Another argument used against compact models of neural representation arises from bulk-activity experiments. A single small stimulus can give rise to activity in a significant fraction of the total population. There are several reasons why this fact does not preclude compact representations. For one thing, the "simplicity" of a stimulus looks different in various encoding schemes. In a Fourier encoding, a small dot activates receptors for all spatial frequencies. In a parameter-space encoding (Ballard 1986a), a single feature provides evidence for many higher-level features, and these may be suppressed more slowly than when more information is present. Finally, there does appear to be some nonspecific gating (Barber 1980) which activates an entire structure when any input appears. None of this is to say that the punctate position is correct, only that arguments from bulk activity do not preclude its viability.

Though the cell-death and bulk-activities arguments against punctate representation are easily accommodated, it is easy to see that there really could not be one neuron for each concept of interest—there are not enough neurons. One clear example arises in early vision. It is well known that the visual system is sensitive to at least the following local stimulus properties: orientation, intensity, hue, depth, motion direction, and size. A system that could resolve ten values for each of the six dimensions would require 10^6 units to represent all combinations of values. But there are about 10^6 separate points at the narrowest (retinal ganglion) level that must be represented, so the total requirement would be 10^{12}—which is too many. Similar combinatorial arguments can be made at higher conceptual levels (e.g., all the memories of one's grandmother). At these higher levels, the structure of the knowledge itself provides considerable encoding economy (section 3); however, early processing requires additional mechanisms. In fact, quite a lot is known about the response properties of cells in visual cortex, and there is a clean computational story that helps to organize the experimental data and contributes to the goal of constraining the possible models of neural encoding.

The basic idea is depicted in figure 3 for the case of two stimulus dimensions. Suppose (as turns out to be the case) that units respond nonuniformly to various stimulus dimensions. For example, the vertical rectangle in the lower left depicts the responsiveness of a cell that is five times more sensitive to size than to orientation, and the horizontal rectangle the opposite. The nice point is that the joint activity of two such cells can code the stimulus space as finely as the finest dimension of either (see the crossed rectangles) while requiring significantly fewer units. This computational mechanism goes by the name "coarse-fine coding" and appears to describe a good deal of neural computation. In general, given K stimulus dimensions, each with a desired resolution of N values, the punctate encoding requires N^K units. A coarse-fine encoding with the coarse dimensions D requires a total of

$$T = K \cdot N \left(\frac{N}{D} \right)^{K-1}$$

units. This is because there will be K separate tilings (covers) of the K-dimensional space, but each will be covered coarsely, and this requires N/D units in all dimensions but one, which has N units. This formula still grows exponentially, but it is significantly smaller for the cases of interest. For example, our early-vision example had $K = 6$ and $N = 10$. With $D = 5$, this yields 1,920 units per point instead of the 1,000,000 for the pure punctate

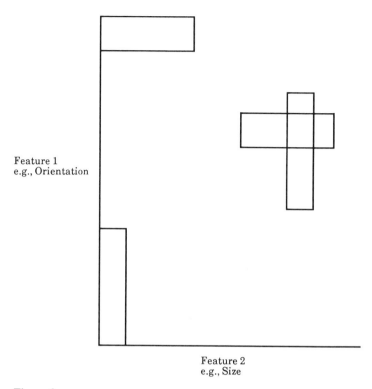

Feature 1
e.g., Orientation

Feature 2
e.g., Size

Figure 3
Coarse–fine coding.

encoding. Since I believe these ideas to be central, I will discuss a number of related issues next.

The critical point in the construction is the overlap of receptive fields, not their asymmetric shape. Essentially the same arguments can be made for symmetric overlapping fields; this is known as "coarse-coding" (Hinton 1981a). Computational ideas of this kind have been known for some time to provide a nice account of hyperaccuity, the ability of humans to resolve details finer than the spacing of their receptors. In both coarse and coarse-fine coding there is a price to be paid for saving all these units. If two stimuli that overlap co-occur, the system will be unable to resolve them. That situation is depicted in figure 4. Suppose one stimulus is encoded by the two rectangles labeled X and the other by the two rectangles labeled Y. The intersections labeled X and Y encode the desired information, but the "ghosts" labeled G would be equally active. One of these expresses the conjunction of Y-size and X-orientation and the other the converse. This is an instance of "cross-talk" in

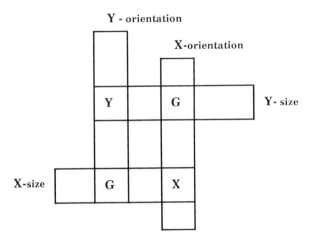

Figure 4
Ghosts in the machine.

neural encodings. Cross-talk, the fundamental problem of shared encodings, appears to be a critical limiting factor on distributed models, as we will see. For the simple case of coarse coding, some analysis of the trade-offs has been carried out (Sullins 1985).

A final point on coarse coding is that the multiple-dimension, fine-grained information is left implicit in the representation. The joint activity of several units encodes the desired information, but how can subsequent computation make use of it? This is another critical issue in shared encodings and a major reason why no holographic model has gone to more than one level. In the case where the information is carried by the activity of a small number of units ($K \sim 10$), there is a simple and biologically plausible solution. Suppose that the inputs to a unit (a neuron) were not all treated uniformly but were grouped into "sites," each of which computed separately a combined input value. If each site computed the logical AND of all its inputs, this would be an ideal receiver for the joint output of coarse coding. Figure 5 (a cartoon of how this might go) shows a fragment of an abstract multiplication table for integers between 1 and 9. Only one inhibitory link is shown. Units representing possible answers (e.g., 12) have separate conjunctive receiving sites and take on the activation of the maximum (or logical OR) of the sites. There are two reasons why this general idea provides a major saving over punctate encodings. One reason is that one computational role of units has been brought down to sites, significantly increasing the feasible numbers (by perhaps 1,000). The other is that not all combinations of outputs need to be

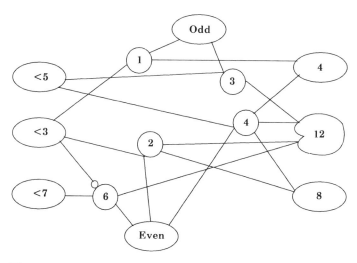

Figure 5
Multiplication table for integers.

explicitly represented. Although it is well beyond the current story, one can envision how the coarse-fine coding units could combine to represent the feature space with different resolutions.

It is interesting to consider if we could eliminate the circular nodes carrying the punctate number representations and deal directly with the distributed representation on the basis of number range and odd-even parity. The obvious solution is to link directly the appropriate combinations to the receiving sites. This works fairly well, but it does encounter some problems. Suppose 1 and 4 were simultaneously active. Our distributed representation of 2 is <3 and even, both of which are active in this case, and this could lead to activation of the answer 8. This problem can be fixed (e.g., by having separate sites for the first and second arguments), but it does point out the delicacy of doing computation with distributed representations.

One final discussion will close off this path of consideration. The examples of coarse-fine coding used overlapping encodings but were based on the minimum possible number of cells to cover some feature space. Suppose instead we allowed for redundancy in the coverage, say three separate tesselations of the space. In terms of figure 3, a second covering could be similar bars at 45° and 315° to the axes (Ballard 1986b). We could still use separate receiving sites for each desired stimulus, but the computation would be not just a logical AND. In fact, a thresholded sum of activity might be quite plausible as the sites' way of computing the likelihood of its combination being present.

This would combine the ideas of error tolerance and information reduction in a simple and plausible way. Edelman (1981) has come to essentially the same kind of model through a very different route, starting from his expertise in immunology. Since this is how I believe the brain really works, I will next attempt to show how the holographic approach narrows down (*sic*) to the same solution.

2   Holographic Models

Holographic models have been fervently supported by biologists, psychologists, and theoreticians. There is no comparable fervor for compact models. In fact, several researchers preach fully distributed models while employing punctate ones, often in the same work. One well-known example is the elegant "traveling salesman" model of Hopfield and Tank (1985), which is purely punctate and cannot be mapped to Hopfield's holographic memory proposals (1982). One major factor in the popularity of this view was the early work of Karl Lashley, who found that, for a variety of tasks, the deficit exhibited by lesioned rats was best explained by the total amount of cortex removed—the "law of mass action." Lashley summarized his view of memory representation in the classic 1950 paper "In Search of the Engram." The following passage in that paper continues to motivate much work:

It is not possible to demonstrate the isolated localization of a memory trace anywhere within the nervous system. Limited regions may be essential for learning or retention of a particular activity, but within such regions the parts are functionally equivalent. The engram is represented throughout the area. . . . Briefly, the characteristics of the nervous network are such that when it is subject to any pattern of excitation, it may develop a pattern of activity, reduplicated throughout an entire functional area, by spread of excitations, much as the surface of a liquid develops an interference pattern of spreading waves when it is disturbed at several points. . . . Consideration of the numerical relations of sensory and other cells in the brain makes it certain, I believe, that all of the cells of the brain must be in almost constant activity, either firing or actively inhibited. There is no great excess of cells which can be reserved as the seat of special memories. The complexity of the functions involved in reproductive memory implies that every instance of recall requires the activity of literally millions of neurons. The same neurons which retain the memory traces of one experience must also participate in countless other activities.

Recall involves the synergic action or some sort of resonance among a very large number of neurons. . . . From the numerical relations involved, I believe that even the reservation of individual synapses for special associative reaction is impossible.

Since Lashley's time, the intricate specialized structure of mammalian cortex has been elucidated. No one currently holds the view that all of cortex is holographic. (Reading Lashley's article makes it clear that he would reach very different conclusions on the basis of current experimental evidence.) Since all the primary sensory and motor areas have been found to have specialized structures, the holographic hypothesis is currently restricted to "higher" brain areas whose functional organization is not yet understood. Another historical source of motivation for diffuse models was the wonderful 1949 book *The Organization of Behavior,* by Donald Hebb. Hebb introduced the notion of cell assemblies, but was (appropriately for the time) vague about how they actually encode knowledge. Hebb definitely envisioned a dynamic pattern of activity, but there are two interpretations of this. The most literal would be to assume that concepts are purely dynamic and are not tied to any particular tissue; this idea has been pursued a bit (von der Marlsberg 1987; Bienenstock 1985), but without much success, and the experimental data are not encouraging. A more general notion of dynamic activity of cell assemblies is inherent in all current connectionist theories; the compact-diffuse question is about what fraction of a system is involved. A closely related question is structure; it does not seem useful to think of a computer as a "chip assembly." We will return to this after examining theoretical hologram models.

Holographic models are theoretically attractive because of two properties: fault tolerance and generalization. The brain clearly has these properties, and it is easy to see informally why holographic models do also. If all the units of a large system are involved in coding one concept, the failure of some of them can be tolerated. Furthermore, two concepts that share much of their activity patterns will tend to behave similarly. More technically, the theoretical hologram models have all been based on one form or another of mathematical correlation. An excellent compendium of holographic-style models can be found in Hinton and Anderson 1981, and I will often cite this rather than the original papers.

The purest holographic model is, unsurprisingly, the optical hologram itself. A nice presentation can be found in Willshaw 1981, where it is also shown that the purely linear hologram is undesirable on both computational and biological grounds. The models typically studied are large rectangular matrices representing all the possible connections between m input units and n output units, which need not be distinct (see figure 6). The most common case, and one of the easiest to consider, is where each unit compares the sum of its weighted inputs against its threshold and emits 1 if the sum of inputs is greater and 0 otherwise. A concept is represented as a binary vector over all the input lines. Each element of the vector may be uninterpreted or may be thought of as the presence or absence of a microfeature characterizing the

Feldman

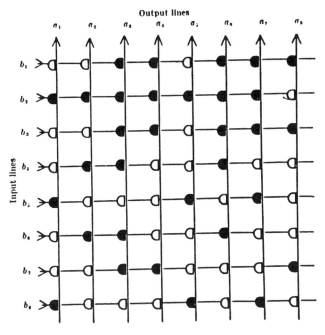

Figure 6
An associative net. The nodes that have been activated in the storage process are
colored black. Source: Willshaw 1981.

concept. (In a punctate view of this, one would imagine each output unit as
responsible for computing one bit of the output, using all the inputs according
to its weights on them.) If the input and the output are identified, the matrix
becomes a pattern-completion machine. The basic idea is simple and derives
from the mathematical notion of correlation. The correlation of two binary
vectors u and v is simply

$$\sum_{j=1}^{n} u_j v_j,$$

and this is obviously maximized when $u = v$. In a well-distributed set of
vectors, an input distorted by modest noise or omission will correlate best
with the appropriate complete vector. This is the basic source of error resistance and generalization in holographic-style models. What makes them interesting is that a connection matrix with the appropriate weights can be learned
with a simple, local procedure. Most of my discussion of learning is in section 3, but this case is so central that it will be discussed here.

For the auto-associative, pattern-completion case, we want weights w_{ij} such that

$$X_j = \sum w_{ij} X_i|_0^1,$$

assuming that the threshold is included as another weight. The natural local weight-change rule is to increase the weight between two units when they both are active (output = 1). This is essentially Hebb's rule, and it can be interpreted as increasing the weight of units whose firing is correlated. Symbolically,

$$\Delta w_{ij} = (X_i \cdot X_j) \cdot \delta, \quad \text{where } \delta \text{ is a constant.}$$

If all the weights are initially set to zero and the auto-association matrix is trained on some P sequences, then

$$w_{ij} = \delta \cdot \sum_{k=1}^{p} X_i^{(k)} \cdot X_j^{(k)}.$$

The resulting matrix can be shown to be optimal in some cases (orthonormal vectors) and is a good estimator in many others (Kohonen 1984). Thus, a simple and biologically plausible local learning rule yields a matrix that reliably finds the best match to an input pattern under some distortion conditions (but not others). The binary, linear auto-associator is the simplest of a wide variety of essentially similar models. Many variations on all aspects of the model have been tried (Hinton and Anderson 1981; Kohonen 1984; Barto and Anandan 1984). The more refined models use a variant of Hebb's rule that allows feedback from some external result to affect the weight-change process (Kohonen 1984; Barto et al. 1981; Anderson and Murphy 1986). The shortcomings of the methodology do not lie in the learning rules; they demonstrate that essentially anything that can be represented as a linear threshold matrix can be learned by correlation. The problem is that the representation itself is much too weak. There is a well-known relation between correlation matrices and classical pattern recognition, and the same basic inability to deal with structure, occlusion, and invariance applies in both cases.

There are a number of computational considerations that rule out any existing holographic encoding and make it extremely unlikely that one will be discovered. Before examining these in detail, we must eliminate a trivial path of escape sometimes sought by defenders of the holographic models. It is a truism of computation theory that any universal mechanism can simulate any other if computational costs are ignored. Since a large enough (associative or other) memory can be made universal, one can find a way to encode any computation as a holographic memory plus a small interpreter. But ignoring

computational costs is precisely what we cannot do in the current enterprise—computational costs are among the principle constraints on the viability of neural representation schemes. Much of the holographic work has been
directed to purely passive memory networks, and we will examine these, but
it is important not to forget that no passive memory will satisfy the basic time
and competence constraints for conceptual knowledge. A sequential machine
with a fast associative memory is still orders of magnitude off the required
performance.

When computational issues are taken seriously, the holographic model is
fatally deficient, even as a passive associative memory. The basic problems
with any holographic representational scheme are cross-talk, communication,
invariance, and the inability to capture structure. Essentially the same problems have prevented the development of holographic computer memories or
recognition systems despite considerable effort. Consider the problem of representing a concept like 'grandmother' as a pattern of activity in all the units
in some memory network. We can assume that different parts of the network
represent various input modalities (e.g. vision), and that they all lead to the
same overall pattern. But notice what would happen if two or more concepts
were presented at the same time (e.g., 'grandmother at the White House').
The encodings for the two concepts would normally overlap, and the system
would get garbled. This is a massive instance of the cross-talk problem of
figure 4. Of course, we can reduce the probability of cross-talk by having
fewer units active for each pattern. Suppose that there are punctate output
detectors for each pattern in the holographic memory (nothing becomes easier
if there are not). Willshaw (1981) addressed the question of how one could
arrange the coding and detector thresholds so that only the desired detector
would respond to each pattern. If one assumes that the cross-talk is randomly
distributed (the best case), the system will be reliable for individual retrievals
only if the number of units active for each pattern is proportional to the log-
arithm of the number of units in the diffuse memory. This means that a network of 1,000,000 units should use an encoding with about 20 active units
per concept—suspiciously close to the number that would arise from a redundant, coarse-coded compact approach.

If a fully distributed encoding is used for concepts, there is an unsolved
problem of how conceptual information could move from one subsystem
(e.g. vision) to another (e.g. speech). The obvious encoding would be with
a "bus" or group of links as wide as the holographic representation, which is
unrealistic. In fact, there are many fewer long-distance than local connection-
ions in the cortex. If only some of the units were linked, they would constitute a more compact representation of the concept, which violates the

holographic assumption. Even so, unless these encodings were largely disjoint, communication over the bus would have to be sequential to avoid cross-talk. If cross-talk were present, people would make mistakes like seeing a horse and a chair and mistakenly saying something irrelevant (e.g. "apple sauce"). If microfeatures were the basis of the representation, then something like "rocking horse" should result. The idea that visual information is conveyed to other parts of the brain one concept at a time clearly violates timing constraints by orders of magnitude. The notion that "attention" can restrict the system to one concept at a time is not tenable. Consider how a cowboy movie is mapped from vision to concepts. What is the concept for each frame: the posse, the horse and rider and saddle and hat, etc.? How do they fit together to keep a gestalt of the scene and the scenario? What is happening with all the other visual information? How does attention know what to transmit unless the structure of the scene and the story line are already known at the vision end? And, of course, we would be back at a sequential machine model. There appears to be no alternative to assuming that, at least for communication, the representation of concepts must be largely disjoint and thus compact.

The same communication problem would arise within the concept memory itself if one tried to build a knowledge structure like figure 1 with a diffuse representation. If a concept like "salty" were represented only by a large pattern, the links for this entire pattern would have to go to all the places that related to saltiness—and be treated correctly at each place. If a concept encoded by N units had to be linked to M other concepts, a total of $M * N$ links would be needed. One punctate intermediate unit can reduce the requirement to $N + M$ connections. The more distributed the representation, the more serious this problem becomes. Again, any serious reduction in this wiring requirement would constitute a compact representation. And, as in the intermodal case, unless these representations were largely disjoint, concept processing would have to be sequential to avoid cross-talk. This eliminates the spreading activation and massively parallel processing that motivated the whole idea.

Even so, no one has suggested how to represent any but the simplest concepts in the holographic style. For example, the problem of all the different historical views of one's grandmother is as difficult for the hologram as for the punctate model. In fact, it is far from obvious how to make the same distributed pattern active for alternative views of a chair, even without occlusion. One could, I suppose, assume that there are essential invariant features of one's grandmother that are derived (magically) from all the different pictures, stories, etc. involving her. Even so, how would one express the structure of concepts such as that grandma has two legs, the left of which is slightly shorter? All concepts in any holographic structure that I know of are totally without internal structure. There is an idea of associating the components of a representation with microfeatures (and this will be discussed later), but these are still unstructured. Nor does any of the holographic proposals provide a way of answering even a simple question, such as "What color is grandmother's hair?" (let alone at different ages). There are a number of other problems with holographic models, but this should suffice to show that this end of the compact-diffuse spectrum is no more viable than the punctate end.

The biological evidence against anything vaguely like a holographic model is equally compelling. This is only fair, since the holographic hypothesis denies any relevance to neuroanatomy and physiology. Since intricate specificity and detailed visuotopic, tonotopic, etc. maps have been discovered everywhere in the brain that has been examined, the only hope for the hologram is for some higher association areas. Even there, the anatomical structure has been found to be much like the sensory areas (Goldman-Rakic and Schwartz 1982) and nothing like the connection of each input to each output required by matrix models. Simple counting arguments show that at most 10,000 neurons could be in a matrix-like network, and the local connectivity precludes this possibility as well. Neurosurgery relies upon precision stimulation and recording to localize lesion sites. There may be a point to studying fully distributed encodings, but direct mapping to the brain is not among them. Even Kohonen, a major figure in holographic-style modeling, says that "there are good experimentally verified reasons to assume that for a particular sensory experience or other occurrence, the pattern of activity over the complete memory field consists of only a few activated local areas" (1980, p. 132).

Another argument for highly distributed representations derives from the large number of input fibres ($\sim 10^4$) to cortical neurons. If all these fibers participate actively, then, *ipso facto,* the representation is diffuse. There are three reasons why this argument fails: Though there has been no definitive study on the number of pre-synaptic events required for neural firing, estimates gleaned from papers and conversations run from one event to a few dozen. No one has suggested that several thousand synapses must fire at once for an action potential. Also, as can be seen from figures 5 and 7, many of the connections could represent alternative ways of activating the same concept (e.g., from different points in space). Another way of looking at this is that the thousandfold connectivity is capturing an "OR" of activation conditions rather than an "AND." Finally, as we will see in section 3, learning in a connectionist system requires the potential for many more connections than are ever made functional. The most striking physiological demonstration of this principle is in the neural-reorganization studies of Merzenich *et al.* (1984).

All this may seem like flogging a dead horse; however, purely holographic theories continue to be seriously proposed. Recently there has been a flurry of interest in spin glasses as holographic memory models among theoretical physicists (see Hopfield 1982; Toulouse et al. 1985). Any physical system will, in isolation, reach some stable state, and each of these states could be looked upon as encoding a different concept; this is obviously a massively parallel system. The spin-glass story is beyond the scope of this chapter, but the key idea is that spin glasses are idealized materials that can take on many stable states in ways that are mathematically interesting. The hope is that analysis of these will provide insights into the behavior of the brain and/or the design of parallel hardware. This might well happen, but the current spin-glass models share the inherent deficiencies of all holographic representations and have no direct applicability to the neural representation of concepts.

There are two basic ways of adding the required structure to hologram-like models: to add structure to the collection of units (see figure 7), and to try to construct structures out of unstructured cell assemblies. Both approaches lead to systems quite like the redundant, coarse-coded approach. Consider the latter idea. Nothing as concrete as figure 1 has been attempted, but one envisions about 100 (Palm) units in an assembly jointly encoding some unspecified number of concepts. But we know that the cross-talk and coarse-coding constraints limit the range of possible number of concept nodes to a few hundred. Of course, the units in the assembly cannot represent the detailed structure of the concept, because they are shared by unrelated concepts. The structure is represented by connections (also never specified) among cell assemblies, which presumably play a role equivalent to that of the evidence links in figure 1. This move preserves the sovereignty of the cell assembly, but only in a titular fashion; the work is all done by the connections among assemblies.

The alternative move, adding structure to the assembled masses, comes in many variants and is treated in the next section.

3 The Middle Ground and Beyond

It is difficult to interpret such findings, but I think that they point to the conclusions that the associative connections or memory traces of the conditioned reflex do not extend across the cortex as well-defined arcs or paths. Such arcs are either diffused through all parts of the cortex, pass by relay through lower centers, or do not exist. (Lashley 1950, p. 461)

It is clear that various forms and aspects of learning and memory involve particular systems, networks and circuits in the brain and it now apppears possible to identify these circuits, localize the sites of memory storage and analyze the cellular and molecular mechanisms of memory. (Thompson 1986)

We have seen that neither the purely punctate model nor the fully holographic model is at all plausible as a theory of how the brain represents conceptual knowledge. A variety of arguments have all converged on the idea that concepts are represented by overlapping activity among a modest number of units (from 3 to 100), and that the structure within and across these groups cannot be uniform or arbitrary. This is all fairly close to the compact end of the original spectrum, but the story is more complex than that. There are important lessons to be learned from the work on highly distributed models, and there are many difficult problems that have eluded all theories. To simplify the discussion, let us adopt the standard convention and treat all compact representations as punctate. As was shown above, the purely punctate theory cannot be biologically valid, and the redundant coarse-coded variant is plausible and computationally very close to punctate version. It is simply much easier to understand punctate systems, and all current models—however distributed—use punctate encodings of some elements for clarity. It is understood that direct neurobiological applications will have to take the detailed encoding more seriously.

From my perspective, there is only one conceptual difference between the current compact and diffuse models of neural knowledge representation, and this difference can be seen as one of research strategy. Consider the punctate model of the appearance of horses shown in figure 7. This is taken from a paper of mine that attempts to show how vision yields such hierarchical conceptual descriptions (Feldman 1985). At the lowest level are feature pairs, which we assume are derived by early vision networks. (The fact that there are feature pairs rather than individual features or n-tuples of them arises from technical considerations that are not relevant here; see Feldman 1985 and McClelland et al. 1986.) The remaining structure is organized as a hierarchy in which activation propagates toward the top pontifical cell which is active when a horse is recognized. Even in this unrealistically punctate version, the recognition of a horse is a "pattern of activation" in many of these units. Since the connections are two-way, mentioning the name of a horse will cause some activation in all the nodes comprising visual and other descriptions of horses. Looking at this another way, we see that it makes no sense to talk about the activation of a single concept in such structure—activation automatically

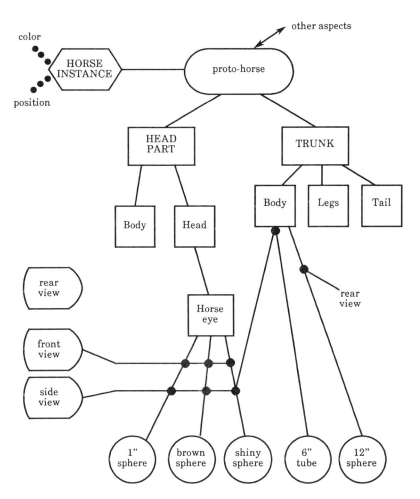

Figure 7
Punctate model of a horse.

spreads to encompass a subnetwork. Notice also that this structure will recognize a horse—even when some features are missing or garbled—if the
other features plus the context are sufficiently strong. This captures the error
tolerance and some of the generalization ability that were most attractive
about correlation matrices. Computer experiments of moderate complexity
along these lines have been successfully carried out (Sabbah 1985; Shastri
1985). The current version of holographic correlation theory uses microfeatures (and feature pairs) essentially identical to the bottom row of figure 7.
The difference is that a correlation model would not have the hierarchical
structure but would represent a horse exclusively by the pattern of activity of
the feature-pair units. But consider how one might expand the correlation
model to represent horses' heads, eyes, etc., as well. No one has done this,
but it is hard to imagine any solution that did not separate out groups of
features and combine them to form higher groups. Now, we have seen that
combining diffuse encodings is a problem whose only known solution is to
focus the representation. So why are all these smart people so excited about
highly distributed representations?

There are two important problems that have been effectively studied using
diffuse encodings: generalization and learning. Some insight into the situation
can be gained by examining the reading model of figure 8, which is taken
from McClelland et al. 1981. This is one of the earliest and most successful
applications of connectionist modeling to psychology. The model is basically
punctate, incorporating units for specific shapes, letters, and words in a

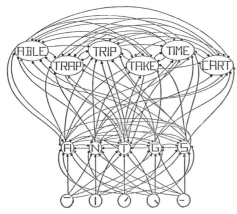

Figure 8
Reading model: a few of the neighbors of the node for the letter T in the first position in a word, and their interconnections. After McClelland and Rumelhart (1981).

highly structured excitation-inhibition network. The model was used to successfully model a wide range of experimental data, including the word-superiority effect previously considered paradoxical. Subjects can more reliably recognize a letter (e.g. A) in the context of a word (e.g. FAST) than in isolation, and the model shows clearly how feedback from the word level can aid decisions at the letter level. But the model did more than this, and therein lies our tale. It turns out that the model (and the subjects) can also recognize letters better in the context of pronounceable nonwords than in isolation. There is no explicit representation of these nonwords, but the units for the similarly spelled words combine to provide enough boost to the target letter. Anderson and Hinton describe this in the following way: ". . . the pronounceable non-words are represented by distributed patterns of activity at the word level." (1981, p. 28)

There is much to be learned from an examination of this statement. It is, of course, not literally true. Many aspects of the nonwords (length, pronunciation, etc.) are not represented at all, and one would not expect someone to recognize repeated occurrences of a nonword from this model. What is true is that *for this task* the network behaves as if it had a representation of the pronounceable nonwords. In fact, it is not just pronounceable nonwords that show the enhancement effect. The concepts with the distributed representation would have to be something like "collections of common pieces of words." It seems to me to be much better to understand this "emergence" as a general property of evidential networks than to postulate extra concepts having a distributed representation. In general, the research that has been described as studying diffuse representations can be understood as really concerned with system properties of neural networks. Structured networks of punctate elements (like an electronic circuit) have "emergent properties," as anyone who has tried to understand or repair one can testify.

What actually happens in the demonstrations of distributed representations is the following: A problem is picked in which certain properties (e.g., surface syntactic categories) are the ones required for a particular class of general answers (e.g., case roles). The distributed representation is chosen to be the required properties, and thus the system shows (or learns) the appropriate generalization. Since the rule for combining inputs is always the simple linear-threshold rule, care must be taken with the choice of primitives and some precoding may be necessary. Other generalizations over the same domain (e.g., past-tense formation) are based on different properties and are thus studied in separate experiments using entirely different distributed representations. A great deal of elegant and important work has been done in this style, but the basic relation between properties and generalizations seems to have been misunderstood.

The generalizations based on property vectors do capture relations that would not arise naturally from hierarchical representations such as figure 7. In the horse example, one might want to capture the generalization that animals with hair are mammals. We could link horse to mammal, but this is of no direct use in classifying novel hairy animals. The point is that if all uses of a concept were forced to go through some focus, the system would be unable to yield many crucial generalizations. There are systematic relationships among properties that are best captured directly. The relations between syntactic and case roles, between pronunciation and morphology, and between hairiness and mammalhood are systematic and are most compactly encoded by circumventing particular instances of words or mammals. There is an interesting duality here: If one knew enough hairy mammals, it is likely that activation of hairy would lead (indirectly) to the activation of 'mammal'. One could view this as all the individual mammals constituting a distributed representation of the hairy-mammal relation; however, this is a bad way to view network properties, which in general are rather complex evidential relations (Shastri 1985).

4 Learning

All of the preceding discussion has explored the ways in which conceptual knowledge might be represented in neural networks, ignoring the critical problem of learning. The question of the relative role of learning in intelligent behavior is as old and as basic as they come. It is now clear that humans come with an enormous amount of pre-wired structure, develop a great deal more in environmentally driven ways, and (except for administrators) continue to learn throughout life. The problem this presents for connectionist learning studies is a severe methodological one.

The basic difficulty is that we know human learning is based on an elaborate existing structure, but we know very little about the exact nature of this structure—particularly in the area of conceptual knowledge. Any study of learning either assumes some existing structure (at the risk of trivializing the learning aspects) or assumes no existing structure and is restricted to quite simple problems. The correlation-matrix models of memory have presented an attractive research vehicle. The total initial connectivity and the linear-threshold rule constitute a minimal *a priori* structure, and the correlation method of updating is an easily analyzed learning rule. The results of such studies often take on a structure-from-chaos aspect which many people find attractive.

Obviously enough, these correlation matrices employ a diffuse encoding, and the appeals of the two ideas are strongly connected. But the ideas of correlation, feedback, and weight change are not restricted to diffuse representations, linear-threshold rules, or complete connectivity matrices. In fact, complete connectivity is not biologically plausible, and the other assumptions are also problematic. A great deal of recent work (Belew 1986; Rumelhart et al. 1986; Parker 1985) involves using correlation-type ideas on networks with much richer structure while preserving domain independence.

It has been known for some time that any effective learning rule will have to include an input from the ultimate result of the computation. (Hebb's correlation rule has no way to punish a connection that leads to a disaster.) In a network that directly links inputs and outputs, such as a matrix model or a one-layer perceptron, it is easy to punish the offending links. For a system with more structure and indirect links, it has not been obvious how to assess who deserves the credit and who deserves the blame. Recent developments in learning theory, while not totally solving this problem, have made it possible to study learning in much richer structures (Rumelhart et al. 1986).

The basic idea is to "back-propagate" error signals from the output (which is directly corrected) to successively lower levels of input. A simple version would have the weight change at layer n, $\Delta w_{ij}^{(n)}$, given by

$$\Delta w_{ji}^{(n)} = \varepsilon \, \delta_i^{(n+1)} \, X_j^{(n)},$$

where $\delta_i^{(n+1)}$ is the error attributed to unit i in layer $n + 1$, $X_j^{(n)}$ is the output of units in layer n (now continuous valued), and ε is a learning constant. One can view this as changing w_{ji} in proportion to how the output of unit j *correlates* with the error attributed to unit i. The back-propagation algorithm has been used in a variety of studies and has been quite successful (McClelland et al. 1986). There are still problems with its range of application, convergence rate, and biological plausibility, but it does provide the best way known to study learning in structured networks. For all the reasons discussed above, this is a critical problem for our enterprise.

Learning in compact connectionist systems involves some additional considerations. A major problem in this formulation is "recruiting" the compact representation for new concepts (Wickelgren 1979; Feldman 1982; Shastri 1985; Fanty 1988). It is all very well to show the advantages of representational schemes such as figures 1, 7, and 8, but how could they come about? This question is far from settled, but there are some encouraging preliminary results. The central question is this: How could a system that grows essentially no new connections find (recruit) compact groups of units to capture new concepts and relations? One relevant result concerns the probability of finding compact groups that link nodes in a random graph (Feldman 1981). It turns out that, for biologically reasonable parameters, the probability of a compact cluster ($\sim$ 20 units) is quite high. (Incidentally, the probability of finding a single unit is essentially zero, and this provides another argument against punctate theories.) The brain is not random, except perhaps very locally, but that actually is good news for recruiting concept representations. Current work on learning in more structured networks (Fanty 1988; Hinton, in press) is examining this more closely.

Another question is: When does the system need to recruit descriptions of new concepts? A connectionist system can recognize a new concept (e.g. 'pink Bentley') without having an explicit representation for it; the joint activity of the components will suffice. But if specific names, properties, or relations of the new concept are required (pink Bentleys are native to Los Angeles), then a specific compact representation is required and is presumably recruited as described above.

5 Structure and Relations

Questions of structure have played a major role throughout the chapter. The structure of the nervous system, the structure of domains of knowledge, and the structure of concepts themselves have been central concerns. Despite the initial disclaimer, some consideration of relations has also appeared. Structure, in my opinion, is the dominant issue in neural knowledge representation. Most of the shortcomings of holographic-style models can be traced to their unstructured nature. This has been recognized for some time, and attempts have been made to correct the problem. One idea is to identify the components of the giant vector with microfeatures of concepts. The cleverest choice is to make the microfeatures follow a conceptual hierarchy so that more specific concepts (e.g. 'horse') share features with more general ones ('mammal', 'animal') (Hinton 1984; Anderson 1983). This implicitly captures one kind of structural relation among concepts, but it leaves all the others untouched. And if properties are all microfeatures of the representation, how could one incorporate new information (such as the fact that early horses were a few inches tall, or the fact that a particular horse has broken a leg)? This move, like the generalization demos, can be seen as another way of exploiting relationships that exist among properties (see Shastri 1985) and has nothing to do with holography.

When it comes to more general relations, there are two ways to try. One, which was mentioned above, assumes that relations among concepts are represented by links (axons) connecting the representations of the concepts involved. This inherently requires compact representations for the concepts, although many authors who talk about the idea in general terms would be repelled by the thought. I believe that resource considerations make this the only viable option, but no one has figured out how to make it work except in simple cases. We do know that hierarchical compact representations (such as figure 7) can capture internal structural relations defining concepts, and that this goes far toward solving the questions of how to treat all the different views of a horse or your grandmother. Briefly, the conceptual knowledge about, e.g., horses is a largely shared structure that derives much of its content from its relationship to other concepts. This is a kind of distributed representation, but it is not at all what is usually meant by the term. There is also strong evidence that we do not retain all the detailed memories of our grandmothers, but recreate them with a significant tendency toward regularization (Neisser 1982).

If one is committed to the diffuse, unstructured representation of concepts, there is no direct way to realize relationships among them. Ignoring computational costs, one can design a holographic memory to store relational information in symbolic form—e.g., as triples like (Brother Billy Jimmy) (Hinton 1981a; Kohonen 1980). But this is a move of desperation in neural modeling, since all the problems of sequential symbolic computing reemerge. A sequential machine with a fast relation store will show none of the performance or the context sensitivity that characterizes connectionist models.

In summary: Connectionist studies of pure learning minimize the preexisting structure and tend to study diffuse models. This has turned out to be very valuable, and it will continue to be. Like the studies of overall convergence (e.g., Wilson and Cowan 1972; Hopfield 1982; Cohen and Grossberg 1983), these studies are best done assuming no particular structure of the network. But the structure is there, and only compact representations can capture it.

Conclusions

Let us return to the analogy of the contrast between atomic physics and thermodynamics. Atomic physics (and chemistry) is concerned with precise structures and their interactions. Because of the complexity involved, cell biology would be an even better analogue for the detailed structural concerns of compact models. Modern thermodynamics (statistical mechanics) derives its power from abstracting, from enormous systems of units, a very small number of state variables that characterize certain questions of interest. Although the abstraction is strictly true only for systems without structure, the results of the theory have much wider application. One cannot do chemistry without knowing thermodynamics, but thermodynamics is a formalism that contains no way to say anything about chemistry on our planet. Similarly, bulk models of neural activity are likely to continue to yield valuable insights into neural functions, but it is fatal to ignore the detailed structure present. The challenge is to get global results into such a form that they can be used to advantage in working out how conceptual knowledge is represented and exploited by the brain.

Structured networks of evidence-combining simple units have a number of attractive computational properties. Error resistance, context dependence, and the ability to assimilate conflicting information are natural properties of such systems. A reasonable degree of generalization follows from these properties. Simple weight-change rules can enable these systems to improve their performance significantly. The collective behavior of such systems can produce powerful computations not easily anticipated, as is true of any complex circuit. Though certain concepts are represented explicitly, the system is not restricted to dealing only with those. A properly structured network can behave, in certain situations, as if it had concepts and relations implicitly represented. An explicit, compact handle on concepts is required when they have disjunction or internal structure or when they participate in relations or are communicated among subsystems. In addition, the nature of any emergent system properties depends heavily on which concepts are explicitly represented and on the detailed structure of the representation.

This suggests the following research priorities for the question of neural representation of knowledge: The detailed anatomy and physiology of nervous systems remains a top priority. The computational properties of connectionist models must be better understood, both in specific circuits and as mass systems. Plasticity and learning, of course, remain important, but the central problem is change of existing structure (Hinton 1988). The most difficult problems, however, appear to lie at the higher conceptual levels. All the concepts and relations treated in this chapter are extremely simplistic. The technical level of research on concept and knowledge representation among linguists, philosophers, and symbolic AI types is enormously more sophisticated (see, e.g., Brachman and Levesque 1985). If it is true that our brains do these things directly with neural nets, connectionist formulations should yield better characterizations of higher-level thought than symbolic logic—perhaps through the mediation of new scientific languages. Expectations that this will happen without detailed consideration of the structure of the tasks and of the underlying hardware should be based on a time frame of evolutionary scale. More likely, we will need to exploit many structural insights from artificial intelligence, neurobiology, and cognitive science and try to synthesize connectionist models that combine the strengths of each approach. Figure 9 depicts this idea graphically.

Acknowledgments

Many of the ideas in this chapter arose in discussions with Geoff Hinton over the years and were crystallized in working with Mark Fanty on his dissertation proposal. Also providing valuable feedback on early drafts were Dana Ballard, Gary Dell, Horst Greilich, Brian Madden, and John Maunsell.

This work was supported in part by ONR Grant N00014-84-K-0655, and in part by NSF Coordinated Experimental Research Grant DCR-8320136.

Appendix: Interim Neuron Doctrine (quoted from Barlow 1972)

The following five brief statements are intended to define which aspect of the brain's activity is important for understanding its main function, to suggest the way that single neurons represent what is going on around us, and to say how this is related to our subjective experience. The statements are dogmatic and incautious because it is important that they should be clear and testable.

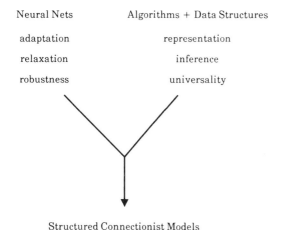

Figure 9
Two approaches to artificial intelligence.

First dogma

A description of that activity of a single nerve cell which is transmitted to and influences other nerve cells, and of a nerve cell's response to such influences from other cells, is a complete enough description for functional understanding of the nervous system. There is nothing else looking at or controlling this activity, which must therefore provide a basis for understanding how the brain controls behavior. *Since significant behaviors involve many individual nerve cells, functional understanding of the nervous system will require scientific languages for characterizing the behavior of networks of neurons.*

Second dogma

Efficient coding of information is a central problem of the sensory system. At progressively higher levels in the sensory pathways, information about the physical stimulus is more abstract and is represented by progressively fewer active neurons.

Third dogma

Trigger features of neurons are matched to the redundant features of sensory stimulation in order to achieve greater completeness and economy of representation. This selective responsiveness is determined by the sensory stimulation to which neurons have been exposed, as well as by genetic factors operating during development.

Fourth dogma

Just as physical stimuli directly cause receptors to initiate neural activity, so the active *networks of intermediate and* high-level neurons directly and simply cause the elements of our perception.

Fifth dogma

Frequency coding is the primary basis of neural communication. Sensory neurons respond with high-frequency discharge to external stimuli which fit into a narrow range of possibilities; the higher the discharge, the more narrow the range of possible causes.

Zeroth dogma

Intelligent behavior and its neural realization are incredibly complex. A functional understanding of this will require organizational principles from the behavioral and computational sciences as well as biology.

References

Allman, J., F. Miezen, and E. McGuiness. 1985. Stimulus specific responses from beyond the classical receptive field: Neurophysiological mechanisms for local-global comparisons in visual neurons. *Annual Review of Neuroscience* 8: 407–430.

Anderson, J. A. 1983. Cognitive and psychological computation with neural models. *IEEE Transactions: Systems, Man, and Cybernetics* 13: 799–815.

Anderson, J. A., and G. E. Hinton. 1981. Models of information processing in the brain. In *Parallel Models of Associative Memory,* ed. G. E. Hinton and J. A. Anderson (Hillsdale, N.J.: Erlbaum).

Anderson, J. A., and G. L. Murphy. 1986. Comments on concepts. In *Proceedings of NSF Connectionism Workshop.*

Ballard, D. H. 1986a. Cortical connections and parallel processing: Structure and function. *Behavioral and Brain Sciences* 9(1): 67–120.

Ballard, D. H. 1986b. Interpolation Coding: A Representation for Numbers in Neural Models. Technical Report 175, Department of Computer Science, University of Rochester.

Barber, C. 1980. *Evoked Potentials.* Baltimore: University Park Press.

Barlow, H. B. 1972. Single units and sensation: A neuron doctrine for perceptual psychology? *Perception* 1: 371–392.

Barto, A. G., and P. Anandan. 1984. Pattern Recognizing Stochastic Learning Automata. Technical Report 84-30, Department of Computer and Information Science, University Massachusetts, Amherst.

Barto, A. G., R. S. Sutton, and P. S. Brouwer. 1981. Associative search network: A reinforcement learning associative memory. *Biological Cybernetics* 40: 201–211.

Belew, R. K. 1986. Learning to Use Symbols in Connectionist Network. Unpublished manuscript.

Bienenstock, E. 1985. Dynamics of central nervous system. In *Proceedings of the Workshop on Dynamics of Macrosystems,* Laxenburg, Austria, ed. J. P. Aubin and K. Sigmund (Berlin: Springer-Verlag).

Brachman, R., and H. Levesque. 1985. *Readings in Knowledge Representation.* Palo Alto: Morgan-Kaufman.

Charniak, E., and D. McDermott. 1985. *Introduction to Artificial Intelligence.* Reading, Mass.: Addison-Wesley.

Cohen, M. A., and S. Grossberg. 1983. Absolute stability of global pattern formation and parallel memory storage by competitive neural networks. *IEEE Transactions: Systems, Man, and Cybernetics* 13: 815–825.

Edelman, G. M. 1981. Group selection as the basis for higher brain function. In *The Organization of Cerebral Cortex,* ed. F. O. Schmitt et al. (Cambridge, Mass.: MIT Press).

Fanty, M. A. 1988. Learning in Structured Connectionist Networks. Ph.D. dissertation, Computer Science Dept., University of Rochester.

Feldman, J. A. 1981. A connectionist model of visual memory. In *Parallel Models of Associative Memory,* ed. G. E. Hinton and J. A. Anderson (Hillsdale, N.J.: Erlbaum).

Feldman, J. A. 1982. Dynamic connections in neural networks. *Biological Cybernetics* 46: 27–39.

Feldman, J. A. 1985. Four frames suffice: A provisional model of vision and space. *Behavioral and Brain Sciences* 8: 265–289.

Gardner, J. C., R. M. Douglas, and M. S. Cynader. 1985. A time-based stereoscopic depth mechanism in the visual cortex. *Brain Research* 328: 154–157.

Goldman-Rakic, P. S., and M. L. Schwartz. 1982. Interdigitation of contralateral and ipsilateral columnar projections to frontal association cortex in primates. *Science* 216: 755–757.

Hebb, D. O. 1949. *The Organization of Behavior.* New York: Wiley.

Hillis, W. D. (1985). *The Connection Machine.* Cambridge, MA: MIT Press.

Hinton, G. E. 1981a. Implementing semantic networks in parallel hardware. In *Parallel Models of Associative Memory,* ed. G. E. Hinton and J. A. Anderson (Hillsdale, N.J.: Erlbaum).

Hinton, G. E. 1981b. Shape representation in parallel systems. In *Proceedings of the Seventh International Joint Congress on Artificial Intelligence,* Vancouver, B. C.

Hinton, G. E. 1984. Distributed Representations. Report CMU-CS-84-157, Department of Computer Science, Carnegie-Mellon University.

Hinton, G. E. 1988. Connectionist learning procedures. *AI Journal.*

Hinton, G. E., and J. A. Anderson. 1981. *Parallel Models of Associative Memory.* Hillsdale, N.J.: Erlbaum.

Hopfield, J. J. 1982. Neural networks and physical systems with emergent collective computational abilities. *Proceedings of the National Academy of Sciences* 79: 2554–2558.

Hopfield, J. J., and D. W. Tank. 1985. Neural computation in optimization problems. *Biological Cybernetics,* 52, no. 3: 141–152.

Hubel, D. H., and T. N. Wiesel. 1979. Brain mechanisms of vision. *Scientific American* 241(3): 150–162.

Kohonen, T. 1980. *Content-Addressable Memories.* Berlin: Springer-Verlag.

Kohonen, T. 1984. *Self-Organization and Associative Memory.* Berlin: Springer-Verlag.

Lashley, K. 1950. In search of the engram. In *Physiological Mechanisms in Animal Behavior* (New York: Academic).

Lynch, G. 1986. *The Neurobiology of Learning and Memory.* Cambridge, Mass.: MIT Press.

McClelland, J. L., and D. E. Rumelhart. 1981. An interactive activation model of the effect of context on language learning (part I). *Psychological Review* 88: 375–401.

McClelland, J. L., D. E. Rumelhart, and the PDP Research Group. 1986. *Parallel*

Distributed Processing: Explorations in the Microstructure of Cognition. Volume 2: Applications. Cambridge, Mass.: MIT Press. A Bradford Book.

Merzenich, M. M., R. J. Nelson, M. P. Stryker, M. S. Cynader, A. Schoppmann, and J. M. Zook. 1984. Somatosensory cortical map changes following digit amputation in adult monkeys. *Journal of Comparative Neurology* 224: 591–605.

Neisser, U., ed. 1982. *Memory Observed.* San Francisco: Freeman.

Parker, D. B. 1985. Learning-Logic. Technical Report 47, Center for Computational Research in Economics and Management Science, Massachusetts Institute of Technology.

Roediger, H. L. III. 1980. Memory metaphors in cognitive psychology. *Memory and Cognition* 8(1): 231–246.

Rumelhart, D. E., J. L. McClelland, and the PDP Research Group. 1986. *Parallel Distributed Processing: Explorations in the Microstructure of Cognition. Volume 1: Foundations.* Cambridge, Mass.: MIT Press. A Bradford Book.

Sabbah, D. 1985. Computing with connections in visual recognition of Origami objects. *Cognitive Science* 9: 25–50.

Shastri, L. 1985. Evidential Reasoning in Semantic Networks: A Formal Theory and Its Parallel Implementation. Ph.D. thesis (Technical Report 166), Computer Science Department, University of Rochester.

Smith, E. E., and D. L. Medin. 1981. *Categories and Concepts.* Cambridge, Mass.: Harvard University Press.

Sullins, J. 1985. Value Cell Encoding Strategies. Technical Report 165, Computer Science Department, University of Rochester.

Thompson, R. F. 1986. The neurobiology of learning and memory. *Science* 233: 941–947.

Toulouse, G., S. Dehaene, and J.-P. Changeux. 1985. A Spin Glass Model of Learning by Selection. Unpublished manuscript.

von der Malsberg, C. 1987. Nervous structures with dynamical links. *Berichte der Bunsen-Gesellschaft für Physikalische Chemie.*

Wickelgren, W. A. 1979. Chunking and consolidation: A theoretical synthesis of semantic networks, configuring in conditioning, S-R versus cognitive learning, normal forgetting, the amnesic syndrome, and the hippocampal arousal system. *Psychological Review* 86: 44–60.

Willshaw, D. 1981. Holography, associative memory, and inductive generalization. In *Parallel Models of Associative Memory,* ed. G. E. Hinton and J. A. Anderson (Hillsdale, N.J.: Erlbaum).

Wilson, H. R., and J. D. Cowan. 1972. Excitatory and inhibitory interactions in localized populations of model neurons. *Biophysical Journal* 12: 1–24.

Chapter 4

| Internal Representation of Universal Regularities: A Challenge for Connectionism | Roger N. Shepard |

We interpret and anticipate significant events by means of a system that has internalized the enduring constraints that govern such events in the world. Undoubtedly, some of these constraints are internalized through learning, and connectionist systems provide a promising medium and set of principles for such learning. Like other systems, however, connectionist systems are capable of nontrivial learning (including appropriate generalization and transfer to new situations) only to the extent that they are endowed with an appropriate structure that is not itself learned. Moreover, there is reason to believe that in systems that have evolved through natural selection, the features of the world that are both biologically significant and absolutely invariant in the world have tended to become genetically internalized. But in what form might such universal regularities of the world be accommodated within connectionist systems?

1 Observations Concerning Connectionist Systems

1.1 Advantages of Connectionist Systems over Symbol-Processing Systems

For the modeling of mental processes that represent natural objects and events, connectionist systems appear to have some significant advantages over the discrete symbol-manipulation systems that once dominated cognitive theorizing. In particular, connectionist systems offer a dense, massively parallel processing medium that both facilitates interpretation in terms of the neuronal substrate and appears more suited to subserving representational processes of an analog character—for example, those representing the transformations of objects in space (see Cooper 1976; Shepard and Cooper 1982; Shepard and Metzler 1971).

In addition, connectionism promises to furnish, for what has been a largely *ad hoc* approach to cognitive modeling (akin to that of engineering), a more deeply principled ground (akin to that of physics). Thus, there is some hope that connectionism could elevate cognitive science above the status of what might, after P. S. Churchland, be described as a kind of mechanized "folk psychology" (see Churchland and Sejnowski [chapter 1 of the present volume] and Smolensky [chapter 2]). Instead of stimulating human capabilities by larger and larger patchworks of heterogeneous, domain-specific heuristics based on introspection and verbal protocols, connectionism provides a uniform framework within which diverse performances and competencies arise from a small set of general principles. I am, thus, heartened in my own quest for universal psychological laws such as might eventually approximate a kind of "Newtonian mechanics" of mind (Shepard 1984, 1987b).

Three Essential Processes of Adaptation
Although they operate on different time scales, all three of the following processes are required in order for systems, including connectionist systems, to achieve behavioral adaptation to a given environment.

Inference   On the shortest time scale, in which an individual system encounters a single environmental situation, that system must adapt its internal representation and its overt response to the requirements of that particular situation. This is a nontrivial task because a situation is never completely revealed in the available sensory input and is rarely, if ever, identical to one encountered before. In a connectionist system, such inferential processes of perceptual completion, interpretation, categorization, and prediction are achieved by a passage through state space of the vector specifying the momentary activation levels of all elements in the processing network to a stationary vector (or "eigenstate"). The passage may be determined, for example, by relaxation methods for the satisfaction of "soft constraints." Incidentally, the set of situations giving rise to the same stationary vector would ideally correspond to what, in a recently proposed theory of generalization (Shepard 1987b), I have termed a "consequential region in psychological space."

Learning   On an intermediate time scale, in which an individual system encounters a series of situations from the environmentally given ensemble of possible situations, that system must adapt its internal representations and responses to the requirements of that ensemble. In connectionist systems, such adaptation is achieved through principles governing the (slower) passage through weight space of a matrix specifying the strengths of all connections between the elements in the processing network. This passage may be

achieved by means of a process such as that of "backwards error propagation," proposed by Rumelhart, Hinton, and Williams (1986a, 1986b). Thus,
an initially chosen matrix of weights is gradually adjusted or "tuned" so as to
yield increasingly refined trajectories and final states for the vector of activations. The result is increasingly effective inference relative to the reference
ensemble of situations.

Evolution   On the longest time scale, in which systems differing in initial
structure encounter series of environmental situations from a given ensemble,
those initial structures that are to be perpetuated in ensuing systems must be
adapted to the requirements of that ensemble. In connectionist systems, such
adaptation might arise through joint processes of (i) generation of systems
with different topological connectivities and initial weights and (ii) elimination of those systems that prove less effective in learning to draw inferences
appropriate to the reference ensemble of situations. In living systems, such
evolution is achieved through natural selection among hereditarily propagated
spontaneous mutations. In artificial systems, such evolution has, at best, been
crudely approximated through a much more limited and idiosyncratic process
of guess and test by particular system builders. (For an engaging, if fanciful,
portrayal of how artificial systems might evolve by a kind of natural selection,
see Braitenberg 1984.) Whether the initial connectivities and weights of a
given system are determined by natural or by artificial selection, those connectivities and weights then determine what inferences are learnable by the
system and what sequences of situations are sufficient for such learning.

1.3   The Importance of the Problem of Initial Structure
The general principles so far proposed by connectionists concern primarily
the first two of these three processes of adaptation. Indeed, the major appeal
of the connectionist approach has been that, through error-driven tuning of
their own weights, connectionist networks manifest a capability of "programming" themselves. Closer consideration reveals, however, that nontrivial self-
programming can take place only if sufficient knowledge about the world in
which the system is to learn is already built into that system.

By hypothesis, the principles that initially govern the learning cannot
themselves have been learned. Moreover, in nature, because an individual
rarely if ever confronts exactly the same situation twice, virtually every action
must be chosen in a new context. But without initial structure, a system has
no basis for generalization from one situation or context to another (Shepard
1964b, 1981, 1987b). Only by virtue of ecologically valid constraints that
have already been internalized is a system empowered to make generaliza-

tions that are appropriate to its world and, thus, to achieve some efficiency in learning. To the extent that it lacks such constraints, a connectionist system, in fact, is a notoriously slow learner and/or is critically dependent on the provision of a carefully tailored sequence of training stimuli by a beneficent "tutor" (see, e.g., Hinton, Sejnowski, and Ackley 1984).

Of course, representations of particular objects and their specific properties cannot be rigidly pre-wired in each individual. Because foods, predators, or places of safety or danger have varied from one epoch or locale to another, representations of such objects must be flexible enough to be shaped through individual experience. Adjustments and retunings may also be necessary to compensate for growth-induced changes in the physical scale of the organism and its sensory receptors (see, e.g., Fernald 1984), as well as to compensate for alterations that may occur through accident or disease.

However, there are general constraints that have uniformly governed the form and the transformation of all terrestrial objects and situations throughout evolutionary history. Some obvious examples are that material objects are conserved, that space is locally Euclidean and three-dimensional with a grav-itationally conferred unique upright direction, and that periods of relative light and warmth alternate with periods of relative dark and cold in a regular cycle (currently 24 hours). Presumably, individuals that had to learn about these pervasive constraints from scratch would be at a disadvantage relative to an individual that came into the world with a representational system that had already took account of them in its processes of inference and generaliza-tion and, hence, did not have to learn them by "trial and possibly fatal error" (Shepard 1987a). Indeed, there is compelling evidence that a circadian clock has been genetically internalized in most animals (see, e.g., Rusak and Zucker 1975), and the constraints concerning the conservation and transfor-mation of objects in space clearly underlie some powerful capabilities for visual inference and generalization.

In short, connectionists who focus on a system's achievement of represen-tations of the external world solely through the two processes of learning and inference are neglecting what may be one of the most challenging problems facing cognitive science: the problem of the internalization of those con-straints that, because they are universally valid in the world, confer an advan-tage on any individuals in which they are innately embodied.

1.4   Why the Problem of Initial Structure Has Been Neglected

One can perhaps understand why cognitive and behavioral scientists, in gen-eral, have so little pursued the possibility that the universal constraints of our world may have been internalized. Such constraints have become so deep, pervasive, and automatic in ourselves that we are quite unaware that they structure our every perception and thought. We may frequently be aware that our office is too small; seldom that it is only three-dimensional. Nor does observation of the behavior of other animals immediately reveal the operation of such internalized constraints. Indeed, the operation of the internalized circadian clock was established only by maintaining animals under highly artificial conditions of constant light and temperature (Rusak and Zucker 1975).

Universal regularities do not call for any particular, specifiable behavior; they merely place subtle constraints on large classes of behaviors serving widely different functions. For example, that space is three-dimensional and Euclidean says little about the shapes of objects that may be edible or dangerous for a given animal; however, it does significantly constrain the relations among the different projections that any such object can cast on a sensory surface as it assumes different relative positions in space. Likewise, that objects that lead to the same biologically significant consequences are similar but rarely identical does not say which particular objects are edible or dangerous. Yet every individual must have some basis for deciding whether any particular new object is similar enough to one previously found to have a significant positive or negative consequence that the individual should approach or take flight. In short, every individual must have internalized an appropriate metric of similarity and principle of generalization with respect to that metric (Shepard 1987b).

1.5 The Difficulty of Specifying Initial Structure for Connectionist Systems

For connectionist systems, a characterization of the form in which any internalized constraints are embodied faces special difficulties. In previous symbol-processing models, internal representations were cast in a form that kept the semantics of the conceptual level accessible to introspection and verbal formulation. In connectionist systems, however, internal representations reside in vast numbers of shifting connection weights. As Smolensky (1988) has made particularly clear (see also chapter 2 of the present volume and Shepard 1988), this "subconceptual" level does not manifest an accessible semantics. This is the root of the objection sometimes raised against connectionist systems—that even if such a system were to exhibit intelligent behavior, its workings might remain as inscrutable and unspeakable as the workings of mind itself.

Perhaps the force of this objection is somewhat mitigated if the *principles* of learning and inference that govern the internal representations can be explicitly stated—even if the forms of the internal representations themselves cannot. Still, if significant structure must be built into a connectionist system before it is capable of effective learning and inference, we are left with a choice between two formidable challenges: Either we must formulate how the required structure is to be implemented at the subconceptual level or we must formalize explicit principles for evolution in species of connectionist systems (just as we have formalized explicit principles for learning in individual such systems).

2   Functions that May Be Served by Internalized Constraints

I turn now to a consideration of some fundamental capabilities of humans and other animals that appear to reflect enduring regularities of the world, that do not appear to be learned *de novo* in each individual, and that may be fully realized in connectionist systems only by the imposition of initial structure (whether evolutionarily or by design).

2.1   Recognition of an Object Regardless of Its Position in Space

A fundamental problem faced by any adaptive system is, of course, the problem of representing an external object as the same when the information available about that object at the sensory surface varies widely depending on the object's relative position in space. It is true that, through changes in the weights of connections between local elements in the sensory array and representational "hidden units," a connectionist system may gradually form a particular internal representation for an object that repeatedly appears in more or less the same relative position and hence repeatedly stimulates more or less the same local pattern of sensory units. But if the object is now presented in an entirely new position, or if it projects on an entirely different portion of the sensory array, there may be no transfer of the previous hard-won but merely local learning about that object.

If the object is to be recognized regardless of its relative direction, distance, and orientation, the internal structure needed to mediate such generalization or transfer must already have been—in some relative balance—acquired or pre-wired. At one extreme, we might laboriously have "tutored" the system by going through the entire training procedure again for each possible relative position of the object. At the other extreme, we might have endowed the system with an initial "micro-architecture" that is massively replicated in parallel across the entire sensory array, such that anything learned about an object appearing in one position immediately transfers to every other position in which that object might appear.

However, the first alternative—ensuring the internalization of the necessary structure solely through learning—seems quite unsatisfactory for at least three reasons: (i) Even a rigid object has six degrees of freedom of position (three of location and three of orientation). Consequently, a prohibitive amount of training would be required in order for the system to learn the appearance of the object in every possible position. (ii) Even if such training were successfully completed for that one object, the entire training regime would have to be undertaken anew for each sufficiently different object. (iii) A system requiring such tailored tutoring fails as a model of the recognition capabilities of humans and other animals. After a single significant experience with a novel object, such individuals may recognize that object when it subsequently appears in an entirely different relative position—with obvious benefits for the individual's chances of survival.

Unfortunately, the opposite extreme, in which the necessary internal structure is entirely hard-wired at the outset, requires provision of an explicit specification of that initial micro-architecture. A few connectionists have made some promising suggestions about possible architectures that could mediate transfer of learning from one relative position of an object to another (see, e.g., Hinton 1981; McClelland 1986). Little agreement has yet been achieved, however, concerning even such basic issues as whether efficiency of performance dictates that the structure required for the processing of shape be massively reduplicated across an entire sensory array, or whether parsimony of hardware dictates that performance be achieved by some kind of multiplexing of the sensory array to one centralized structure of that kind (D. E. Rumelhart, personal communication, November 1987).

Moreover, although the sensory surface is two-dimensional, there are reasons for believing that the mechanisms underlying shape constancy in humans arose as an evolutionary accommodation to the three-dimensional world. For example, human adults readily discriminate rigid from nonrigid motion of a configuration of points in three dimensions, even when presented only with a nonrigid two-dimensional projection of the rotating configuration (Green 1961; Wallach and O'Connell 1953), and the capacity for such a discrimination is evidently well established by early infancy (Gibson and Spelke 1983). I take it as significant (Shepard 1981, 1984) that no one has yet manifested a similar ability to discriminate rigid from nonrigid motion of a configuration of points in four-dimensional space (as in the computer-generated display introduced by Green [1961]), even when presented with its stereoscopic, three-dimensional projection (see Noll 1965).

2.2 Recognition of an Object Regardless of Its Illumination

The visual information available at the sensory surface about an external object varies not only with the relative position of that object in space but also with the composition of the light falling on that object. Just as mechanisms of size and shape constancy enable us to determine the geometrical structure of a rigid object despite enormous variations in the way that structure projects on the retina, mechanisms of color constancy enable us to determine the intrinsic spectral reflectance properties of the surfaces of an object despite enormous variations in the composition of the light that falls on those surfaces and is scattered back to the retina.

Maloney and Wandell (1986), taking a significant step beyond Land's "retinex" theory of color perception (see Brainard and Wandell 1986; Land 1964, 1983; Land and McCann 1971), have clarified this problem of color constancy in a way that is of fundamental relevance here because it indicates further aspects of the world that, having been invariant throughout evolutionary history, may have become hard-wired into the visual system.

Much as the complete physical specification of an arbitrary shape could require an unlimited number of degrees of freedom, the complete physical specification of the spectral reflectance of an arbitrary surface could require an unlimited number of degrees of freedom—namely, those giving, for each wavelength within the visible spectrum, the proportion of the incident energy at that wavelength that is scattered back from the surface rather than absorbed by it. However, much as a rigid shape, being constrained to an invariant three-dimensional space, has only six degrees of freedom of position (three of location and three of orientation), the spectral power distribution of natural illumination, deriving from the invariant sun, has only a few degrees of freedom of spectral composition.

In fact, empirical functions describing the spectral distribution of natural daylight measured over a wide range of times of day and atmospheric conditions have been found to be closely approximated by linear combinations of no more than about three properly chosen spectral basis functions (Dixon 1978; Judd, MacAdam, and Wyszecki 1964; Maloney and Wandell 1986). One degree of freedom is certainly needed to accommodate variations in the overall level of illumination, as when an object moves between open daylight and deep shade. One or two more degrees of freedom suffice to accommodate variations in the spectral balance between the longer and shorter wavelengths in the light: The longer wavelengths are more subject to absorption by water vapor but more readily penetrate dust and other particles suspended in the air, so that illumination is typically redder at sunset, when the nearly horizontal rays must penetrate a longer and denser column of atmospherically suspended small particles. The shortest wavelengths are more subject to scattering by the (even smaller) molecules of the air itself, so that on a clear day the rays reaching an object indirectly through scattering from the surrounding sky are relatively bluer, while the rays reaching an object from the sun directly, if not blocked by another object or cloud, are relatively yellower.

In short, what has been invariant over evolutionary history is neither the shapes nor the spectral reflectance properties of particular objects. Instead, what has been invariant has been, in the former case, the constraints governing projective transformations in three-dimensional Euclidean space and, in the latter case, the constraints governing the terrestrial transformations of the constant radiation of the sun. On the bases of these latter constraints, Maloney and Wandell (1986) show how a linear model permits the recovery of an invariant characterization of the spectral reflectances of surfaces in the absence of independent knowledge of the momentary state of the ambient illumination. Their results have some interesting implications for what must be built into a connectionist visual system if that system is to attain color constancy.

• Such a system must analyze the input into a few color channels—say, a long-wavelength, a medium-wavelength, and a short-wavelength channel (as proposed by Helmholtz [1856/1962]). Remarkably, this remains true even if these channels are ultimately to be recombined into a final internal representation that is itself colorless. That is, even if the surrounding surfaces are to be internally represented only in shades of gray (as in a "black-and-white" photograph), constancy of color—in this case, constancy merely of lightness—nevertheless requires an initial analysis into separate color channels in order to compensate for the independent longer- and shorter-wavelength degrees of freedom of the terrestrial transformation.

• It may not be arbitrary that human vision has just three degrees of freedom of color representation, as is ensured by the presence of just three classes of color receptors (namely, cones sensitive to longer, shorter, and intermediate wavelengths) and as is reflected in the three dimensions of color space (whether the polar-coordinate dimensions of lightness, hue, and saturation or the Cartesian dimensions of light-dark, red-green, and blue-yellow opponency). The linear model proposed by Maloney and Wandell suggests to me that this three-dimensionality may be neither an arbitrary design feature of the human visual system nor a consequence of the surface spectral reflectances of the particular objects that were significant at various stages of our ancestral line. Three-dimensional color representation may have been

favored because three degrees of freedom are needed to compensate for natural variations in terrestrial lighting and, thus, to achieve color constancy.
• However, because this evolutionary accommodation has been specifically to the natural environment on earth, it has not furnished us with a mechanism yielding color constancy in any arbitrary environment—such as modern technology can now impose upon us. This is why, in a parking lot illuminated at night by sodium vapor lamps, we may walk right past our car. Our visual system is not prepared to compensate for illumination that deviates so markedly from that achievable within the few degrees of freedom that have prevailed in nature. True, we may learn that the colors of objects appear different under such lighting. But because the compensatory circuitry is built in, we never learn to *see* colors correctly under such lighting.

2.3   Determination that Two Objects Are Identical in Shape

The intrinsic shapes of some objects—such as objects that are enantiomorphic or "mirror images" of each other (Cooper 1975; Shepard and Metzler 1971) or objects whose differences in global shape are sufficiently subtle (Cooper and Podgorny 1976)—evidently cannot be discriminated in arbitrary orientations. The discrimination of such shapes seems to require a voluntary analog simulation of a rigid motion of one object into the position of the other followed by a test for a match or mismatch of shape (Cooper 1976; Shepard and Cooper 1982; Shepard and Metzler 1971). Moreover, when two such identical objects are presented in alternation (with a sufficiently slow rate of alternation and a sufficiently short interstimulus interval), observers experience an involuntary perceptual illusion of a single such object rigidly moving back and forth between the two positions in three-dimensional space (Farrell and Shepard 1981; Shepard 1984; Shepard and Judd 1976).

Data concerning these cases of imagined and apparent motion have consistently revealed two regularities: First, the time required for the completion of the imagined or perceptually experienced motion increases linearly with the extent of that motion (Shepard and Cooper 1982; Shepard and Metzler 1971; Shepard and Zare 1983). Second, the motion tends to be represented over one of the particular (generally helical) paths prescribed as simplest by principles of kinematic geometry for three-dimensional Euclidean space (Foster 1975; Shepard 1984; Carlton and Shepard, in preparation). In a current line of work, my co-workers and I are also finding evidence that real motions are judged to be simplest when they traverse these same paths.

I have taken these findings as evidence for the internalization of fundamental principles of object conservation and least action—with the latter principle interpreted in an abstract sense of kinematic geometry (Shepard 1984). Carlton and I have been developing the idea (earlier outlined in Shepard 1981 and Shepard and Farrell 1985) that psychologically preferred paths take their most economical form when expressed as geodesics (the analogs of great circles on the surface of a sphere) in a curved psychological space that is isomorphic to the six-dimensional manifold of possible locations and orientations of an object in three-dimensional Euclidean space (Carlton and Shepard, in preparation). Thus, at a sufficiently abstract level, the implied mental mechanics may be analogous to physical mechanics in which, too, a system follows a least-action or geodesic path in a space-time manifold.

2.4 Determination that Two Objects Are of the Same Natural Kind

I have already noted that because situations rarely if ever exactly recur in our world, every individual must come into the world with an initial metric of similarity and an innate principle of generalization. The constraints here are even more general than those of kinematic geometry for three-dimensional space. Objects or situations with the potential for the same important consequence need not be identical in three-dimensional shape. They need merely be of the same *natural kind,* and they often differ more or less among themselves in intrinsic shape, color, texture, posture, expression, and motion, as well as in other (auditory, olfactory, gustatory, or even amodal, semantic, or syntactic) properties. In connection with this ubiquitous problem of generalization, I have advanced two claims (Shepard 1987b).

The first claim is empirical: If the metric of similarity is specified as the one for which generalization (defined in terms of probability of response) falls off in accordance with an invariant monotonic function of the distance between stimuli in the "psychological space" of possible stimuli (Shepard 1957, 1962), then the following two things are true: (i) The (initially unknown) monotonic function approximates a simple exponential decay function, and does so for all stimulus domains and for all animals (Shepard 1958, 1965, 1987b). (ii) The initially unknown metric of that psychological space approximates the Euclidean metric (or L_2 norm) if the dimensions of the stimuli have one kind of relation (called "unitary" or "integral"), as in the case of colors differing in lightness and saturation, and approximates the "city-block" metric (or L_1 norm) if the dimensions of the stimuli have another kind of relation (called "analyzable" or "separable"), as in the case of geometrical figures differing in size and orientation (Shepard 1964a; Attneave 1950; Garner 1974; Lockhead 1966; Torgerson 1958).

My second claim is theoretical: The exponential function and the two metrics are mathematically derivable for an individual who assumes (i) that the set of stimuli leading to any given important consequence corresponds to a region in its psychological space that is suitably regular (e.g., convex and centrally symmetric) but that otherwise has an unknown position, size, and shape in that abstract space and (ii) that the correlation between the possible extensions of a consequential region along the underlying dimensions of that space is +1 for integral dimensions and 0 for separable dimensions (Shepard 1987b).

I suggest, then, that the result of natural selection has been twofold, consisting of (i) an internalization of these invariant principles of generalization and (ii) a gradual adjustment, in each evolutionary line, of the psychophysical transformation from physical parameter space to a psychological space in which these principles can take on an invariant form—namely, a psychological space in which the regions that have been consequential for that evolutionary line, whatever the individual shapes of those regions, do not systematically tend to be elongated or compressed in any particular directions in the space.

2.5 Two Fundamentally Different Types of Representational Continua

The separable-integral distinction is a distinction that pertains to the *relation* between dimensions of stimulus representation; it is not a distinction that applies to any one dimension individually. The dimension of lightness, taken by itself, is neither integral nor separable. It has, nevertheless, an integral relation to the dimension of saturation and a separable relation to that of size.

There is, however, an equally fundamental distinction that does apply to individual continua. This further distinction can probably be traced back, through Locke and perhaps even Aristotle, to the distinction between primary and secondary qualities. However, it has emerged most sharply in the contrast that Kubovy (1981) has drawn between "dispensable" and "indispensable" attributes.

A dispensable attribute of stimuli is one that can be eliminated (or made identical) in those stimuli without destroying their separate identities. In vision, spatial location is an indispensable attribute, whereas color is a dispensable attribute. Thus, a red spot and a blue spot of light projected at the same location are no longer distinguishable but become a single, purple spot, whereas spatially separated spots of light remain distinguishable even when they are identical in color. In audition, the facts seem to be just the reverse: Spatial location is dispensable but pitch is indispensable. Thus, two tones of different pitch are still distinguishable, even when emitted from the same spatial location; but two auditory sources that are emitting exactly the same (steady-state) pitch, to the left and to the right, subjectively fuse into a single tone that is heard as straight ahead.

Although we speak of literal space and of color space as if these two "spaces" were on the same perceptual footing, the relation between them is fundamentally asymmetric. Colors retain their individual identities only by virtue of their differences in location, whereas locations retain their identities regardless of their colors. Three separated places are not made indistinguishable by rendering them the same color, nor are they made to constitute a different place. Rather they become something quite different from a place. They become an emergent form, namely a triangle. In contrast, three different colors are rendered indistinguishable by confining them to the same place. They neither retain their original identities nor constitute any analog of a form (in color space). They simply become a different color—that is, a different point in color space.

Indispensable attributes thus correspond to what Attneave called *morphophoric media*—that is, continua capable of supporting form (see Attneave and Olson 1971; Kubovy 1981; Shepard 1981, 1982). These are the continua along which objects can undergo perceptual or mental transformations while preserving their inherent structures—for example, the medium of literal space in which visual objects preserve their shapes under translations or rotations (Shepard 1984; Shepard and Cooper 1982), or the medium of auditory pitch in which melodies, scales, or chords preserve their "shapes" under musical transposition (Attneave and Olson 1971; Jordan and Shepard 1987; Shepard 1982, 1984; Shepard and Jordan 1984).

In contrast, color space does not appear to admit an analog of form. Certain shades of red, orange, and pink may define an abstract triangle in color space, but we are hard pressed to determine whether it is a triangle of the same "shape" as that defined by particular shades of lavender, navy, and turquoise. And certainly an attempt to imagine a rigid transformation of the triple of colors from the one part of color space to the other does not seem to help us make such a determination. Moreover, the phenomenon of apparent motion is readily demonstrated in auditory pitch, just as in visual space (McAdams and Bregman 1975), but it reportedly has no analog in color space (Kolers and von Grünau 1975, 1976).

The distinction between these two types of continua seems relevant here for three reasons. First, the abilities I have discussed (i) of recognizing an object despite variations in its position in space, (ii) of determining that two objects are identical in shape by mentally transforming one into the position of the other, and (iii) of traversing the geodesic path prescribed by kinematic geometry—in such imagined transformations as well as in apparent motion—evidently are possible only in those continua classified as morphophoric. Second, I believe that the distinction ultimately derives not from an arbitrary design feature of the sensory or representational systems but from a fundamental difference in the world, to which those systems have accommodated through natural selection. Surely the fact that the same surface reflectance can simultaneously reside in distinct locations whereas the same location cannot simultaneously retain distinct surface reflectances is a fundamental fact about the physical world that antedated the emergence of perceptual systems. And third, the internal representation of these two fundamentally different kinds of continua will presumably be best realized in connectionist subsystems with different microarchitectures. This leads me to a consideration of the physical constraints that necessarily apply to any physical system, including any connectionist system.

3 Consequences of Unavoidable Physical Constraints

Connectionist systems are subject to general physical constraints not only because these constraints hold in the external world and hence confer an advantage on those individuals in which they have been internalized through natural selection and learning; connectionist systems are also subject to physical constraints simply because each such system is itself a part of the physical world and must therefore comply with universal physical constraints. Two such constraints appear particularly relevant for connectionist systems in general and for the brain in particular: (i) Because physical space is three-dimensional, all macroscopic systems, including the brain, are limited to at most three dimensions. (ii) Because causal processes propagate with a finite velocity determined by their physical medium, propagation times in a neuronal network necessarily increase linearly with an appropriate measure of distance through that network. Indeed, the linear increase must be relatively steep in the case of the brain, owing to the relatively slow velocities achievable by the electro-chemical processes of neural conduction and synaptic transmission.

In some contexts, connectionists have discussed networks as though they might be endowed with any connectivity that would serve the adaptive needs of the system (including, for example, a connectivity in which every element has a direct connection to every other), without taking explicit account of physical limitations on dimensionality or rate of propagation. In other contexts, however, such limitations have been at least implicitly invoked—as in positing regular spatial arrays with nearest-neighbor interactions to account for certain cooperative phenomena in, for example, vision (Julesz 1971; Marr 1982; Marr and Poggio 1976; Mead 1987; Szeliski and Hinton 1985), motor control (Eckmiller 1986), and mental transformation (Kosslyn and Schwartz

1977; Mel 1986; Trehub 1977). Moreover, neurophysiological investigations have shown that sensory and motor regions of the brain are topographically organized with respect to some sensory dimensions—including dimensions that are not literally spatial, such as that of pitch. At the same time, many other sensory dimensions, including those of color, do not seem to be topographically represented.

Accordingly, we must confront some new questions: What psychological phenomena arise directly, in compliance with universal constraints such as those concerning dimensionality and propagation, rather than indirectly, as evolutionary or learned accommodations to external regularities? Is the choice of a topographic or a nontopographic representation of a dimension merely an arbitrary accident of phylogenetic development, or does it ultimately stem from some combination of unavoidable dimensional restrictions of the brain and enduring regularities of the world (such as those pertaining to the two fundamentally different types of continua already discussed)?

3.1 Consequences of the Limited Dimensionality of the Neural Medium

The advantage of topographic organization for a connectionist system is, of course, that things that are closely related in the world have neighboring and, hence, readily connectable representations in the system. But because dimensionality is a topological property, the advantage is realized only if dimensionality is preserved. We cannot map an intrinsically higher-dimensional domain to a lower-dimensional representational medium without disrupting local neighborhoods and hence disrupting connectivity. The massive communication that such a dimension-reducing mapping would require between widely separated units is prohibited by the presence of other units and their local interconnections (which already fill the intervening space) and, possibly, by the additional time required for transmission of signals over the greater distances. Thus, the relative rarity of long-range neural connections in the brain, noted by Feldman in chapter 3 of this volume, has arisen not through exercise of option but through necessity.

True, the brain, being part of the world, is three-dimensional, just as is the external world that it must represent. However, there are at least three reasons why this circumstance does not provide grounds for a wholesale recourse to topographic representation of that world:

• The three-dimensional world is not directly available, as such, to the internal system. It is available only in the reduced form of its projection onto a sensory array that (forming, as it must, a part of the bounding surface of the system [Shepard 1981]) is generally of no more than two dimensions.

Hence, even if a three-dimensional representation were to be internally constructed, the construction would have to be based on a lower-dimensional input (see Marr 1982).

• Neuroanatomical examination reveals that the brain cannot really be a three-dimensional homogeneous modeling medium—in which a scale model of the world might be reconstructed as if in a kind of three-dimensional "sand box" (to use the metaphor of Attneave [1972]). In fact, the major portions of the brain subserving cognitive functions, especially in the cortex, consist, rather, of layers or sheets of neural tissue that, though highly convoluted (in order to be accommodated within the limited diameter of the skull), are each essentially two-dimensional. (This anatomical two-dimensionality may have been favored at the outset, when these sheets originated as rather direct maps of the two-dimensional sensory surfaces. In addition, however, it may have been perpetuated by the necessity of leaving space for the neuronal interconnections between spatially separated circuits within the brain and between these and remote sensory and motor organs. Similar requirements seem to have favored the organization of computers into interconnected but essentially two-dimensional circuit boards or chips.)

• Most stimuli of biological significance nevertheless differ along many more than two or even three dimensions—including the numerous visual dimensions of location, orientation, shape, texture, color, and motion as well as the many nonvisual dimensions of feel, sound, smell, and taste. A topographic representation of the values that an object simultaneously takes on all these dimensions is impossible within a single, two- or even three-dimensional modeling medium.

3.2 Representation of a Three-Dimensional World in a Two-Dimensional Medium

In the particular case of the visual representation of surrounding objects in our three-dimensional environment, however, there is one mitigating circumstance. Because the surfaces of most objects are opaque, our direct visual experience is not really of the entire three-dimensional world, as such. Rather, for each direction from the vantage point we occupy at any given moment, our view is generally only of the first two-dimensional surface intersected by the straight line from that vantage point in that particular direction. There may well be an unlimited number of other opaque bodies behind that first surface in any given direction, but they all remain invisible from that vantage point.

Because light travels in straight lines until intercepted by a solid surface, an adequate representation of the three-dimensional world, as it appears from any one vantage point, may therefore be possible, after all, within an essentially two-dimensional neural medium. At each location within such a neural sheet, all that is required is that the distance to the external visible surface in the particular direction corresponding to that location within the sheet be coded by a scalar quantity definable in terms of the neural activity at that point. (The distance itself is generally computable from the many distance indicators contained within the available visual pattern, including linear perspective, optic flow patterns, and—with particular accuracy in the case of nearby objects—binocular parallax [Julesz 1971; Marr and Poggio 1979; Sperling 1970; Szeliski and Hinton 1985]).

We do in fact generally experience the world as if from a particular vantage point (Metzler and Shepard 1974). Although the internal construction of an observer-independent, object-centered representation of an external object has advantages (Hinton 1981; Marr 1982; Marr and Nishihara 1978), we must also retain a representation of our own spatial relation to the object and, indeed, to our surrounding environment as a whole. Moreover, if we did fully represent the intrinsic structure of objects independently of their relative positions, we should be able to determine whether two objects were the same or different in shape immediately. In fact, however, we may first have to imagine a normalizing transformation of the one object into the orientation of the other, taking an additional time proportional to the degree of difference in their positions (Shepard and Cooper 1982).

Nevertheless, what we mean when we say that we experience the world as three-dimensional cannot be entirely captured by computing and assigning a depth to each direction from our momentary vantage point. What we mean, even more fundamentally, I believe, is that we are able to anticipate how our visual experience of the world will change as we freely move our vantage point in that world. In a subsequent section of this chapter I consider a connectionist theory, recently proposed by Mel (1986), that indicates one way in which we may acquire the ability to do this within an essentially two-dimensional neural medium.

3.3 Topographic and Nontopographic Forms of Internal Representation
In addition to their positions, objects have countless other degrees of freedom of shape, texture, color, sound, taste, smell, and so on. Even the position of a three-dimensional object in physical space, including as it does three degrees of freedom of orientation as well as three degrees of freedom of location, could not have a fully topographic representation in a medium having fewer than six dimensions (Shepard 1984; Carlton and Shepard, in preparation). Accordingly, in a three-dimensional brain or, *a fortiori,* in a merely

two-dimensional layer of that brain, we must allow for an encoding in terms of some nontopographic variable of neural activity—such as relative rates of firing of groups of cells that are distinguished only by their functions and not by their spatial locations. For example, the color of the surface visible in a particular direction from a given vantage point might be encoded, at the corresponding location in the neural sheet, by the relative levels of activation in mutually inhibitory cells in each of three opponent systems of such cells— representing, say, degrees of light versus dark, red versus green, and yellow versus blue.

What are the consequences for mental representation, connectionist learning, and behavior of these two (topographic and nontopographic) types of neural encoding? Perhaps most fundamentally, in a topographic representation the same patterns of activity at different locations retain, by virtue of their spatial separation, their separate identities. But in a nontopographic representation, a particular cell or group of functionally equivalent cells, being capable of only one level of activity at a time, cannot simultaneously represent two different values of a variable. This suggests that topographic representation may be the preferred form for morphophoric media or indispensable attributes, whereas nontopographic representation may be appropriate for nonmorphophoric continua or dispensable attributes. If so, the choice of topographic versus nontopographic representation of a continuum is not an arbitrary design feature or an accident of phylogenetic development; is a reflection of a fundamental difference in the types of continua along which objects vary in the world. However, to the extent that the dimensionality or morphophoric variation in a given domain exceeds two or three, the history of phylogenetic development may also play a role in the determination of which dimensions of morphophoric variation become entrenched in a topographic form—presumably with some consequences for the efficiency with which the different morphophoric variations are internally represented.

3.4 Consequences of the Limited Velocity of Neural Propagation
In a topographic representation, propagation time should exhibit a particular orderly relation to distance within the neural medium. To the extent that form-preserving transformations are simulated within a topographic representation, then, orderly relations might be expected to emerge between time and distance. The phenomenon of apparent motion, in particular, should reveal such a relation.

In the simplest form of apparent motion, namely that between two alternately presented visual dots, the minimum stimulus-onset asynchrony yielding a strong illusion of motion between the locations in which the two dots are displayed increases when the distance between the two locations increases (see Korte's third law). Indeed, to a good approximation, this critical time increases linearly with the distance of separation in physical space (Corbin 1942; Shepard 1984; Shepard and Cooper 1982). Similarly, in rotational apparent motion (Shepard and Judd 1976) and in mental rotation (Shepard and Metzler 1971), the critical times increase linearly with the angular difference between the orientations of the two presented three-dimensional objects (Shepard and Cooper 1982).

A closely analogous relation also holds for apparent motion in pitch. The greater the pitch separation of two tones, the more slowly must they be alternately sounded in order to be heard as an up-and-down melody rather than as a high tone and a low tone going on and off independently (Jones 1976; McAdams and Bregman 1979; Shepard 1981; van Noorden 1975). Indeed, owing to the presence of a circular component of pitch, called "chroma," there are even analogs of rotational apparent motion and mental rotation in the domain of auditory pitch (Shepard 1982, 1983, 1984). There is also evidence for apparent motion of tactile position (Kirman 1983), though its compliance with Korte's law may remain to be tested.

In the domain of color, however, there does not seem to be an analog of apparent motion. When two different colors have been presented alternately, the appearance has been described not as a continuous passage through intermediate colors but as a discontinuous switching from each actually presented color to the other (Kolers and von Grünau 1975, 1976). If there is no critical stimulus-onset asynchrony between the experiences of discontinuous switching and continuous variation, no functional relation between time and difference, analogous to Korte's law, can be determined for color. Perhaps this is because color, unlike space and pitch, is nonmorphophoric, dispensable, and (perhaps for that reason) represented nontopographically in the brain.

For those domains that do give rise to apparent motion and that do support imagined transformations, I have suggested that the rates of translational and rotational motion implied by the slopes of the functions relating the critical times to distances and angles do not reflect the rates at which objects typically move or rotate in the physical world. (After all, the rate of relative motion of an object is not an inherent property of the object but depends on such arbitrary and variable things as the force with which the object has been propelled and the independent velocity of the observer.) I have conjectured, rather, that these estimated rates of mental transformation are determined by the limiting velocities of propagation of representational activity in the neural substrate (Shepard 1981, 1984; for what may be a similar kind of propagation underlying motor control, see Eckmiller 1986). What is perhaps generally most adaptive for an individual who has experienced two glimpses of a visual object or snatches of an auditory source is to instantiate the continuing existence of that object or source, as quickly as possible, in the concrete form of an interpolated path of simple transformation.

The required time is necessarily greater for longer paths of transformation, provided that length of path is defined in terms of extent of transformation in the external world, not in terms of distance on the sensory surface (Attneave and Block 1973; Corbin 1942; Farrell 1983; Metzler and Shepard 1974; Ogasawara 1936; Shepard and Judd 1976; Shepard and Zare 1983; Shepard 1984, p. 427). For a given path of transformation, moreover, the time evidently is also greater when the transformation must be internally planned, voluntarily simulated, and checked, step by step, as in imagined rotation, than when it is externally and involuntarily driven, as in apparent motion (Shepard and Cooper 1982). I suggest that, whereas the *path* of an internally simulated transformation is determined by an evolutionary internalization of the kinematic geometry of rigid motion in the world, the *rate* of the simulated transformation over that path is determined by the velocity of propagation of the representational activity within the neural substrate. However, the total time required to complete such a transformation must depend on both the length of the path and the rate of propagation over that path (Shepard and Zare 1983).

3.5 Possible Mental Analogs of Relativistic and Quantum Phenomena

The fact that the brain (being itself a physical system) is directly constrained by the laws of physics widens the range of physical principles that may have applications to mental phenomena. One would not expect all facts about the physical world to become internalized through biological evolution alone. For example, some of these facts are on a biologically inaccessible scale. This is why I could speak of space as Euclidean and three-dimensional. The possibility (in accordance with general relativity) that at the scale of the universe as a whole or in the vicinity of supermassive objects space is markedly curved, and the possibility (in accordance with recent quantum theories) that at a scale well below that of elementary particles space may be of much higher dimensionality or extremely contorted are both irrelevant here. The departures from Euclidean three-dimensionality at cosmological distances or at Planck distances are, respectively, too vast or too minuscule to affect biological systems as such. However, this does not mean that principles of relativistic and quantum mechanics have no counterparts in mental mechanics.

The limitation on the velocity of neuronal propagation can be seen as an analog (on a vastly different scale) of limitation, according to the theory of relativity, of the velocity of any causal propagation to the speed of light. Some support has already been obtained for the inference that neural processes in topographically organized systems should therefore conform to analogs of the Lorenz transformation equations of relativity theory—with the velocity of light, c, replaced by the appropriate velocity of causal propagation through the neuronal medium (Caelli, Hoffman, and Lindman 1978).

Indeed, the linear dependence on distance of separation of the minimum onset-to-onset time yielding apparent motion (Korte's law) can readily be interpreted in accordance with such an extension of special relativity. The two alternately presented events are causally connected (by the representation of motion over a connecting path) only if the second event falls within the cone of causal propagation of the first event (the analog of the "light cone" in special relativity). Otherwise the two events are separated by a spacelike rather than a timelike interval in space/time and hence cannot be causally connected (Jones 1976; Shepard 1981). Moreover, I claim that the connecting paths over which such motions are experienced, when the causal connection can be made, are in the general case geodesic paths in the curved manifold of possible positions (Shepard 1981; Carlton and Shepard, in preparation), just as light traverses a geodesic path in the curved space/time manifold of general relativity.

Even quantum mechanics may have its mental analogs. There is evidence that, upon the presentation of an ambiguous stimulus, all the possible alternative interpretations are momentarily activated in parallel, until (through a kind of lateral inhibition) one interpretation quickly gains ascendancy and suppresses all the others before those others are able to leave a trace in memory (Swinney 1979; Tanenhaus, Leiman, and Seidenberg 1979). This seems in some ways analogous to the "collapse of the wave function" in quantum mechanics, in which, upon the making of a measurement, the possible outcomes (which were until then only probabilistically represented, as a linear superposition, in the propagating wave function) collapse nonlinearly into a single outcome.

An example from apparent motion would be the selection of which dot in one visual display is represented as moving into which dot in the immediately succeeding display. Dots tend to be identified with their nearest neighbors in successive displays; however, when more than one dot is equally close to another, something like an exclusion principle tends to prevent two dots in one display from being identified with the same dot in the other. The apparent motion of a dot between two actually presented dots also seems in some ways analogous to the transit of a "virtual particle" in quantum physics.

Here, I am merely pointing to some analogies between brain function and principles of relativistic and quantum physics that may be useful even if brain processes can adequately be described, at the neurophysiological level, solely in terms of classical physics. Whether truly quantum-mechanical phenomena in the brain, perhaps akin to macroscopic quantum phenomena that occur in physical systems at very low temperatures, are psychologically significant (as has been proposed by Eddie Oshins in a personal communication; see also Oshins and McGoveran 1980) remains a separate and intriguing question.

3.6   Possible Synergy between Direct and Evolutionarily Internalized Constraints

I have been distinguishing sharply between those constraints that have been internalized through natural selection and learning and those constraints that necessarily apply directly to the processing system as a physical system. However, some parallelisms between the forms taken by these two types of constraints are also implicit in my remarks. Thus, the brain, which has to represent the layout in a surrounding three-dimensional space, is itself a three-dimensional system. Or, perhaps more accurately, the brain, which has to represent the distance to the first opaque surface in each direction in a two-dimensional manifold of directions, is composed of neural manifolds that are themselves two-dimensional. Likewise, the brain, which must simulate external transformations that (in accordance with principles of object conservation and finite velocity) must pass through a dense series of intermediate states, does so by an activity that propagates with restricted velocity through a topographically organized neural network and, hence, must itself pass through intermediate states.

Evidently, direct physical constraints have already biased the development of the nervous system toward some of the minimum properties appropriate for the representation of external objects and events. This bias may therefore have facilitated the evolutionary internalization of the much richer and more refined properties that now manifest themselves as an intuitive wisdom about such things as shortest paths of transformation and possible consequential regions in psychological space. In addition, the structure and connectivity of the neuronal system, as directly constrained by physics and as gradually shaped by natural selection, provides, in turn, the initial conditions necessary for judicious generalization and, hence, for nontrivial and efficient learning. (Hinton and Nowlan [1987] have recently indicated how a synergy may also obtain between evolutionary and learning processes.) Accordingly, I will turn in the following section to a consideration of how connectionist mechanisms of learning might capitalize on the already-shaped structure of a processing system to achieve more refined approximations to environmentally determined consequential regions and paths of transformation.

4   Connectionist Tuning of Internalized Constraints

4.1   Classification Learning through Adjustment of Weights of Candidate Regions

In an earlier section, I suggested that connectionist systems are particularly suited to the mechanization of learning. However, I also argued that learning will necessarily be of an entirely trivial and hopelessly inefficient kind in the absence of some built-in metric of similarity or "psychological space" governing how what is learned about any one situation should generalize to other possible situations.

The theory of generalization that I outlined briefly here (and more fully in Shepard 1987b) was strictly intended for the highly idealized situation in which an individual who has had a single learning experience with a novel object then confronts another object that more or less differs from the first. The problem of generalization for an individual in that situation, I have claimed, is just the problem of inferring the conditional probability that a consequential region thus found to overlap the first stimulus in psychological space also overlaps the second. That generalization decreases with distance in psychological space according to an exponential function, and a certain metric is, then, a consequence of integrating over all possible candidates for the consequential region. In this integration, each candidate, which constitutes an alternative hypothesis as to the location, size, and shape of the consequential region in psychological space, has an associated prior weight. In the absence of any knowledge about this location, size, and shape, the weights are presumed to be those that maximize the Shannon-Weiner measure of entropy (Shepard 1987b).

We cannot specify what is learned, even on a single trial, in the absence of a psychological space and principles of generalization with respect to that space. However, such a space and set of principles, once established, should provide a suitable basis for the development of a theory of discrimination and classification learning. In particular, if we treat each alternative hypothesis as to the disposition of a consequential region in psychological space as a "hidden element" in a connectionist system, then principles for the modification of connection weights (such, perhaps, as those of backwards error propagation, proposed by Rumelhart, Hinton, and Williams [1986a, 1986b]) should permit the system to adjust those weights from an initial (e.g., maximum-entropy) set of values to the values that best fit the evidence in a series of positive and negative encounters with different stimuli. Ultimately, the system could converge on the correct hypothesis as to even a quite sharply bounded consequential region. However, because the elements are here given a geometrical interpretation as overlapping regions in a psychological space, that space must confer on those elements a definite (innate) structure or connectivity beyond that usually ascribed to the elements of connectionist systems.

4.2 Mel's Proposal for a Connectionist Representation of Spatial Transformations

Especially because this volume is dedicated to the memory of Donald Hebb, it seems fitting to devote the final section of this chapter to a proposal that Bartlett Mel has recently made for a way in which a connectionist learning mechanism of the sort originally set forth by Hebb (1949) might assist an essentially two-dimensional sheet of neural tissue to represent the way in which one's view of the surrounding three-dimensional world would transform as a result of any given shift in one's vantage point (Mel 1986).

Gibson (1979) has emphasized that most motions of objects in the world, relative to the self, are in fact relative motions induced by one's own movements in the world. I have noted that such relative motions, even of an object as nonrigid as a curl of smoke, are rigid motions, with the same six degrees of freedom of translation and rotation already mentioned (Shepard 1984). I have also observed that, upon encountering any solid object, we have an immediate, intuitive appreciation of these six degrees of freedom of possible relative motion of that object—even before we have had time to recognize what the object is (Shepard 1981, p. 327).

Now, whenever a viewer moves, the projection of the world onto any two-dimensional representational medium must shift in a way that is highly constrained by the principles of kinematic geometry and perspective projection. But, in whatever form such principles may come to be represented within the neural medium, the isomorphism between the geometry of that two-dimensional medium and the geometry of the two-dimensional optic array associated with a single vantage point must considerably facilitate the representation of those principles.

Through computer simulation, Mel (1986) has demonstrated how such a connectionist system can learn spatial transformations through the Hebbian principle that neurons that are activated in appropriate spatio-temporal contiguity become more strongly connected. Neuronal programs for movement initiation come in this way to be associatively connected with the corresponding shifts in the perceptual projection that they induce. Thus, without ever constructing any truly world-centered representation of the three-dimensional environment as such, the freely mobile individual may be able to achieve a representation that is adequate from its own point of view because that representation is able to anticipate the perceptual consequences of initiating any particular movement in space.

Incidentally, if some neural sheets have come to represent transformations induced by movements that are only imagined rather than physically initiated (as, perhaps, in the phenomenon of mental rotation), an individual can presumably imagine the world from a point of view that differs from that individual's own momentary, real point of view. Blindfolded subjects have demonstrated the ability to point in the relative directions in which different objects in their environment would be from themselves if they were to station themselves in different specified locations and orientations in that environment (Attneave 1972; Attneave and Farrer 1977; Attneave and Pierce 1978; Thomson 1983). In this way, individuals might attain something like the viewer-independent representation advocated by Marr (1982). Presumably, however, the resulting environment-centered viewpoint or frame would not be achieved automatically, but only as the result of the completion of a voluntary mental transformation.

In any case, some learning mechanism along the lines proposed by Mel (1986) may play an important role in our ability to anticipate the changes in the view of the three-dimensional world that would result from a particular self-induced motion. As Mel suggests, it may also contribute to our ability to imagine such spatial transformations. Certainly, a considerable degree of plasticity has been demonstrated in the visual system (Held 1965; Stratton 1896). However, this plasticity is not unlimited. The system can learn to correct for certain transformations, such as global inversion or distortion; but transformations that disrupt topology (such as a scrambled fiber-optics channel that permutes the elements of the visual display according to some fixed but arbitrary rule), even though it preserves the pictorial information, must completely defeat the local connectivities of the topographically organized system. Thus, the learning mechanism considered by Mel depends for its effectiveness on the preceding existence of a topographically organized neuronal medium.

Moreover, whatever is both learnable in the individual and invariant in the world is, in principle, genetically internalizable in the species as well. Indeed, as I have implied, there should be a pervasive selection pressure for the genetic internalization of those biologically relevant things, such as kinematic geometry, that are always true in the world. Still, as I have noted, some plasticity is needed in order for each developing individual to correct for changes entailed by growth, injury, or disease. Thus, the Hebbian learning mechanism proposed by Mel, even if not entirely responsible for our internalization of kinematic geometry, may nevertheless provide the fine tuning and the developmental plasticity that make our representation of space and of spatial transformations so precise and so robust.

Conclusion

The framework offered by connectionism prompts the question of how regularities of the world have come to determine the structure of the brain and, hence, the functioning of the mind. In order to exhibit adaptive generalization and, hence, efficient learning, a connectionist system must already possess a structure that captures some fundamental regularities of the world. As primary examples, I have discussed the representations of objects as identical despite variations in their positions in space or their conditions of illumination and as belonging to the same biologically significant natural kind despite variations in their many other attributes of size, shape, color, odor, movement, and so on. My central questions have concerned how and in what form this initial structure is established in a system in which representations of external objects and regularities exist only in the weights of connections among vast numbers of hidden elements. I have tried to indicate how a start might be achieved by recognizing that, although the initial connectivity of the system may not preserve the to-be-learned semantics of individual objects and events, it may preserve something of the abstract constraints that uniformly govern all such objects and events in the world—as these constraints might be formalized in terms of appropriate psychological spaces together with the psychologically significant geodesic paths and consequential regions in these spaces.

Acknowledgments

The preparation of this chapter was supported by National Science Foundation Grant BNS 85-11685. I am indebted to several colleagues for their clarification concerning connectionist issues. I thank, particularly, Mark Gluck, Misha Pavel, David Rumelhart, Paul Smolensky, and Brian Wandell.

Note

Subsequent to the preparation of this chapter, I learned of additional proposals as to how, through experience, connectionist learning mechanisms might contribute to the formation of topographic maps in the cortex (Kohonen 1984) and to the development of capabilities for the representation of rigid transformations of objects in space (Goebel 1987).

References

Attneave, F. 1950. Dimensions of similarity. *American Journal of Psychology* 63: 516–556.

Attneave, F. 1972. Representation of physical space. In *Coding Processes in Human Memory*, ed. A. W. Melton and E. Martin (Washington, D.C.: Halsted).

Attneave, F., and G. Block. 1973. Apparent movement in tridimensional space. *Perception and Psychophysics* 13: 301–307.

Attneave, F., and P. Farrar. 1977. The visual world behind the head. *American Journal of Psychology* 90: 549–563.

Attneave, F., and R. K. Olson. 1971. Pitch as a medium: A new approach to psychophysical scaling. *American Journal of Psychology* 84: 147–166.

Attneave, F., and C. R. Pierce. 1978. Accuracy of extrapolating a pointer into perceived and imagined space. *American Journal of Psychology* 91: 371–387.

Brainard, D., and B. Wandell. 1986. An analysis of the retinex theory of color vision. *Journal of the Optical Society of America* 3: 1651–1661.

Braitenberg, V. 1984. *Vehicles*. Cambridge, Mass.: MIT Press. A Bradford Book.

Caelli, T., W. C. Hoffman, and H. Lindman. 1978. Subjective Lorentz transformations and the perception of motion. *Journal of the Optical Society of America* 68: 402–411.

Carlton, E. H., and R. N. Shepard. In preparation. Geometrical Bases for Psychologically Simplest Motions of a Rigid Object in Space.

Cooper, L. A. 1975. Mental rotation of random two-dimensional shapes. *Cognitive Psychology* 7: 20–43.

Cooper, L. A. 1976. Demonstration of a mental analog of an external rotation. *Perception and Psychophysics* 19: 296–302.

Cooper, L. A., and P. Podgorny. 1976. Mental transformations and visual comparison processes: Effects of complexity and similarity. *Journal of Experimental Psychology: Human Perception and Performance* 2: 503–514.

Corbin, H. H. 1942. The perception of grouping and apparent movement in visual depth. *Archives of Psychology* 38 (series no. 273): 5–50.

Dixon, E. R. 1978. Spectral distribution of Australian daylight. *Journal of the Optical Society of America* 68: 437–450.

Eckmiller, R. 1986. Topological and dynamical aspects of a neural network model for generation of pursuit motor programs. In Proceedings of the Eighth Annual Conference of the Cognitive Science Society.

Farrell, J. E. 1983. Visual transformations underlying apparent movement. *Perception and Psychophysics* 33: 85–92.

Farrell, J. E., and R. N. Shepard. 1981. Shape, orientation, and apparent rotational motion. *Journal of Experimental Psychology: Human Perception and Performance* 7: 477–486.

Fernald, R. D. 1984. Vision and behavior in an African Cichlid fish. *American Scientist* 72: 58–65.

Garner, W. R. 1974. *The Processing of Information and Structure*. Hillsdale, N.J.: Erlbaum.

Gibson, E. J., and E. S. Spelke. 1983. The development of perception. In *Handbook of Child Psychology. Volume 3: Cognitive Development,* ed. J. H. Flavell and E. M. Markman (New York: Wiley).

Gibson, J. J. 1979. *The Ecological Approach to Visual Perception*. Boston: Houghton Mifflin.

Goebel, P. 1987. Toward a Mental Mechanics of Neural Systems. Unpublished manuscript.

Green, B. F., Jr. 1961. Figure coherence in the kinetic depth effect. *Journal of Experimental Psychology* 62: 272–282.

Hebb, D. O. 1949. *The Organization of Behavior*. New York: Wiley.

Held, R. 1965. Plasticity in sensory-motor systems. *Scientific American* 213: 84–94.

Helmholtz, H. von. 1962. *Treatise on Physiological Optics*. New York: Dover. (Original German publication: 1856.)

Hinton, G. E. 1981. A parallel computation that assigns canonical object-based frames of reference. In Proceedings of the Seventh International Joint Conference on Artificial Intelligence.

Hinton, G. E., and S. J. Nolan. 1987. How learning can guide evolution. *Complex Systems* 1: 495–502.

Hinton, G. E., T. J. Sejnowski, and D. H. Ackley. 1984. Boltzmann Machines: Constraints Satisfaction Networks that Learn. Technical Report CMU-CS-84-119, Department of Computer Science, Carnegie-Mellon University.

Jones, M. R. 1976. Time, our lost dimension: Toward a new theory of perception, attention, and memory. *Psychological Review* 83: 323–355.

Jordan, D. S., and R. N. Shepard. 1987. Tonal schemas: Evidence obtained by probing distorted musical scales. *Perception and Psychophysics* 41: 489–504.

Judd, D. B., D. L. MacAdam, and G. Wyszecki. 1964. Spectral distribution of typical daylight as a function of correlated color temperature. *Journal of the Optical Society of America* 54: 1031–1040.

Julesz, B. 1971. *Foundations of Cyclopean Perception*. University of Chicago Press.

Kirman, J. H. 1983. Tactile apparent movement: The effects of shape and type of motion. *Perception and Psychophysics* 34: 96–102.

Kohonen, T. 1984. *Self-Organization and Associative Memory*. New York: Springer-Verlag.

Kolers, P. A., and M. von Grünau. 1975. Visual construction of color is digital. *Science* 187: 757–759.

Kolers, P. A., and M. von Grünau. 1976. Shape and color in apprent motion. *Vision Research* 16: 329–335.

Kosslyn, S. M., and S. P. Schwartz. 1977. A simulation of visual imagery. *Cognitive Science* 1: 265–295.

Kubovy, M. 1971. Concurrent pitch-segregation and the theory of indispensable attributes. In *Perceptual organization*, ed. M. Kubovy and J. Pomerantz (Hillsdale, N.J.: Erlbaum).

Land, E. H. 1964. The retinex. *American Scientist* 52: 247–264.

Land, E. H. 1983. Recent advances in retinex theory and some implications for cortical computations: Color vision and the natural image. *Proceedings of the National Academy of Sciences* 80: 5163–5169.

Land, E. H., and J. H. McCann. 1971. Lightness and retinex theory. *Journal of the Optical Society of America* 61: 1–11.

Lockhead, G. R. 1966. Effects of dimensional redundancy on visual discrimination. *Journal of Experimental Psychology* 72: 95–104.

McAdams, S., and A. Bregman. 1979. Hearing musical streams. *Computer Music Journal* 3: 26–43.

McClelland, J. L. 1986. The programmable blackboard model of reading. In J. L. McClelland, D. E. Rumelhart, and the PDP Research Group, *Parallel Distributed Processing: Explorations in the Microstructure of Cognition, Volume 2: Applications* (Cambridge, Mass.: MIT Press. A Bradford Book).

Maloney, L. T., and B. A. Wandell. 1986. Color constancy: A method for recovering surface spectral reflectance. *Journal of the Optical Society of America* 3: 29–33.

Marr, D. 1982. *Vision*. San Francisco: Freeman.

Marr, D., and H. K. Nishihara. 1978. Representation and recognition of the spatial arganisation of three-dimensional shapes. In *Proceedings of the Royal Society* B 200: 269–294.

Marr, D., and T. Poggio. 1976. Cooperative computation of stereo disparity. *Science* 194: 283–287.

Mead, C. 1987. Silicon models of neural computation. In Proceedings of the IEEE First International Conference on Neural Networks.

Mel, B. W. 1986. A connectionist learning model for 3-dimensional mental rotation, zoom, and pan. In Proceedings of the Eighth Annual Conference of the Cognitive Science Society.

Metzler, J., and R. N. Shepard. 1974. Transformational studes of the internal representation of three-dimensional objects. In *Theories in Cognitive Psychology: The Loyola Symposium*, ed. R. Solso (Potomac, Md.: Erlbaum).

Noll, A. M. 1965. Computer-generated three-dimensional movies. *Computers and Automation* 14: 20–23.

Ogasawara, J. 1936. Effect of apparent separation on apparent movement. *Japanese Journal of Psychology* 11: 109–122.

O'Leary, A., and G. Rhodes. 1984. Cross-modal effects on visual and auditory object perception. *Perception and Psychophysics* 35: 565–569.

Oshins, E., and D. McGoveran. 1980. . . . thoughts about logic about thoughts . . . : The question "Schizophrenia?" In *Systems, Science, and Society* (Proceedings of the 24th Annual North American Meeting of the Society for General Systems Research), ed. B. H. Banathy (Louisville: Society of General Systems Research).

Rumelhart, D. E., G. E. Hinton, and R. J. Williams. 1986a. Learning internal representations by error propagation. In D. E. Rumelhart, J. L. McClelland, and the PDP Research Group, *Parallel Distributed Processing: Explorations in the Microstructure of Cognition, Volume 1: Foundations* (Cambridge, Mass.: MIT Press. A Bradford Book).

Rumelhart, D. E., G. E. Hinton, and R. J. Williams. 1986b. Learning representations by back-propagating errors. *Nature* 323: 533–536.

Rusack, B., and I. Zucker. 1975. Biological rhythms and animal behavior. *Annual Review of Psychology* 26: 137–171.

Shepard, R. N. 1957. Stimulus and response generalization: A stochastic model relating generalization to distance in psychological space. *Psychometrika* 22: 325–345.

Shepard, R. N. 1958. Stimulus and response generalization: Deduction of the generalization gradient from a trace model. *Psychological Review* 65: 242–256.

Shepard, R. N. 1962. The analysis of proximities. Multidimensional scaling with an unknown distance function. I and II. *Psychometrika* 27: 125–140, 219–246.

Shepard, R. N. 1964a. Attention and the metric structure of the stimulus space. *Journal of Mathematical Psychology* 1: 54–87.

Shepard, R. N. 1964b. Review of *Computers and Thought*, ed. E. Feigenbaum and J. Feldman. *Behavioral Science* 9: 57–65.

Shepard, R. N. 1965. Approximations to uniform gradients of generalization by monotone transformations of scale. In *Stimulus Generalization*, ed. D. J. Mostofsky (Stanford University Press).

Shepard, R. N. 1981. Psychophysical complementarity. In *Perceptual Organization*, ed. M. Kubovy and J. Pomerantz (Hillsdale, N.J.: Erlbaum).

Shepard, R. N. 1982. Geometrical approximations to the structure of musical pitch. *Psychological Review* 89: 305–333.

Shepard, R. N. 1983. Demonstrations of circular components of pitch. *Journal of the Audio Engineering Society* 31: 641–649.

Shepard, R. N. 1984. Ecological constraints on internal representation: Resonant kinematics of perceiving, imagining, thinking, and dreaming. *Psychological Review* 91: 417–447.

Shepard, R. N. 1987a. Evolution of a mesh between principles of the mind and regularities of the world. In *The Latest on the Best: Essays on Evolution and Optimality*, ed. J. Dupré (Cambridge, Mass.: MIT Press. A Bradford Book).

Shepard, R. N. 1987b. Toward a universal law of generalization for psychological science. *Science* 237: 1317–1323.

Shepard, R. N. 1988. How fully should connectionism be activated? Two sources of excitation and one of inhibition. *Behavioral and Brain Sciences* 11: 52.

Shepard, R. N., and L. A. Cooper. 1982. *Mental Images and Their Transformations.* Cambridge, Mass.: MIT Press. A Bradford Book.

Shepard, R. N., and J. E. Farrell. 1985. Representations of the orientations of shapes. *Acta Psychologica* 59: 104–121.

Shepard, R. N., and D. Jordan. 1984. Auditory illusions demonstrating that tones are assimilated to an internalized musical scale. *Science* 226: 1333–1334.

Shepard, R. N., and S. A. Judd. 1976. Perceptual illusion of rotation of three-dimensional objects. *Science* 191: 952–954.

Shepard, R. N., and J. Metzler. 1971. Mental rotation of three-dimensional objects. *Science* 171: 701–703.

Shepard, R. N., and S. Zare. 1983. Path-guided apparent motion. *Science* 220: 632–634.

Smolensky, P. 1988. On the proper treatment of connectionism. *Behavioral and Brain Science* 11: 1–23.

Sperling, G. 1970. Binocular vision: A physical and neural theory. *American Journal of Psychology* 83: 461–534.

Stratton, G. M. 1896. Vision without inversion of the retinal image. *Psychological Review* 3: 611–617.

Swinney, D. A. 1979. Lexical access during sentence comprehension: (Re)consideration of context effects. *Journal of Verbal Learning and Verbal Behavior* 18: 645–659.

Szeliski, R., and G. Hinton. 1985. Solving random-dot stereograms using the heat equation. In Proceedings of the Conference on Computer Vision and Pattern Recognition.

Tanenhaus, M. K., J. L. Leiman, and M. S. Seidenberg. 1979. Evidence for multiple stages in processing of ambiguous words in syntactic context. *Journal of Verbal Learning and Verbal Behavior* 18: 427–440.

Thomson, J. A. 1983. Is continuous visual monitoring necessary in visually guided locomotion? *Journal of Experimental Psychology: Human Perception and Performance* 9: 427–443.

Torgerson, W. S. 1958. *Theory and Methods of Scaling.* New York: Wiley.

Trehub, A. 1977. Neuronal models for cognitive processes: Networks for learning, perception, and imagination. *Journal of Theoretical Biology* 65: 141–169.

van Noorden, L. P. A. S. 1975. Temporal Coherence in the Perception of Tone Sequences. Doctoral dissertation, Technishe Hogeschool, Eindhoven.

Wallach, H., and D. N. O'Connell. 1953. The kinetic depth effect. *Journal of Experimental Psychology* 45: 205–217.

PART II
Neurobiology

Chapter 5

Some Arguments for a Theory of Cell Assemblies in the Cerebral Cortex

Valentino Braitenberg

I am about to conclude a period of involvement in the cerebral cortex, the results of which have been published in various papers concerned with the quantitative anatomy of the mouse cortex (Braitenberg 1978a,b, 1981a,b, 1982) and in some comments on the physiology of the monkey striate area (Braitenberg 1985a,b). In this chapter I try to justify the philosophy underlying these studies, and I point out some of the more controversial tenets.

1 Critique of the Wiring Concept

Fascinating aspects of the latest technology are always creeping into science and being turned into subconscious motives for theory. For brain science, in the nineteenth century it was optics, with its idea of projection, and in the twentieth century it was radio engineering, with the idea of wiring, followed by computer engineering, with its logical circuits. The influence of electronics has been particularly misleading.

Components in an electronic device are connected by wires, whose main virtue is constancy in time. In contrast to this, it is likely that the connecting scheme in the brain is subject to changes as long as life lasts. Many synapses, perhaps the majority in mammals, obey something like Hebb's law which governs the transformation of the statistics of coincidences into changes of synaptic strength.

Furthermore, electronic equipment has very little tolerance for aberrant wiring. In many cases a single disconnected or wrongly connected wire among thousands renders an entire operation completely useless. Much information is needed to set up such equipment. In contrast, in brains the growth of many fibers, and hence the pattern of their connections, is governed by chance to a large extent; it is constrained, but not determined in detail, by a relatively small amount of information in the "blueprint" (another misleading concept). Details are evidently unimportant for function, and many changes of the connections brought about by age or disease can easily be absorbed by a vast amount of built-in tolerance.

Most important, we are accustomed to explaining the action of an electronic machine in terms of functional units consisting of a few shrewdly connected components of different kinds: an oscillator is composed of a solenoid and a condenser, an amplifier of a transistor and some resistors, and so on. In striking contrast to this, the cerebral cortex is, to a first approximation, an enormous collection of components *all of one kind* (the pyramidal cells), and is not easily separable into small meshes of standard structure (in spite of claims to the contrary: modules, columns). All these neurons are held together by an even greater number of synapses, which again mediate influences of one kind only, very likely of the nature of "excitation."

I know very well that the cortex contains stellate ("nonpyramidal") interneurons of various kinds, possibly equipped with different kinds of transmitters, but these represent only a minority in comparison with the large number of pyramidal cells with their homogeneous connections. Also, there may be an uneven distribution of stellate cells in the cortex, a feature we want to discuss only after we have fully grasped the meaning of the homogeneous wiring in the preponderant population of pyramidal cells.

It is important to emphasize that this picture of the cortex is not just one instance of a general feature that sets apart all nerve matter from conventional technical equipment. The homogeneity of the wiring in the cerebral cortex is quite characteristic for that part of the brain and must be explained in terms of the special function it performs, for there are other kinds of nerve tissue where the neural connections are just as precise, just as diversified, and just as constant and predetermined as the wiring in the machine. The fibers emanating from the fly's compound eye are distributed on the first optic ganglion according to a complicated scheme, which is completely understood and absolutely precise. There are more instances of such precise wiring at other levels of the visual ganglia of insects.

The cortex is very different. Having looked at very many neurons in Golgi, silver, and electron-microscopic preparations of the mouse cortex over the years, I should be very surprised indeed if anybody were to come up with a convincing scheme resembling the diagrams of electronics. The neurons in the cortex—tens of millions or billions, depending on the size of the animal—are all similar in the overall pattern of distribution of dendritic and axonal processes, but no two are exactly alike. A description of their geometry in statistical terms seems the only appropriate one. The technical counterpart, statistical electronics, has hardly been explored yet.

2 Weak and Strong Connections

When a number of measurements and quantitative estimates obtained from our study of the mouse cortex (Braitenberg 1978a,b; Schüz and Münster 1985; Schüz and Dortenmann 1987) were put together, the most surprising result turned out to be the tenuous synaptic connection between any given pair of neurons in the system of cortical pyramidal cells. A typical pyramidal cell in the mouse has about 5,000 synaptic contacts through which it is affected and about as many through which it affects other neurons. In larger animals this figure may be twice as high. The following question immediately suggests itself: How much convergence and divergence is present in these connections; do most of the synapses on the axonal tree of one pyramidal cell contact just one or a very few other pyramidal cells, or does the pyramidal cell achieve the maximal dispersion of its signals by contacting as many different neurons as it has synapses on its axonal branches? The same question can, of course, be asked inversely about the number of different neurons that provide the synaptic afferents for any given neuron: as many as there are afferent contacts, or much fewer? The answer to both questions is "Almost as many." In fact, the most likely connection between a pair of neurons is by just one synaptic contact. Two or three contacts may happen, but this should be rare according to our calculations. Our quantitative arguments are based on the morphology of the cortical neurons. For a neuron to make multiple synaptic contacts with other neurons, its axonal tree should match in its shape, at least partially, the dendritic tree of the neurons which it contacts. This is what is observed in the cerebellum (in the synaptic relation of climbing fibers and Purkinje cells), but nowhere in the cerebral cortex. The majority of the intrinsic fiber population of the cerebral cortex (and this means the majority of all fibers there, since the afferents are orders of magnitude fewer in number) consists in axon collaterals of pyramidal cells, some millimeters per neuron. The straight course of these axon collaterals through the neuropil, at all possible angles, is their salient morphological feature. Such a straight fiber, traversing the dendritic tree of another pyramidal cell, may hit that particular cell once, twice, or perhaps more often, with probabilities comparable to those of a bullet shot at the crown of a tree hitting the tree once, twice, or more often. These probabilities depend, of course, on the density of the crown and the thickness of the branches. In the case of cortical pyramidal cells both are quite low, yielding very low probability for multiple hits.

There is the possibility of an axon collateral running in close proximity exactly parallel to a dendrite. In this case there could be multiple contacts, but the situation is quantitatively unimportant for two reasons. First, it is a rare case. For any given pair of neurons, the probability of the direction of any one collateral's coinciding exactly with the direction of any of the dendrites of the other neuron is very low. Second, even if such a close parallel arrangement of an axon collateral and a dendrite does occasionally happen, the collateral is not likely to contact many synapses along the dendrite, since the synapses, in the case of pyramidal cells, reside at the tips of the spines and are thus distributed in a sort of probabilistic sleeve around the dendrite. In fact, the spines protrude on all sides of the dendrite and have varying lengths.

We have a good case for a system of widespread, very weak excitatory contacts between pyramidal cells forming the main synaptic network in the cortex.

But there are also strong contacts in the cortex. Some of the stellate cells distribute their efferent synapses within the narrow region defined by their dense axonal tree. Multiple synaptic contacts with any one postsynaptic neuron are much more likely there than in the system of synapses between pyramidal cells. Some other stellate cells concentrate their terminations in the immediate neighborhood of cell bodies of pyramidal cells, forming the so-called baskets (Ramon y Cajal 1911), and another type grasps the initial segment of pyramidal-cell axons with specialized endings, forming the so-called chandeliers (Somogyi 1977). All these are almost certainly inhibitory— strongly so in the case of baskets and even more strongly, one would expect, in the axo-axonal contacts of the chandelier axon.

The overall picture is this: a majority of excitatory neurons connected by a vast number of very weak, very widespread synaptic contacts. Interspersed among these we find a minority of neurons whose action is inhibitory, narrow in range, and very strong.

3 Cell Assemblies

We argue that the cortex is essentially a deposit of acquired information, a gigantic memory store. The material substrate of the message "learned" is a change in the pattern of the connections. Having excluded both the growth of new axonal or dendritic branches as the mechanism of these changes and the establishment of new synaptic contacts on the basis of work on guinea pigs, in which all the synapses are already present at birth, Schüz (1981) pointed out the possibility that dendritic spines modify synaptic strength by changing their shape. This idea is in keeping with our picture of the cortex as a vast collection of neurons of one kind—the pyramidal cells—interconnected by long- and short-range connections which all produce synapses of one kind localized on dendritic spines. In fact, pyramidal cells are the only neurons in the cortex for which the typical "spines," with all their electron-microscopic characteristics, have been convincingly demonstrated. The observation that counts of spines in the cortical tissue reveal their number to be almost as great as that of all cortical synapses also fits the picture, since numerical estimates based on the shape of dendritic and axonal arborization of all cortical neuron types indicate the majority of synapses in the cortex to be synapses between pyramidal cells and therefore localized on spines.

Thus we complete a skeleton picture of the cortex as a widely interconnected system of pyramidal cells (with some other cells interspersed among them), where all the synapses may change with experience. The individual synaptic change, of course, contributes only a tiny fraction of the global change that manifests itself as "learning" in behavior, since we have already seen that the contacts between pyramidal cells are of the weak kind.

If we now ask ourselves what the use of such a network could possibly be, the answer is in terms of the theory of cell assemblies—proposed by Hebb (1949), out of fashion for some time, and now again favored by many. The essence of this theory is that the representation of meaningful things and events within the brain is in terms of the activity of sets of neurons rather than of individual neurons, and that such sets of neurons (called "cell assemblies") are held together by excitatory connections which are built up through a process akin to "associative learning." It is remarkable that Hebb and his contemporaries seemed to have no doubt about the localization of cell assemblies in the cerebral cortex, despite the fact that the properties of the cortical "wiring" which the theory requires had not yet been demonstrated at that time. Today we know that the connections are weak, excitatory, and plastic. The fact that a single connection between a pair of neurons is so weak that it can hardly raise the target neurons above threshold implies that information in the brain must be carried by quite large sets of neurons in order to be effective. The fact that 80 percent of the synapses in the cortex are excitatory, which is quite astonishing at first, becomes comprehensible when we recognize that their main business is to keep cell assemblies together. Finally, recent demonstrations of plasticity of the cortical connections depending on their activity (Wiesel and Hubel 1965) are in accordance with the idea that cell assemblies are molded by experience.

If cell assemblies represent things of the outside world within the brain, the ignition of a cell assembly (i.e., the activation of all of its member neurons aided by their reciprocal connections) represents "getting the idea" of that thing, and the ignition of a number of assemblies in succession is the physiological counterpart of a "train of thought." We have elaborated this in some detail (Braitenberg 1978, 1984; Palm 1982). The main point is a global feedback on cortical activity necessary for preventing the ignition of one cell assembly from spreading to all the others via the excitatory network. This has interesting consequences, since it embodies the principle of a quasi-random walk from cell assembly to cell assembly, dictated by successive phases of an oscillation in the threshold control mechanism.

4 Cortical Architectonics

Our view of the cortex as an associative matrix is disappointingly simple in comparison with the high-level operations that have been occasionally purported to occur in that part of the brain. It is, in fact, only one part of the story. The associative network of the cortex requires input and output devices of various kinds, besides the threshold control already mentioned. High-level operations will be understood once the role of the cortex is defined within the entire central-nervous-system circuitry, and this implies an understanding of the dynamic relations between cortex and the basal ganglia, cortex and thalamus, cortex and cerebellum, and so on.

But even within the cortex there is more structure than one would expect in a simple associative matrix. Clearly, not all the connections can be pre-established in the cortex between billions of neurons. Where there is no fiber, the coincidence of activity in a pair of neurons, which according to Hebb modifies the strength of their connection, cannot be detected, let alone translated into a change of synaptic coupling strength. The preexisting structure of the hemispheric white matter thus determines what can be learned by the cortex and embodies genetically fixed constraints on the acquisition of knowledge by the individual. The presence of a variety of discrete bundles within the white substance indicates that the pattern is indeed far from random. Moreover, as is well known, different "areas" of the cortex differ in the fine structure of their gray substance in spite of the basic uniformity of their composition in terms of neuronal types. Both the pyramidal cells and the stellate interneurons show considerable morphological variation depending on their position in different layers and in different areas. The result is a local variation of the "style" of the neuropil (in some cases very obvious; in other cases subtle and visible only to the expert in cortical architectonics, whose eyes are trained to catch small differences in the patterns formed by neural cell bodies or by myelinated fibers). This variation in the geometry of the cortical nerve net probably again reflects built-in knowledge from evolution, determining for each area—i.e., for each sensory (motor, etc.) context—what aspects of the input are available to the learning process.

To illustrate, I quote an interpretation that I have given for the cortical network in the monkey visual area (Braitenberg 1985a, b, 1986).

5 Area 17 and Hubel-Wiesel Effects

I have shown that oriented receptive fields, their excitatory and inhibitory subfields, and their rotation as the electrode proceeds through the cortex are features that follow quite naturally from the lumping of inhibitory interneurons in patches about 0.5 mm apart. These patches may well be identified with the Cytochrome-oxidase "blobs" described by Humphrey and Hendrikson (1980) and by Horton and Hubel (1981). The pyramidal cells in this model play quite the same role as in the rest of the cortex; i.e., they build up associations between themselves. The model I have proposed makes a general point. In this case, and perhaps in many others, minor variations of the statistics of a random network may produce effects that at first sight would seem to require a great deal of specific "wiring."

In short, the idea is this: I assume nests of inhibitory neurons semiregularly spaced at distances of about 0.5 mm throughout area 17. These strongly inhibit pyramidal cells in a surrounding region about 0.5 mm in width, called a hypercolumn. The input fibers contact both the inhibitors and the pyramidal cells. A row of active input fibers, representing a line in the visual field, will have different effects depending on its orientation within the hypercolumn. If it is radially oriented, it will pass through the inhibitory center of the hypercolumn, which in turn will block the responses of the surrounding pyramidal cells. If it goes tangentially through the hypercolumn, it will miss the inhibitory centers and activate the pyramidal cells in the part of the hypercolumn which it traverses. Thus, each pyramidal cell responds preferentially to orientations perpendicular to the radius connecting it to the nearest hypercolumn center. A regular succession of orientations will be encountered by a physiologist pushing an electrode across a hypercolumn, as will breaks in the sequence of orientations between one hypercolumn and the next. This scheme provides a good interpretation for the charts obtained by voltage-sensitive-dye techniques in the visually stimulated monkey cortex (Blasdel and Salama 1986).

The connection of this model with the theory of cell assemblies is as follows: The mechanism that makes the orientation of cortical neurons rotate around inhibitory centers, described in the preceding paragraph, is confined to one hypercolumn. In fact, as is shown by many published records (e.g., Hubel and Wiesel 1974), a complete cycle of 180° rotation corresponds to the width of one hypercolumn—about 0.5 mm in the monkey area 17. However, the size of a "simple" or "complex" receptive field, expressed in cortical coordinates, is at least twice as great. This suggests that each of the Hubel-Wiesel-type receptive fields is made up of several elementary fields belonging to neurons housed in several neighboring hypercolumns, all having the same orientation and bound together into a cell assembly by their excitatory axon collaterals. Many more results of area-17 physiology are well accounted for by this model, as I have already shown in a more detailed analysis (Braitenberg 1985a). The point here is that anatomy may be much simpler than physiology suggests. Our model does not require any preferential orientation of fibers in the visual cortex, and still it fully explains the "sequence regularity and geometry of orientation columns" described by Hubel and Wiesel (1974).

References

Blasdel, G. G., and G. Salama. 1986. Voltage-sensitive dyes reveal a modular organization in monkey striate cortex. *Nature* 321: 579–585.

Braitenberg, V. 1978a. Cortical architectonics: General and areal. In *Architectonics of the Cerebral Cortex,* ed. M. A. B. Brazier and H. Petsche (New York: Raven).

Braitenberg, V. 1978b. Cell assemblies in the cerebral cortex. In *Approaches to Complex Systems,* ed. R. Heim and G. Palm (Berlin: Springer-Verlag).

Braitenberg, V. 1981a. Anatomic basis for divergence, convergence and integration in the cerebral cortex. *Advances in Physiological Science* 16: 411–419.

Braitenberg, V. 1981b. A selection of facts and conjectures about the cerebral cortex inspired by the theory of cell assemblies. *Advances in Physiological Science* 30: 287–289.

Braitenberg, V. 1982. Outline of a theory of the cerebral cortex. In *Biomathematics in 1980,* ed. L. M. Ricciardi and A. C. Scott (Amsterdam: North-Holland).

Braitenberg, V. 1984. *Vehicles: Experiments in Synthetic Psychology.* Cambridge, Mass.: MIT Press.

Braitenberg, V. 1985a. Charting the visual cortex. In *Cerebral Cortex, volume 3,* ed. A. Peters and E. G. Jones (New York: Plenum).

Braitenberg, V. 1985b. An isotropic network which implicitly defines orientation columns: Discussion of an hypothesis. In *Models of the Visual Cortex,* ed. D. Rose and V. G. Dobson (New York: Wiley).

Braitenberg, V. 1986. Two views of the cerebral cortex. In *Brain Theory,* ed. G. Palm and A. Aertsen (Berlin: Springer-Verlag).

Hebb, D. O. 1949. *The Organization of Behavior.* New York: Wiley.

Horton, J. C., and D. H. Hubel. 1981. Regular patchy distribution of cytochrome oxidase staining in primary visual cortex of macaque monkey. *Nature* 292: 762–764.

Hubel, D. H., and T. N. Wiesel. 1974. Sequence regularity and geometry of orientation columns in the monkey striate cortex. *Journal of Comparative Neurology* 158: 267–294.

Humphrey, A. L., and A. E. Hendrikson. 1980. Radial zones of high metabolic activity in squirrel monkey striate cortex. *Society for Neuroscience Abstracts* 6: 315.

Palm, G. 1982. Neural assemblies: An alternative approach to artificial intelligence. Berlin: Springer-Verlag.

Ramon y Cajal, S. 1911. *Histologie du systeme nerveux de l'homme et des vertebres.* Paris: Maloin.

Schüz, A. 1981. Prenatal formation of synapses and dendritic spines in guinea-pig cortex and their postnatal changes. *Advances in Physiological Science* 30: 279–285.

Schüz, A., and M. Dortenmann. 1987. Synaptic density on non-spiny dendrites in the cerebral cortex of the house mouse. A phosphotungstic acid study. *Journal für Hirnforschung* 28: 633–639.

Schüz, A., and A. Münster. 1985. Synaptic density on the axonal tree of a pyramidal cell in the cortex of the mouse. *Neuroscience* 15: 33–39.

Somogyi, P. 1977. A specific axo-axonal neuron in the visual cortex of the rat. *Brain Research* 136: 345–350.

Wiesel, T. N., and D. H. Hubel. 1965. Comparison of the effects of unilateral and bilateral eye closure on cortical unit responses in kittens. *Journal of Neurophysiology* 28: 1029–1040.

Chapter 6

A Population Approach to the Neural Basis of Perceptual Categorization	Leif H. Finkel, George N. Reeke, Jr., and Gerald M. Edelman

In this chapter we present a view of the operation of the nervous system that is based on the theory of neuronal group selection (Edelman 1978). This theory holds that the fundamental operations of the nervous system are based on population principles, and that neural function must be understood in a developmental and ecological context. The theory is motivated by the following questions: How are the connections between regions developmentally determined and evolutionarily constrained? What is the relationship between anatomy, physiology, and pharmacology in determining function? How are the responses of various brain regions (both mapped and nonmapped) coordinated? How do neural networks perform categorizations, and how do these categorizations form the basis of learning? What are the mechanisms of short-term and long-term memory at different levels of neural organization, from the molecular level to that of the entire system? Any theory of central-nervous-system function must confront these issues. We will show that an approach based on somatic neuronal group selection has particular advantages for this purpose.

The above questions serve to point out the differences between a global theory aimed at understanding the operation of whole nervous systems and models of single neural processes such as stereopsis or associative memory. A global theory, however intellectually satisfying, is of little practical use unless it motivates a program of detailed models coupled to experimentally testable questions. We have constructed a number of such models that are consistent with the theory and focused at several different levels of organization of the nervous system. We will present three of these models here: one dealing with the molecular mechanisms of synaptic plasticity, one dealing with the plasticity of organization of mapped representations under such synaptic mechanisms, and one concerned with the modes by which categorization by repertoires of neural elements can take place. These models are interlocking, and their construction is driven by the rationale that only by considering the interactions between the different functional levels of the nervous system can the operations of selection be fully understood. We begin by briefly reviewing the outlines of the theory and the problems it addresses; then we return to the issue of selection after considering the individual models.

1 Overview of the Theory

The theory of neuronal group selection holds that the nervous system is a selective system operating according to population principles similar to those governing natural selection acting on organisms, but by means of special mechanisms transacted through groups of neurons in somatic time. Selection in the nervous system during development results in organized anatomy. Selection acting later during experience results in physiologically active groups of neurons chosen from that anatomy.

According to the theory (Edelman 1978, 1981; 1988; Edelman and Finkel 1984), the units of selection in the nervous system are groups of neurons. These groups are envisioned to be compact, local clusters of hundreds to thousands of neurons, which maintain strong synaptic connections to one another and weaker connections to cells outside the group. The cells in a group function as a collective, and they share many functional properties, such as mean receptive field location. The main mechanism of selection involves modifications of the strengths of synapses of the individual neurons in a group.

Groups participate in three major processes, as diagrammed in figure 1. First, during development, a *primary repertoire* of neuronal groups is formed through an initial phase of selection. Due to the epigenetic nature of the mechanisms of development, variations in anatomical connectivity are introduced, particularly at the level of the finer ramifications of neurites. A major mechanism in the formation of these connections involves a small set (no more than dozens) of cell-adhesion molecules (CAMs) (Edelman 1984). These molecules are involved in the dynamic control of morphogenesis, and they undergo changes in amount and distribution at all sites of embryonic induction (Edelman 1986). So far, several CAMs have been found in the nervous system. Each shows different schedules of regulation in different brain regions (Chuong and Edelman 1984). In addition, CAMs participate in migration of cells, as shown in the developing cerebellum (Chuong et al. 1986), and they are also related to changes seen in regenerating nerves (Daniloff et al. 1986).

A second selective process, group selection, leads to the formation of a

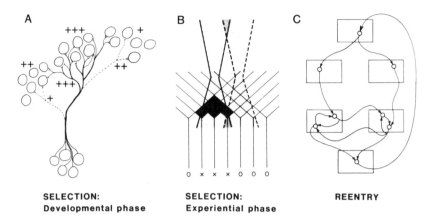

| SELECTION: | SELECTION: | REENTRY |
| Developmental phase | Experiential phase | |

Figure 1
Schematic of the major processes of neuronal group selection. (A) During development, a primary repertoire of neuronal groups is formed. These groups arise from an
initial phase of selection in the formation of neuronal connections. Variability in the
anatomy is due to epigenetic mechanisms involving cell-adhesion molecules. Plus
signs indicate the relative amount or distribution of CAMs on cells and fibers; solid
lines are stabilized connections; broken lines are connections that have not been stabilized. (B) Selection of neuronal groups by patterns of extrinsic inputs. Hourglass
figures represent groups that extend through all cortical laminae. Branching "Y's"
represent thalamic afferents; those marked x receive coactive stimulation, those
marked O do not. Group selection depends upon local coactivated input over time
(see figure 5). (C) Reentry—anatomical projections between different repertoires
(involving, but not limited to, reciprocal connections) carry out phasic signaling that
coordinates the responses of the repertoires in space and time, allowing a unitary
object to be recognized from the background and categorized.

secondary repertoire of functioning groups (figure 1b). During experience,
particular groups are selected over others in a competitive fashion. The selection is accomplished by enhancing the synaptic strengths of the selected
groups and weakening those of others. Once formed, groups can compete for
cells that belong to other groups. This competition determines functional
properties, such as the size, location, or modality of their receptive fields. It
consequently plays a major role in the organization of the topographic maps
found so widely throughout the nervous system. We will present a model of
this process below.

   The final process essential to functional group selection, indicated in figure
1c, is *reentry*. Reentry is the mechanism that coordinates the separate representations of individual mapped brain regions into a unitary basis for events
of perceptual categorization. The process involves phasic signaling along re-

ciprocally connected projections. Reentry can also involve loops of three or more stages of connected regions. Since the anatomical connectivity between regions is fixed in adult life, the flow of signals between various repertoires is controlled by changes within individual groups. Reentry may serve to refine further the properties of the receptive fields in various maps and, in particular, can act to sharpen topography and modality.

2 Variability

An often-neglected feature of brain organization, the existence of widespread variability, provides strong though indirect support for the group selection theory. The existence of extensive variability is a burden for information-processing views of the brain that require the possible meanings (or "codings") of signals to be decided upon before they are received. On the other hand, variability is a requisite property of all selective systems, inasmuch as it provides the population distribution upon which selection acts.

Although the structure of identifiable brain areas appears to be modally similar among conspecific animals, an enormous degree of variation exists. Variability is seen at the gross level; for instance, the size of visual cortical area V1 has been observed to vary by a factor of 2 in macaques (Van Essen et al. 1984), and there are marked differences in the relative area of sulci and gyri on individual primate brains (Sherman et al. 1982), not to mention the large variance in total size of individual brains. At the microscopic level there is tremendous variability in the pattern of axonal and dendritic connectivities (Macagno et al. 1973; Pearson and Goodman 1979; Kramer et al. 1985).

Variability also exists at the physiological level. It has traditionally been assumed that the topographic receptive-field maps found throughout the brain reflect the topography of the underlying anatomical connections. Recent experiments in several laboratories, particularly on the maps in somatosensory areas 3b and 1 in monkeys, have shown that cortical maps are in fact dynamic and can be dramatically altered (Devor and Wall 1981; Kaas et al. 1983; Merzenich et al. 1983a, b and 1984). Similar effects have been seen in other species and at other levels of the nervous system (see Mountcastle 1984).

It has been reported that the receptive-field maps in cortical areas 3b and 1 of squirrel monkeys vary greatly from animal to animal, and also vary over time in each animal. Furthermore, the locations of receptive fields and the magnification factors of body areas can be changed by various perturbations, such as repeated stimulation. Most dramatic, perhaps, are the changes seen after transection of a peripheral nerve. The cortical area formerly devoted to representation of the denervated part, such as the glabrous surface of a finger, switches to a representation of a new portion of the hand. The evidence suggests that this change does not involve sprouting of neuronal processes but instead reflects the emergence of anatomical connections which, although present, were previously too weak to be effective.

We have proposed a model based on neuronal group selection that accounts for these changes (Edelman and Finkel 1984). In this model, the receptive-field properties of neurons are determined by the neuronal group to which they belong. Group boundaries arise through a process of *confinement* in which the balance between the tendencies of neuronal groups to expand and to contract is determined by the relative influence of intrinsic excitatory and inhibitory inputs in the various layers of the developing cortex. Some of these groups are then *selected* over others, depending upon the location and characteristics of their receptive fields and the amount of stimulation received. In primary areas, the receptive fields of nearby neuronal groups normally overlap, and the groups continually compete for representation of these overlap regions and also for control of neighboring cells in the cortex. This competition operates by means of modifications in the synaptic strengths of the extrinsic and intrinsic connections of the group. Using the processes of confinement, selection, and competition, we have been able to account for many of the experimentally reported findings on the reorganization of somatosensory maps (Edelman and Finkel 1984). We have more recently developed a computer simulation of this process of map plasticity (Pearson et al. 1987) and we shall review it here. This simulation is itself based upon a detailed model of plasticity of synaptic efficacies, to which we shall turn first.

3   Rules for Synaptic Plasticity

After the developmental period of establishment of neuronal connectivity, the main mechanism of selection in the nervous system is the modification of synaptic efficacy. The view that neural activity carries information, that synapses store this information, and that memory is replicative (i.e. a homomorphic representation of the details of an object) is naturally associated with a class of synaptic models designed for information transfer and storage. This information-processing view of synaptic function is not consistent with current experimental findings. To approach these findings in a neuronally based system, we have proposed a new model of synaptic modification that provides a detailed basis for the operations of neuronal group selection (Finkel and Edelman 1985; Finkel 1985; Finkel and Edelman 1987).

The model proposes that there are multiple mechanisms for synaptic modification operating in parallel upon *populations* of synapses in the nervous

system. We assume that presynaptic efficacy (the amount of transmitter released per depolarization) and postsynaptic efficacy (the locally generated
voltage per amount of transmitter) are *independently* controlled by separate
mechanisms, which we discuss in turn. Given what is known about the actions of different transmitters, receptors, and second messenger systems, it is
natural to consider that multiple mechanisms may exist within a neuronal
population. However, for simplicity, we consider here just one presynaptic
modification rule and one postsynaptic rule, both of which are intended as
exemplary of the totality of possible rules.

3.1 The Presynaptic Rule

The presynaptic rule addresses the problem of how long-term changes can be
stored by synaptic modifications. The rule faces a double difficulty in that it
must account for the substantial phenomenology which has been reported
concerning short-term presynaptic changes in transmitter release, and yet
must also deal with long-term changes at synapses (a phenomenon about
which almost nothing is known). We therefore have made a simple assumption about the coupling between short-term and long-term changes in presynaptic efficacy.

Figure 2 shows a schematic of the presynaptic rule. Presynaptic efficacy
depends upon two factors: the baseline efficacy (i.e., the amount of transmitter released under normal activation) and the short-term facilitations and
depressions of transmitter release that occur in response to the recent history
of stimulation. We model the transient facilitations and depressions with first-
order rate equations (Finkel and Edelman 1985, 1987). There is substantial
experimental evidence for this approach, based particularly on transient
changes in transmitter release at the frog neuromuscular junction (Magleby
and Zengel 1982). In fact, Magleby and Zengel give evidence for multiple,
parallel, transient presynaptic changes with different decay constants and
stimulation requirements.

The main assumption of the rule, indicated in figure 2, is that long-term
synaptic change is effected by changes in the steady-state value of the baseline efficacy. We have studied alternative implementations of the long-term
change—for example, the effects of alterations in various rate constants of
the transient presynaptic changes. Whatever the relative contribution of these
factors, the critical aspect of the rule is that *all* presynaptic terminals of a
particular cell are modified together. This property is chosen to reflect the
effect of a change in gene expression, which would ostensibly affect all presynaptic terminals equally. The effect of the long-term change is therefore
usually manifested at terminals across the entire extent of the axonal arbori-

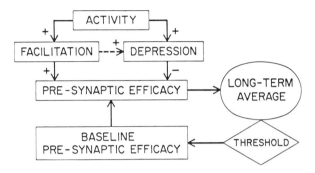

Figure 2
Flow chart of the presynaptic rule. The presynaptic efficacy ξ (the amount of transmitter liberated for a given depolarization) is given by the product of the baseline efficacy, ξ^0, multiplied by the effects of facilitation and depression. Efficacy is increased by facilitation and decreased by depression. Activity increases the degree of both facilitation and depression, which are coupled as greater facilitation increases depression. The presynaptic rule states that a long-term average is kept of ξ as it fluctuates with the temporal pattern of activation. If this long-term average reaches a threshold, the baseline value or presynaptic efficacy is reset to a new value, reflecting a change in gene expression. This affects all presynaptic terminals of the cell, and changes the response of the cell to future inputs.

zation of the neuron sustaining the change. In general, such a long-term change cannot maintain specificity with respect to individual stimuli, since it reflects both a temporal average over the shorter-term presynaptic changes and a spatial sum of these changes at the various presynaptic terminals of the cell. Since the synaptic change is not stimulus-specific and since its effect is widespread across the arborization and connectivity of a cell, it is clear the presynaptic rule cannot be used to store "information" in the conventional sense. However, we have shown (Finkel and Edelman 1985) that the rule does have two very useful population properties in connection with the postsynaptic rule: It serves as a generator of variability in the nearby and distant patterns of postsynaptic changes, and it can differentially enhance particular local postsynaptic patterns in a given group (which themselves maintain a high degree of specificity). Before discussing these effects, we consider the postsynaptic rule.

3.2   The Postsynaptic Rule
There are two general properties that any postsynaptic rule must have in order to account for reported experimental results. First, it must account for how changes can take place at specific synapses, yet be dependent in some fashion

on the *spatial* pattern of inputs to the cell. Second, the rule must account for the time window of synaptic modification—i.e., the fact that modifications can depend on two sets of inputs, received hundreds of milliseconds apart (Ito et al. 1982; Levy and Steward 1983; Kelso et al. 1986). Furthermore, the rule must incorporate the growing body of experimental evidence on the molecular basis of synaptic modifications (Hawkins et al. 1983; Alkon 1984; Changeux 1981). There is some preliminary experimental evidence supporting the particular example of the postsynaptic rule we will discuss here; however, regardless of its verisimilitude, this example is illustrative of a class of rules that satisfy these minimal explicatory requirements.

In its most general form, the postsynaptic rule states that the change in postsynaptic efficacy of a given synapse is governed by the positional pattern and relative timing of heterosynaptic inputs (those to other synapses) on the neuron with respect to the homosynaptic inputs on that neuron (i.e., those to the synapse in question). Such a mechanism requires two components: one sensitive to homosynaptic inputs and one sensitive to heterosynaptic inputs. Table 1 shows various possible components of postsynaptic rules. As a result of diffusional constraints, the substances responsible for the biochemical modifications (Ca^{++}, cAMP, etc.) must be produced locally or at nearby

Table 1
Possible component mechanisms for postsynaptic modifications.

Local modifier
- Receptor-associated second messenger
- Ca^{++}
- Voltage
- pH
- Direct structural interaction between target molecules

Heterosynaptic mediator
- Voltage (electrotonic or active conduction)
- Ca^{++} diffusion
- Second messenger diffusion (cytosolic or intramembranous)
- External paracrine diffusion of transmitter
- Global cell-surface modulation

Target
- Receptors
- Ionophores
- Other ultrastructural or regulatory proteins

Effect
- Change in effective number of channels or receptors
- Change in conductance of channels or binding or receptors
- Change in kinetics of state transitions for channels or receptors

synapses. However, the influences of heterosynaptic inputs can be communicated through electrotonic or active conduction.

Unlike the presynaptic rule, the postsynaptic rule allows for specific individual changes at each synapse. Owing to the operation of other mechanisms, there may in addition be cell-wide postsynaptic changes (for example, in the numbers of postsynaptic receptors, channels, or second messengers); however, here we will consider only the effects of local biochemical modifications.

The example we will consider here is illustrated in figure 3. Local modifications are produced by a modifying substance, M, produced postsynaptically in response to homosynaptic inputs. This substance modifies voltage-sensitive channels. However, we assume that channels are differentially modifiable depending on their functional state. Thus, for example, open channels may be more easily modified than closed or inactivated channels (e.g., because of steric factors). There is ancillary evidence for such an assumption (Catteral 1979; Huang et al. 1982; Huganir et al. 1986). Conducted voltages from heterosynaptic inputs change the states of voltage-sensitive channels at the synapse, increasing or decreasing the fraction of channels in modifiable states. Using parameter values from various experimental preparations, we have calculated that the proposed mechanism could generate a severalfold increase in postsynaptic efficacy (Finkel and Edelman 1987).

Thus, the nature and the timing of heterosynaptic inputs can modulate the effect of homosynaptic inputs in producing a local modification. The neuron can be imagined to be a "synaptic archipelago" consisting of islands of local modifications coupled by long-distance conducted voltages. Large depolarizing or hyperpolarizing inputs to the cell (which in some cases might follow from the types of presynaptic changes discussed above) can effectively change the "sea level" and create new island configurations. This would allow interactions between previously isolated synapses, thus changing the set of contexts that can affect a given stimulus.

The state-dependent assumption provides a molecular mechanism for coordinating heterosynaptic and homosynaptic inputs. Other postsynaptic rules, using different mechanisms (table 1), would each require an analogous coordinating step. For example, another possible mechanism might involve the selective modification (e.g. by intracellular Ca^{++}) of those transmitter receptors that had recently bound transmitter; or a subclass of receptors (e.g. NMDA receptors) might be rendered modifiable by intense homosynaptic inputs, and the modification could then depend upon heterosynaptic effects. This last possibility is similar to the mechanism for synaptic modifications proposed by Lynch and his colleagues (see Lynch and Baudry 1984).

(A)

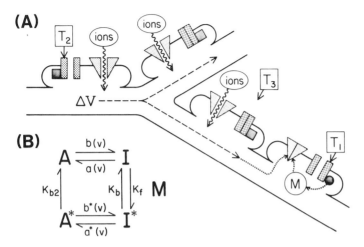

(B)

Figure 3
Operation of the postsynaptic rule. (A) Schematic of four synapses on a branching
dendritic tree. Shaded triangles represent voltage-sensitive channels (VSCs); shaded
rectangles represent receptor-operated channels (ROCs). A transmitter (T_1) has
bound to the synapse at lower right, leading to opening of the ROCs and also to
the production of a modifying substance, M, through activation of a membrane-
associated protein (small shaded circle). M modifies VSCs which are in the modifiable state. A potentially different transmitter, T_2, has bound to the leftmost synapse,
opening local ROCs and VSCs. The resulting change in membrane potential (ΔV) is
propagated through the dendritic tree (broken line), changing the states of VSCs as
they are reached. If the potential reaches the bottom right synapse (dotted line) at a
time when the concentration of M is still high, the fraction of VSCs in the modifiable
state at the synapse will be altered, and consequently so will the number of channels
modified by M. Synapses that have not yet bound transmitter (e.g. T_3) and synapses
that have not yet been reached by the potential will not be affected. (B) Kinetics of
state-dependent modification. Two-state model of a VSC. A represents lumped activated states; I represents lumped inactivated states, which we take to be the modifiable states. Channels in state I can be modified, in the presence of modifying
substance M, to the modified inactivated state, I^*. Forward and backward rate constants for the modification are K_f and K_b. Modification changes the voltage-
dependent state-transition rates from $a(V)$ and $b(V)$ to the modified rates $a^*(V)$ and
$b^*(V)$. Other effects of modification, such as a change in the conductance of the
channel, are possible (see table 1). Modification is short-term, and decays from I^*
according to K_b and by the potentially different rate constant K_{b2} from the modified
activated state A^*.

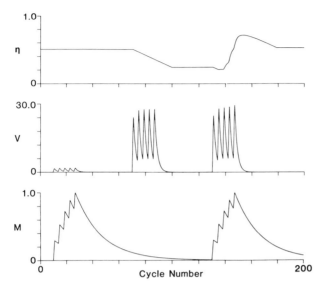

Figure 4

Computer simulation of the postsynaptic rule showing plots of modifying substance *M* (bottom panel), voltage at the postsynaptic terminal *V* (middle panel), and postsynaptic efficacy η (top panel). From cycle 10 to cycle 30, the homosynaptic input was stimulated in five short bursts. This produced a large change in *M*, only a small change in *V*, and consequently no change in η (because virtually no channels switched into the modifiable state). From cycle 70 to cycle 90, heterosynaptic inputs to the cell were stimulated in five bursts, causing a large increase in *V* but no change in the homosynaptically produced *M*. This led to a decrease in η (since channels switch into the modifiable states, but, in the absence of *M*, demodification occurs). From cycle 130 to cycle 150, both the homosynaptic and the heterosynaptic inputs were stimulated, causing increases in both *M* and *V*. This led to a large increase in η.

An illustrative simulation of the proposed rule is shown in figure 4. The three graphs display, respectively, the postsynaptic efficacy, η, the voltage at the postsynaptic terminal, *V*, and the local concentration of modifying substance, *M*. The voltage is produced in this case, by the sum of the local homosynaptic input and the (possibly attenuated) heterosynaptic inputs. The modifying substance is assumed to build up linearly with the amount of transmitter released from the presynaptic terminal (given by the presynaptic efficacy, ξ, multiplied by the activity of the presynaptic terminal, S_i), and *M* decays with a rate constant, δ. Thus,

$$M(t) = m_0 \cdot \xi \cdot S_i + (1 - \delta) \cdot M(t - 1),$$

where m_0 is a constant of proportionality. The change in postsynaptic efficacy is given by

$$\Delta\eta = k_f \cdot \text{(fraction of channels in state } I) \cdot M(t)^4$$
$$- k_b \cdot \text{(fraction of channels in state } I^*),$$

where k_f and k_b are the rate constants given in figure 3. The fact that the modifying substance enters as M^4 makes postsynaptic changes nonlinearly dependent on large presynaptic inputs and is intended to reflect a degree of cooperativity in one of the chemical reactions between transmitter binding and channel modification. Finally, the postsynaptic efficacy itself is given by

$$\eta = g \cdot \text{(fraction of unmodified channels)}$$
$$+ g^* \cdot \text{(fraction of modified channels)},$$

where g and g^* are the conductances of unmodified and modified channels, respectively. It is assumed that the modified conductance exceeds the unmodified conductance.

As figure 4 shows, when M is produced but the voltage is low, there is little change in η (left side of figure). When the voltage is high but there is no M, η actually decreases (middle of figure). This is because channels are switching to the I and I^* states, but only the demodification ($I^* \rightarrow I$) transition can occur in the absence of M, thereby decreasing the fraction of channels in the modified (higher conductance, g^*) state. When both M and V are high (right of figure), there is a large increase in η, as channels in the I state are modified to the I^* state.

The formal logic of this postsynaptic rule resembles that of the Hebb rule (see Hebb 1949). In fact, the postsynaptic rule can be made to mimic a Hebb rule by (1) making the voltage-dependent transitions occur as step functions, with the transition occurring at the cell's firing threshold, and (2) letting M be produced in large quantities with every presynaptic firing but also letting M decay very quickly. The postsynaptic rule is more general than the Hebb rule, however, and the two rules normally differ greatly in their actions. This can be seen in figure 5, which shows the pattern of synaptic modifications in a network of seven interconnected cells. Connections that do not exist are shown by shaded boxes. We assume that cells 1, 2, 5, and 7 are firing, and that the postsynaptic rule requires that a neuron receive at least three active inputs to raise the voltage high enough to transfer channels into a modifiable state. The boxes marked H would correspond to synapses modified under the Hebb rule, and those marked P would be modified by the postsynaptic rule. Clearly, the patterns are quite different.

The postsynaptic rule presented here has several significant advantages over the Hebb rule and certain of its modern derivatives (Bienenstock and

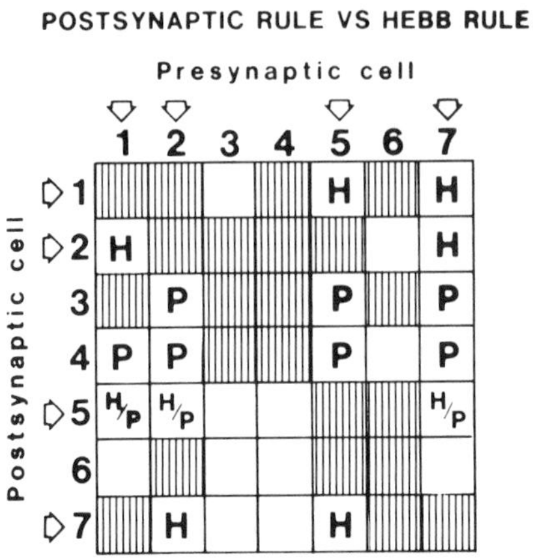

POSTSYNAPTIC RULE VS HEBB RULE

Presynaptic cell

	1	2	3	4	5	6	7
▷1					H		H
▷2	H						H
3		P			P		P
4	P	P			P		P
▷5	H/P	H/P					H/P
6							
▷7		H			H		

Postsynaptic cell

Figure 5
Comparison of the postsynaptic rule with the Hebb rule for a hypothetical network
of seven cells. The matrix shows connections between cells, with darkened boxes
representing absent connections. Cells 1, 2, 5, and 7 are assumed to be firing. The
boxes marked with P are synapses that would be strengthened according to the postsynaptic rule; those marked with H would be strengthened by the Hebb rule. The
Hebb rule strengthens synapses if and only if both pre- and postsynaptic cells are
firing; the postsynaptic rule strengthens a synapse if the homosynaptic input occurs
at an appropriate time with respect to the firing of the heterosynaptic inputs. Here we
assume that the "appropriate time" is simultaneity, and that at least three heterosynaptic inputs are necessary to raise the voltage enough to switch channels into modifiable states. Note the very different distribution of synapses strengthed by the two
rules. The distribution of weakened synapses would also differ.

Cooper 1982; von der Malsburg 1981) for explaining certain aspects of plasticity in the nervous system. The postsynaptic rule is purely voltage-
dependent and (unlike the Hebb rule) does not depend upon cell firing. This
is consistent with the recent experimental evidence of Carew et al. (1984),
which shows that cell firing is neither necessary nor sufficient for synaptic
modifications. The postsynaptic rule depends upon coactivation of heterosynaptic inputs to the postsynaptic cell rather than upon correlation of presynaptic and postsynaptic activation across an individual synapse. This
allows for more subtle context-dependent effects. The Hebb rule requires
rather strict temporal correlations, whereas in the present population rule
there can be significant (up to hundreds of milliseconds) delays between presynaptic and postsynaptic events, inasmuch as the effect of the presynaptic
input is effectively integrated by the production of modifying substance. This
allows the present rule to account for certain timing effects seen in synaptic

modifications in the hippocampus (Kelso et al. 1986; Gustafsson and Wigstrom 1986) and in the cerebellum (Ito et al. 1982). Finally, the postsynaptic rule differs from previous formal models in that it provides a schematic molecular mechanism based on biochemical and biophysical data, which is then reduced to a set of formal equations, and does not simply assume an abstract description alone.

4   The Rules in Action

To show the relation of such formulations in a selective system, we have recently incorporated the postsynaptic rule into a detailed computer model of cortical-map plasticity (Pearson et al. 1987). The simulation involves a large neural network which receives two superposed, individually topographic projections from two sensory surfaces representing the projections from the glabrous and dorsal surfaces of the hand. Owing to the properties of the postsynaptic rule, this initially disorganized network robustly organizes into neuronal groups when stimulated by any of a large variety of stimulation patterns. The rule coordinates the changes in the strengths of extrinsic and intrinsic connections through its heterosynaptic properties. The postsynaptic rule then serves as the mechanism for groups to compete for receptive-field sizes and locations.

The computer model simulates the three neuronal group processes involved in the formation and maintenance of topographic maps (Edelman and Finkel 1984). As shown in figure 6 and discussed above, these processes are group confinement, group selection, and group competition. In the present model, confinement is reflected in the tendency of complex networks to self-organize into groups with the size and distribution of the groups chiefly dependent upon the density of intrinsic connections and the ratio of excitatory to inhibitory synapses. Selection occurs when repeated presentations of inputs on one set of extrinsic connections to a group lead to a sharpening of the groups' boundaries and to the *effective* elimination (through synaptic weakening) of other extrinsic inputs to the group. Such selection is mediated by the heterosynaptic properties of the postsynaptic rule (figure 6.6b). Various stimuli can alter intrinsic and extrinsic connection strengths through group competition, but once groups have been selected they strongly influence the types of changes that can occur.

The computer model satisfactorily accounts for the experimental findings on cortical-map plasticity discussed above. We have shown how receptive fields can shift on the hand, and how the receptive-field organization of the observed map can be changed by perturbing the input. Thus, the physiologi-

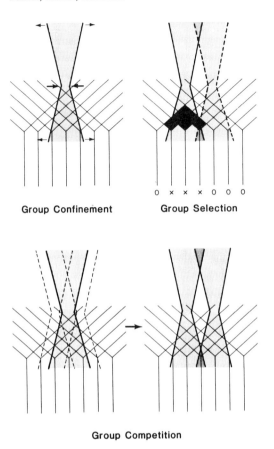

Group Confinement   Group Selection

Group Competition

Figure 6
The three components of map formation. Ascending Y-shaped figures represent ar-
borizing thalamic afferents; hourglass figures represent groups with narrow waist in
layer IV. Group confinement restricts activity to local areas because of the interplay
of expanding excitation in supra- and infra-granular layers with constricting inhibition in layer IV. Group selection depends upon coactive heterosynaptic and homosynaptic inputs, denoted by the x's, according to the postsynaptic rule. In this case the
group on the left is selected because it contains a region (blackened) that receives
coactive inputs but not uncorrelated inputs (denoted by the O's) from the adjacent
afferents. Repeated or intense stimulation will lead to presynaptic changes as well.
Group competition among three previously selected groups leads, in this hypothetical case, to dissolution of the central group (perhaps due to lack of overlap of its
receptive field with those of the surrounding groups).

cally recorded map is but one of many that are possible given the underlying anatomy, and it is the forces of selection and competition under the organizing influences of neuronal group dynamics that result in any particular map.

We have also investigated the interactions within a neural network of the presynaptic and postsynaptic rules operating in parallel (Finkel and Edelman 1985, 1987). The main finding is that the interactions between the rules depend crucially upon the architecture of the network. In randomly organized networks, there is no significant interaction between the two rules. However, in networks that are organized into neuronal groups, the two rules interact to give a "memory" mechanism arising from population properties. Short-term changes in a neuronal group, if repeated or intense, give rise to a long-term presynaptic change. Because of the widespread arborizations of the presynaptic axon, these changes affect neurons both inside and outside the group. However, there are two quite different effects of the long-term change. Inside the group, where recursive connections have a high probability, certain patterns of short-term postsynaptic changes are differentially enhanced, such that they occur more easily when the same or similar stimuli are presented again. Secondly, the long-term change acts as a generator of diversity, introducing variance into the patterns of short-term changes. This latter effect occurs both inside and outside the group; however, inside the group the increased variance is outweighed by the differential enhancement of particular short-term changes under the specific operation of the postsynaptic rule. Thus, the long-term change strengthens certain short-term changes and "scrambles" others. This scrambling is a critical requirement for any selective system, since continued selection may act to reduce variability in the population, leading to a loss of adaptability. Thus, long-term changes based on the presynaptic rule act to ensure that the system can competitively maintain the ability to respond to novel stimuli in novel ways.

The combined action of the two rules provides a useful mechanism for a system of memory. Long-term changes do not "store" activity patterns. They are necessarily crude because of the biochemical and molecular constraints on long-term storage. Instead, long-term changes have a population property by which they can differentially bias the system toward recreating short-term changes similar to those that originally precipitated the long-term change. The constant introduction of variability makes perfect recall unlikely, but it allows for continued adaptability and paves the way for generalization.

Our view of memory, in fact, is not one of storage of replicated images with more or less added noise, but rather one of enhanced bases for *recategorization* of objects or situations (Edelman 1986). According to this view (which is closest to the views of the reconstructionist school; see Oldfield and Zangwill 1942a, b; Bartlett 1964), perception involves categorization of the environment into objects, and memory involves a recreation of that categorization by a variety of means and circuits—not all of them necessarily identical.

To consider how selective systems can perform categorizations, we have developed a series of selective automata, Darwin I, II, and III, each of which deals with successively more difficult problems in categorization. But before we discuss how these automata go about simulating perceptual categorizations, we first briefly review what we mean by categorization.

5 The Problem: Categorization

The central problem facing the nervous systems of higher vertebrates, if not all animal species, is how to categorize the rush and plenitude of environmental stimuli received over time. There is considerable biological evidence that categorization is an innate and widespread ability. Spelke and her colleagues have shown that preverbal human infants have well-defined schemes for categorization of objects (see Kellman and Spelke 1983). Moreover, Herrnstein and his collaborators have shown that pigeons are capable of recognizing sophisticated categories of objects never before encountered, such as fish or the cartoon figure Charlie Brown (see Herrnstein et al. 1976; Cerella 1979).

The fundamental problem is that the world is unlabeled—categories are the adaptive creations of individuals or species and do not follow strictly from the physical properties of the environment. For example, imagine that you are presented with two types of objects: large red objects and small blue objects. You could construct a two-dimensional attribute space, with one dimension being color and the other being size. Each object could be represented by a point in this space, and there would be a boundary line (perhaps it would have to be curved in some regions) that would separate the points into large and red versus small and blue. Now, clearly, if asked to classify a small red object, one could not fit it into the previous classification scheme. Bongard (1970) has generalized this point (namely, that categories cannot always be defined as separable regions of attribute spaces of higher dimensionalities). This point is simple but significant, as most models of memory or perception (McClelland and Rumelhart 1986; Hopfield 1982; Anderson and Hinton 1981) involve the implicit assumption that categories can be so defined, *a priori*.

Another body of facts reinforces this analysis. There is a large literature (see Smith and Medin 1981) on alternative schemes for categorization, most of which involve either a probabilistic or an exemplar approach. In probabilistic schemes, objects in a category have particular attributes with defined probabilities; for example, the category 'firetruck' contains objects of which 90 percent are red, 85 percent carry ladders, 65 percent have sirens, and so on. One can then calculate the probability that a particular object belongs to the class. This notion has some psychological support, but there is also support for categorization based on exemplars. In exemplar schemes, objects in a category are all similar to one or several prototypical examples. There is, in fact, evidence that humans use both types of schemes.

These schemes are important, but they do not stress a critical aspect of categorization that was emphasized by Wittgenstein (1958). Many natural categories are *polymorphous;* there are no singly necessary or jointly sufficient characteristics for membership. For example, what do the following *games* have in common: baseball, solitaire, and war games? Dennis et al. (1973) have formalized the notion of a polymorphous category as a set of objects each of which possesses some threshold number (m) out of a set of N possible attributes, where $m < N$. An example of a polymorphous category is shown in figure 7. Category I is defined as any object with at least two of the three following properties: dark-centered, double-edged, and round. Thus, no single property is necessary for inclusion, nor is any particular combination of properties jointly sufficient for class membership. Furthermore, in examples with $M < N/2$ two objects in the same category may have *no* properties in common.

Even the polymorphous set formulation misses some obvious features of natural categories. For instance, either the inclusion or the lack of certain attributes can sometimes rule an object out of a category. Also, most objects in a category usually share many features with one another. Most critically, categories must be amenable to several operations: division into subcategories, inclusion into supercategories, association with related categories, and generalization. Nonetheless, they need not obey logically based superordinate or subordinate relations.

These notions of categorization concern higher-order, cognitively based, perceptually defined objects, and might be performed by highly specialized modules in the nervous system. That such is not the case, however, is a central tenet of the theory of neuronal group selection (Edelman 1985). In our view, categorization reflects the initial and primary operation of the nervous system, in that it is required for all other neural operations (particularly

I   II

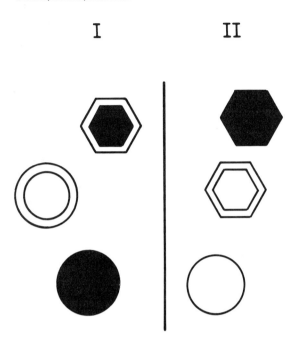

Figure 7
Polymorphous sets. Set I is a polymorphous set defined by objects with at least two
of the following properties: round, dark, double-edged. Objects in set II do not meet
this condition.

learning). To make this point more trenchant, we now turn to a description of
the categorizations performed by the set of automata we have constructed.

6 Selective Automata

The first selective automaton we constructed, Darwin I, was based on the
selective operations of the immune system. The automaton dealt with the
process of recognition itself, using strings of binary digits as recognizers and
recognizands. It demonstrated that the recognizing and generalizing ability of
a system can be improved by the introduction of variability into the memory
mechanism. This finding is a population property: if some variability is introduced into the population selected for a possible match to a stimulus under a
rule, then not only will that particular stimulus elicit enhanced responses in
the future, but (because of the variability) other, similar stimuli will also be
recognized by the selected population. We shall not describe Darwin I here
(see Edelman 1981), as the results have been incorporated in the later au-

tomata, to which we now turn. It is useful to point out, however, that the recognitions it carried out were of polymorphous sets.

Darwin II is much more similar to nervous systems and is concerned with the classification of two-dimensional patterns, most usually various geometrical shapes, presented on a retina-like array. The schematic design of construction for Darwin II is shown in figure 8. The recognizing elements of the automaton are simulated neuronal groups, idealized versions of those considered earlier. The groups are connected in a series of interconnected repertoires. Once established, the connectivity between repertoires remains fixed, but the strengths of connections vary in accord with the rules for synaptic modification that serve as the mechanism of group selection.

The automaton consists of two parallel concatenations of repertoires making classifications according to quite different principles. These subsystems, named "Darwin" and "Wallace," interact by reentry to give associative func-

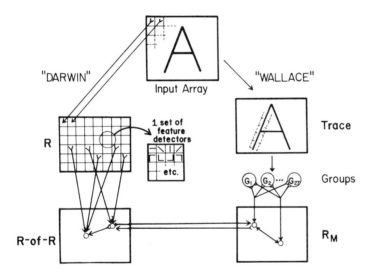

Figure 8
Simplified plan of construction for "Darwin II." Boxes represent repertoires, circles represent neuronal groups, and arrows represent synaptic connections. The inset to the right of the **R** repertoire is an expanded view of one of the topographically mapped subrepertoires, indicated by the circle and curved arrow. The specific functions of the individual repertoires are described in the text. In this typical instantiation, **R** contains 3,840 groups (a 10 × 12 topographic map with 32 kinds of feature detectors at each point) with 16 inputs each, **R-of-R** contains 4,096 groups with 96 connections each, and **R$_M$** contains 2,048 groups with 15 inputs each, for a grand total of about 500,000 connections. (Reprinted from Reeke and Edelman 1984, with permission.)

tions not possessed by either set alone. The "Darwin" network is designed to respond differently to each individual stimulus pattern. The Wallace network, on the other hand, is designed to respond in the same way to different objects in the same class. However, no specific information about the stimulus objects to be presented is built into the system when it is constructed.

The two subsystems both have a hierarchical structure. Each has, connected to the input array, a first level (which deals directly with features of the stimulus) and, connected to the first level, an abstracting or combining level. The two abstracting repertoires are connected in a reentrant fashion to form what we call a classification couple. It is important that in such a couple the earlier levels are not connected, for then the separate modes of disjunctive sampling upon which subsequent classification is based would be confounded, and their distinct characteristics would be lost.

The first part of "Darwin" is the **R,** or "recognizer," repertoire. It has groups that respond to local features on the input array, such as line segments oriented in certain directions or with certain bends. Multiple sets of these groups are connected to the input array in a topographic map (suggested by the parallel arrows from the input array to **R** in figure 8). As a result, patterns of response in **R** spatially resemble the stimulus patterns. The abstracting network connected to **R** is called **R-of-R,** or "recognizer-of-recognizers." Groups in **R-of-R** are connected to multiple **R** groups distributed over the **R** sheet, so that each **R-of-R** group is capable of responding to an entire pattern of response in **R.** In the process, the topographic mapping of **R** is destroyed and **R-of-R** gives an abstract transformation of the original stimulus pattern. If the stimulus undergoes a change, such as a translation to a new position on the input array, the pattern of response in **R-of-R** will be quite different. It is the responsibility of "Wallace" to deal with these perceptual-constancy problems, whereas "Darwin" deals with local individuating properties.

"Wallace" begins with a tracing mechanism designed to scan the input array, to detect object contours, and to trace along them. It responds to correlations of features that distinguish objects as entities from the background by their spatial continuity. (This is something like the operation the eye does when it rapidly scans a scene to detect the objects present.) The result of the trace is the excitation of a subset of a set of groups (G_1, G_2, . . . , G_{27} in figure 8) that represent by their activity the particular correlations of features or contours present in the input. These correlative responses are connected, in turn, to an abstracting network, $\mathbf{R}_M$, that responds to patterns of activity in G_1–G_{27} in much the same way that **R-of-R** responds to patterns of activity in **R.** Because the tracing mechanism responds to the presence of lines or junctions of lines in the environment with little regard for their lengths and orientations, $\mathbf{R}_M$ is insensitive to both rigid and nonrigid transformations of stimulus objects and tends to respond to certain class characteristics of whole families of related objects. Perforce it must fail to individuate objects.

The neuronal groups in all the repertoires of "Darwin II" are constructed according to a common principle, with parametric differences. The output of each group depends on a sum over its synaptic inputs, weighted by their individual synaptic efficacies and subject to noise and exponential decay. "Darwin II" does not implement the presynaptic and postsynaptic rules described above, but it does allow a number of rules based on variations of the Hebb principle. These rules have the advantage of computational simplicity, but they deprive the automaton of the versatility conferred by heterosynaptic effects. The Hebb-type rules are adequate for the simple recognition and categorization tasks studied with "Darwin II," and they were therefore used in the experiments presented here.

6.1   Results Obtained with "Darwin II"

With appropriate stimulation protocols, "Darwin II" is capable of producing responses corresponding to behaviors such as categorization, generalization, and association. We shall present examples of only the first two of these here; for a more detailed treatment see Edelman and Reeke 1982 and Reeke and Edelman 1984.

Figure 9 shows the responses obtained when three stimuli—two different A's and an X—were presented on the input array under conditions in which the reentrant connections between "Darwin" and "Wallace" were inactive. The **R** responses (left column) resemble the shapes of the stimulus letters as a direct consequence of the topographic mapping built into the connections between the input array and **R**. The **R-of-R** responses (second column) are different for the three letters, corresponding to individual representations of the letters. In contrast, the $\mathbf{R}_M$ responses (third column) are very similar for the two stimuli that are in the same class (the two A's), and different for the other class (the X). In short, these patterns of response meet the criteria set out earlier for the "Darwin" and "Wallace" networks. It should be noted that the particular categories arrived at by $\mathbf{R}_M$ for the different stimuli are dependent on the particular choice of trace correlations that $\mathbf{R}_M$ groups respond to, and might or might not agree with the categories we define for the letters.

Synaptic modifications improve the ability of the system to categorize, as table 2 shows. The numbers given in this table are ratios, before and after synaptic amplification, of the numbers of groups responding to two stimuli in the same class to the numbers responding to two stimuli in different classes. (The class-membership information used to derive these statistics is

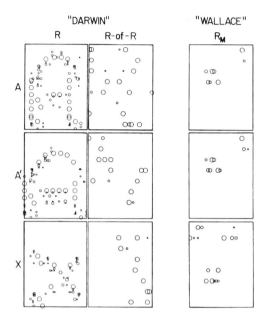

Figure 9
Responses of individual repertoires (**R, R-of-R,** and **R$_M$**) to three different stimuli.
Circles represent groups; the radius of each circle is proportional to the response of
the group. Groups responding at less than 0.5 of maximal response are omitted,
leaving blank areas in the plots. The stimuli were a tall narrow A (top row), a lower
wider A (middle row), and an X (bottom row). (Reproduced from Reeke and Edelman 1984, with permission.)

Table 2
Classification in Darwin II.

	Repertoire	
Time tested	Darwin [**R-of-R**]	Wallace [**R$_M$**]
Initially	1.21	90.93
After selection*	1.41	241.30

Repertoire sizes: **R**, 3,840 groups; others, 4,096 groups. Total connections: 368,840;
no Darwin-Wallace connections. Stimuli used: 16 letters, 4 each of 4 kinds. Quantity
shown is ratio of number of groups responding to two stimuli in same class to number of groups responding to two stimuli in different classes, corrected for numbers
that would respond in each case by chance alone.
*Each of four stimuli was presented for eight cycles, then the entire set was repeated
three times.

not known to the automaton during the test.) The ratios, which are corrected for the numbers of common responding groups that would be obtained by chance alone under the various conditions, measure the degree of commonality in the responses to stimuli that are in the same class. As such, they indicate, in agreement with the results shown in figure 9, that "Wallace" is far more effective at categorizing under these conditions than is "Darwin," but that nonetheless the "Darwin" responses to each stimulus are not entirely idiosyncratic. They also show that, after selective amplification, the classifying ability of "Wallace" is improved nearly threefold, with a smaller improvement apparent in the results for Darwin. This occurs even though there is no feedback from the environment that would enable the system to "learn" which responses are "correct."

One can look for generalization by making similar tests with letters related to *but not included in* the set used during selective amplification. Generalization occurs if the responses to the novel letters are more like those to the training letters than would have been the case without amplification. In "Wallace," generalization is already present without amplification as a consequence of the class-responding property of that network; in "Darwin," generalization is not built in and cannot occur without the help of "Wallace." Reentrant connections from R_M to R-of-R permit R_M to give this help in the following way: Among the groups in R-of-R responding to different stimuli of the same class will be some that happen to receive connections from R_M groups responding to these same stimuli. The extra input to these groups will increase their likelihood of exceeding the modification threshold, thus amplifying not only their connections from R_M but also those from R. Because of the class-response property of R_M, these groups will tend to be the same ones for the various stimuli. Therefore, groups in R-of-R that respond to multiple members of the class will be favored for amplification. After a number of repetitions of this process, with letters from several different classes, the R-of-R responses will become more alike within each class. To the extent that novel stimuli in the same class share features in R with the stimuli used during amplification, responses to them will also become more similar, consistent with generalization.

Results for a typical experiment of this type are shown in table 3. Sixteen different stimuli from four different classes (different letters of the alphabet) were used. Selective amplification was allowed to occur while each stimulus was presented for four cycles. The entire set of sixteen letters was repeated four times (256 cycles in all). A separate set of test letters, different but of the same four kinds, was presented before and after this process. (During these tests, amplification and the reentrant connections from R_M to R-of-R

Table 3
Generalization in R-of-R.[a]

Stimuli	Intraclass Chance	Interclass Chance	Intraclass Interclass
Initially			
Training set	2.09	0.72	0.90
Test set	2.89	1.63	1.77
Control set	—	1.96	—
After selection[b]			
Test set	6.10	1.00	6.10
Control set	—	1.00	—

a. Repertoire sizes: **R**, 3,840 groups; others, 1,024 groups. Connections to each **R-of-R** group: 96 from **R**, 64 from **R-of-R**, 128 from R_M. Stimuli used: 16 letters, 4 each from 4 classes.
b. Each of 16 stimuli was presented for 4 cycles, then entire set was repeated 4 times.

were disabled.) For these particular test letters, the degree of commonality of response within classes, as compared to that between classes, increased by a factor of 3.4, from a ratio of 1.77 to 6.10, as a result of selective amplification. With a set of unrelated control letters, no such increase was seen; this shows that the effect is specific, and that it is not due to a general increase in similarity of response to all stimuli. **R-of-R** thus displays generalization, in that, after it has had some experience with a number of letters of a particular kind, its response to novel letters of the same kind is more like that to the letters already "seen" than would have been the case without that experience.

"Darwin II" has no mechanism for generating motor output; performance is evaluated by examination of its internal states, directly or by means of appropriate statistics. More recently, however, we have begun to explore a new class of selective-recognition automata incorporating the ability to interact with the environment through motor output. Such interactions allow an appropriately designed automaton to signal its responses without need for the experimenter to interpret its internal states, but they are in fact important for a more fundamental reason: Interaction with the environment completes a global reentrant loop (figure 1) by which the responses of the automaton affect its own sensory input, giving it access to much more powerful selective paradigms. Its responses can now be interpreted as having varying degrees of adaptive value for it, leading to the generation of more complicated behavioral sequences and the possibility of learning. These automata are being used to study problems involving motion, perceptual invariance, figure-ground discrimination, memory, and other phenomena. One such experiment will be discussed briefly in the next subsection.

6.2 Preliminary Experiments with a New Class of Selective Automaton

The network architecture for one instantiation of "Darwin III" capable of developing visual tracking skills by selection is shown schematically in figure 10. Familiar from "Darwin II" are the input array and the Darwin and Wallace networks with **R** and **R-of-R** at the upper left. R_M is replaced by a pair of simple "visual scanning" repertoires that respond to objects on the input array at larger or smaller distances from what corresponds to the central fovea. A rather elaborate **R-out** repertoire controls the motor system. There are no prearranged motor skills; performance can develop and improve only by selection from spontaneous movements generated by pairs of mutually inhibitory pattern-generating layers of groups in repertoires. Separate layers are provided for large jumps (saccades) and fine tracking movements of the "head." Connections from the scanning cells in "Wallace" are made indiscriminately to motor cells in these layers corresponding to all directions of head movement. Amplification of these connections is modulated by value schemes based, respectively, on the appearance of activity in an area outside the foveal region and in the foveal region itself. Thus, connections from a particular point on a scanning repertoire to a particular motor area tend to be strengthened when the appearance of an object at that point is correlated with activity in the motor area that leads to foveation of the stimulus, and weakened when it does not. After a suitable period of experience with various moving stimuli, the system comes to make the appropriate saccades and fine tracking movements with no further specification of its task than that implicit in a "value scheme" given *a priori* that foveation is favored over random movement.

How this all works out in practice is shown in figure 11. The key to this rather complex figure is given in the legend; the important thing to note is the modification of the connection strengths from scanning repertoires to motor areas represented in the large crosses in each frame. Early in the experiment (figure 11a), these connections are weak, and motions are generated mainly as a result of activity in the pattern-generating layers. As time goes on (11b and 11c), the strengths of these connections are selectively modified, and activity in the scanning repertoires increasingly comes to dominate the motion of the head. The automaton finally displays a system of behavior in which the head scans at random when no stimulus is visible, makes a rapid saccade to any stimulus that appears within the outer limits of its widest visual field, and finely tracks any stimulus that has successfully been foveated. During fine tracking, **R** and **R-of-R** are able to respond to the now centered object, permitting position-independent categorization to occur. Habituation eventually sets in, permitting occasional saccades to other parts of

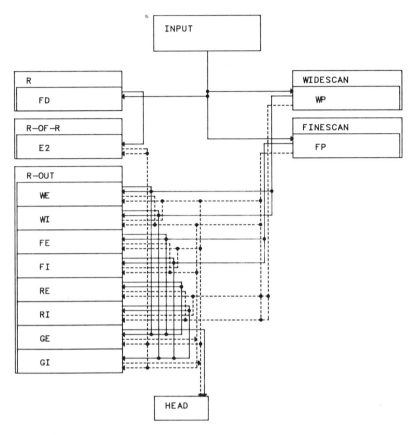

Figure 10
Network architecture for visual tracking. The input array is at the top; the motor
output to the movable head is at the bottom. At either side are the neuronal repertoires (large boxes) with their various cell layers (smaller included boxes). Predominantly excitatory connection tracts are shown as solid lines, inhibitory tracts as
dashed lines.

the visual field. After such a saccade, a new stimulus object, if present, may take precedence for new tracking movements.

Of course, this system makes mistakes, and a better tracking system could surely be *engineered* in which the correct motions for a spot of light at any location on the visual field would all be *calculated* in advance and incorporated in the logic of the design. The selective system takes longer to get its actions right. But since the machinery "doesn't know what it is for," the same networks can accomplish various tasks depending on what we, acting as external agents of "evolution," decide they should find "adaptive." Equally simple training regimes should work for a wide variety of harder tasks, such as finding a desirable object in a background of distracting objects and picking it out with a suitably designed independent arm. The modular combination of subsystems capable of carrying out recognition tasks provides an attractive approach to the construction of automata with increasingly complex perceptual capabilities that should have eventual significance for efforts at machine vision. On the output side, the corollary for motor control is the ability to generate complex behavioral sequences by selection from simple and innate motion patterns, with obvious significance for developments in robotics and the control of complex systems.

In work carried out since this chapter was prepared, Darwin III has been extended by the addition of a multijointed arm capable, after selection, of reaching to objects placed in its environment and exploring them with its sense of touch, providing information for categorization similar to that provided by "Wallace" in Darwin II.

Conclusions

We have considered models concerned with phenomena at three levels of organization of the nervous system. At the level of synaptic plasticity, we have shown how consideration of the biochemical and biophysical constraints on possible mechanisms leads to a new population model of synaptic modifications useful for selective responses. The presynaptic and postsynaptic rules combine to yield novel population properties when embedded in realistic neural architectures. But the action of the rules depends upon the details of the architectures; they work best in networks that are organized into neuronal groups. Here, then, is an example of a requisite interlinking of different levels required to model a selective system.

We have also considered, briefly, evidence that topographic maps in nervous systems are dynamic structures that emerge through a competitive

a

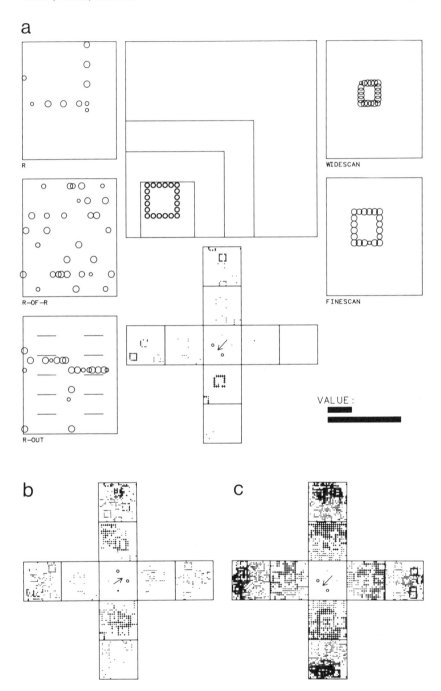

R

R—OF—R

R—OUT

WIDESCAN

FINESCAN

VALUE:

b

c

process from the much richer possibilities allowed for by the underlying anatomy. We discussed two versions of a model of this process, both of which depend upon the formation of neuronal groups, which, once formed, serve as the organizers of the map. Such neuronal groups give rise to the functional properties of maps and, through reentry, coordinate the representations in separate brain areas.

Changes in these maps must be related to the categorizations and recategorizations we view as central to higher brain function. To exemplify how such complex phenomena may be modeled without instructionistic assumptions, we reviewed a series of selective automata concerned with the general problem of categorization. The automata presented here are intended to illustrate certain aspects of the theory of selective recognition systems without attempting to model real nervous systems in detail. These models do not provide evidence for the applicability of the theory to real nervous systems; such evidence can only come from experiments. Nonetheless, as instantiated in such models, the theory provides satisfying explanations for the whole panoply of perceptual processes involving categorization. These models of aspects of selective systems can help to demonstrate the self-consistency of

---

Figure 11

State of "Darwin III" at three stages in a visual tracking task: after 42 cycles (a), 182 cycles (b), and 796 cycles (c). At top center in (a) is the input array, with the stimulus (a square) delineated by small circles and the visual fields of the two scanning (R_M) and one foveal (R) repertoires outlined by successively smaller squares. Down the left and right sides of (a) are shown the activities in the various repertoires, keyed to their relative positions in figure 10 and represented as in figure 8. Dashed lines separate pairs of cell layers in **R-out**. The behavioral values for saccade and fine-tracking motions are shown at the bottom right in (a). The measures of value and the activity in **R** and **R-of-R** are large only when the stimulus has been foveated, as is the case here. The large cross at bottom center in (a) displays the strengths of the connections from the wide-range scanning repertoire (WIDESCAN) to the motor areas (outer four squares), from the narrow-range scanning repertoire (FINESCAN) to the motor areas (inner four squares), and finally the activities of the up, right, down, and left motor neurons and the resultant motion of the head (circles and arrow in central square). The four arms of the cross correspond (clockwise from top) to the up, right, down, and left motor areas. Connection strengths are shown for excitatory and inhibitory connections as $+$ or $-$ signs, respectively, with sizes proportional to the connection strengths. (b) and (c) show only the connection strengths at cycles 182 and 796, as in the bottom center part of (a). In a perfectly engineered system, the outer halves of the eight squares forming the arms of the cross would contain excitatory connections ($+$ signs) and the inner halves would contain inhibitory connections ($-$ signs). The actual development of the connections under selective amplification closely approaches this ideal arrangement by the end of the experiment.

the theory as an abstract description of these processes. Such demonstrations are important for understanding complicated biological systems and, at the same time, can provide real insight into the redoubtable problem of designing artificial systems with brain-like capabilities.

Selection provides an explanation for the operation of the brain at what Mayr (1982) has called the level of ultimate causation. According to the theory, the nervous system *is* a selective system. Although the theory itself would be consistent with a large variety of possible mechanisms at the level of proximate causation, it does motivate a set of self-consistent and mutually reinforcing models of proximate neural processes that will eventually be important in designing experiments.

In terms of our initial list of requirements to be met by a general theory of the brain, many significant areas still remain to be explained. We believe that the theory outlined here can eventually provide at least initial guidance in these remaining areas. Whether cogent models of all these processes can be developed that lead to experimentally testable predictions for direct neuroscientific experimentation remains a challenge for the future.

References

Alkon, D. L. 1984. Calcium-mediated reduction of ionic currents—A biophysical memory trace. *Science* 226: 1037–1045.

Anderson, J. A., and G. E. Hinton. 1981. Models of information processing in the brain. In *Parallel Models of Associative Memory,* ed. G. E. Hinton and J. A. Anderson (Hillsdale, N.J.: Erlbaum).

Bartlett, F. C. 1964. *Remembering: A Study in Experimental and Social Psychology.* Cambridge University Press.

Bienenstock, E. L., and L. N. Cooper. 1982. Theory for the development of neuron selectivity—Orientation specificity and binocular interaction. *Journal of Neuroscience* 2: 32–48.

Bongard, M. M. 1970. *Pattern Recognition.* New York: Spartan.

Carew, T. J., R. D. Hawkins, T. W. Abrams, and E. R. Kandel. 1984. A test of Hebb's postulate at identified synapses which mediate classical conditioning in *Aplysia. Journal of Neuroscience* 4: 1217–1224.

Catterall, W. A. 1979. Binding of scorpion toxin to receptor sites associated with sodium channels in frog muscle—Correlation of voltage-dependent binding with activation. *Journal of General Physiology* 74: 375–391.

Cerella, J. 1979. Visual classes and natural categories in the pigeon. *Journal of Experimental Psychology (Human Perception)* 5: 68–77.

Changeux, J.-P. 1981. The acetylcholine receptor: An "allosteric" membrane protein. *Harvey Lectures* 75: 85–254.

Chuong, C.-M., and G. M. Edelman. 1984. Alterations in neural cell adhesion molecules during development of different regions of the nervous system. *Journal of Neuroscience* 4: 2354–2368.

Chuong, C.-M., K. L. Crossin, and G. M. Edelman. 1987. Sequential expression and differential functions of multiple adhesion molecules during the formation of cerebellar cortical layers. *Journal of Cell Biology* 104: 331–342.

Daniloff, J. K., G. Levi, M. Grumet, F. Rieger, and G. M. Edelman. 1986. Altered expression on neuronal cell adhesion molecules induced by nerve injury and repair. *Journal of Cell Biology* 103: 929–945.

Dennis, I., J. A. Hampton, and S. E. G. Lea. 1973. New problem in concept formation. *Nature* 243: 101–102.

Devor, M., and P. D. Wall. 1981. Effects of peripheral nerve injury on receptive fields of cells in the cat spinal cord. *Journal of Comparative Neurology* 199: 227–291.

Edelman, G. M. 1978. Group selection and phasic reentrant signalling: A theory of higher brain function. In *The Mindful Brain*, ed. G. M. Edelman and V. B. Mountcastle (Cambridge, Mass.: MIT Press).

Edelman, G. M. 1981. Group selection as the basis for higher brain function. In *Organization of the Cerebral Cortex*, ed. F. O. Schmitt, F. G. Worden, G. Adelman, and S. G. Dennis (Cambridge, Mass.: MIT Press).

Edelman, G. M. 1984. Modulation of cell adhesion during induction, histogenesis, and perinatal development of the nervous system. *Annual Review of Neuroscience* 7: 339–377.

Edelman, G. M. 1985. Neural Darwinism: Population thinking and higher brain function. In *How We Know: The Inner Frontiers of Cognitive Science* (Proceedings of Nobel Conference XX), ed. M. Shafto (San Francisco: Harper & Row).

Edelman, G. M. 1986. Cell adhesion molecules in the regulation of animal form and tissue pattern. *Annual Review of Cell Biology* 2: 81–116.

Edelman, G. M. 1988. *Neural Darwinism: The Theory of Neuronal Group Selection.* New York: Basic Books.

Edelman, G. M., and L. H. Finkel. 1984. Neuronal group selection in the cerebral cortex. In *Dynamical Aspects of Neocortical Function*, ed. G. M. Edelman, W. E. Gall, and W. M. Cowan (New York: Wiley).

Edelman, G. M., and G. N. Reeke, Jr. 1982. Selective networks capable of representative transformations, limited generalizations, and associative memory. *Proceedings of the National Academy of Science* 79: 2091–2095.

Finkel, L. H. 1985. Selection in synaptic regulation and neural mapping. In *Molecular Basis of Animal Form*, ed. G. M. Edelman (New York: Alan R. Liss).

Finkel, L. H., and G. M. Edelman. 1985. Interaction of synaptic modification rules within populations of neurons. *Proceedings of the National Academy of Sciences* 82: 1–1295.

Finkel, L. H., and G. M. Edelman. 1987. Population rules for synapses in networks. In *Synaptic Function,* ed. G. M. Edelman, W. E. Gall, and W. M. Cowan (New York: Wiley).

Gustafsson, B., and H. Wigstrom. 1986. Hippocampal long-lasting potentiation produced by pairing single volleys and brief conditioning tetani evoked in separate afferents. *Journal of Neuroscience* 6: 1575–1582.

Hawkins, R. D., T. W. Abrams, T. J. Carew, and E. R. Kandel. 1983. A cellular mechanism of classical conditioning in *Aplysia*—Activity-dependent amplification of pre-synaptic facilitation. *Science* 219: 400–405.

Hebb, D. O. 1949. *The Organization of Behavior* (New York: Wiley).

Herrnstein, R., D. Loveland, and C. Cable. 1976. Natural concepts in pigeons. *Journal of Experimental Psychology (Animal Behavior Processes)* 2: 285–301.

Hopfield, J. J. 1982. Neural networks and physical systems with emergent collective computational abilities. *Proceedings of the National Academy of Sciences* 79: 2554–2558.

Huang, L.-Y. M., N. Moran, and G. Ehrenstein. 1982. Batrachotoxin modifies the gating kinetics of sodium channels in internally perfused neuroblastoma cells. *Proceedings of the National Academy of Sciences* 79: 2082–2085.

Huganir, R. L., A. H. Delacour, P. Greengard, and G. P. Hess. 1986. Phosphorylation of the nicotinic acetylcholine receptor regulates its rate of desensitization. *Nature* 321: 774–776.

Ito, M., M. Sakurai, and P. Tongroach. 1982. Climbing fiber-induced depression of both mossy fiber responsiveness and glutamate sensitivity of cerebellar Purkinje cells. *Journal of Physiology (London)* 324: 113–134.

Kaas, J. H., M. M. Merzenich, and H. P. Killackey. 1983. The reorganization of somatosensory cortex following peripheral-nerve damage in adult and developing mammals. *Annual Review of Neuroscience* 6: 325–356.

Kellman, T. J., and E. S. Spelke. 1983. Perception of partly occluded objects in infancy. *Cognitive Psychology* 15: 483–524.

Kelso, S. R., A. H. Ganong, and T. H. Brown. 1986. Hebbian synapses in hippocampus. *Proceedings of the National Academy of Sciences* 83: 5326–5330.

Kramer, A. P., J. R. Golden, and G. S. Stent. 1985. Developmental arborization of sensory neurons in the leech *Haementeria-ghilani*. Origins of natural variations in the branching pattern. *Journal of Neuroscience* 5: 759–767.

Levy, W. B., and O. Steward. 1983. Temporal contiguity requirements for long-term associative potentiation/depression in the hippocampus. *Neuroscience* 8: 791–797.

Lynch, G. S., and M. Baudry. 1984. The biochemistry of memory: A new and specific hypothesis. *Science* 224: 1057–1063.

Macagno, E. R., V. Lopresti, and C. Levinthal. 1973. Structure and development of neuronal connections in isogenic organisms: Variations and similarities in the optic system of *Daphnia magna*. *Proceedings of the National Academy of Sciences* 70: 57–61.

McClelland, J. L., D. E. Rumelhart, and the PDP Research Group. 1986. *Parallel Distributed Processing. Volume II: Psychological and Biological Models.* Cambridge, Mass.: MIT Press.

Magleby, K. L., and J. E. Zengel. 1982. Quantitative description of stimulation-induced changes in transmitter release at the frog neuromuscular junction. *Journal of General Physiology* 80: 613–638.

Mayr, E. 1982. *The Growth of Biological Thought: Diversity, Evolution, and Inheritance.* Cambridge, Mass.: Harvard University Press.

Merzenich, M. M., J. H. Kass, J. T. Wall, R. J. Nelson, M. Sur, and D. J. Felleman. 1983a. Topographic reorganization of somatosensory cortical areas 3b and 1 in adult monkeys following restricted deafferentation. *Neuroscience* 8: 33–55.

Merzenich, M. M., J. H. Kaas, J. T. Wall, R. J. Nelson, M. Sur, and D. J. Felleman. 1983b. Progression of change following median nerve section in the cortical representation of the hand in areas 3b and 1 in adult owl and squirrel monkeys. *Neuroscience* 10: 639–665.

Merzenich, M. M., R. J. Nelson, M. P. Stryker, M. Cynader, A. Schoppman, and J. M. Zook. 1984. Somatosensory cortical map changes following digit amputation in adult monkeys. *Journal of Comparative Neurology* 224: 591–605.

Mountcastle, V. B. 1984. Central nervous mechanisms in mechanoreceptive sensibility. In *Handbook of Physiology,* vol. 3 (Bethesda, Md.: American Psychological Society).

Oldfield, R. C., and O. L. Zangwill. 1942a. Head's concept of the schema and its application in contemporary British psychology. II. Critical analysis of Head's theory. *British Journal of Psychology* 33: 58–64.

Oldfield, R. C., and O. L. Zangwill. 1942b. Head's concept of the schema and its application in contemporary British psychology. III. Bartlett's theory of memory. *British Journal of Psychology* 33: 111–129.

Pearson, J. C., L. Finkel, G. M. Edelman. 1987. Plasticity in the Organization of Adult Cortical Maps: A Computer Model Based on Neuronal Group Selection. *Journal of Neuroscience* 7: 4209–4223.

Pearson, K. G., and C. S. Goodman. 1979. Correlation of variability in structure with variability in synaptic connections of an identified interneuron in locusts. *Journal of Comparative Neurology* 184: 141–165.

Reeke, G. N., Jr., and G. M. Edelman. 1984. Selective networks and recognition automata. *Annals of N.Y. Academy of Sciences* 426: 181–201.

Sherman, G. F., A. M. Galaburda, and N. Geschwind. 1982. Neuroanatomical asymmetries in non-human species. *Trends in Neuroscience* 5: 429–431.

Smith, E. E., and D. L. Medin. 1981. *Categories and Concepts.* Cambridge, Mass.: Harvard University Press.

Van Essen, D. C., W. T. Newsome, and J. H. R. Maunsell. 1984. The visual field representation in striate cortex of the macaque monkey: Asymmetries, anisotropies, and individual variability. *Vision Research* 24: 429–448.

von der Malsburg, C. 1981. The Correlation Theory of Brain Function. Internal Report 81–2, Department of Neurobiology, Max Planck Institute for Biophysical Chemistry, Göttingen.

Wittgenstein, L. 1958. *Philosophical Investigations.* English text of third edition. New York: Macmillan.

Chapter 7

| Cortical Encoding of Memory: Hypotheses Derived from Analysis and Simulation of Physiological Learning Rules in Anatomical Structures | Gary Lynch, Richard Granger, John Larson, and Michel Baudry |

How neural networks in cerebral cortex encode and utilize information constitutes one of the most poorly understood yet crucially important questions confronting the brain and behavioral sciences. Pertinent experimental studies on this issue have largely been the province of physiologists analyzing the activity of individual cells while stimuli are presented or behavioral responses elicited. A very different and far more theoretical approach has recently appeared in which the operations of networks composed of computational nodes with some neuron-like properties are explored with mathematical tools (in large part derived from physics) as well as with computer simulations. While the latter pursuit may be of questionable biological validity, it does have the great advantage of dealing with the ensemble activity of the network—and it is surely at this level that behaviorally recognizable phenomena emerge from brain.

The line of inquiry described in this chapter relates to these approaches but differs from them in several important respects. We are attempting to understand information storage and processing in cortical networks by determining the physiological rules that govern cellular activity and synaptic modifications (which we assume to be the substrate of memory) and then incorporating these rules into simulations of a particular cortical region. This program thus involves three very different levels of investigation:

1. experimental studies of the physiological mechanisms that trigger synaptic changes with properties expected of a memory substrate (e.g., rapid onset, extreme duration),

2. selection and description of a cortical region, whose anatomical circuitry is to be used as the basis for constructing a simulation that incorporates the information obtained in the physiological studies, and

3. analysis of the simulation itself in terms of the network-level behaviors manifested by the physiological rules embedded in these cortical structures.

While there are many evident differences between this approach to the study of cortical functioning and those employed in behavioral neurophysiology and computer modeling, a most important point of departure may not be obvious: Our strategy does not take as its starting point a set of prespecified functional operations (e.g., perception of angles, detection of moving objects, or recognition of degraded cues) and then seek to explain how a network (cortical or otherwise) might solve these operations. Rather, we are attempting to identify and characterize the physiological and behavioral properties of learning and memory that emerge when detailed neurobiological features are incorporated into circuitries containing salient anatomical characteristics found in specific areas. In essence, we do not attempt to reduce behavior to neurobiology; rather, we attempt to predict behavior from neurobiology.

This three-tiered strategy (which does have points of contact with the work of Cooper, Edelman, and their colleagues; see Cooper et al. 1979; Cooper 1984; Finkel and Edelman 1985) for exploring the nature of memorial processes in simple cortical circuits is reflected in the present chapter. Section 7.1 discusses experimental work on the physiological operations that produce stable synaptic changes of a type linked by pharmacological studies to memory storage. For reasons discussed below, we use long-term potentiation (LTP) as the model storage mechanism. A description of the olfactory cortical area selected for modeling work, and the reasons for choosing it, make up section 7.2. Section 7.3 deals with simulations of the network model. There we will emphasize, by example, a crucial aspect of the research program— namely, that the different levels of analysis are interactive. As will be seen, the types of memory operations that emerge when physiological rules are implemented in computer models of anatomical networks are somewhat unexpected; furthermore, specific questions that have been raised directly by examination of the simulation's behavior have prompted us to look experimentally for, and to find, some striking and previously unsuspected physiological properties of LTP induction.

A fourth and logically necessary layer of research to the program we are attempting is now only beginning and is not critically discussed in this chapter. That is, a program seeking to move from an understanding of biological rules and network properties, as gained in simulations, succeeds to the degree that it makes nontrivial predictions about the physiological events that occur during learning in the cortical regions that serve as guides for the simulation and about the types of behavioral learning that emerge from these events. Testing those predictions constitutes the fourth phase of the program. We will return to this point at the end of the chapter.

1   Learning Rules for Neural Networks

1.1   Results from Connectionist Models

The field of parallel networks has identified interesting learning algorithms that strengthen and weaken connections among neural-like processing elements; these rules, in combination with particular performance rules, enable systems with certain architectures to learn to minimize errors on specified tasks over trials. Much excitement has been generated by the recognition that the Rescorla-Wagner (1972) rule for behavioral learning during classical conditioning is formally equivalent to a special case of the "delta" network learning rule developed by Widrow and Hoff (1960), despite the fact that these two rules were derived independently and from completely distinct considerations (Sutton and Barto 1981). The Widrow-Hoff rule states that the change in connection weight between two neural elements i and j depends on the input and output activity in those two elements as well as upon the *desired* activity of the output, which must be provided as input to the algorithm

$$\Delta T_{ij} = k(\lambda_j - B_j)a_i,$$

where T_{ij} is the change in the weight of the connection between units i and j, a_i is the activity of unit i, B_j is the activity of unit j, λ_j is the desired target activity of unit j, and k is a constant. In this rule, the activity of unit j is simply calculated as the weighted sum of its inputs:

$$B_j = \sum_i a_i T_{ij}.$$

The Rescorla-Wagner rule states that on each trial, the change in weight of the expectancy or hypothetical associative strength value V_{ij} of a particular CS i for a US j is proportional to the difference between the actual occurrence of the US on that trial and the total expectation of the US on that trial, where the total expectation of the US is calculated as the sum of the expectancies of each of the CSs present on that trial; that is,

$$\Delta V_{ij} = k\alpha_i(\lambda_j - E_j),$$

where ΔV_{ij} is the change in associative strength between CS i and US j, α_i is the intensity of the CS presentation, λ_j is the occurrence of the US j, and E_j, the expectancy of the US, is calculated as the (unweighted) sum of the expectancies of all present CSs for this US:

$$E_j = \sum_i V_{ij}.$$

Each of these two rules is guaranteed to reduce the error of the performance of the system over trials; in the case of the Widrow-Hoff rule this means reducing the difference between the desired and the actual activity of each output cell, and in the case of the Rescorla-Wagner rule it means reducing the difference between the US expectancy and occurrence. Because these two rules both reduce the mean-squared error of these terms over trials, they can collectively be referred to as LMS (least-mean-square) rules.

The direct mapping of a learning rule such as an LMS rule from psychology to synaptic change is easily achieved. For each CS, a population of cells might fire in a configuration characteristic of that CS, whereas for each US, a distinct population could fire in its own configuration. Furthermore, these two populations of cells must be connected with each other such that the outputs of the first population of cells are compared against the firing patterns of the second population of cells, and the difference is transmitted back to the synapses of the first population. In the absence of such an anatomy, the apparent mapping between the Widrow-Hoff and Rescorla-Wagner rules is not necessarily indicative of any deeper connection between behavior and neurobiology; rather, the Widrow-Hoff rule may more fruitfully be thought of as a behavior-level rule itself.

Although it may prove useful to search for physiological correlates of behavioral (or computational) learning rules, it should also be possible to study synaptic changes of the type expected for the substrates of learning and to ask if characterizations of the physiological mechanisms that produce these synaptic changes can be developed into learning rules. If this could be done, then the implementation of such rules in anatomically realistic network simulations would provide novel and well-specified descriptions of the learning process. We will proceed by outlining the known physiology of a particular form of synaptic change which we will use as a candidate mechanism underlying learning.

1.2 Hippocampal Long-Term Potentiation as a Guide for Developing Learning Rules

Long-term potentiation (LTP) is a well-studied form of synaptic modification with many properties that render it an excellent candidate for the substrate of certain forms of memory (see Landfield and Deadwyler 1987 for reviews):

• Selectivity: Studies using multiple inputs to the same dendritic tree have shown that LTP occurs only on synapses experiencing high-frequency bursting activity, while neighboring contacts are unchanged (Lynch et al. 1977; Andersen et al. 1977).

• Time course: Studies in chronic animals indicate that synaptic potentiation can last for weeks (Barnes 1979). We have recently confirmed this point (see below). Despite its longevity, LTP is elicited by events lasting fractions of seconds and appears to develop and stabilize in seconds to minutes.

• Cooperativity: The induction of LTP requires near-simultaneous activation of some minimal number of contacts on a cell; in other words, LTP requires the association of activity in several input axons (McNaughton et al. 1978; Levy and Steward 1980).

• Structural changes in synapses: The induction of LTP is correlated with changes in the shape of spines and an increase in the numbers of certain classes of synapses, as was shown by our laboratory and replicated by other groups (Lee et al. 1980; Chang and Greenough 1984; Desmond and Levy 1983; Wenzel and Mathies 1985). This effect provides an explanation for the extraordinary persistence of LTP.

• Two very different types of drugs that block the induction of LTP also produce a selective impairment of certain forms of learning (Morris et al. 1986; Staubli et al. 1984, 1985).

Long-term potentiation thus provides a well-documented physiological phenomenon with analogues of several of the salient features of associative memory. The time course is appropriate, since memories certainly form in response to momentary events and persist for indefinite time periods. The selectivity of LTP tells us that the effect occurs at synapses. This is a vital point, since the vast capacity of human memory implies that the storage elements must be available in staggering numbers and there are orders of magnitude more synapses than neurons in brain. Beyond this, the argument that associative memory involves quasi-random networks (Lynch 1986) has as a corollary the requirement that synaptic change is the encoding agent. Finally, the cooperativity rule indicates that associativity is an intrinsic property of LTP: the effect requires the convergence of input events.

The following section outlines a coherent set of results amassed over the past decade of work investigating the conditions that give rise to LTP; our goal is to specify these conditions in sufficient detail to enable the development of a physiologically accurate formal learning rule. It will be seen later in the chapter that the necessary rigor imposed by simulation work quickly pushes us beyond the extant bounds of physiological data on LTP; indeed it has already suggested new experiments, some of which have uncovered the existence of heretofore unsuspected physiological aspects of LTP induction.

1.3   Activity Patterns and the Induction of LTP
Naturally occurring activity patterns provide a logical starting point for the development of a learning rule based on long-term potentiation. Hippocampal

pyramidal cells in freely moving animals often emit very short (30–40 msec) high-frequency bursts consisting of 3–5 action potentials ("complex spikes") (Ranck 1973; Fox and Ranck 1981). Single stimulation bursts (i.e., 4 pulses at 100 Hz) designed to mimic this pattern do not elicit LTP when delivered to the Schaffer-commissural projections connecting fields CA3 and CA1 in hippocampal slices. However, LTP does occur when several bursts are given in rapid succession, i.e., with a frequency greater than one burst per second. Quantitative studies using a fixed number of bursts have shown that the optimal inter-burst interval for producing LTP is 200 msec; shorter or longer intervals elicit less LTP and reduce the likelihood that it will occur (Larson et al. 1986). The 200-msec interval is particularly intriguing because it corresponds to the period of the theta rhythm, an EEG pattern that is prominent in the hippocampus of animals (rats, rabbits, cats) engaged in exploratory activity (Landfield 1976; Bland 1986). It thus appears that the coupling of two commonly occurring aspects of hippocampal physiology—burst discharges and the theta rhythm—produces conditions that are optimal for the induction of LTP. These results reinforce the suggestion that LTP occurs during certain behaviors and also provide us with the first temporal parameters for the construction of LTP learning rules.

There is no consensus regarding the stability of LTP—which is surprising, since duration is crucial to ideas regarding both the behavioral significance and the underlying cellular substrates of the potentiation effect (see Baudry et al. 1987). It is also the case that synaptic facilitations lasting for several minutes (which have in some reports been labeled as "LTP") might well be due to different processes than those responsible for effects persisting for days or weeks. Accordingly, we have attempted to measure the time course of LTP elicited by the "theta burst" pattern using rats implanted with chronic electrodes positioned so as to stimulate and sample the same pathways used in the above-described slice experiments. The stimulation parameters employed were also virtually identical to those of the slice studies (i.e., 10 four-pulse bursts, with each burst lasting 30 msec and with 200 msec between successive bursts). A second electrode was used to stimulate a group of control inputs terminating in the same dendritic field as those given theta bursting. LTP was selectively induced in groups receiving theta bursting and persisted without evident change until the evoked responses began a rapid decline to below baseline values, an event that required from one to several weeks to occur and that in all likelihood was due to electrode deterioration (Staubli and Lynch 1986). We interpreted these data as indicating that LTP elicited by the theta paradigm is stable for at least several weeks.

Further *in vitro* slice experiments using stimulation of different collections of inputs to the same cell or collection of cells have gone far toward explaining why the theta bursting pattern of stimulation is so effective in producing LTP. When the single 30-msec high-frequency bursts are given in sequence to two distinct sets of afferents, only the synapses activated on the target cell by the second of the two inputs exhibit LTP (figure 1). The magnitude of LTP is again dictated by the interburst interval, with maximum effects occurring when the burst to the second input follows that to the first by 200 msec. It thus appears that the first input elicits a kind of "priming" effect such that subsequent bursts to synapses on the same cell occurring 200 msec later result in LTP. The priming event is postsynaptically global in that it affects much of the dendritic tree of the target cell. That is, stimulation of afferents terminating on apical dendrites is capable of priming basal dendritic synapses. LTP, in contrast, is restricted to the synapses activated on a primed background. Further study revealed that primed EPSPs were substantially prolonged over controls, probably because the feedforward IPSPs that normally truncate excitatory responses are suppressed by the priming input (Larson and Lynch 1986). Thus far, only indirect evidence for the IPSP suppression has been collected (Larson and Lynch, in prep.), but others have reported effects of this type in hippocampus and in piriform cortex (McCarren and Alger 1985; Haberly 1985).

How do prolonged EPSPs occurring during theta burst stimulation produce LTP? A useful clue is found in the observation that single stimulation pulses to inputs to primed dendrites do not cause potentiation. However, temporal summation of responses to short bursts is much greater in primed neurons precisely because the individual EPSPs evoked by the burst are prolonged as described above; in essence, priming and bursting result in a synergistic interaction such that the net depolarization observed in the target cell is much greater than the depolarization produced by a burst without prior priming stimulation. Pharmacological studies have shown that this enhanced response is sufficient to activate the voltage-dependent N-Methyl-D-Aspartate (NMDA) receptor-channel complex, thus adding an additional conductance to that normally present (Larson and Lynch 1988). Collingridge et al. (1983) discovered that blockers of the NMDA receptors selectively prevent the induction of LTP, and this has been confirmed by several laboratories (Harris et al. 1984; Morris et al. 1986). It also proves to be true for the LTP produced by theta bursting (Larson and Lynch 1988).

It has been shown that intracellular injections of EGTA, a calcium chelating agent, into hippocampal pyramidal cells also suppresses the development of LTP (Lynch et al. 1983)—a result that confirms earlier suggestions (Dun-

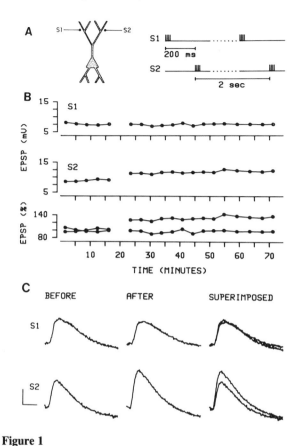

Figure 1
LTP induction by short high-frequency bursts involves sequential "priming" and
"consolidation" events. (A) S1 and S2 represent separate groups of Shaffer/commis-
sural fibers converging on a single CA1 pyramidal neuron. The stimulation pattern
employed consisted of pairs of bursts (each four pulses at 100 Hz) given to S1 and
S2 respectively, with a 200-msec delay between them. The pairs were repeated ten
times at 2-second intervals. (B) Only the synapses activated by the delayed burst
(S2) showed LTP. The top panel shows measurements of amplitudes of intracellular
EPSPs evoked by single pulses to S1 before and after patterned stimulation (given at
20 minutes into the experiment). The middle panel shows the amplitude of EPSPs
evoked by S2. The bottom panel shows EPSP amplitudes for both pathways expressed as a percentage of their respective sizes before stimulation. (C) Records of
EPSPs evoked by S1 and S2 5 minutes before and 40 minutes after patterned burst
stimulation. Calibration bar: 5 mV, 5 msec. (From Larson and Lynch 1986.)

widdie and Lynch 1979) that an influx of calcium is the triggering event for LTP. This is particularly pertinent to the present discussion, since the NMDA-linked conductance channel has been shown to pass calcium when the receptor channel complex is depolarized (MacDermott et al. 1986). Taken together, the experimental evidence points to the sequence summarized in table 1 as the route through which theta bursting causes LTP. To the extent it is correct, this set of events provides the first description of the manner in which naturally occurring brain rhythms could be linked to cellular events that result in synaptic modification.

A point of potential computational significance should be emphasized here. The priming process inherent in the theta mode of activity does not eliminate the convergence requirement for LTP; weak inputs stimulated by themselves in the theta bursting pattern do not typically potentiate. By reducing the normally very potent inhibitory responses, priming allows those cells receiving a sufficiently large number of bursting afferents to cross a depolarization threshold for entry into a state in which synaptic plasticity can occur. Work from other laboratories has convincingly demonstrated a link between cellwide depolarization and the induction of LTP (Wigstrom and Gustaffson 1983; Wigstrom et al. 1986; Malinow and Miller 1986; Kelso et al. 1986). Theta bursting in a sizeable number of converging afferents appears to be a device for achieving the appropriate level of depolarization. LTP thus emerges from a peculiar combination of global (net depolarization resulting from IPSP suppression, convergence, and bursting) and synapse-specific (i.e., calcium entry into those postsynaptic sites at which transmitter is released onto NMDA receptors) events.

Table 1
Sequence of events in the triggering of LTP by "theta pattern" activity.

1. A burst of afferent activity "primes" the postsynaptic neurons.
2. Loss of inhibition produced by priming results in the prolongation of EPSPs evoked 200 msec later.
3. Prolonged EPSPs exhibit enhanced spatial and temporal summation during a high-frequency burst.
4. Enhanced depolarization releases NMDA receptors from voltage-dependent magnesium blockade.
5. Transmitter interaction with NMDA receptors causes postsynaptic influx of calcium.
6. Calcium triggers biochemical reactions resulting in structural changes in dendritic spines and/or new synapse formation.

1.4   Reversal of Long-Term Potentiation?

A commonly raised question concerning LTP, and one of great significance for its use as a learning algorithm in networks, is whether the synaptic potentiation is reversible and/or balanced in some way by a long-term depression. The utility of synaptic weakening is well illustrated by the delta rule (see above) which converges toward a solution (i.e., reduces the error between desired and observed outputs over trials) by reducing as well as strengthening connection strengths (see Cooper et al. 1979 for another example). Long-term depressions were described early in the course of experiments on LTP (Lynch et al 1976, 1977) and were subsequently shown to be independent of the processes that generate LTP (Dunwiddie and Lynch 1978). This effect may not be computationally desirable—at least in terms of algorithms like the delta rule—because it is generalized in distribution and affects synapses throughout the dendrite (Dunwiddie and Lynch 1978). Subsequent experiments have confirmed these observations and indicate that the depression can be very long lasting and can be induced by a variety of stimulation paradigms (Levy and Steward 1980; Abraham and Goddard 1983). However, evidence that a selective form of LTP reversal exists was obtained in an experiment in which low-frequency stimulation was applied to a population of hippocampal synapses before and after the induction of LTP. The stimulation substantially reduced the potentiation in about 80 percent of the cases but had little effect on "naive" responses (Barrionuevo et al. 1979). The reduction of LTP persisted for a 30-minute test period. As was stressed in the report describing these effects, chronic studies would be needed to determine if the observed effect was a true reversal of LTP (that is, does LTP reappear several hours later?), and to date no experiments of this type have been attempted. In sum: It is possible that some type of reversal of LTP or a functionally equivalent depressive effect is present in hippocampus, but conclusive evidence on this point is lacking.

2   Olfactory Cortex as a Model System for Testing the Functional Consequences of LTP

The results thus far collected suggest the foundations of an LTP-based learning rule. Further developments will depend on still more detailed physiological analyses, but will also require the formalization of available information by means of computer simulations. Simulations provide constraints that arise from anatomical/network considerations and thus raise questions and indicate experiments that would not otherwise be apparent. While the wealth of anatomical and physiological data associated with the hippocampus makes this region an excellent subject for simulations, it will be easier to build behaviorally predictive models using brain structures that have more direct linkages with the environment and thus have more easily specified behavioral functions. We have selected olfactory cortex for reasons outlined below.

Implicit in most theories of memory and explicit in many is the assumption that the storage and the processing of associations, at least as they are used in human cognition, reside in the cerebral cortex. Indeed cortical involvement is one of the most resilient of themes in memory research, and there are good reasons for this. Neocortex expands much more rapidly with increasing brain size than other regions and, in the very large human brain, accounts for the great majority of brain volume (Jerison 1973). In light of this it is reasonable to assume that neocortex is responsible for higher-order associational and cognitive memorial functions. Moreover, neocortex possesses the vast number of synapses needed to account for the capacity of memory and clearly has the anatomical potential for forming associations between virtually any group of complex representations. The great difficulty in using neocortex for neurobiological or computer simulations of memory networks lies in its extraordinary complexity. This has a number of consequences. For one, it is exceedingly difficult to specify in more than the most general of terms how a given neocortical region anatomically projects to hippocampus or any other region thought to be crucial for memory processing. Similarly, how hippocampus might physiologically interact with a particular neocortical area is essentially a complete mystery. The complexity of neocortex also means that inputs converge and diverge continuously, thereby producing exceptional problems in defining, even in qualitative terms, the precise architectural organization of any putative matrix network. Similarly, links between different layers have resisted analysis, and there are few hypotheses concerning the anatomical-physiological interactions among the cortical layers.

Olfactory cortex (piriform–lateral entorhinal cortex) has not figured prominently in discussions of cortical memory networks but nonetheless has many features that make it particularly appropriate for psychological studies, computer simulations, and neurobiological investigations (Lynch 1986; Lynch and Baudry 1988). Some of these are the following:

• Direct, well-defined linkages with hippocampus: The entorhinal wing of olfactory cortex projects monosynaptically and massively into dentate gyrus, the first of the successive stages that constitute hippocampus.

• Simpler anatomical design: The internal anatomy of olfactory cortex possesses fewer layers than neocortex and is not embedded in interweaving thalamic and neocortical connections.

• Disynaptic inputs from external receptors: The olfactory receptors project
to the mitral cells of the olfactory bulb, the axons of which terminate in
layer I of piriform-entorhinal cortex. Given this proximity to odorants, we
can assume that olfactory cortex is involved in constructing representations
of odors. The overall architecture of the system is thus simple enough that it
predicts functions—something that cannot be said for neocortex.

2.1 Telencephalic Connections of the Olfactory Cortex
In this subsection, we will describe the location and telencephalic relationships of olfactory cortex and then turn to its internal anatomy.

Figure 2 summarizes the projections of the olfactory system through the
telencephalon. The piriform-entorhinal cortex is monosynaptically innervated
by the mitral cells of the olfactory bulb, which themselves receive the terminals of the olfactory nerve (Shepherd 1979). The connections between nasal
epithelium and the bulb exhibit a degree of topography (Jourdan 1982; Lancet
et al. 1982), but those from the bulb to olfactory cortex carried in the lateral
olfactory tract (LOT) have little if any order; that is, a small region in the
bulb projects to most of the cortex and small regions of cortex receive input
from all parts of the bulb (Price 1973; Skeen and Hall 1977; Haberly and

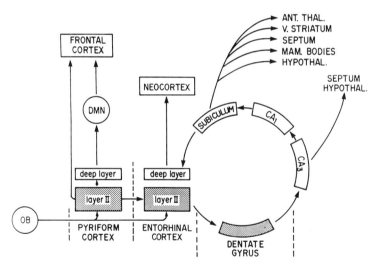

Figure 2
Schematic diagram of the major telencephalic connections of olfactory (piriform)
cortex. The layer II cells we have chosen to model have extensive connections with
two structures thought to be important for memory processing: hippocampus and the
dorsomedial nucleus of thalamus. See text for discussion. (From Lynch 1986.)

Price 1977). The LOT axons and their dendritic targets thus constitute a random combinatorial matrix. It is likely that the piriform-entorhinal complex unifies activation of different regions of the bulb (as presumably occurs when odors composed of many chemicals are present) into a single representation, and that this representation is distributed, consisting of activity in a collection of neurons scattered throughout the cortex (Lynch 1986).

The piriform/entorhinal cortex projects to dorso-medial nucleus of thalamus (DMN), frontal cortex, hippocampus, and amygdala (Krettek and Price 1977; Carlsen et al. 1982; Kosel et al. 1981; Price and Slotnick 1983; Luskin and Price 1983). The hippocampus receives nonolfactory input from the medial entorhinal cortex, and it seems only reasonable therefore to assume that it is a site at which olfactory representations are associated with other sensory representations of objects in the environment. Unfortunately we have not been able to find experimental work in the literature bearing on this fundamental point. However, patient H.M., with severe temporal-lobe damage (including hippocampus), is reported to be unable to associate odors with their names (Eichenbaum et al. 1983).

The second system leading out of olfactory cortex is targeted for DMN and frontal cortex. The significance of these projections for olfactory learning has been investigated by two groups, and we have also conducted investigations on this question. Slotnick and Kaneko (1981) showed that DMN lesions impair rats on successive reversal learning using a two-odor discrimination task; more specific, while the rats showed improvement over days, they never reached the very rapid acquisition phase seen in normal animals after several days of training. Eichenbaum et al. (1980) report that either DMN or frontal cortical lesions (in the area innervated by piriform cortex and DMN) severely impair the animals on a "go–no-go" problem involving odors. Though there are several possible interpretations of these results, it will be noted that both impairments involve a type of learning set (e.g., reverse if not rewarded). In any event, it seems reasonable to assume that the DMN–frontal system linkages serve to relate a now-present odor with *some* aspect of the animal's repertoire of responses.

To summarize: Anatomical and neurobehavioral studies suggest the following hypotheses (see Lynch 1986 for further discussion):

• Piriform cortex serves to represent complex odors.
• Hippocampus associates odors with environmental objects.
• The projections of piriform cortex through DMN and frontal cortex serve to link the olfactory system to the response-organizing mechanisms of the brain.

2.2 Internal Organization of Olfactory Cortex

The piriform is composed of three layers of neurons. The outermost (layer II) contains cells whose dendrites form the relatively homogeneous molecular zone (layer I) that encircles the cortex; the lateral-olfactory-tract axons from the bulb travel at the top of layer I and innervate its outer half in a quasi-random fashion (Haberly and Price 1977). Layer III is a zone containing several types of neurons, including many small pyramidal cells, a sizeable number of which have dendrites extending into layer I. The layer III cell bodies are not tightly packed; dendrites, cell bodies, and axons are intermingled. The dendrites, however, have a predominantly vertical orientation. The deepest layer is usually referred to as the endopiriform nucleus, although in fact it is more properly thought of as a cortical layer (layer IV). It contains large pyramidal cells and numerous polymorph cells, whose widely radiating dendrites give the layer its "nuclear" appearance (Lorente de No 1934).

A great deal is known about layers I and II, but very little attention has been given the deeper layers. Layer I is subdivided into Ia and Ib, the former innervated by the LOT and the latter by a feedback system originating in the layer II neurons and a group of deeper cells. Anatomical studies have shown that this feedback projection is diffuse and exhibits little topography (Haberly and Price 1977); in essence, it constitutes a second, quasi-random combinatorial array lying beneath that generated by the LOT input. Layers I and II thus present an anatomical arrangement that bears some remarkable similarities to the associative memory networks simulated by connectionist theorists (Lynch 1986). There are, however, some important differences. For one, the layer I matrices are sparse in the sense that a given axon has a low probability of encountering a given dendrite. There are about 10^5 axons in the LOT, and it is unlikely that the short dendrites of the layer II neurons contain much more than 10^4 spines; hence, each cell can sample no more than 10 percent of the potential input. Similarly, if there are 10^5–10^6 neurons in layer II and if most of these contribute to the feedback system, then only a small percentage of the total feedback array can contact a given dendrite. Most network theories employ much denser arrays. Another feature of layer I is the presence of small interneurons that appear to be feedforward inhibitory elements. (See Lorente de No 1934 for a description of the interneurons; see also Valverde 1965.) Feedforward inhibition is a potent factor in hippocampal physiology (Lynch et al. 1981; Alger and Nicoll 1982; Buzsaki 1984), and it is known to be present in the piriform as well (Haberly 1985). The status of feedback inhibition in the layer II system is uncertain. The pericellular basket plexus morphology that characterizes inhibition at several sites in the brain (e.g. hippocampus, cerebellum) has not been described for layer II in all aspects of the piriform; nonetheless, symmetric synapses (usually thought to be inhibitory) are found on the cell bodies and initial axon segments of layer II cells. This is a point that requires resolution. Finally, Valverde in his elegant Golgi studies describes projections from deeper polymorph cells to the layer I associational system; this opens the possibility for a direct influence of layer IV cells on events in the zone receiving LOT inputs.

2.3 Behaviorally Relevant Inputs to the Piriform Cortex

Though olfactory cortex possesses a number of attractive features for simulation work, it also has a very serious drawback: Much less is known about the physiology of olfaction than is the case for the other sensory modalities. The paucity of physiological data is deeply confounded by the fact that the olfactory bulb is the target of powerful centrifugal projections and its activity is undoubtedly regulated by the behavioral state of the animal. This presents a serious difficulty for the construction of behaviorally predictive models, because chronic recordings of bulb and cortex across sets of relevant behaviors are virtually nonexistent. The upshot of this is that we cannot form an experimentally grounded set of assumptions about the activity patterns that transmit information from bulb to cortex, to say nothing of whether theta bursting modes of firing and LTP are used in the system.

In an effort to obviate this problem, we asked whether theta bursting applied to a subset of LOT axons would be detected as an odor by the animal and, if so, whether such "electrical" odors would be learned and remembered. It will be helpful to briefly consider certain aspects of olfactory learning and memory in rats before discussing the results of these electrical odor experiments.

Experiments in our laboratory using mazes as well as simple operants have been directed specifically at the issues of acquisition, capacity, duration, and types of memory involved in olfaction (Staubli et al. 1987). The design is relatively simple: Rats are trained over days on two-odor discriminations, with a new pair of cues used each day. The animals learn the first discrimination very slowly (taking up to hours, depending on the task), but they improve over days until after four to six days they are able to master a new discrimination in fewer than five trials. As was suggested earlier by Slotnick and Katz (1974), it seems that the rats learn something about the nature of the olfactory task over days and then make use of this information to deal with each novel discrimination. While learning is rapid in these paradigms, it nonetheless has great stability, since the rats remember previously learned odors even after delays of several weeks. Moreover, the capacity of the system must be very large, since the rats are able to learn new discriminations each day for a month and then exhibit excellent recall of any of the elements in the group (Staubli et al. 1987).

Many of the odors used in these experiments were composites of three chemicals, suggesting that some stage of the olfactory circuitry carries out associations of disparate cues. Work in our group (Staubli et al. 1987) has demonstrated that rats are capable of distinguishing between two composite odors with overlapping components (e.g., ABC and ABD) but do not recognize the distinguishing components (e.g., C vs. D) when these are given alone. These last experiments point to the conclusion that complex odors are treated as unitary cues by the olfactory system, an operation that would be predicted for a quasi-random combinatorial system (Lynch 1986).

Having established a paradigm for measuring olfactory learning, we began using electrical stimulation of the lateral olfactory tract in place of odors in the successive-olfactory-discrimination problem. The rats were first trained on a series of odor discriminations before attempts were made to substitute electrical stimulation; they did not respond well behaviorally to single-pulse stimulation of the LOT, but they did behave as though an odor were present when short bursts of pulses were applied with the bursts occurring at five per second (i.e., the theta burst pattern). Moreover, they quickly learned to discriminate between "positive" and "negative" electrodes (i.e., stimulation followed by reward or no reward). The size of the monosynaptic extracellular responses in piriform cortex to single pulses was measured before and after a learning episode; in a great majority of cases, these responses were potentiated after learning—an effect that did not dissipate over 24 hours. The responses to control electrodes (i.e., electrodes that were not used as "cues") did not change during or after the learning episodes (Roman et al. 1987). That rats will learn electric odors has also been demonstrated by Mouly et al. (1987), who used arrays of stimulating electrodes on the surface of the olfactory bulb.

One of the most surprising results from our experiments was that the patterned stimulation used as an odor did not produce potentiation when applied outside the learning task. Apparently the learning situation in some way exerts an extrinsic influence on the piriform cortex such that patterns of electrical activity are able to impress an extremely stable potentiation of synapses. These experiments may be providing clues about interaction of "procedural" and "data" memory systems (Squire 1986), in that prior learning acquired over several days seems to be needed to produce plasticity in response to a particular datum (in this case, an electric odor). Finally, we should not overlook the fact that the electric odor experiments provide us with experimental evidence that a group of cortical synapses in a defined larger population actually change selectively during learning.

3 Simulations of Olfactory Cortex

We have constructed a computer simulation of layer II of piriform cortex that incorporates many of its anatomical features as well as the physiological rules governing LTP induction. Our findings indicate that the network tends to produce a coherent set of behaviors under a range of biologically plausible parameter settings. In particular, the network simulation performs specific categorization functions on its inputs—not simply generalization of learned cues (e.g., recognition of degraded cues) or simply "orthogonalization" of cues to allow maximal differentiation of quite similar cues, but rather an experience-dependent combination of categorization and differentiation that enables the network to yield information about both the similarity among learned cues and their individual differentiating characteristics. Before we describe these results, it is necessary to turn to certain questions about the LTP effect that arose from the modeling work.

3.1 Computationally Motivated Questions about LTP
In the course of running simulations, we found that the description of LTP given earlier, while adequate for preliminary modeling of cortex, was not sufficiently detailed to generate decision rules (e.g., to strengthen synapses or not) that deal with a number of frequent occurrences in the network. Construction of the simulation required the precise formalization of necessary and sufficient conditions for LTP induction, which in turn forced us to ask many more specific physiological questions about these events than had been tested so far. This represents a clear case in which a network model has raised specific testable physiological questions about the rules and characteristics of LTP induction, with specific implications for the outcomes of those experiments. The issues raised by the simulation had not been systematically discussed in the literature; as the following subsections show, we have begun to explore certain of them.

Timing and Presynaptic Activity Rules   As was described above (see also Wigstrom et al. 1986), LTP induction depends on both the global state of postsynaptic depolarization and the presynaptic release of the transmitter onto NMDA receptors. Although the theta rhythm provides a degree of synchronization of neuronal activity, it remains the case that individual neurons will not be perfectly synchronized with one another and will fire different frequencies and numbers of spikes. Thus, it becomes necessary to ask how the temporal patterns of activity at different synapses on depolarized neurons affect the degree of LTP induced at the individual synapses.

Questions of this type relate to the nature of the information that is likely to be encoded by circuitries using LTP, because frequency of firing and arrival times reflect the structure of the input being processed. That is, within-burst firing frequency will be determined in part by the number and activity of the inputs to the cell that generates the bursts. An exponential relationship between activity and degree of potentiation on a cell innervated by multiple inputs therefore tends to exclude inputs that were only weakly driven by the extrinsic stimuli. The rules relating time of arrival and degree of LTP also have very powerful effects on the encoding properties of a system using LTP. Consider the piriform cortex network shown in figure 3, in which extrinsic (LOT) and feedback inputs terminate on the same cells. This is a very common anatomical arrangement, and it is characteristic of many neural network models (see Lynch 1986 for a discussion of this point). In general, the feedback connections will be activated several milliseconds after the extrinsic synapses. Do we assume that the former will promote LTP in the latter, or vice versa? The answer to this question has profound implications for the types of operations executed by the network. For example, the use of the network as an autocorrelation matrix would be facilitated if the extrinsic inputs were to promote LTP in the feedback connections.

Preliminary experiments directed at the above issues have been conducted. Figure 4A illustrates the design of a study in which three groups of afferents terminating in a common dendritic field were stimulated with four pulse bursts, with the onsets of the bursts staggered by 20 msec. Surprisingly, the first burst produced robust LTP and the third input did not. The second input appeared to produce intermediate effects; however, quantitative analysis using larger samples are needed before this conclusion can be accepted (J. Larson et al., unpublished data). But in any event, the preliminary findings strongly suggest that powerful order effects do exist and that late-arriving inputs are far less likely to cause LTP than are initial bursts. (Note that all of the target zone was primed approximately 200 msec prior to all bursts—the results described here are concerned with closely spaced bursts delivered to primed dendrites.)

The design of a related experiment is shown in figure 4B. Two relatively strong inputs were used, with one of these receiving four pulses in a burst and the second only two pulses. The two-pulse afferents induced about 60 percent of the LTP found in the inputs given four pulses. Further experiments in which input frequency and number of pulses are varied are in progress.

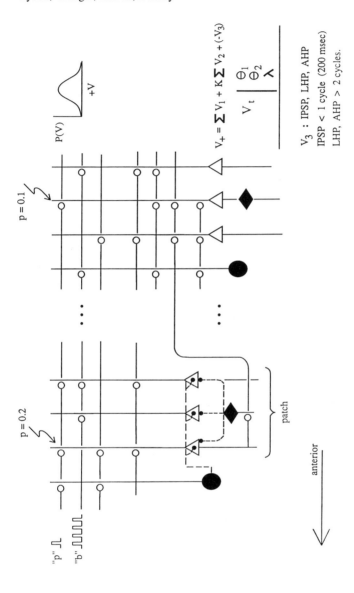

Figure 3

Organization of extrinsic and feedback inputs to layer II cells of piriform cortex. The axons constituting the lateral olfactory tract (LOT), originating from the bulb, innervate distal dendrites, whereas the feedback or associational fibers contact proximal dendrites. Layer II cells in anterior piriform are depicted as dominated by extrinsic (LOT) input, whereas feedback inputs are more prominent on cells in posterior piriform.

A

 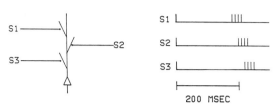

B

 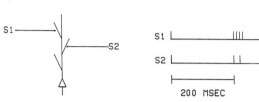

Figure 4
Stimulation patterns to test effects of differential input activity patterns on LTP induction. (A) Experimental design to test sequential ordering effects of partially overlapping bursts. Three separate groups of fibers are given a priming pulse; S1 receives
a burst 180 msec later, the S2 burst begins 200 msec after priming (i.e., 20 msec
after the onset of the S1 burst), and the S3 burst begins 220 msec after priming. (B)
Experiment to test role of input frequency and number. Both S1 and S2 receive a
priming pulse; S1 then receives a four-pulse burst (with 10 msec inter-pulse interval)
and S2 a two-pulse burst (20 msec inter-pulse interval) 200 msec after the priming
pulse.

These studies should provide us with a more explicit formulation of an LTP
rule to use in future simulations.

Interactions between Past and Present Plasticity Episodes   Central to any
hypothesis or model of neural-network operation are the provisos describing
how experience influences current encoding. It is on this point that learning
rules derived from LTP may differ most strikingly from those used in connectionist models. Networks—whether biological or purely hypothetical—must
have operating rules for both performance and learning. Network models use
the same synaptic weights in both performance and learning modes, but this
may not be true for circuitries employing LTP. As noted, theta bursting introduces a brief period in which EPSPs are prolonged and thus can temporally
summate to a far greater extent than is observed under control conditions. In
essence, then, the learning mode in LTP involves modifying synaptic sum-

mation properties for a brief period so as to induce a state that is conducive to the production of long-term changes. The question then arises as to how preexisting synaptic strengths, presumably reflecting earlier LTP episodes, interact with the transient changes in strength that are obtained during theta-bursting stimulation.

The simplest means of addressing this question is to measure the net de-polarization produced by a given set of synapses during theta bursting before and after the induction of LTP. Studies of this type have been conducted using extracellular recording, and the preliminary results are of the type illustrated in figure 5. LTP as measured by the slope or amplitude of dendritic-popu-lation EPSPs evoked by single-pulse stimulation represents a 40 percent in-crease in synaptic strength; when delivered as a burst to a primed background, previously potentiated synapses generate a net response that is only 20 per-cent larger than that produced by naive contacts activated in a comparable fashion (J. Larson et al., unpublished data). Thus, it is possible that the ef-fects of prior experience are more pronounced in the performance mode of network operation than during learning.

The extent to which prior increments in synaptic strength are manifested during encoding strongly affects what is learned by the network simulation. Consider for example a case in which two groups of overlapping inputs (A and B) are potentiated in succession on a pool of target neurons. Assume that the synapses involved in the first array become maximally potentiated to a value X, and that all other synapses (not utilized by the first input) have strength Y. The depolarization in any given cell in the network will thus de-pend upon the number of synapses it receives and the relative balance of X versus Y contacts. For cells receiving a given number of contacts, those with the greatest proportion of X synapses will experience the greatest degree of depolarization and hence be more likely to cross the threshold at which syn-aptic modifications can occur. Naive contacts landing on cells that already have a sizeable population of previously potentiated (and active) synapses will therefore be more likely to become potentiated. Note that cells with large numbers of X synapses are precisely those neurons on which LTP had oc-curred during the first learning period; in fact, these cells form the represen-tation associated with the first input array. In all, neurons responsive to the first cue are probabilistically more likely to become part of the second rep-resentation than other neurons innervated by the second input to the network; prior learning will tend to produce "attractor" target cells. The magnitude of this effect will depend upon the percentage of potentiation produced by the first learning episode that is present during LTP induction in the second epi-

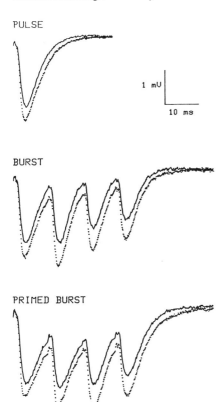

Figure 5
Relative difference in net postsynaptic depolarization produced by stimulation between naive and potentiated synapses in three different stimulation conditions. The top panel illustrates the relative increase (≈ 40%) in depolarization for single-pulse stimulation before (solid line) and after (dashed line) potentiation. The next two panels depict the increases in depolarization for burst (four-pulse) stimulation before and after potentiation; in both primed (bottom panel) and unprimed (middle panel) conditions, bursts elicit approximately 20% more depolarization after synaptic potentiation than before.

sode. Incorporating the same degree of synaptic potentiation during learning as is present during performance will thus tend to merge representations, whereas excluding past potentiation during current LTP episodes will favor the formation of distinct representations. The results of our preliminary experiments suggest that the hippocampus takes a middle course. Additional work mixing naive and potentiated synapses should provide a more computationally useful picture. In the simulations described below, past LTP contributed little to the priming-bursting interactions during a now-present learning episode.

3.2 Probabilistic Analysis of Cell "Recruitment"

Our study of the behavior of these networks has been almost exclusively empirical, i.e., we have run the simulation under various conditions and observed its behavior; analytical work on the nature of the piriform matrix is still in its infancy. We have focused so far on a probabilistic analysis of cell firing. Even without any mechanisms for learning via synaptic plasticity, the anatomical connectivity characteristics of the sparse matrix in piriform layer Ia predetermine the firing patterns of the layer II cells in response to any particular input pattern of activity in the LOT, given a known layer-II-cell firing threshold.

That is, for any particular spatial pattern of activated LOT axons, there will be certain dendrites that, solely by virtue of the pattern of synaptic connections in the network, will be "recruited" to fire in response to that axonal activation pattern, given any specified threshold for postsynaptic cell firing. To see this, imagine a particular pattern of activation in the LOT. For each dendrite in piriform, the probability of its firing will be a (relatively steep) step function that depends on the convergence of the active axons onto that dendrite (assuming that all synapses are initially of equal strength). For a dendrite with sufficient convergence of active axons to cause its cell to be depolarized over the cell firing threshold, that cell will have been recruited, i.e., will participate in the output firing pattern in response to this input. Dendrites with fewer synapses activated by the active set of axons will not be recruited, since their depolarization will be insufficient to bring them over firing threshold. Hence, before learning, we could in principle determine in advance the piriform layer II cells that will participate in the representation of any particular known LOT axon pattern of activation (i.e., in response to some olfactory input). For each axonal activation pattern, then, the set of cells having a particular level of convergence defines a "bin" from which cells may be recruited. Those bins of cells that contain at least the number of active synapses to put the cell over firing threshold will always fire in response to this input pattern; any cell with just under the necessary number of synapses is in a bin that may be recruited for this input, either by additional noise in the input (which may activate an additional LOT axon and hence activate a synapse on this cell's dendrite that was not initially activated by the original LOT pattern alone) or by feedback collaterals activating additional synapses on the dendrite. We term those bins of cells that receive sufficient convergence from an LOT pattern alone *first-order bins* for that input; bins that require additional synapses to fire are second-order bins for the input. A cell in a second-order bin for a particular input can of course become part of the first-order bin for that input by synaptic potentiation. This can be seen by imagining that the second-order cell is fired by a combination of (insufficiently large) LOT convergence plus convergence of, e.g., feedback collaterals, and that the resulting firing gives rise to potentiation of the synapses on that cell. For large enough percentage conduction increase per synapse due to potentiation, the convergence of the identical LOT pattern may then be sufficient to fire the cell without any feedback, effectively boosting the cell into the first-order bin for this pattern of LOT activation. Lowering the resting potential of the cell via extrinsic effects on inhibition can prevent some cells in even the first-order bin from firing, and raising the resting potential can recruit second-order bin cells without feedback. The physiological effect of afterhyperpolarization (AHP) of those cells that are firing most strongly tends to "turn off" strongly firing cells in proportion to their firing strength; in combination with the inhibitory resting-potential effects, this provides a "window" of synaptic convergence that determines cell recruitment: Too little convergence prevents cell recruitment, since the cell will be unable to fire; too much prevents cell recruitment after initial firing, since the cell will then be in a refractory afterhyperpolarized state.

A useful task for analysis, then, is to determine the probabilistic percentage of cells that will have precisely κ active synapses given appropriate physiological characteristics of the firing patterns of the LOT axons and given the anatomical connectivity characteristics of the network matrix. In particular, if we know the number of axons in the LOT (n), which is the same as the total number of possible connection sites in any given dendrite, the probability of firing of axons (a_p), i.e., the average percentage of axons that will fire in response to a stimulus, which allows determination of the average number of firing axons ($a_p n$); and if we know the probability of synaptic contact between the axons and dendrites in layer Ia (s_p), which in turn determines the average number of synapses per dendrite ($s_p n$), then we can determine the probability of a cell's having a particular number κ of *active* synapses on its dendrite:

$$p(\kappa \text{ active synapses}) = \frac{\binom{a_p n}{\kappa} \binom{n - a_p n}{s_p n - \kappa}}{\binom{n}{s_p n}}.$$

This formula is easiest to understand by taking an example. Assume that we wish to identify the percentage of cells that are likely to have a single active synapse in response to an LOT input, i.e., $\kappa = 1$. Then we wish to first find the number of combinations or ways in which we can take one active axon out of the total $a_p n$ active axons; this corresponds to the first element in the equation. We then must find the number of combinations or potential ways of connecting the remaining, nonactivated synapses on a dendrite ($s_p n - \kappa$) to the remaining, nonfiring axons ($n - a_p n$); this is the second element of the equation. Their product denotes the total number of ways in which this set of axons can give rise to a single active synapse on a dendrite; the product must then be divided by the total number of ways of taking $s_p n$ synaptic connections out of n potential synaptic sites (i.e., out of n potential axonal connections with the dendrite). The resulting quotient then can be seen to yield the probability or percentage of cells with precisely κ active synapses, i.e., synapses receiving input from a firing axon. Examination of the successive values of this function over increasing values of κ gives a probability density function for the probability of cells with certain firing strengths; then assuming a firing threshold enables calculations of the average number of cells that will respond to an input vector (LOT activation pattern) of particular size. It is the case, of course, that

$$\sum_{\kappa \geq 0} \left[\frac{\binom{a_p n}{\kappa} \binom{n - a_p n}{s_p n - \kappa}}{\binom{n}{s_p n}} \right] = 1;$$

that is, the sums of the probabilities of cells that have no active synapses, one active synapse, two active synapses, etc., must equal 1, as a consequence of the simple fact that each cell must have some number of active synapses.

The value of a_p has been estimated to be about 0.2 for piriform cortex; i.e., approximately 20 percent of the LOT axons are active in response to olfactory stimuli. We also estimate that the approximate probability of contacts between the LOT axons and the layer-II-cell dendrites (s_p) is about 0.1 (Haberly and Price 1977); i.e., there will be an average of $0.1n$ synapses per dendrite in layer Ia. Assuming that there are about 50,000 LOT axons, there are then about 10,000 firing LOT lines per average stimulus and about 5,000 synapses per layer-II-cell dendrite. Using these values, we have performed some initial calculations of the probability density of the average convergence of active synapses per dendrite, and have based our simulation convergence requirements (i.e., simulated resting potentials and firing thresholds) on these values for 100 LOT axons, 20 of which fire per stimulus, and a synaptic density of 0.2, since 0.1 was prohibitively low for our purposes. The resulting behavior of the model is discussed in the following subsections.

3.3 Behavior of the Model

Most of our simulation work has been done on a model with 100 excitatory LOT input lines and 100 layer II target cells, with the density of connections between them being $p = 0.2$. The layer II cells in the model, as in the brain, generate an associational feedback system, with the probability of a given axon's contacting a particular dendrite again 0.2. Connections were placed at random with certain statistical constraints (e.g., limits on the total number of synapses that an axon can form or that a dendrite can accept). Stimulation of an axon in the LOT or feedback system causes simulated EPSPs to appear in the dendrites of the cells innervated by the axon; EPSPs summate linearly (in the model), and the target cell discharges one or more action potentials when a threshold voltage value is exceeded (the performance rule). LOT and feedback axons also activate inhibitory cells that raise the voltage threshold of the cells in the network; the number of simulated IPSPs of a given hyperpolarizing value that appears at a cell is dependent upon the number of input and/or feedback lines that are active. In many cases it proves useful to simulate two inhibitory events: a short and very potent IPSP and a long hyperpolarizing event. The first of these events effectively terminates a firing episode; the second serves to raise the threshold of the cell and hence the amount of convergent excitatory input needed to activate it. The excitatory events (EPSPs) are quite brief relative to either of these inhibitory responses. It is important to note that neurons in the simulation are simple voltage-summing devices and do not incorporate length and time constants or current shunting.

An "odor" input to the network consists of activating contiguous groups of axons, with each group representing one component of the odor. The relative intensity of the component is reflected in the number of LOT lines it stimulates; we assume that the bulb seeks to normalize its output and that hence the total number of axons constituting an odor does not vary much from 20 percent of the entire LOT (i.e., 20 axons in the simulation). We are rather faithfully simulating the events that occur in the "electric odor" experiments described above; we are also using these to generate hypotheses about characteristics of bulb outputs that enable these electric odors to serve as successful physiological and behavioral substitutes for bulb activity.

The learning mode of the simulation incorporates several prominent features of LTP and, in particular, the synergistic facilitation of responses that results from bursting discharge patterns and priming. Thus, synaptic strength increases transiently during a learning episode and there is a voltage threshold that must be reached for synaptic change to occur. As discussed earlier, this type of LTP rule does not linearly incorporate existing synaptic strengths into synaptic strengths present during a learning episode. A further complexity is that the inputs and feedback lines do not sum linearly during learning in terms of achieving the voltage threshold for change and do not influence each other equivalently (i.e., feedback promotes LTP in the LOT synapses to a greater extent than the LOT promotes change in the feedback). As in the "electric odor" experiments, the LOT operates rhythmically and activity in the target cells is time locked to this. Thus, the simulated inputs are activated three to four times at 5 Hz either with single pulses (performance) or with short bursts that generate facilitated EPSPs (learning).

The sparseness of synaptic connections in layer Ia of the model, together with the recruiting of "attractor cells" as described above, cause the model to generate spatial patterns of layer-II-cell responses that denote a representation of the input. It is likely that these representations may be encoding population characteristics of the input patterns that are not otherwise readily derivable from the individual inputs themselves. One major set of relevant population characteristics involves the similarities and differences among learned odor patterns. Training the model strengthens the reliability of layer II output responses to an input, thereby enabling the network to generate a recognition response to a "degraded" version of a learned cue. This is a nearly ubiquitous ability of standard neural-network learning models (see, e.g., Anderson and Mozer 1981; Hinton and Anderson 1981; Rumelhart and Zipser 1986). A "degraded" cue is simply a novel cue that is sufficiently similar to a learned cue; hence, learned recognition of degraded or noisy versions of cues can be viewed as learned *categorization* of similar cues (see, e.g., Andersen et al. 1977; Rumelhart and Zipser 1986; Rumelhart et al. 1986). This raises two related questions: (1) How are both the similarities among cues and the differences among similar cues encoded in the network? (2) What overlap must two cues have in order to be confused with each other—i.e., how similar must a novel cue be to a learned cue in order to be treated as a degraded version of that cue? Although it is straightforward for a network to perform either categorization of cues or differentiation of cues, multiple networks or multiple operations are typically required to provide both functions (see, e.g., Kohonen 1984).

Theta-patterned input stimulation, in addition to facilitating induction of LTP, also induces time-varying inhibitory currents, giving rise to a pattern of changing global resting potentials in the network, which in turn can cause different cell-firing patterns in response to identical inputs, depending on whether those inputs arrive against a background of high or low cell resting potentials. Figure 6 shows that the first burst of an input pattern in the LOT induces a short EPSP (lasting up to 20 msec) and IPSPs and other hyperpolarizing currents that are slower to develop but are longer lasting (long hyperpolarizing currents can last for 1–2 seconds). Hence, the second and subsequent bursts of LOT stimulation will land on a background of hyperpolarization that can cause many fewer cells to be driven over firing thresh-

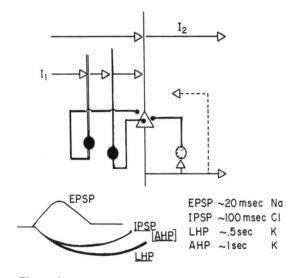

Figure 6
Onset and duration of events constituting stimulation of a layer II cell in piriform cortex. Axonal stimulation via the LOT activates feedforward EPSPs with rapid onset and short duration ($\approx$ 20 msec) and two types of feedforward inhibition: short feedforward IPSPs with slower onset and somewhat longer duration ($\approx$ 100 msec) than the EPSPs, and longer hyperpolarizing potentials (LHP) (lasting $\approx$ 500 msec). These two types of inhibition are not specific to firing cells; an additional, long-lasting ($\approx$ 1 sec) inhibitory afterhyperpolarizing current (AHP) is induced in a cell-specific fashion in those cells with intense firing activity. Finally, feedback EPSPs and IPSPs are induced by activation of recurrent collateral axons.

old. Our piriform simulation models this effect, yielding very different patterns of layer-II-cell firing at different bursts of the same input stimulation pattern and enabling different information to be encoded in different bursts. In particular, after the learning of several odors that are similar to one another (i.e., their spatial patterns overlap significantly), the presentation of a novel odor sharing this overlap with the learned odors will generate an initial burst response that is nearly identical to that for the learned odors, whereas subsequent responses (against a now hyperpolarized background) will yield almost no response. After the learning of this novel odor, the first response will be nearly identical to that for the other similar odors, whereas later responses will be significantly different across different odors. We presume that subsequent brain regions (i.e., those receiving these sequences of piriform-cell firing patterns as their inputs) are similarly sampling at appropriate theta rhythms; it is known that hippocampal areas, the major recipients of these outputs, do indeed fire these patterns. Hence, the network can be thought of as simultaneously encoding similarity and difference information. Late sniffs differentiate cues, whereas early sniffs cluster cues together by similarity. This immediately raises the second question asked above: How similar need two cues be to give rise to identical first responses?

3.4   Learning-Dependent Partitioning of Experience

Clustering cues by similarity can be thought of as *partitioning* the set of trained cues into clusters. Mechanisms and substrates aside, the task of categorization or partitioning can be discussed abstractly. The task is to choose, for each input, whether to "place" it into an existing category (and if so, which one) or to "create" a new category of which it will be the first member. From an information-theoretic point of view, the ideal partitioning of a set of cues into categories is one that maximizes the information that those categories provide about their members. If a category signal that groups cues together is going to be substituted for individual cues, then some information will be lost; an information-optimal partitioning will be one that loses the minimal amount of information in the encoding. This notion has been formalized (Shannon and Weaver 1949; Gluck and Corter 1985; Fisher 1985, 1987), thereby allowing us to measure the information value of a particular encoding of inputs with reference to the inferential task of recognizing similarities and differences among cues and an assumed "cost" for errors in that task.

There is an enormous number of possible partitionings of any given set of cues into similarity classes; the number of possible partitionings grows as the factorial of the number of cues. Furthermore, the partitioning task is non-monotonic with respect to incremental acquisition of cues—that is, the optimal partitioning of n cues is not related in a straightforward way to the optimal partitioning of those n cues plus an $(n + 1)$st cue; merges and splits of existing categories may be required. Hence, the search for the optimal partitioning of a set of cues is computationally very expensive. A serial computer search procedure for incrementally identifying the information-optimal partitioning of arbitrary sets of cues requires factorial time using a beam search of the space of all possible partitionings. That algorithm basically generates all possible divisions of the cues into categories, calculates the information value for each, and chooses the one with the highest value (Fisher 1985, 1987). Since the task is nonmonotonic, this entire process must be repeated with the addition of every new cue.

3.5 Example of Partitioning of Cues

As an example of the optimal partitioning of cues into categories, figure 7 depicts "chromatographic" representations of four different hypothetical odors as inputs to piriform. In the figure, each P1, P2, etc., denotes a different chemical constituent of the odor (and hence each denotes activity in a different area or "patch" of the olfactory bulb), and the height of the bar at each patch denotes the relative intensity of that constituent in the overall compound comprising the odor. For simplicity, assume for the purposes of this example that there are only five patches on the bulb, each of which may have one of three possible intensities: low, medium, and high. Assume further that the animal will sense just these four odors and no others. In terms of this example, the task is to partition these four odors into categories; i.e., to form some set of categories and place each odor into one or the other of these categories in such a way as to maximize the information value of the categories overall.

There exist exactly fifteen different ways in which the four odors can be partitioned into categories:

- (Odor1 Odor2 Odor3 Odor4) [one category containing all four odors],
- (Odor1) (Odor2 Odor3 Odor4) [two categories, one containing only a single odor and the other containing the remaining three odors; there are four possible partitionings like this],
- (Odor2) (Odor1 Odor3 Odor4),
- (Odor3) (Odor1 Odor2 Odor4),
- (Odor4) (Odor1 Odor2 Odor3),
- (Odor1 Odor2) (Odor3 Odor4) [two categories, one containing two of the

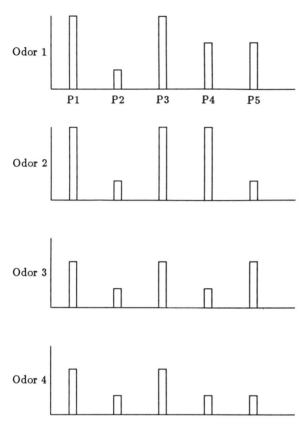

Figure 7
Bar graphs depicting four distinct "simulated odor" activation patterns. The olfactory
bulb is presumed to be divided into five "patches" or regions (P1–P5), each of which
may exhibit any of three possible levels of activation (low, medium, high) in response to a particular olfactory input. Each bar measures the level of response of a
particular patch; an odor corresponds to a spatial activation pattern on the bulb consisting of these levels of firing in each of the five bulb patches.

odors and the other containing the other two; there are three of these partitionings],
• (Odor1 Odor3) (Odor2 Odor4),
• (Odor1 Odor4) (Odor2 Odor3),
• (Odor1) (Odor2) (Odor3 Odor4) [three categories, one containing two odors and the others containing one odor each; there are six of these partitionings],
• (Odor1) (Odor3) (Odor2 Odor4),
• (Odor1) (Odor4) (Odor2 Odor3),
• (Odor2) (Odor3) (Odor1 Odor4),
• (Odor2) (Odor4) (Odor1 Odor3),
• (Odor3) (Odor4) (Odor1 Odor2),
• (Odor1) (Odor2) (Odor3) (Odor4) [four separate categories, each containing only one of the odors].

Similarly, for five odors there are 52 possible partitionings; the number of possible partitionings grows factorially with the number of distinguishable odors in the training set.

The question is this: For a set of odors, how can we tell which of the many possible partitionings or divisions into categories is the best possible division? In particular, for the four odors in this example, how can we tell which of the fifteen possible partitionings or divisions into categories is the best one?

For simplicity, we will consider only the three possible partitionings (out of the possible fifteen) in which there are two categories with two odors each. The calculated information-theoretic values for the three partitionings are as follows:

• Partitioning A (Odor1 Odor2) (Odor3 Odor4): 4.25,
• Partitioning B (Odor1 Odor3) (Odor2 Odor4): 3.50,
• Partitioning C (Odor1 Odor4) (Odor2 Odor3): 3.00.

These calculated values show that Partitioning A contains the highest information value; this jibes with intuition based on observation of the three partitionings of the four odors: It is clear that Odor1 and Odor2 share the features of three patches (P1, P2, and P3), as do Odor3 and Odor4; hence, Partitioning A, which groups these pairs together, should be superior to either of the other two pairwise groupings. Note next that Odor1 and Odor3 share the features of two patches (P2 and P5), as do Odor2 and Odor4; hence, Partitioning B should be superior to Partitioning C, in which only the value of a single patch, P2, is shared across members of the categories.

We have performed a number of experiments on the piriform simulation to test its partitioning behavior. These experiments consist of training the simulation on a series of simulated odors like the above and noting the first-response output after training. These outputs are nearly identical for some odors and are quite different from one another for others (as opposed to the second and subsequent responses, which are quite different from one another for all cues and which tend to individuate or orthogonalize the cues). Our experiments so far show that the simulation tends to produce near-optimal partitionings of the data; as an example, figure 8 gives 22 simulated chromatographs of artificial odor-stimulation patterns in a random order. The simulation, trained on these patterns, learned to produce nearly identical initial responses to subsets of these cues, effectively partitioning them into categories. Examination of figure 8 will illustrate the difficulty of partitioning these cues optimally; it is far from obvious even how many categories there should be, let alone which cues should be in which categories. Yet once they have been categorized by the simulation as described, the resulting categories look intuitively correct by inspection (figure 9), and, more important, they correspond to the optimal partitioning of the cues as measured by a computer program designed to identify the optimal partitioning via beam search (Fisher 1987); furthermore, they are arrived at in linear computational time, as contrasted with the factorial time that the beam-search algorithm requires.

We have not tested the simulation against some of the more subtle yet crucially important requirements for optimal categorization. One of the most intriguing aspects of information partitioning is that it requires a coordination between global experience with the world of cues and behavior in specific instances. That is, a good partitioning scheme (with "good" defined by information-theoretic measures) must be based on the general heterogeneity of the stimuli to be organized rather than on absolute measures of overlap between particular subsets of cues. Thus, two stimuli that are 70 percent similar might be classified together if the population of stimuli (so far sampled) is heterogeneous, but these same two cues might not be placed in the same category if the population is extremely homogeneous, containing many stimuli that are 90 percent similar to one another. In the context of this latter population, small differences among similar input vectors become salient. Note again that categories must be dynamic and susceptible to modification as further sampling—including sampling of stimuli that have no overlap with members of existing categories—is carried out. It will be of great interest to establish the degree to which our current model captures these features of optimal partitioning and to determine if additional properties or further layers of cells are needed for it to do so.

In any event, the simulation work done thus far indicates that a simple cortical layer operating according to empirically derived physiological rules does accomplish the dual functions of forming differential representations of individual stimuli and the grouping of these stimuli into reasonable categories. This leads us to suggest that these operations are the "primitive" or basic functions of layer-II-type cortex, and that the design features as well as the learning and performance rules found there have evolved in response to pressures for simultaneous clustering and individuation of environmental stimuli. Experimental tests of these ideas will be pursued along two paths. First, we will examine layer II of piriform to determine if it possesses those anatomies and physiologies that facilitate the dual representation of information in the simulations; in essence, we will ask if the hypothesized "function" of this type of cortex as observed in computer models successfully predicts the existence of neurobiological properties. Second, we can sample the cortex as it processes natural and electric odors for cellular behaviors that correspond to those exhibited by the simulation. Does the pattern of cell firing on different sniffs change so as to first denote a known group and to then signal the presence of a specific cue? We hope that this cycle of simulation and experimentation will close the gap between computational operations of this one layer of cortex and its organization and physiologies.

Conclusions

Most computational approaches to learning begin with prespecified behaviors and strive to identify either formalisms to characterize these behaviors or mechanisms to compute them. For instance, in the area of classical conditioning, examples of the former case (formal characterizations of behavior) include formal statements of the contingency relations that seem to hold between conditioned and unconditioned stimuli in classical conditioning (Rescorla 1968; Gibbon et al. 1974; Granger and Schlimmer 1987), and the latter case (algorithmic mechanisms) includes, e.g., production-system models (Holyoak and Nisbett 1987) or matrix network algorithms (Sutton and Barto 1981) that may underlie and give rise to those contingency relations. At their most successful, such approaches can only identify correspondence between their formalisms and the already-identified behaviors that they were intended to account for. To the extent that these behavioral-level effects are accurate reflections of the behavioral data, the formalisms aid in characterization and possibly in deeper understanding of the nature of these data. However, even accurate statements of behavioral data capture only the effects examined in the behavioral experiments. Determination of the deeper underlying "primitives" that may give rise to such behaviors, or the crucial distinctions between

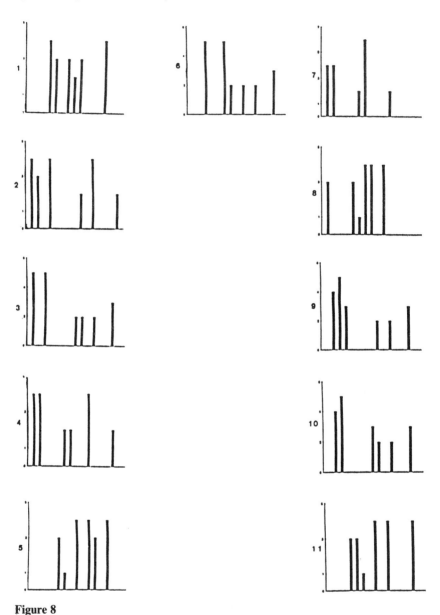

Figure 8

Bar graphs depicting 22 distinct "simulated odor" activation patterns given in a random order (1–22) as input to the piriform computer simulation. Each bar graph corresponds to an odor. The position of each bar represents a particular simulated "patch" or region of the bulb. The height of each bar corresponds to the number of simulated bulb cells firing within the patch. Hence, each graph constitutes the spatial bulb cell firing pattern "signature" for a given input odor.

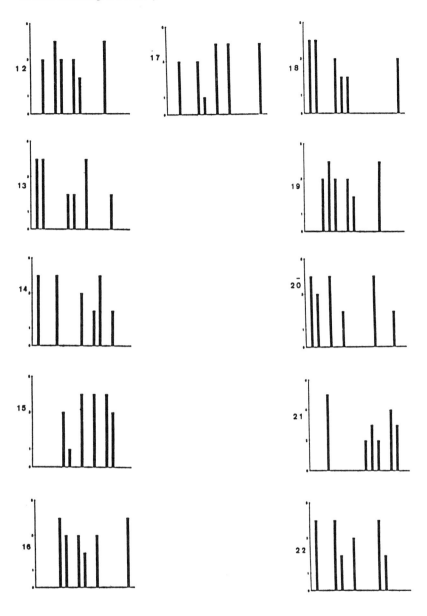

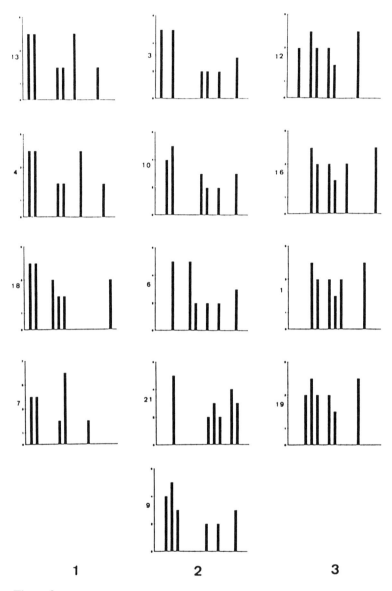

Figure 9
The same 22 "simulated odor" graphs as in figure 8, sorted according to the simulated layer-II-cell firing patterns elicited by the piriform simulation after training. Sets of input patterns eliciting nearly identical layer-II-cell spatial firing patterns are clustered together, revealing patterns of similarities in the inputs that were difficult to detect among the randomly ordered cues in the previous figure; i.e., after training, the layer-II-cell spatial firing pattern identifies similarities among inputs.

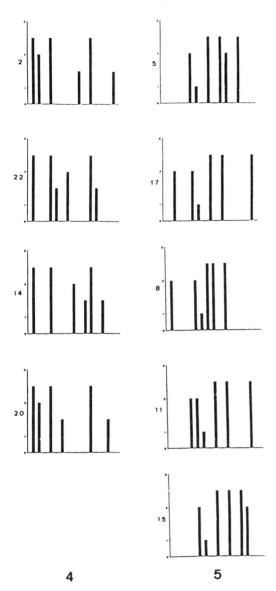

4   5

apparently similar forms of behavior, must ultimately be identified as emergent functional properties of the substrate that gives rise to them.

We are engaged in a program of research that is attempting to directly model the structural and functional characteristics of cortical networks and to elucidate their emergent network-level behaviors. This approach contrasts with yet complements approaches above and below this level, which serve either to uncover more "molecular" properties of brain structure and function (e.g., at the biophysical and biochemical levels) or to provide formal statements more clearly characterizing the available behavioral-level data. Our initial efforts have already generated some small contributions in both directions; for example, identification of the behavioral-level differences that would emerge from differential potentiation of LOT versus feedback axons led to our physiological experiments on delay dependencies among multiple inputs to a single cell, thereby identifying a previously unsuspected physiological property of LTP induction. Furthermore, embedding known physiological rules for LTP induction in a real anatomical network pointed out the potentially central role of training-dependent partitioning of experience as one of the major emergent functions of olfactory cortex. We could have put any learning rule into a network and gotten different results; e.g., if we had intentionally picked a rule designed to perform associative learning, we might well have forced the network to do so. In contrast, we did not suspect or preconceive that this network, using empirically derived LTP rules, would give rise to training-dependent partitioning of experience; it simply did so. This suggests to us that this particular network-level (and behavioral-level) function may be a true primitive of cortical operation, emerging directly from the anatomies and physiologies inherent in these networks.

We explicitly hope by our efforts to augment the terminology applied to describe behavioral effects by identifying those behaviors and computations that emerge as primary functions from cortical operation, and by using these fundamental mechanisms to inform the still-developing descriptive language of the behavioral field. This difficulty in identifying the correct underlying functions of a set of behaviors, and hence appropriately taxonomizing those behaviors, occurs in other areas of psychology as well as in the subfield of learning and memory. For instance, in discussing the difficulty of formally characterizing what constitutes a human natural language, and therefore being able to distinguish such a language from ape languages in a principled way, Premack (1986, p. 5) asks: ". . . are types of locutions a secondary consideration, not at all at the heart of what makes a system language? Suppose the ape could not be taught a system exactly duplicating the human one. Are there ways in which the ape's system could fall short and still remain interesting? Are there other ways in which failure would immediately disqualify the system, robbing it of all interest? In short, one needed a discussion of criteria that make a system language and even a weighting of these criteria." Analogously, we focus on types of learning that seem to be present in both rat and human: the rapid (< 5 trials) and long-lasting (> weeks) acquisition of data (as opposed to procedures). Are these distinctions crucial differences among different types of learning (Squire 1986)? Is it significant that acquisition of a learning set is possible in rats in olfactory tasks, though it is extremely difficult and often impossible for rats in tasks dealing with other sensory modalities (Slotnick and Katz 1974)? Might experience-dependent clustering of cues be a primitive function underlying learning and memory organization? In the absence of examples of carefully specified behavioral and network-level abilities such as these, potentially central questions like this tend not to be raised. We recognize that the field is still in its infancy, and we hope to be able to contribute specific experimental questions at both the physiological and the behavioral level and to suggest fundamental emergent brain network functions that may aid in the ongoing construction of the bridge between biology and behavior.

References

Abraham, W. C., and G. V. Goddard. 1983. Asymmetric relationships between homosynaptic long-term potentiation and heterosynaptic long-term depression. *Nature* 305: 717–719.

Alger, B., and R. Nicoll. 1982. Feed-forward dendritic inhibition in rat hippocampal pyramidal neurons studid *in vitro*. *Journal of Physiology* 328: 105–123.

Andersen, P., S. H. Sundberg, O. Sveen, and H. Wigstrom. 1977. Specific long-lasting potentiation of synaptic transmission in hippocampal slices. *Nature* 226: 736–737.

Anderson, J. A., and M. Mozer. 1981. Categorization and selective neurons. In *Parallel Models of Associative Memory*, ed. G. Hinton and J. A. Anderson (Hillsdale, N.J.: Erlbaum).

Barnes, C. A. 1979. Memory deficits associated with senescence: A neurophysiological and behavioral study in the rat. *Journal of Comparative Physiology and Psychology* 93: 74–104.

Barrionuevo, G., F. Schottler, and G. Lynch. 1979. The effects of repetitive low frequency stimulation on control and "potentiated" synaptic responses in the hippocampus. *Life Sciences* 27: 2385–2391.

Baudry, M., J. Larson, and G. Lynch. 1987. Long-term changes in synaptic efficacy: Potential mechanisms and implications. In *Long-Term Potentiation: From Biophysics to Behavior*, ed. P. Landfield and S. Deadwyler (New York: Alan Liss).

Bland, B. H. 1986. The physiology and pharmacology of hippocampal formation theta rhthms. *Progress in Neurobiology* 26: 1–54.

Buzsaki, G. 1984. Feed-forward inhibition in the hippocampal formation. *Progress in Brain Research* 22: 131–153.

Carlsen, J., J. DeOlmos, and L. Heimer. 1982. Tracing of two-neuron pathways in the olfactory system by the aid of transneuronal degeneration: Projections of the amygdaloid body and hippocampal formation. *Journal of Comparative Neurology* 208: 196–208.

Chang, F. L. F., and W. T. Greenough. 1984. Transient and enduring morphological correlates of synaptic activity and efficacy change in the rat hippocampal slice. *Brain Research* 309: 35–46.

Collingridge, G. L., S. J. Kehl, and H. McLennan. 1983. The antagonism of amino-acid-induced excitation of rat hippocampal CA1 neurones *in vitro*. *Journal of Physiology* 334: 19–31.

Cooper, L. N. 1984. Neuron learning to network organization. In *J. C. Maxwell, the Sesquicentennial Symposium* (Amsterdam: Elsevier).

Cooper, L. N., F. Lieberman, and E. Oja. 1979. A theory for the acquisition and loss of neuron specificity in visual cortex. *Biological Cybernetics* 33: 9–28.

Desmond, N. L., and W. B. Levy. 1983. Synaptic correlates of associative potentiation/depression: An ultrastructural study in the hippocampus. *Brain Research* 265: 21–30.

Dunwiddie, T., and G. Lynch. 1978. Long-term potentiation and depression of synaptic responses in the rat hippocampus: Localization and frequency dependency. *Journal of Physiology* (London) 276: 353–367.

Dunwiddie, T., and G. Lynch. 1979. The relationship between extracellular calcium concentrations and the induction of hippocampal long-term potentiation. *Brain Research* 169: 103–110.

Eichenbaum, H., K. J. Shedlack, and K. W. Eckmann. 1980. Thalomocortical mechanisms in odor-guided behavior. I. Effects of lesions of the mediodorsal thalamic nucleus and frontal cortex on olfactory discrimination in the rat. *Brain Behavior and Evolution* 17: 255–275.

Eichenbaum, H., T. H. Morton, H. Potter, and S. Corkin. 1983. Selective olfactory deficits in case H.M. *Brain* 106: 459–472.

Finkel, L. H., and G. M. Edelman. 1985. Interaction of synaptic modification rules within populations of neurons. *Proceedings of the National Academy of Sciences* 82: 1291–1295.

Fisher, D. 1985. A Hierarchical Conceptual Clustering Algorithm. Technical Report 85–21, ICS Dept., University of California, Irvine.

Fisher, D. 1987. Knowledge acquisition via incremental conceptual clustering. *Machine Learning* 2: 139–172.

Fox, S. E., and J. B. Ranck, Jr. 1981. Electrophysiological characteristics of hippocampal complex—spike cells and theta cells. *Experimental Brain Research* 41: 399–410.

Gibbon, J., R. Berryman, and R. L. Thompson. 1974. Contingency spaces and measures in classical and instrumental conditioning. *Journal of the Experimental Analysis of Behavior* 21: 585–605.

Gluck, M., and J. Corter. 1985. Information, uncertainty and the utility of categories. In *Proceedings of the Seventh Annual Conference of the Cognitive Science Society* (Irvine, Calif.: Erlbaum).

Granger, R. H., and J. C. Schlimmer. 1987. The computation of contingency in classical conditioning. *Psychology of Learning and Motivation* 20: 137–192.

Haberly, L. B. 1985. Neuronal circuitry in olfactory cortex: Anatomy and functional implications. *Chemical Senses* 10: 219–238.

Haberly, L. B., and J. L. Price. 1977. The axonal projection of the mitral and tufted cells of the olfactory bulb in the rat. *Brain Research* 129: 152–157.

Harris, E. W., A. H. Ganong, and C. W. Cotman. 1984. Long-term potentiation in the hippocampus involves activation of N-Methyl-D-Aspartate receptors. *Brain Research* 323: 132–137.

Hinton, G. E., and J. A. Anderson. 1981. *Parallel Models of Associative Memory.* Hillsdale, N.J.: Erlbaum.

Holyoak, K., and R. Nisbett. 1987. Induction. In *The Psychology of Human Thought,* ed. R. J. Sternberg and E. E. Smith (Cambridge University Press).

Jerison, H. J. 1973. *Evolution of the Brain and Intelligence.* New York: Academic.

Jourdan, F. 1982. Spatial dimension of olfactory coding: A representation of ^{14}C-2-deoxyglucose patterns of glomerular labeling in the olfactory bulb. *Brain Research* 240: 341–344.

Kelso, S. R., A. H. Ganong, and T. H. Brown. 1986. Hebbian synapses in hippocampus. *Proceedings of the National Academy of Sciences* 83: 5326–5330.

Klemm, W. R. 1976. Hippocampal EEG and information processing: A special role for theta rhythm. *Progress in Neurobiology* 7: 197–214.

Kohenen, T. 1984. *Self-Organization and Associative Memory.* Berlin: Springer-Verlag.

Kosel, K. C., G. W. Van Hoesen, and J. R. West. 1981. Olfactory bulb projections to the parahippocampal area of the rat. *Journal of Comparative Neurology* 198: 467–482.

Krettek, J. E., and J. L. Price. 1977. Projections from the amygdaloid complex and adjacent olfactory stimulus to the entorhinal cortex and the subiculum in the rat and cat. *Journal of Comparative Neurology* 172: 723–752.

Lancet, D., C. A. Greer, J. S. Kaver, and G. M. Shepherd. 1982. Mapping of odor-related neuronal activity in the olfactory bulb by high-resolution 2-deoxyglucose autoradiography. *Proceedings of the National Academy of Sciences* 79: 670–674.

Landfield, P. W. 1976. Synchronous EEG rhythms: Their nature and their possible function in memory. In *Molecular and Functional Neurobiology,* ed. W. H. Gispen (Amsterdam: Elsevier).

Landfield, P., and S. Deadwyler. 1987. In *Long-Term Potentiation: From Biophysics to Behavior* (New York: Alan Liss).

Larson, J., and G. Lynch. 1986. Synaptic potentiation in hippocampus by patterned stimulation involves two events. *Science* 232: 985–988.

Larson, J., and G. Lynch. 1988. Role of N-Methyl-D-Aspartate receptors in the induction of synaptic potentiation by burst stimulation patterned after the hippocampal theta rhythm. *Brain Research* 441: 111–118.

Larson, J., D. Wong, and G. Lynch. 1986. Patterned stimulation at the theta frequency is optimal for induction of long-term potentiation. *Brain Research* 368: 7–35.

Lee, K., F. Schottler, M. Oliver, and G. Lynch. 1980. Brief bursts of high-frequency stimulation produce two types of structural change in rat hippocampus. *Journal of Neurophysiology* 44: 247–258.

Levy, W. D., and O. Steward. 1980. Synapses as associative memory elements in the hippocampal formation. *Brain Research* 175: 233–245.

Lorente de No, R. 1934. Studies on the structure of the cerebral cortex. II. Continuation of the study of the ammonic system. *Journal of Psychology and Neurology* 46: 113–177.

Luskin, M. B., and J. L. Price. 1983. The laminar distribution of intracortical fibers originating in the olfactory cortex of the rat. *Journal of Comparative Neurology* 216: 292–302.

Lynch, G. 1986. *Synapses, Circuits, and the Beginnings of Memory.* Cambridge, Mass.: MIT Press.

Lynch, G., and M. Baudry. 1988. Structure-function relationships in the organization of memory. In *Perspectives in Memory Research,* ed. M. S. Gazzaniga (Cambridge, Mass.: MIT Press).

Lynch, G. S., V. K. Gribkoff, and S. A. Deadwyler. 1976. Long-term potentiation is accompanied by a reduction in dendritic responsiveness to glutamic acid. *Nature* 263: 141–153.

Lynch, G. S., T. V. Dunwiddie, and V. Gribkoff. 1977. Heterosynaptic depression: A postsynaptic correlate of long-term potentiation. *Nature* 266: 737–739.

Lynch, G., R. A. Jensen, J. McGaugh, K. Davila, and M. Oliver. 1981. Effects of enkephalin, morphine and naloxone on the electrical activity of the hippocampal slice preparation. *Experimental Neurology* 7: 527–540.

Lynch, G., J. Larson, S. Kelso, S. Barrionuevo, and F. Schottler. 1983. Intracellular injections of EGTA block the induction of hippocampal long-term potentiation. *Nature* 305: 719–721.

McCarren, M. and B. E. Alger. 1985. Use-dependent depression of IPSPs in rat hippocampal pyramidal cells *in vitro*. *Journal of Neurophysiology* 53: 557–571.

McClelland, J. L., D. E. Rumelhart, and the PDP Research Group. 1986. *Parallel Distributed Processing.* Cambridge, Mass.: MIT Press.

MacDermott, A. B., M. L. Mayer, G. L. Westbrook, S. J. Smith, and J. L. Barker. 1986. NMDA-receptor activation increases cytoplasmic calcium concentration in cultured spinal cord neurones. *Nature* 321: 519–522.

McNaughton, B. L., R. M. Douglas, and G. V. Goddard. 1978. Synaptic enhancement in fascia dentata: Cooperativity among coactive afferents. *Brain Research* 157: 277–293.

Malinow, R., and J. P. Miller. 1986. Postsynaptic hyperpolarization during conditioning reversibly blocks induction of long-term potentiation. *Nature* 320: 529–530.

Morris, R. G. M., E. Anderson, G. Lynch, and M. Baudry. 1986. Selective impairment of learning and blockade of long-term potentiation by an N-methyl-D-aspartate receptor antagonist, AP-5. *Nature* 319: 774–776.

Mouly, A. M., M. Vigouroux, and A. Holley. 1987. On the ability of rats to discriminate between microstimulations of the olfactory bulb in different locations. *Behavioral Brain Research* 17: 45–58.

Premack, D. 1986. *Gavagai!, or, the Future History of the Animal Language Controversy.* Cambridge, Mass.: MIT Press.

Price, J. L. 1973. An autoradiographic study of complementary laminar patterns of termination of afferent fibers to the olfactory cortex. *Journal of Comparative Neurology* 150: 87–108.

Price, J. L., and B. M. Slotnick. 1983. Dual olfactory representation in the rat thalamus: An anatomical and electrophysiological study. *Journal of Comparative Neurology* 215: 63–77.

Ranck, J. B., Jr. 1973. Studies on single neurons in dorsal hippocampal formation and septum in unrestrained rats. *Experimental Neurology* 41: 462–531.

Rescorla, R. 1968. Probability of shock in the presence and absence of CS in fear conditioning. *Journal of Comparative Physiology and Psychology* 66: 1–5.

Rescorla, R., and A. R. Wagner. 1972. A theory of Pavlovian conditioning: Variations in the effectiveness of reinforcement and nonreinforcement. In *Classical Conditioning II*, ed. A. H. Black and W. F. Prokasy (New York: Appleton-Century-Crofts).

Roman, F., U. Staubli, and G. Lynch. 1987. Evidence for synaptic potentiation in a cortical network during learning. *Brain Research* 418: 221–226.

Rumelhart, D., and D. Zipser. 1986. Feature discovery by competitive learning. In D. Rumelhart et al., *Parallel Distributed Processing,* volume 1 (Cambridge, Mass.: MIT Press).

Rumelhart, D., G. Hinton, and R. Williams. 1986. Learning internal representations by error propagation. In D. Rumelhart et al., *Parallel Distributed Processing,* volume 1 (Cambridge, Mass.: MIT Press).

Shannon, C., and W. Weaver. 1949. *The Mathematical Theory of Communication.* Chicago: University of Illinois Press.

Shepherd, G. M. 1979. *The Synaptic Organization of the Brain.* Second edition. Oxford University Press.

Skeen, L. C., and W. C. Hall. 1977. Efferent projections of the main and accessory olfactory bulb in the tree shrew (*Tupaia glis*). *Journal of Comparative Neurology* 172: 1–36.

Slotnick, B. M., and N. Kaneko. 1981. Role of mediodorsal thalamic nucleus in olfactory discrimination learning in rats. *Science* 214: 91–92.

Slotnick, B. M., and H. M. Katz. 1974. Olfactory learning-set formation in rats. *Science* 185: 796–798.

Squire, L. S. 1986. Mechanisms of memory. *Science* 232: 1612–1619.

Staubli, U., and G. Lynch. 1987. Stable hippocampal long-term potentiation elicited by "theta" pattern stimulation. *Brain Research* 435: 227–234.

Staubli, U., M. Baudry, and G. Lynch. 1984. Leupeptin, a thiol-proteinase inhibitor, causes a selective impairment of spatial maze performance in rats. *Behavior and Neural Biology* 40: 58–69.

Staubli, U., M. Baudry, and G. Lynch. 1985. Olfactory discrimination learning is blocked by leupeptin, a thiol-proteinase inhibitor. *Brain Research* 337: 333–336.

Staubli, U., D. Fraser, R. Faraday, and G. Lynch. 1987. Olfaction and the "data" memory system in rats. *Behavioral Neuroscience,* 101: 757–765.

Sutton, R. S., and A. G. Barto. 1981. Toward a modern theory of adaptive networks: Expectation and prediction. *Psychological Review* 38: 135–171.

Valverde, F. 1965. *Studies on the Piriform Lobe.* Cambridge, Mass: Harvard University Press.

Wenzel, J., and H. Matthies. 1985. Morphological changes in the hippocampal formation accompanying memory formation and long-term potentiation. In *Memory Systems of the Brain* ed. N. Weinberger, J. McGaugh, and G. Lynch (New York: Guilford).

Widrow, G., and M. E. Hoff. 1960. Adaptive switching circuits. *Institute of Radio Engineers, Western Electronic Convention Record,* Part 4, pp. 96–104.

Wigstrom, H., and B. Gustaffson. 1983. Facilitated induction of long-lasting potentiation during blockade of inhibition. *Nature* 301: 603–605.

Wigstrom, H., B. Gustaffson, Y. Y. Huang, and W. C. Abraham. 1986. Hippocampal long-term potentiation is induced by pairing single afferent volleys with intracellularly injected depolarizing current pulses. *Acta Physiologica Scandinavica* 126: 317–319.

Chapter 8

Computations the Hippocampus Might Perform	John O'Keefe

In 1978, Lynn Nadel and I put forward the theory that the hippocampus acts as a cognitive mapping system (O'Keefe and Nadel 1978). We ascribed several properties to this system and tried to show, on the one hand, how these properties might relate to the known anatomy and physiology of the hippocampus and, on the other, how they would provide animals with certain behavioral and cognitive capacities. These latter were used to analyze and explain the effects of hippocampal lesions. In the present chapter I will review and update the properties attributed to the cognitive map, taking into account recent evidence on the activity of hippocampal neurones during spatial memory tasks. Next I will consider the way in which some of these properties could be generated by operations performed on parallel systems of the sort found in the hippocampus. In the final section I will try to map these operations onto the anatomy and physiology of the hippocampus.

The cognitive-map theory of hippocampal function postulates that the hippocampus and associated areas (septum, subiculum, and perhaps entorhinal cortex) provide the rat with a spatial representation of its current environment. It locates the animal's position within that environment, and it contains the information that will allow it to calculate the behavior necessary to move from its current location to a desired location (e.g., one containing a reward). The motivation for building or modifying maps is a purely cognitive one. A mismatch system calculates disparities between the sensory input and the current stored representation of an environment. If the disparity is large enough, either because no map exists or because there has been an environmental change since the last update, exploration is triggered. Exploration is the systematic acquisition of information to build and modify maps. Once a map has been constructed, the animal can use the information it contains to satisfy biological needs as they occur; however, the reduction of such needs is not the motivation for constructing the maps. In this section I will discuss evidence demonstrating some of the properties of cognitive maps that will need to be taken into account when devising models of hippocampal function.

Recording from neighboring hippocampal neurons, either in succession (O'Keefe 1976; Muller et al. 1987) or simultaneously (O'Keefe and Speakman 1987a) has led to the conclusion that the fields of these neurons bear no necessary spatial relation to one another; that is, they are as likely to represent distant patches of an environment as to represent close ones. The fields of three hippocampal place units recorded at the same time during a spatial memory task are shown in figure 2. It is clear that the three represent different parts of the environment. Simultaneous recording from larger groups of neurons leads to the conclusion that as the number increases, more and more areas of the maze are represented. Figure 3 shows a composite of the place fields of eight neighboring units recorded from the CA1 field of the hippocampus. The firing rate of these place units, averaged across an environment, is uniformly low (<1 per second). This, combined with the distributed nature of the place fields in neighboring units, means that multiunit recording from the hippocampus should show a constant firing rate as the animal moves about a familiar environment and from one familiar environment to the next. The environment is represented by changes in the pattern of firing across the neurons and not by the summed rate of firing.

The unit recordings in these studies have all been taken from the dorsal hippocampus of the rat, and there remains the possibility that the ventral hippocampus has a different organization. As we shall see in the subsection on hippocampal anatomy, there are differences in the cell density and wiring of the dentate and cornu ammonis in dorsal and ventral hippocampus.

If the representation of each environment is spread across the entire array of hippocampal neurons, it follows that different environments must be represented across the same array, different environments being represented by different firing patterns. Kubie and Ranck (1983) have reported that the same hippocampal neuron can have place fields in three different environments but that there appears to be no relationship between the fields in these environments. In more similar environments (such as cylinders differing only in diameter), some neurons have similar fields (Muller et al. 1987).

Since the classic studies of Scoville and Milner (1957) on the amnesic patient H.M., the hippocampus has been implicated in some aspect of memory, although it is still not clear whether the memories are permanently stored in the hippocampus itself. The cognitive-map theory suggests that in animals such as the rat, the hippocampus is a *specific memory system* dealing only with the representations of environments and not with other types of information or memories. I will review recent studies which demonstrate that the

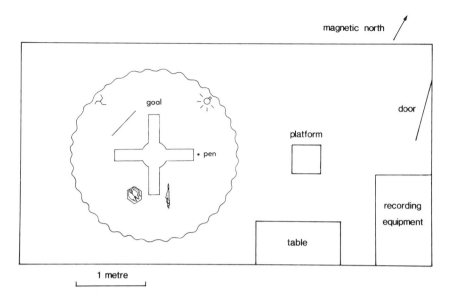

Figure 1

Layout of the cue-controlled environment. An elevated +-maze was isolated from the rest of the laboratory by a set of black curtains. Six cues inside the enclosure provided spatial information by which the rat could locate itself and the goal. The cues were (clockwise from the upper right) a light, a marker pen, a towel, a cage with two rats, a white card, and a fan. On each trial the cues were rotated as a constellation by multiples of 90°. The goal was always located in the arm between the fan/card and the light. The door to the room was arbitrarily labeled the North direction (it was not true north), and the configuration shown has the goal in the west. On spatial reference memory trials, these controlled cues were present throughout the trial and the animal's task was to remember the relationship of the goal to the cues. On spatial working memory trials, the cues were present for the first part of the trial (30 or 60 seconds) and the animal was locked in the start arm by the lowered central platform. After this period the cues were removed and the animal was kept in the start arm for a memory delay interval of 30 or 60 seconds. Only then was it allowed to choose. Since the location of the controlled cues and the goal was changed from trial to trial according to a pseudo-random schedule, the animal had to remember the location of the cues and/or the goal on each trial. During the intertrial interval the animal was held on the platform outside the cue-controlled environment.

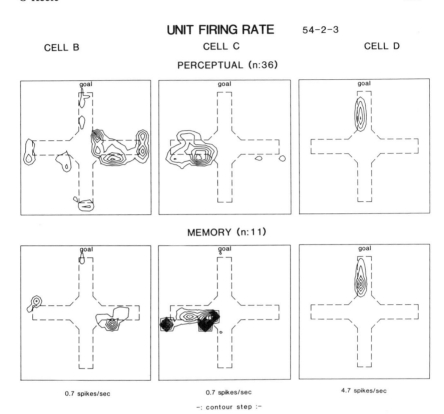

UNIT FIRING RATE   54-2-3

Figure 2

Place fields of three CA1 hippocampal complex spike units in the cue-controlled environment. The three units were recorded simultaneously using a dual-electrode technique (the "stereotrode"). Each picture was constructed from a number of trials by rotating the data so that the goals were at the top of the picture. The data from a trial in which the goal was in the west was rotated 90° clockwise; that from an east-goal trial was rotated 90° anticlockwise. The three upper pictures show the firing rates (as isorate contour plots) during entire spatial reference memory trials together with the first part of the spatial working memory trials. During both of these the cues were present and the cells might have been responding to perceptual inputs. The lower three pictures show the firing pattern of the same three units during the second part of the spatial working memory trials after the controlled cues had been removed. The firing patterns of the three units remain approximately the same, demonstrating that these units maintain a "memory" of the location of the controlled cues on that trial. Source: O'Keefe and Speakman 1987a.

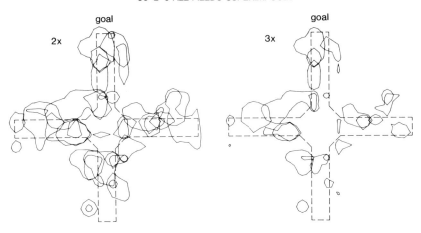

Figure 3
Contours of the fields from eight neighboring place cells. Only the contours at 2 times (left) and 3 times (right) the mean rates across the entire maze are shown. It appears that the fields of as few as eight neighboring place cells are sufficient to map a large proportion of an environment.

hippocampal place cells either store information about the current environment and the animal's location within it or receive inputs from neural areas which store such information.

After lesions of the hippocampus, rats are no longer able to perform correctly on spatial working memory tasks (see, e.g., Olton et al. 1978; Nadel and MacDonald 1979) although they are unimpaired on nonspatial working memory tasks (see, e.g., Nadel and MacDonald 1979; Aggleton et al. 1986; see Barnes 1988 for a recent review). They are also impaired on the acquisition of those spatial reference memory tasks—such as the Morris water maze (O'Keefe et al. 1975; Morris et al. 1982; Sutherland et al. 1982)—that cannot be solved using a simple direction or cue guidance strategy. This is an important point, since Ranck et al. (1987) have found that in the post-subiculum— an area closely related to but independent of the hippocampus—there are neurons that are sensitive to the direction in which the rat's head is pointing irrespective of its location in the environment.

Memory deficits after hippocampal damage could result from several different involvements in the mnemonic process. The hippocampus may be the site of storage of the information; it may be part of the system for the encoding or retrieval of information stored elsewhere; it may be important for the successful retrieval and manipulation of information stored elsewhere. As we shall see, one interpretation of the evidence from single-unit studies is that spatial information is being manipulated in the hippocampus.

There are also several possibilities as to the types of information that could be stored or represented in the hippocampus. The environment itself may be represented in the hippocampus, or only the locations of rewards or punishments. In the latter case, damage to the hippocampus would still lead to failure in most spatial tasks, since the animal's ability to locate reward or avoid punishment is the experimenter's primary source of information about its knowledge of the environment. In the next section I will briefly review recent studies of hippocampal unit activity in freely moving rats, with particular attention to results that suggest the computations the hippocampus might perform.

1 Recent Single-Unit Evidence on the Role of the Hippocampus in Spatial Memory

Andrew Speakman and I have recently studied the firing pattern of hippocampal place cells during different types of memory tasks (O'Keefe and Speakman 1987a). The recordings took place in a cue-controlled environment (see figure 1) where we could manipulate the spatial cues which the rat used to solve the task. At the beginning of each trial, the rat was confined to one of three arms of a four-arm + -shaped maze and allowed to observe the spatial cues spread around the testing environment. After a period of 30 or 60 seconds, the animal was allowed to choose the goal. The locations of the cues and the goal remained constant from trial to trial but were rotated by multiples of 90° relative to the laboratory. The place fields of hippocampal complex spike neurons were recorded within this environment and shown to relate primarily to the controlled spatial cues, although there was also evidence that some of these neurons were influenced by the static background cues (which were not being changed from trial to trial) as well.

In order to test the role of these cells in one-trial learning (or spatial working memory) we included trials during which the controlled spatial cues were shown to the animal at the beginning of the trial but were removed before it was allowed to make its choice. On these trials we could compare the place fields of the neurons in the start arm after the controlled cues were removed with those when the cues were present. Most of the neurons tested (27 of 30) exhibited a firing pattern which was similar during these two periods; the place cells either maintain the spatial representation as a memory trace or receive inputs from neurons which do so (see figure 2).

We next asked whether the representation of the environment which was activated during the perceptual periods (when the controlled cues were present) and was maintained during the memory periods (when the cues had been removed) was limited to the start arm of the maze or incorporated other areas as well. To test this we forced the animal to make a detour at the end of the memory period so that it had to enter a nongoal arm and remain there for 30 seconds before being allowed to choose the goal. Eleven of the twelve units tested in this way showed a significant correlation between the place fields recorded on the detour trials and those recorded on perceptual trials (see figure 4 for an example). We conclude that the process of retrieving the spatial representation of the start arm also retrieves the representation for the rest of the environment. The maintenance of appropriate place fields in the goal arm during memory periods is taken as further demonstration of this effect (see figure 2, unit D). An adequate computational model for the hippocampus must account for this "holistic" property.

Another property of the hippocampal cognitive map which the theory must address derives from the observation that place units can encode not only the animal's position relative to the controlled spatial cues but also the relationship of these cues to the background environmental cues not manipulated during the experiment. We noticed that the strength of the place field of some neurons varied with the orientation of the controlled cues relative to the fixed background environment. Figure 5 shows an example of this effect. The neuron is the same as shown in the center panels of figure 2. Although the firing was localized to the arm 90° anticlockwise from the goal irrespective of the goal location relative to the static background cues, the strength of the firing varied from a rate of 2.46 spikes per second in the hottest orientation (goal in the north) to 0.41 spike per second in the coolest orientation (goal in the south). The other two place units recorded at the same time showed a similar variation in firing rate as a function of the location of the controlled environment relative to the static background cues. (See figure 6.) These and similar findings in other animals provide evidence for the following:

• There is an influence of the static background cues on the firing of the units, and it interacts with the influence of the controlled cues.
• The influence of these background cues is exerted on several units at the same time and, by implication, on all the units representing an environment,
• The lower firing rate in some orientations of the controlled cue environment is due in part to the longer latency for the onset of the firing in the place fields in these orientations. It takes longer to set up the appropriate firing patterns with some orientations. For some units this time can be as long as 20 seconds.

UNIT FIRING RATE   55-2-3A'

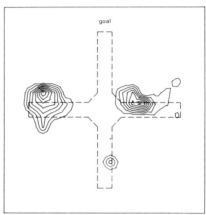

MEMORY (n: 19)   1.5 spikes/sec   PERCEPTUAL (n:24)   0.2 spikes/sec

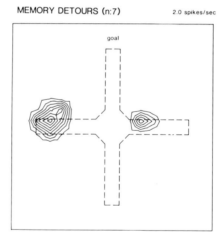

MEMORY DETOURS (n:7)   2.0 spikes/sec

Figure 4

Firing patterns of a place unit during memory detour trials. The two upper pictures show the pattern during perceptual and memory periods, respectively. The lower picture shows the pattern during the detours. These periods were taken from trials which were identical to working memory trials except that the animal was not allowed to run to the goal at the end of the usual memory periods but instead was forced into a nongoal arm for an additional period. The cell fired with the appropriate pattern on these trials, indicating that the exposure to the controlled cues at the start of the trial had set up the firing pattern for the entire maze and not just for the start arm.

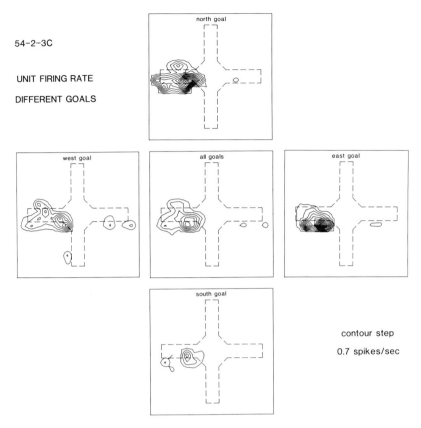

Figure 5

An example of the influence of the orientation of the controlled cues with respect to the static background cues on the firing rate but not the firing pattern of a place cell. The cell is one of those shown in figure 2 (54-2-3C). The firing rate for all orientations is shown in the center panel. For all orientations, the goals have been rotated to the top of the panel.

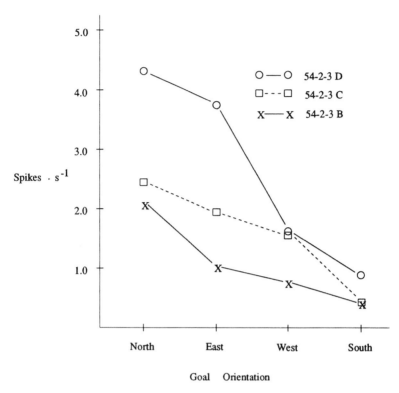

Figure 6
Graph of the firing rates of three units as a function of goal orientation. The units are those whose fields are shown in figure 2. Each rate is for the arm containing the place field. Notice that the rate decreases with goal location in a similar way for the three units.

• One reason that firing in the north or the east goal orientation is higher may be that the rats enter the environment on each trial with that orientation in mind; this is the default orientation. If the controlled cues match this pre-ferred orientation, then it is maintained. If not, then the representation is manipulated to bring it into register with the actual cue orientation *or* sev-eral other representations are searched until the appropriate one found. In either case, the "correct" representation is latched and maintained even after removal of the controlled cues. The existence of a default or preferred repre-sentation is confirmed by the pattern of unit activity when the rats were placed into the environment without the controlled cues. On these control trials, the place fields maintained the appropriate relationship to the maze configuration (i.e., they continued to fire in a small area, such as at the end of one of the four arms), but as might be expected these fields were not related to the controlled cues. They varied from trial to trial in location, but in general they were oriented with respect to a goal in the North or the East arm. At the end of each control trial, the animal chose as its goal the arm that was appropriate to the representation of the environment encoded in the hippocampus during that trial.

• Although the representation predicted the animal's behavior (it went to the arm designated as goal in that representation), the cells were not signaling the intended motor response. This was shown in experiments (O'Keefe and Speakman 1987b) in which the location of the goal was changed halfway through the recording session and the animal retrained to the new goal. Under these circumstances, most of the place cells maintain their fields in relation to the controlled cues and do not change to reflect the relocation of the goal. We assume that the animal can use its map to calculate the location of the goal, but that the location of the goal is not represented within the hippocampus itself (at least not as a major influence on the firing patterns of CA1 neurons).

The ability of prominent distal stimuli to control the orientation of a place field within an environment was also shown by Muller et al. (1987), who recorded place cells while rats were chasing food pellets in a cylinder which was undifferentiated except for a white card on one part of the wall. In their study, place fields maintained a constant relation to the cue card when it was rotated, and they maintained this orientation relative to the last position of the card after its removal. The results of O'Keefe and Speakman and those of Muller et al. are equivalent despite differences in experimental details.

2 Computations the Hippocampus Might Perform

The single-unit and lesion studies summarized above give us some indication of the types of information available to the hippocampus and the types of operations performed there or in adjacent areas. In the absence of information about these adjacent areas, the actual transformations occurring in the hippocampus can only be guessed at. In this section I will make explicit the operations which I believe are carried out in the hippocampus on the inputs it receives.

2.1   The Representation of an Environment Is Distributed across Large Numbers of Neurons in the Hippocampus

I have discussed elsewhere the evidence that the representation of an environment is distributed across the hippocampus (O'Keefe 1985). In addition, it is clear that the same cells can participate in the representation of numerous environments (Kubie and Ranck 1983). If we assume that all the synapses of a neuron are activated when the neuron fires, it follows that the same synapses can participate in the representation of different environments. In this chapter I will assume that the distributed nature of the hippocampal representation is a fundamental and not an incidental aspect of the function of the hippocampus, and that this method of representation is different from that found in the neocortex (including those parts of the neocortex that provide the sensory inputs to the hippocampus via the entorhinal cortex). On this view, the neocortical representations are topographic, being mapped onto the receptor surfaces or egocentric taxon spaces which travel with the animal as it moves. The transform to a distributed representation is assumed to take place at the entorhinal cortex or between the entorhinal cortex and the dentate gyrus. Several aspects of this distributed representation should be noted.

The distributed nature of the representation is assumed to result from the way that the representation is built up during exploration and from the nature of the encoding processes within the hippocampus. In turn, it allows the hippocampus to minimize metabolic functions by allowing it to operate with low firing rates and to transform global operations into local ones. An incidental benefit of the distributed nature of the representations is that they are relatively resistant to degradation after localized or distributed physical damage to the hippocampus.

One of the major differences between representing an egocentric space and a nonegocentric one is the higher levels of uncertainty involved in the latter. In egocentric spaces the frame within which the representation must fit is known and remains relatively constant and predictable. For example, the location of a visual stimulus on the retinal surface is constrained in advance. Exactly the opposite pertains to the mapping of an environment. When an animal enters a new environment, there is no pre-established isomorphic framework. The animal does not know how large the environment will be, how much information it will contain (in terms of complexity), and how much time it will have in which to map it. It may have considerable leisure in which to do so, or it may have to flee after a short time (for example, if it is disturbed or senses a predator). All these considerations suggest that the best strategy for maximizing the amount of information about an environment would be to store the representation as a set of connected vectors each consisting of a pattern of activity across a large number of pyramidal cells. As each new vector comes in, it is compared with the previous vector and the difference is stored in the same set of neurons. The first inputs differentiate the present environment from some subset of previously stored maps; each new input further restricts the subset. Less information about the environment is stored with each successive vector as the animal moves through the environment, since it is being differentiated from fewer and fewer stored representations.

Since groups of neighboring cells represent the entire environment, calculations and constraints relating to the entire environment can be done on a local basis. For example, if the system is designed to minimize the total firing rate, this can be accomplished piecemeal through the inhibitory interaction of neighboring cells. Similarly, the information about translocation from one part of an environment to another might only involve short-distance interactions among neighboring neurons.

2.2 The Representation Is Nondirectional

I assume that the finding in some experiments that the firing of some of the place cells is relatively independent of the direction in which the animal points in the place field indicates that this computation is made before or at the earliest stages of the hippocampus. One way in which this could be accomplished is by taking the equivalent of the autocorrelation of the sensory pattern. This has the effect of freeing the pattern from a particular location within a spatial framework while preserving the internal spatial relationships between the elements of the pattern intact. An alternative would be to associate the different views of an environment from a particular location with one another. It is important to note that in some environments (e.g., the radial-arm maze used in McNaughton et al. 1983) many of the place cells have strongly preferred directions. One possibility is that tactile and olfactory intramaze cues might act as nondirectional cues with which the more directional auditory and visual extramaze cues are associated.

2.3 Memories for Environments Are Stored in the Hippocampus or in a Neighboring Area

Place-field firing remains appropriate after the removal of the relevant spatial cues (see above). Speakman and I have suggested that, rather than representing *de novo* associations formed on each trial, this memory might result from the activation of the previously formed map for that configuration or the manipulation of a paradigmatic map into the "best-fit" configuration. In either case, this best-fit representation is maintained after the relevant information is removed, and this must depend on neural changes. Other neural changes would include those through which different sensory inputs occurring in the same place in an environment are associated with one another and the changes involved in the mechanism by which different places in an environment are connected together via the appropriate distance and direction vectors.

At present there is no hard evidence that any of these neural changes take place in the hippocampus or that they all involve the same underlying mechanisms. It would appear that the basis for the prototype or default map involves relatively long-lasting synaptic changes whereas the changes involved in the modifications of working memory might be more short-lived. Although we have no neurophysiological data on the time course of this latter change, Conway and I have shown that in behavioral tasks well-tained rats can remember the appropriate goal location for each trial for as long as 30 minutes after a 30-second exposure to the controlled cues (O'Keefe and Conway 1980).

The plasticity of hippocampal synapses has been studied intensively (Andersen and Hvalby 1986; Bliss and Lomo 1973; McNaughton 1983). For the purposes of this chapter, let us assume that some such mechanism operates during the construction of the default map. Whether the association formed is between inputs representing different cues or between an input and a framework will be considered below.

2.4 The Representation of an Environment Is Holistic

Physiological and behavioral evidence supports the notion that the matrices representing the different places in an environment are connected together to form a map. The crucial findings are that retrieving the representation of part of an environment retrieves the entire representation and that influences on the firing patterns of the place cells are similar across the entire environment. As was mentioned above, the firing rates of hippocampal units in their place fields varies with the orientation of the controlled cues to the static background cues. Regardless of the cause of this effect, the fact that it applies equally to different units and to the different fields of the same unit suggests that it reflects a global influence and not a local one. It is possible that, in addition to being part of the representation of a particular place or set of places within an environment, each place cell might also signal the entire environment. On this view, the firing field of a place cell may simply be the peak of a continuous intracellular process that codes for the entire environment. As an animal moved around a familiar environment, the membrane potential of a place cell would vary in a consistent and repeatable pattern but only those patches of an environment associated with a suprathreshold depolarization would be signaled by action potentials. Kubie and Ranck (1983) have shown that the overall rate of out-of-field firing varies from one environment to another and have suggested that this may signal the behavioral or motivational context in which the place field firing occurs. The present suggestion is that all hippocampal-complex spike-cell activity is spatially coded but that much of it is normally below firing threshold. One possibility (which will not be explored further in this chapter) is that the firing thresholds of these cells are variable and can be manipulated as part of the search for the best representation of an environment.

2.5 The Motive for Building Maps Is a Cognitive One

Andrew Speakman and I have recently shown that the representation of an environment is not altered by relocation of the goal (O'Keefe and Speakman 1987b). Although the evidence is less direct, it is also unlikely that biological motivations such as reduction of hunger or thirst are the basis for map construction. Rather, the motivation may be the cognitive one of curiosity (O'Keefe and Nadel 1978). Translated into computational terms, this means that the construction of the map of an environment must be guided by principles such as the ability of the representation to predict the subsequent inputs on the basis of the current inputs and parameters internal to the representation itself. I will suggest that one of these goodness-of-fit parameters concerns the relative or absolute firing rates in cell clusters in the hippocampus. These may act as energy functions which the system tries to minimize.

2.6 One Function of the Hippocampus May Be to Manipulate the Default Representation of an Environment to Reduce the Disparity between It and the Incoming Sensory Data

One interpretation of the time delays in setting up the appropriate representation in the spatial working memory trials in the cue-controlled environment task is that the hippocampus needs time to manipulate the default representation to get it to match the present environment. The manipulations that may be performed include filtering, rotation, dilation, and translation. On this view, the hippocampus is a system for the manipulation of matrices which represent environments. I will suggest that the distributed nature of the representation may facilitate these types of manipulations.

2.7 The Representation of Time in the Hippocampus

Unpublished observations by Speakman and me suggest that the strength of the place fields is systematically reduced with repeated trials in the spatial working memory task. This might form the basis for temporal discriminations in which rats are required to judge the relative recency of entry into one of the two arms in the Olton eight-arm maze (Kesner and Novak 1981). Since each place in an environment is postulated to be represented by an equal number of neurons firing at roughly comparable overall rates, a comparison of integrated rates would provide an indication of the relative recency with which the places had been visited.

3   A Computational Model for a Cartesian Navigational System

My purpose in this section is to update the computational model of the Cartesian Navigational System presented in O'Keefe and Nadel 1978 on the basis of the data summarized in the preceding sections. The basic assumptions are the following:

• The brain uses several systems for moving from one part of an environment to another, one of which involves a metric coordinate space (probably Cartesian) in which stimuli are located. Other systems, lumped together under the general category of taxon systems, include an orientation system (see also O'Keefe 1983) that enables an animal to learn the sequence of body turns to specific stimuli and a guidance system that enables an animal to approach or avoid specific cues. Ranck et al. (1987) have discovered a set of directional units in the postsubiculum (or dorsal presubiculum), and I propose that a directional system be included in the above scheme as well.

• The Cartesian mapping system consists of a space within which the coordinates of the stimuli experienced within an environment can be stored and several mechanisms for operating on these stored representations. The first of these mechanisms is one for transforming the information about the stimulus array that is contained in the neocortical sensorium and probably transmitted to the mapping system through the entorhinal cortex. I will assume that these taxon representations are located in an egocentric coordinate frame of the sort shown in figure 7, where the stimulus quality (Q) is identified and the angle (α) within a body-centered (or head-centered) framework is given but the distance of the stimulus from the animal (R) is not. A second mechanism allows maps to be manipulated so as to bring them into correspondence with the present sensory array. A third mechanism allows the representation of the current location to be compared with the representation of a desired location and the translation required to move between the two calculated.

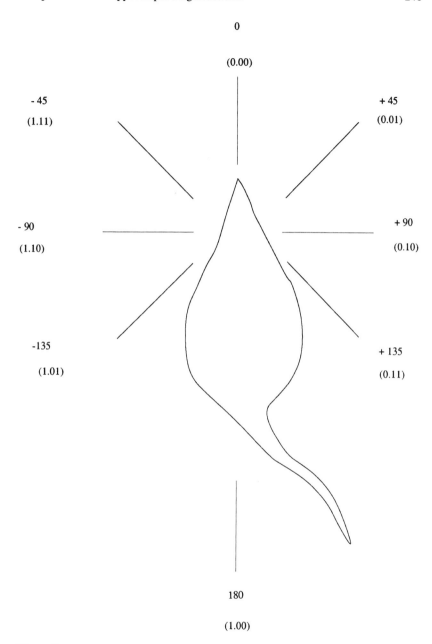

Figure 7
Head-centered axes for locating a stimulus in egocentric space. The upper number gives the angle in degrees; the lower number (in parentheses) gives the angle in binary notation. Locations on the left side of the head are given as negative angles; these are represented in binary notation as the twos complement of the equivalent positive angle.

In this section I will first characterize the representation of an environment within the hippocampus and then discuss the mechanisms by which it can be manipulated and "read."

3.1 The Representation of an Environment within the Cartesian Mapping System

The way in which the taxon systems in the neocortex represent stimuli is shown in figure 7, as is the mode of representing angles in binary notation. As can be seen in the figure, angles on the left side of the head/body axis are represented by negative numbers, which in turn are represented in twos-complement notation. The mapping system transforms the individual stimulus representations of the taxon system into an integrated set of x,y coordinates. It could do this by assigning to each stimulus an appropriate distance (R) and the angle (α) given by the taxon system and then converting these to rectangular coordinates using the following formulas:

$Y = R \cos\alpha,$
$x = R \sin\alpha.$

In this scheme, the representation of an environment would be given by the matrix representing the X,Y coordinates of the stimuli. Figure 8 shows the representation of an environment with three objects: A, B, and C. The matrix representing the objects in homogeneous coordinate form is

$$\begin{bmatrix} -1 & 1 & 1 \\ 2 & 2 & 1 \\ 1 & -2 & 1 \end{bmatrix}.$$

In homogeneous coordinate form, the pairs of numbers in columns 1 and 2 represent the X and Y coordinates of the three objects and the numbers in column 3 represent projection and scaling factors. In figure 8 the reference axes are centered on the rat's head, but this is not necessary. It is the relationship between the objects that defines the environment, not their relationship to a particular set of axes. This is important since it allows the coordinate axes to be altered without changing the representation of the environment. As an animal moves around an environment, it constantly recalculates the location of the stimuli in that environment. I imagine this is done by shifting the axes of the coordinate frame so that it remains centered on the animal's head. In a Cartesian system this is easily accomplished by multiplication of the matrix representing the stimuli by a transform matrix representing the rotation and translation produced by the movement. Figure 9 shows an ex-

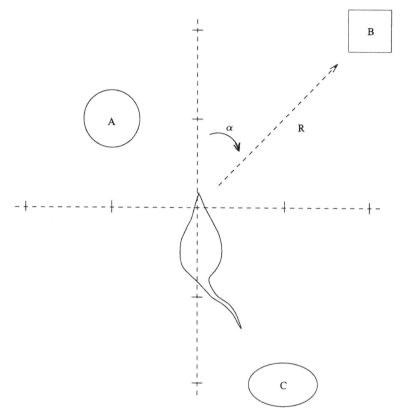

Figure 8
Cartesian axis framework centered on rat's head and location of objects A, B, and C within it. R represents the distance to object B in polar coordinates; α represents the angle.

ample of a movement, and figure 10 shows the changes in the position of the objects as a result of that movement. The appropriate change in the matrix representing the object locations in the head-centered framework is achieved by matrix multiplication of the current matrix (**C**) by the transform matrix (**T**). In matrix notation,

$$\mathbf{C} \qquad \cdot \qquad \mathbf{T} \qquad = \qquad \mathbf{N}$$

$$\begin{bmatrix} -1 & 1 & 1 \\ 2 & 2 & 1 \\ 1 & -2 & 1 \end{bmatrix} \cdot \begin{bmatrix} 0 & -1 & 0 \\ 1 & 0 & 0 \\ 2 & -2 & 1 \end{bmatrix} = \begin{bmatrix} 3 & -1 & 1 \\ 4 & -4 & 1 \\ 0 & -3 & 1 \end{bmatrix}.$$

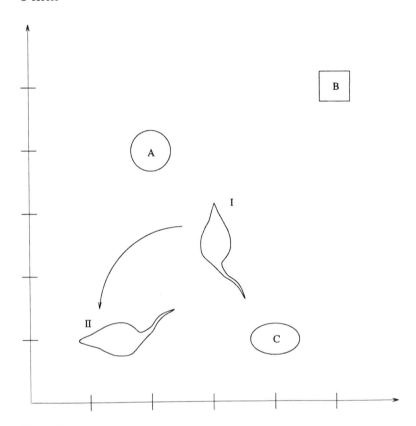

Figure 9
The movement from position I to position II within the environment.

The transform matrix is made up of several factors. The 2 × 2 matrix in the upper left rotates the axes by the required angle:

$$\begin{bmatrix} \cos\alpha & -\sin\alpha & \cdot \\ \sin\alpha & \cos\alpha & \cdot \\ \cdot & \cdot & \cdot \end{bmatrix}.$$

The 2 × 1 row matrix in the lower left produces the translation

$$\begin{bmatrix} \cdot & \cdot & \cdot \\ \cdot & \cdot & \cdot \\ -X & -Y & \cdot \end{bmatrix}.$$

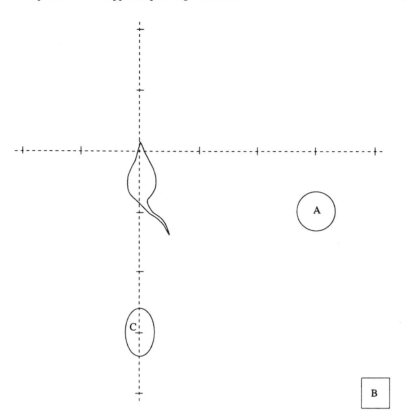

Figure 10
The new locations of the three objects in the rat's rotated and shifted framework after
the movement.

The 1 × 2 column matrix on the right projects the matrix onto the Z axis:

$$\begin{bmatrix} \cdot & \cdot & 0 \\ \cdot & \cdot & 0 \\ \cdot & \cdot & \cdot \end{bmatrix}.$$

The 1 × 1 matrix in the lower right corner scales the representation globally:

$$\begin{bmatrix} \cdot & \cdot & \cdot \\ \cdot & \cdot & \cdot \\ \cdot & \cdot & s \end{bmatrix}.$$

Although I have represented the X and Y coordinates in digital form, I assume that they are represented in the nervous system by a pattern of firing across fibers. Furthermore, I assume that in most natural environments many more than the three stimuli represented in figures 8–10 will be encoded within the map of that environment. Notice that the matrix transformations which rotate and translate the reference frame can operate in parallel (as shown above) or in sequence. In the section on the hippocampal model (section 6), I will assume that the two operations are performed sequentially, the reference frame being first rotated and then translated.

3.2   Generation of the Inverse Matrix to Guide Behavior

Once a map of an environment has been established, it can be used not only to predict the changes in location of objects as the rat moves around a familiar environment but also to generate the translations and rotations necessary to move from the current location to a desired location. One way to do this is to make use of the inverse matrix (Zipser 1986). In this section I will show how the present model does this. I assume that during exploration of a new environment or during patroling of a familiar environment, encounters with incentives are treated differently from other stimuli even if the animal is not deprived or biologically motivated. For example, the locations of edible and potable objects are noted. These locations are probably stored outside the hippocampus, since there is no evidence for a differential encoding of "goal" or potential "goal" locations by the hippocampal place cells.

These incentive coordinates are stored in other limbic areas, which can be accessed not only by the mapping system but also by inputs from "motivational" systems or from the temporal circadian clocking systems of the hypothalamus. In this way, coordinates corresponding to the location of (e.g.) food can be retrieved and sent to the hippocampus when the animal is hungry or when it is time to eat. The transform required to reach the desired location can be calculated by multiplying the desired location matrix by the inverse of the current location matrix:

$$C^{-1} \cdot N = T,$$

where C^{-1} stands for the inverse of matrix C.

In the example of figures 8–10, let us assume that the rat has noticed food at its second location II and has stored that location in its incentive file. Finding itself at location I again at lunchtime, it need only carry out the inverse calculation,

$$\mathbf{C} \;=\; \begin{bmatrix} -1 & 1 & 1 \\ 2 & 2 & 1 \\ 1 & -2 & 1 \end{bmatrix}$$

$$\mathbf{C}^{-1} \;=\; \frac{1}{11} \begin{bmatrix} -4 & 3 & 1 \\ 1 & 2 & -3 \\ 6 & 1 & 4 \end{bmatrix}$$

and then multiply this by the desired matrix at location II,

$$\begin{array}{ccccc} \mathbf{C}^{-1} & \cdot & \mathbf{N} & = & \mathbf{T} \end{array}$$

$$\frac{1}{11} \begin{bmatrix} -4 & 3 & 1 \\ 1 & 2 & -3 \\ 6 & 1 & 4 \end{bmatrix} \cdot \begin{bmatrix} 3 & -1 & 1 \\ 4 & -4 & 1 \\ 0 & -3 & 1 \end{bmatrix} = \begin{bmatrix} 0 & -1 & 0 \\ 1 & 0 & 0 \\ 2 & -2 & 1 \end{bmatrix},$$

in order to generate the transform matrix required to get back to the desired location. I will discuss in more detail below the operations necessary to generate the inverse transform and the way in which the transform matrix might be used by the neural areas that generate motor programs.

3.3 Construction of a Cartesian Representation of an Environment during Exploration

When an animal such as a rat enters an environment, its cognitive mapping system searches for a representation that captures the spatial features of the sensory input. Let us assume that the animal is placed in a novel environment and therefore has no existing representation.

On the present model, exploration consists in the calculation of the correct R values for each stimulus Q so that it can be combined with the egocentric angles α to yield an accurate Cartesian location. The process, shown in block-diagram form in figure 11, will be described in this section.

At any given location in an environment, the sensory cues impinging upon an animal can be allocated an α within the animal's egocentric space in accordance with the scheme shown in figure 7. In order to locate an object or a cue in a Cartesian-like space, it is necessary to assign a distance measure (R) as well as an angle (α) to each cue. I will assume that for unknown cues this is not done on the basis of size or intensity but is calculated by the hippocampal system during exploration. In fact, exploration of a novel environment can be viewed, on the present theory, as the behavior designed to calculate the R's for the cues in that environment. As we have already seen, on each

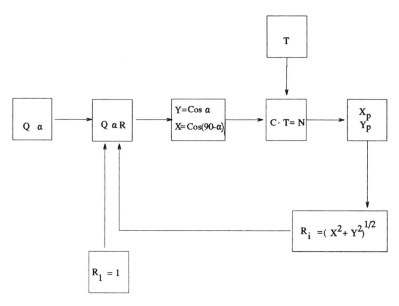

Figure 11

Block diagram of the computational process for calculating the correct R's during exploration of an environment. The stimuli enter from the left and are specified by a quality (Q) and an angle (α) in egocentric space. These are combined with the calculated distance (R) of each stimulus from the previous cycle in the second stage and converted into Cartesian coordinates in the third. In order to calculate the expected new coordinates resulting from each movement the current matrix (C) is multiplied by the movement-derived transform (T) to give a matrix specifying the new X and Y coordinates of each stimulus. These are converted to polar coordinates using the hypothenuse rule, and the new calculated distance is fed back to the second stage, where it enters the calculation for the next cycle. R is arbitrarily set to 1.0 at the beginning of exploration.

cycle the matrix specifying the location of the cues in the environment is transformed on the basis of the direction and distance matrix to produce the new coordinates of the same cues. Since the R's of the cues in a novel environment are not known, they are initially estimated. In the present example they are all set to 1.0. These values and the veridical α's are fed into the hippocampus, where they are converted to the corresponding x and y coordinates. During the exploratory movement, the hippocampus combines these rectangular coordinates with the transform representing the rat's displacement to produce a prediction of the resulting coordinates in the new set of axes. It does this by multiplying the current matrix by the transform. In the early stages of exploration there will inevitably be large disparities between the predicted R's and the actual R's depending on the actual distances of the cues and the direction and distance of the rat's movement relative to them. After the first cycle, the system updates the estimated R's by substituting the calculated R's and combining them with the new input α's. Over a series of cycles, this process leads to successively closer approximations to the actual distances R. Furthermore, it may be possible for the system to use the discrepancy between predicted and experienced angles to guide exploratory behavior to acquire the maximum information on each movement.

As an example of the operation of this process, let us follow the changes in coordinates and the concomitant hippocampal computations during the first exploratory movements of our rat in the environment shown in figure 9. These are listed in table 1, which is divided into three parts. The actual physical locations of the objects A, B, and C in a framework centered on the animal's head are represented in Cartesian and equivalent polar coordinates on the left side of the table, the computations performed by the hippocampal system are shown in the middle of the table, and the differences between the actual and the computed distances of the cues are shown on the right.

At location I, a value of 1.0 is assigned to each object and combined with the egocentric angle (α) to give a calculated set of polar coordinates for each stimulus (column headed *New (polar)*). In order to compute the effects of movement (I→II), these coordinates are converted into rectangular coordinates and represented as the current matrix (arrows from *New polar* column to *Current* column). This is multiplied by the transform matrix generated by the motor programming system to yield the predicted *New* matrix and the equivalent *New (polar)* coordinates. As can be seen in the $\Delta\alpha$ column, the predicted angles differ from the actually perceived angles and this information is available to the animal to be used for guiding exploration. The new *Current* cue location matrix is derived from the calculated distance of the cues (R) and their experienced angles (input α's). These are fed back to form the input stage for the next movement computation and the cycle recurs.

The right side of the table contains information about the differences between the actual distances of the cues and the calculated distances. *RM* is the distance mismatch of each cue, and *RR* is the sum of the relative mismatches. *RM* is calculated by dividing each mismatch by the actual distance to get a relative mismatch and summing across the absolute values of these at each location. It can be seen that the value of *RR* decreases with each cycle as the calculated distances move closer to the actual cues.

In the case of a familiar environment in which the location of an object has

Table 1

Location	Environment Cartesian X	Y	Polar R	α	Current	Transform	New	New (polar) R	α	Input α	Δα	Σ|Δα|	RM	RR
I														
a)	-1	1	1.41	-45°				1.0	-45°	-45°			-0.29	
b)	2	2	2.83	45°				1.0	45°	45°			-0.65	
c)	1	-2	1.73	153°				1.0	153°	153°			-0.42	0.45
I → II					$\begin{bmatrix} -0.71 & 0.71 & 1.0 \\ 0.71 & 0.71 & 1.0 \\ 0.45 & -0.89 & 1.0 \end{bmatrix}$	$\begin{bmatrix} 0 & -1 & 0 \\ 1 & 0 & 0 \\ 2 & -2 & 1 \end{bmatrix} =$								
II	3	-1	3.16	108°			$\begin{bmatrix} 2.71 & -1.29 & 1.0 \\ 2.71 & -2.71 & 1.0 \\ 1.11 & -2.45 & 1.0 \end{bmatrix}$	3.0	115°	108°	+7°		-0.05	
	4	-4	5.66	135°				3.83	135°	135°	0°		-0.32	
	0	-3	3.00	180°				2.69	155.6°	180°	-24.4°	31.4°	-0.10	0.16
								3.0	108°					
								3.83	135°					
								2.69	180°					
II → III					$\begin{bmatrix} 2.85 & -0.93 & 1.0 \\ 2.71 & -2.71 & 1.0 \\ 0.0 & -2.69 & 1.0 \end{bmatrix}$	$\begin{bmatrix} 0.707 & 0.707 & 0 \\ -0.707 & -0.707 & 0 \\ 0 & -4.0 & 1 \end{bmatrix} =$								
III	2.83	-2.59	3.83	132.4°			$\begin{bmatrix} 2.67 & -2.64 & 1.0 \\ 3.83 & -4.00 & 1.0 \\ 1.42 & -5.90 & 1.0 \end{bmatrix}$	3.76	134.7°	132.4°	-2.3°		-0.02	
	5.66	-4.00	6.93	125.2°				5.54	136.2°	125.2°	11.0°		-0.20	
	2.12	-6.12	6.48	160.9°				6.07	166.5°	160.9°	6.4°	19.7°	-0.06	0.09
								3.76	132.4°					
								5.54	125.2°					
								6.07	160.9°					

Table 1

Coordinates and computations at three locations during exploration of a novel environment. The left side of the table gives the actual locations of three objects (A, B, and C) within the rat's head-centered framework as the animal moves successively among locations I, II, and III. Locations I and II correspond to those shown in figure 9. Both the Cartesian coordinates and their equivalent polar coordinates are listed.

been changed, the criterion would also direct the animal's behavior toward the altered stimulus.

One of the predictions of this analysis is that changes in the size of cues should not elicit exploration. Muller et al. (1987) reported that cutting a cue card in half did not change the place fields in their environment. On the other hand, changes in the angle between cues in an environment should have a large effect. This would probably be apparent only in environments in which the cues had been reduced to a small number. The difficulty here is that in most environments the number of cues is large and a change in any two may not be sufficient to alter the place-cell firing pattern. We are hoping that extensions of the cue-controlled environment will enable us to force the animal to use only a small number of cues to locate itself.

At any given location in an environment, only some of the stimuli in that environment will be available to the animal. In large environments some stimuli will be too distant and faint to be perceived. In most environments some stimuli will be occluded by obstructions (other stimuli). Representations of these stimuli are all incorporated into the map of the environment with the appropriate distance calculations, and can be retrieved by subsets of the total representation (i.e., those stimuli available to the animal at any part of the environment). One corollary of this idea is that there is rarely a perfect match between the input sensory data and the stored representation of an environment. Therefore, criteria for accepting less-than-perfect matches must be available.

The discovery by Ranck (1983, 1987) of directional neurons in the postsubiculum suggests that the inputs from the entorhinal cortex might also be used for this calculation. One possibility is that only those stimuli assigned very large R's by the mapping system are routed to the direction system. By definition, movements within an environment would not produce changes in the location of these stimuli or their relation to one another. This would appear to be a simpler method for constructing a direction system than to rely on calculations based on proximal stimuli. See O'Keefe and Nadel 1978, pp. 73–74, for further discussion of the role of distant cues in direction finding.

3.4   The Procedure for Retrieving the Best Map for a Familiar Environment

When an animal enters an environment, it has no means of knowing *a priori* whether the environment is familiar or novel. It is reasonable to assume, therefore, that it engages in the same procedures in order to retrieve a familiar map as it does to construct it initially. In the case of a familiar environment, the activation of a map or a set of possible maps will generate a particular set of distances (R's) or several sets of distances in response to the input of the stimulus qualities (Q's) and egocentric angles (α's). In the case of the stored map, these calculated R's will enable the system to match the subsequent inputs and therefore achieve some criteria and be accepted as veridical. In the case of several maps being stored, the system has to be able to select among them. On the basis of the information available about the hippocampus, it appears that storage of several representations is probably distributed across the same set of neurons and synapses. In the present example this means that the maps that have the same set of stimuli share the same synapses and neurons, and that maps that share some stimuli also share synapses and neurons. The problem of retrieval then involves the selection of the stored map that fits best with the current sensory inputs. This is done in the same way in which the maps were originally constructed: by the assignment of R values to the Q input matrix. The system is assumed to generate a composite set of values for the R's based on the stored maps and then to rapidly choose among these on the basis of the difference between the estimated and actual R inputs. Once the best fit between the input $Q\alpha$ matrix and part of the stored $Q\alpha R$ matrix is found, the whole of the $Q\alpha R$ matrix has been activated on retrieval and can be used to guide behavior.

3.5   Manipulations of the Map of a Familiar Environment to Match the Incoming Sensory Array

One explanation for some of the results of the O'Keefe-Speakman (1987a) experiment is that upon entering the environment the animal activates a version of its map of the environment which is oriented in a particular way relative to the background cues. If the orientation of the controlled cues with respect to the background cues matches the "default" orientation, it is maintained. If there is a mismatch, the two maps are manipulated with respect to each other in order to bring them into correspondence. One possible such manipulation would involve the rotation of one map relative to the other. In terms of the present theory this would be accomplished by a rotation of the reference frame in a manner unconnected with changes of direction of the rat's head in the environment. In the extreme this would mean a rotation of the reference axis while the animal was stationary. More usually for the rat, it would involve a summation of this movement-independent axis rotation with the movement-related rotation described in the previous sections. In the section on the hippocampal model I will suggest that the mechanism for producing reference-frame rotations is the theta system. As we shall see, there are two relatively independent components to the theta system, one of which is movement-related and one of which is independent of movement. It is to the latter component that I will assign the function of behavior-independent map rotation. It should be noted that in an environment such as the $+-$ maze in the cue-controlled enclosure, the rotation of the map should be centered on the center of the environment. Whether this means that the animal can rotate the map only when it is in or near the center of such an environment or whether it can do so at a distance (from the end of an arm) I do not know.

4 Computations with Hippocampal Neurons

Neurons can be conceived as performing logical (Shepherd and Brayton 1987) or mathematical (Blomfield 1974) computations. In the present theory I envisage them as mathematical operators capable, individually or in combinations, of carrying out the calculations postulated in the preceding sections. Section 6 will suggest that the hippocampus and related areas (such as the entorhinal cortex, the subicular area, and the septum) are the parts of the brain that carry out these computations. In order to see how they might do this, it is first necessary to see what kinds of calculations could be performed by individual neurons or by small networks of neurons. I will start with simple calculations such as addition, multiplication, and trigonometric functions and go on to vector rotation, matrix multiplication, and matrix inversion. For these latter algorithms I will rely for ideas on recent work in the computational properties of parallel computers such as systolic array processors and wavefront array processors.

4.1 Arithmetic and Trigonometric Calculations
Langmoen and Andersen (1983) studied the additive properties of two afferent inputs onto different parts of the dendritic tree of CA1 pyramidal cells in hippocampal slices and found that the two inputs together gave less than the sum of the individual epsp's but that the nonlinearity was due to the concomitant inhibition. The use of inhibitory transmitter blockers resulted in a linear summation of the two inputs. The usual contribution of the inhibitory synapses was to reduce the sum by 10–20 percent depending on the membrane potential. It is not possible to draw too many conclusions from the latter figure, since it is recognized that in the slice inhibition is reduced to a greater extent than excitation.

The first computation suggested by figure 11 involves conversion from polar to rectangular coordinates:

$Y = R\cos\alpha,$
$X = R\cos(90 - \alpha).$

This involves the multiplication of a number by the cosine of an angle. It may also involve the subtraction of two numbers. In keeping with the suggestion made in section 3 that negative angles be represented by twos-complement notation, I suggest that two numbers are subtracted by taking the twos complement of the second and adding it to the first.

Cosine calculations are performed by taking advantage of the fact that neurons in the hippocampus are not strictly linear summating devices since they are gated by the theta-wave inputs from the medial septum and therefore have an analog component. It is known that the excitability of hippocampal neurons varies as a function of the local hippocampal theta wave (Rudell et al. 1980; see section 8.6 below). Thus, phase shifts in the temporal relations between the input to a neuron and the peak of its theta-wave excitability will effectively result in the multiplication of the input by the cosine of the phase shift.

Multiplication of two numbers, as is required for matrix multiplication, can be accomplished by one of several methods. If single neurons or small groups of neurons were capable of calculating logarithms, then they could first take the log of the two numbers, then add them, and finally take the antilog of the result. More probably the computation is done by a network of neurons in a fashion similar to that used in digital computers. Here two binary numbers are multiplied by shifting one a number of places to the left as a function of the number of places in the other. For example, to multiply 5 by 4

$$000101$$
$$\times 000100$$

involves shifting the top number by $(3 - 1 = 2)$ two places to the left to get $010100 = 20$. Multiplication by numbers other than multiples of 2 is accomplished by breaking the number into its component multiples of 2, shifting each separately, and adding the products—e.g., $5 \times 7 =$

000101	000101	000101
000100	000010	000001
shift 2R	shift 1R	no shift
010100 +	001010 +	000101

$$+001010$$
$$+000101$$
$$100011 = 35$$

The crucial operation then is the shift operation. This can be accomplished by a delay line where a particular number is delayed relative to another (if the number is represented as a sequence of firing in a single line) or by a lateral skewing or shift (if the number is represented as a pattern across a set of lines).

4.2 Cordic Processors

Many of the manipulations on the vectors representing stimulus locations involve the rotation and scaling of these vectors as the animal moves around the environment. As we saw in the preceding section, this can be accomplished by matrix multiplication. In this section I discuss a method for accomplishing this by successive approximation which does not use multiplication. This method involves the use of the Cordic operators introduced by Volder (1959) for the calculation of coordinate rotations using only addition, subtraction, and binary shift operations. The system receives input from an egocentric polar coordinate such as the one outlined in section 3 above and rotates the vector through a given angle using an iterative process on the rectangular coordinates of the vector. Three intermediate memory buffers are needed: one for storing the x coordinate of the vector, one for the y coordinate, and the third for the angle through which the vector must be rotated. At each step of the iteration, the vector is rotated by plus or minus a fixed angle and the new X and Y coordinates are calculated. The fixed series of rotation angles is chosen so that any angle of rotation (λ) can be approximated by the sum of the series:

$$\lambda = \xi_1\alpha_1 + \xi_2\alpha_2 + \cdots + \xi_n\alpha_n$$

where $\alpha_1 = 90°$ and where, for $i > 1$, $\alpha_i = \tan^{-1}2(2^{-i})$. The first few terms of this series are

$$\alpha_1 = 90°,$$
$$\alpha_2 = \tan^{-1}2^0 = 45°,$$
$$\alpha_3 = \tan^{-1}2^{-1} \approx 26.5°.$$

$\xi_i = +1$ or -1 depending on the current state of the angle register. If the angle in the register is positive, then $\xi = +1$; if the angle in the register is negative (or >1.0 in twos-complement notation), then $\xi = -1$.

The psuedo-rotations of the series are accomplished as follows: The initializing step rotates the vector by $+90°$ in the direction of the desired rotation. This is accomplished simply by swapping the X and Y coordinates:

$$Y_2 = \pm X_1,$$
$$X_2 = \pm Y_1.$$

In subsequent steps the Y and X registers are updated at each step by the formulas

$$Y_{i+1} = Y_i - \xi_i 2^{(2-i)} X_i$$

and

$$X_{i+1} = X_i + \xi_i 2^{(2-i)} Y_i.$$

These formulas state that the new Y coordinate is equal to the previous Y coordinate with the addition or subtraction (depending on the sign of ξ_i) of the previous X coordinate multiplied by $2^{(2-i)}$. The effect of this latter operation, when performed on a binary number, is to shift the term $2 - i$ places to the right. Thus, for example, for $i = 3$, $Y_4 = Y_3 + (X_3$ shifted one place to the right). The number of steps in the series is equal to the number of bits in each word (the level of accuracy).

Table 2 and figure 12 show the sequence of events in the rotation of a vector of 142° through an angle of $90° + 45° + 5.1625° + 1.406 = 142°$.

An alternative use of the Cordic processor is vectoring. In this mode, the X and Y coordinates of the vector are the inputs and the final output is the magnitude (R) and the angle (θ) of the vector. This may be the method by which the predicted R which is fed back to the input of the mapping system is computed from the current X and Y. One of the problems with the Cordic vector-rotating method is that it introduces a scaling factor which depends on the number of iterations in the calculation.

The factor K is equal to

$$\prod_{i=0}^{n-1} (1+2^{-2i})^{1/2}.$$

For example for the eight-bit figures used in the example, $K = 1.65$. For $i > 5$, $K \approx 1.65$.

This scaling factor artificially increases R and needs to be compensated either by division or by the incorporation of extra terms during the rotation. In this chapter it will be assumed that the compensation is performed either by synapse weighting or by interneuron division.

5 Matrix Manipulations

According to the present model, the hippocampus is primarily involved in the manipulation of matrices which represent an environment and the animal's location within that environment. Considerable work has been done recently on the way in which parallel computers might perform matrix operations such as convolutions or matrix multiplication. In this section I wish to discuss several aspects of parallel computers which I believe can teach us about the types of operations that can be expected from a parallel computational device

Table 2

Position	Rotation angle inc. $\xi = (+$ or $-)$	Angle register	X (binary)	Y (binary)	X	Y	R	R/R_1
I		0.1100101	0.0101110	1.1000101	0.3594	−0.4609	0.5845	1.00
	$\tan^{-1}\infty = (+)90.0$	−0.1000000	+1.1000101	−0.0101110				
II		0.0100101	1.1000101	1.1010010	−0.4609	−0.3594	0.5845	1.00
	$\tan^{-1}1 = (+)45.0$	−0.0100000	+1.1010010	−1.1000101				
III		0.0000101	1.0010111	0.0001101	−0.8203	0.1015	0.8266	1.41
	$\tan^{-1}2^{-1} = (+)26.5$	−0.0010010	+0.0000110	−1.1001011				
IV		1.1110011	1.0011101	0.1000010	−0.7734	0.5156	0.9295	1.59
	$\tan^{-1}2^{-2} = (-)14.0$	+0.0001001	−0.0010000	+1.1100111				
V		1.1111100	1.0001101	0.0101001	−0.8984	0.3203	0.9538	1.63
	$\tan^{-1}2^{-3} = (-)7.12$	+0.0000101	−0.0000101	+1.1110001				
VI		0.0000001	1.0001000	0.0011010	−0.9375	0.2031	0.9592	1.64
	$\tan^{-1}2^{-4} = (+)3.58$	−0.0000010	+0.0000001	−1.1111000				
VII		1.1111111	1.0001001	0.0100010	−0.9296	0.2656	0.9668	1.65
	$\tan^{-1}2^{-5} = (-)1.79$	+0.0000001	−0.0000001	+1.1111100				
VIII		0.0000000	1.0001000	0.0011110	−0.9375	0.2343	0.9663	1.65

Table 2
Cordic computations for the rotation of a vector 142° clockwise from +142° to +284° (−76°). The coordinates of the start (I), finish (VIII), and intermediate positions (II–VII) of the vector are listed in binary (X,Y) and Cartesian (X,Y) coordinates. Between each position is shown the angle of rotation (*rotation angle*), whether it is + or − (ξ), the change this causes to the *angle register*, and the Cordic computation that produces the rotation. Notice that the length of the vector (**R**) increases with each rotation except the first, and that the ratio of the rotated vector to its original value (**R/R₁**) rapidly approaches 1.65. Source: Volder 1959.

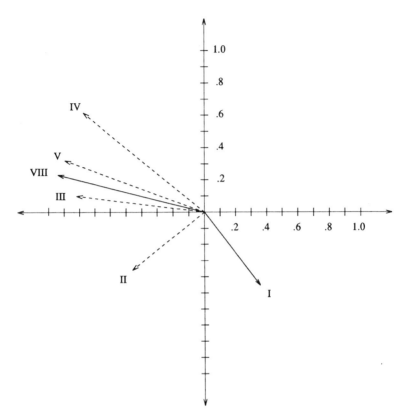

Figure 12
Stages in the rotation of a vector of 142° through an angle of 142°, as described in
the text and in table 2. The first (start) and eighth (finish) vectors are shown in solid
lines, and four intermediate vectors are shown in dashed lines. Note that the size of
the vector grows artificially with each step in the rotation. Source: Volder 1959.

such as the hippocampus. I will begin with a few general remarks and then
describe two types of architecture: the systolic array processor proposed by
H. T. Kung and his colleagues and the wavefront array processor proposed
by S. Y. Kung and his colleagues. My intention here is not to discuss these
from the engineering point of view but rather to extract principles which may
help us to understand the parallel processing networks of the brain.

The type of calculation that can most easily be performed on a parallel
processor is one that is equivalent to or can be reduced to a matrix operation,
for example matrix multiplication or the multiplication of a matrix by a vector. (See Gasson 1983 and Grossman 1984 for elementary introductions to

linear algebra.) This restriction is not particularly severe, since many of the calculations that interest signal-processing engineers and computational neuroscientists (Fourier transforms, convolution, correlation, finite and infinite impulse filters, pattern matching) can be reduced to matrix multiplication. I have proposed elsewhere (O'Keefe 1985) that the hippocampus stores information in a distributed or holographic form and considerable interest in convolution/correlation techniques for information storage and retrieval has been shown by psychologists (see, e.g., Murdock 1982; Eich 1982, 1985).

There are several types of architecture for the use of parallel processors in the performance of numerically intensive computations. The primary strategy is to identify those aspects of the algorithm that involve recursion and to perform these recursive calculations in parallel rather than in series. The second strategy is to minimize the number of transfers between memory and processing elements, thereby reducing considerably the total time involved in memory accesses. In doing this, as many operations as possible are performed on a piece of data once it has been retrieved from memory. Calculations are data-driven rather than instruction-driven. That is, they are performed as soon as the processor has the necessary data rather than being performed in a logical sequence.

The coupling of the independent processors (P.E.'s) can be done in one of two ways. In the first, there is a central clock which synchronizes their operation and forces them to perform each calculation at the same time. This can be the same calculation or execution of the same instruction at each P.E., or it can involve different operations at each processor. An alternative to this is to decentralize control of the processors and to allow each processor to operate from its own clock and to perform its own calculations as soon as it has sufficient data (see above). The processors can perform asynchronously, or the synchrony can be imposed upon them not by a clock but by the data flow itself. Since each P.E. must wait for the output of other P.E.'s, a pattern of data flow across the processors establishes a temporal organization of the whole. I will discuss an example of such an organization (a wavefront array processor) shortly.

In these parallel array processors, each processing element possesses a considerable degree of computational power. (This distinguishes this approach from some of the simpler connectionist models, such as the Perceptron or the Hopfield device.) In addition to an arithmetic and logic unit and several registers, each processor has a few kilobytes of on-board memory and facilities for communicating with several of its neighbors.

5.1 Systolic Array Processors

H. T. Kung has proposed that a set of processing elements could be connected into one or two dimensional arrays and that maximum use of the parallelism could be achieved by pumping either the data or the results through the array in much the way that the heart pumps blood through the body with each beat (hence "systolic"). Each datum is used in repeated calculations once it is retrieved from memory. Typically each processing element multiplies its current input with a stored weight or another input, adds the result to the output from the earlier processor in the chain, and passes its results to a later processor. Kung has suggested several ways in which different architectures of this general nature could be used to solve a range of problems. Let us look at his examples for systolic-array-processor configurations for the calculation of the convolution between a sequence of weights $(W_1, W_2, \ldots, W_k)$ and an input sequence $(X_1, X_2, \ldots, X_n)$ to produce an output sequence $(Y_1, Y_2, \ldots, Y_{n+1-k})$, where $Y_i = W_1X_i + W_2X_{i+1} + \ldots + W_kX_{i+k-1}$.

Arrays can differ in the way in which the weights and data are initially sent to the processors, the types of information passed from one processor to the next, and the manner in which the results (y's) are collected.

In the first design (figure 13) the weights are stored in the processor memory, each datum is broadcast to all of the elements, and the results are accumulated as they are passed from one processor to the next. At every clock tick, each processor multiplies its current input X by the stored weight, adds it to the accumulated y being passed from the processor on its left, and sends the result to the processor on its right. The results emerge from the last processor in the chain as a sequence of y's.

Instead of broadcasting each input to all the processors, the inputs can be pulsed from one processor to the next and the accumulation can be achieved by fanning in the outputs of the processors to an adder (figure 14).

In each of these designs the systolic movement (either of the partial result or of the data) is in the same direction: left to right. An alternative strategy would be to have the data pulsed from P.E. to P.E. in one direction (e.g. rightward) while the accumulating results are pulsed in the opposite direction (figure 15) and the weights remain in the processors. One disadvantage of this scheme is that the opposing streams meet each other only at every other processor (since they jump over each other at each cycle). This means that one stream (e.g. the data stream) must be delayed on every other cycle of the clock. The result is that only half of the processing elements are working on each cycle.

A final design also makes use of two streams with one moving at a different rate from the other. In this configuration (figure 16) the data stream pulses

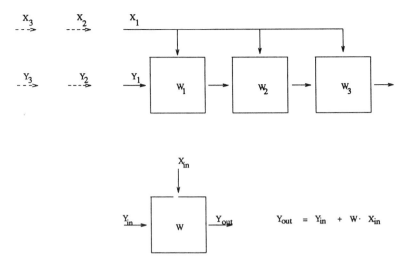

Figure 13
Systolic architecture for computing convolution between X's and W's. The X's are broadcast, the W's stay in each processor, and the Y's move from one processor to the next with each systole picking up the intermediate values as they go. The output of each processor is the input from the left-hand processor added to the product of the weight stored in that processor multiplied by the current X input. After figure 3 of H. T. Kung 1982.

one step with each clock cycle and the results stream pulses two steps. In consequence, the results stream effectively pulses past the data stream, picking up the accumulated results as it goes by.

These differing designs demonstrate several ways in which the same vector computations can be achieved using systolic architecture. In trying to apply these ideas to the understanding of hippocampal function, we will be alerted to look for several things:

• Systolic architectures of the type discussed rely on a central clock which synchronizes the activity of all the processors and ensures the order of movement of data through the array. If timing is an important factor, then care must be taken that the appropriate information arrives at each successive processor at the appropriate time. This either places constraints on the wiring between the processors or requires handshake protocols between neighboring processors so that operations are executed when the necessary data have been received. As we shall see shortly, it is possible to dispense with the central clock and allow a wavefront of operations to flow across the array if elaborate handshaking hardware is built into each processor.

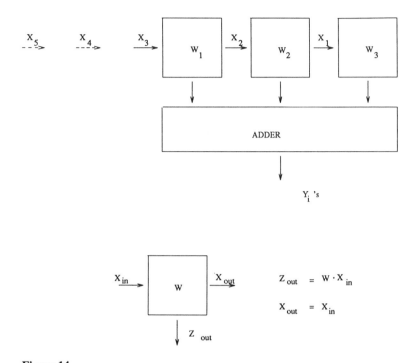

Figure 14
Systolic architecture in which the W's stay in each processor and the X's move systolically from one processor to the next. The results are obtained by summation across all the current outputs of the processors on each cycle. After figure 5 of H. T. Kung 1983.

• Calculations may involve constants which remain within each processor throughout the entire computation. This could be accomplished at a cellular level as well as at a synaptic level. For example, a constant level of hyperpolarization of the soma or a change in the spiking threshold could act as a constant divisor. At a synaptic level, there may be short-term synaptic changes that last only for the duration of each calculation.
• Data for the calculations may move in two streams at the same speed or at different speeds. If different speeds are employed, there may be neurons or neural circuits that have the specific role of introducing delays. Alternatively, delays may be achieved by differing conduction rates. Similarly, data may move in the same direction across the cellular array or they may move in opposite directions. If they move in opposite directions, it is important that the geometry of the circuitry be appropriate. As we shall see, it is possible that the mossy-fiber pathway is a carefully designed system for deliv-

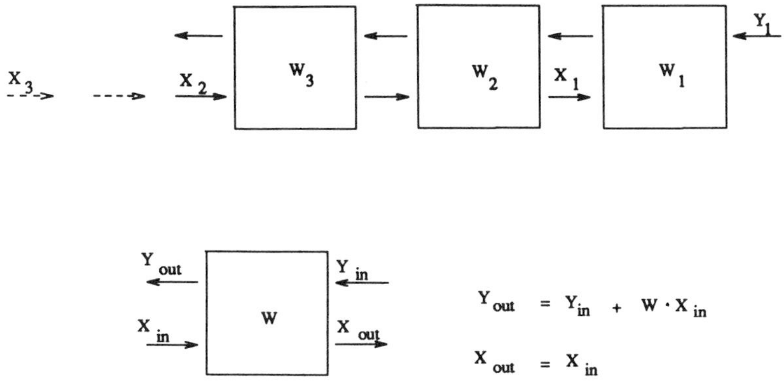
Y1
X3
X2
W3
W2
X1
W1
Y out
Y in
X in
W
X out
Y out = Yin + W · X in
X out = X in

Figure 15
Systolic architecture in which the weights remain in the processors and the *X*'s move from one processor to the next on each cycle. The results (*Y*) move in the opposite direction. After figure 8 of H. T. Kung 1982.

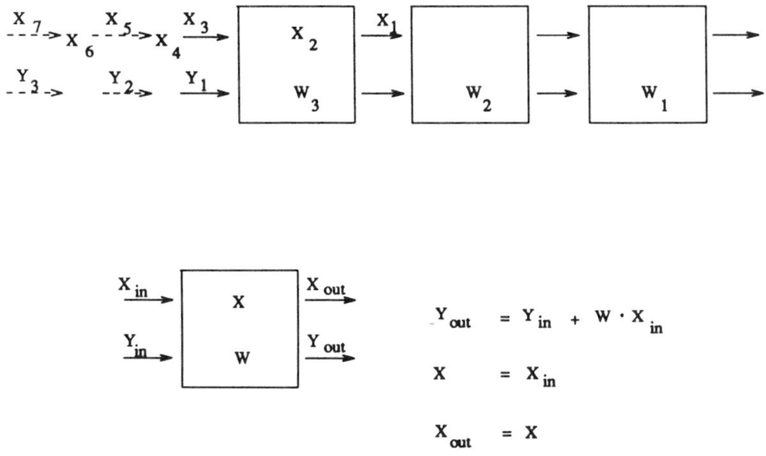
X7
X6
X5
X4
X3
X2
X1
Y3
Y2
Y1
W3
W2
W1
X in
Y in
X
W
X out
Y out
Y out = Y in + W · X in
X = X in
X out = X

Figure 16
Systolic architecture where the *W*'s remain in the processors and the *X*'s and *Y*'s move in the same direction but at different speeds. After figure 9 of H. T. Kung 1982.

ering the same sequence of data across the CA3a array in different directions.

In the next subsection I discuss a slightly more complicated two-dimensional systolic array in which the data moves across the array as a wavefront in the absence of a central clocking system.

5.2   The Concept of the Wavefront Array Processor

Two-dimensional arrays of processors in which each processor communicates with its four immediate neighbors can be used to solve a large number of matrix-based algorithms. S. Y. Kung et al. (1982) have developed a data-flow language for programming such an array so that the computation is broken down into a series of calculation waves which flow across the array (see figure 17). Each processor in a diagonal row operates on the same wavefront, which starts at the upper left processor and moves toward the lower right. No central clock is used, and the wavefront moves asynchronously under the control of the interprocessor handshake protocol. Although the wavefront proceeds in one direction, at the local level there can be data flow in directions other than that of the overall wavefront (for example, backward).

One of the strengths of the wavefront processor derives from the possibility of selectively delaying parts of the wavefront as it progresses through the array. Weiser and Davis (1981) have examined the way in which delay operators can be used to manipulate wavefronts. For example, if as a set of data elements $[A = a(1), a(2), \ldots, a(N - 1), a(N)]$ progresses through a set of processors delays are introduced as a function of N such that the $a(1)$ is not delayed, $a(2)$ is delayed one step, and $a(N)$ is delayed $N - 1$ steps, the effect will be to rotate the wavefront by 45° (figure 18). By such a technique, two wavefronts can be rotated until they reach some relation to each other—for example, until they are shifted 90° relative to each other. At this point the wavefronts can be systoled past each other, multiplying each set of data points at each step and summing the products on the diagonal to give a matrix multiplication.

In summary: The wavefront array processor calls attention to the way in which the ability to move a series of wavefronts through a set of processors can be used to manipulate the array as the computations are being performed. Array rotations as well as translations can be accomplished in this way.

MEMORY MODULES

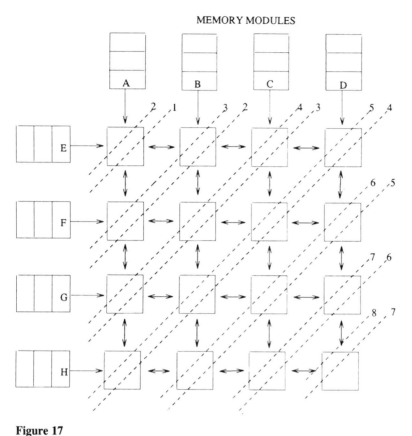

Figure 17
Wavefront array processor. The data are fed into the system from the memory modules at the top and along the left. The progression through the array of two waves of calculations at eight successive times is shown. At time $T = 1$, the upper left processor receives inputs from memory modules A and E. At time $T = 2$, the results from the upper left module are sent to the modules on the right and below, where they interact with inputs from their respective memory modules (B and F). New inputs are delivered to the upper left, where they form the first step in the second wave. The processes continues until both waves have moved through the array. After S. Y. Kung et al. 1982.

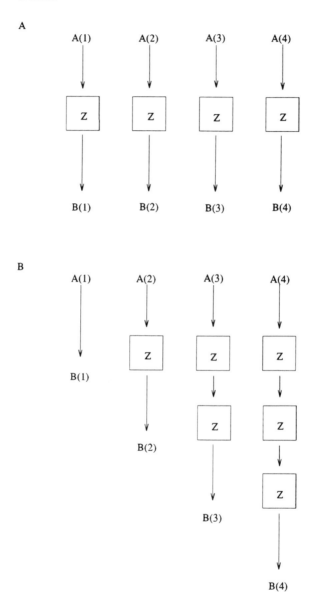

Figure 18
A: Delay lines (Z) interposed in an array. B: The use of different numbers of delays
in different parts of the array to rotate a vector as it moves through the array. After
figures 2-1 and 2-2 of Weiser and Davis 1981.

6   A Computational View of the Hippocampal System

In this section I will attempt to map the modular computational model presented in sections 3 and 4 onto the anatomy and physiology of the hippocampal system. First I will give an overview, then I will go into some of the computations in more detail. The model is summarized in figure 19.

Sensory inputs enter the hippocampus primarily through the entorhinal cortex, and it is there that I shall locate the module that receives the Q^α stimulus information derived from the neocortex and combines it with the distance estimate (R) calculated by the hippocampal system. This information is sent to the dentate gyrus via the perforant path and also to the CA3 and CA1 sectors of the hippocampus proper. The dentate, on this model, rotates the polar coordinates as a function of the animal's changes in direction and also transforms the polar coordinates into rectangular coordinates. In addition, it is one of the sites where delays can be imposed on parts of the matrix and where nonmovement matrix rotations can occur. The area CA3 takes the output of the dentate and multiplies it by the translation matrix derived from the animal's movements in order to predict the new x,y coordinate resulting from the movement. The CA3 area is also where an autoassociation matrix is formed. This allows any part of the sensory input pattern to recall the entire matrix for an environment. The CA3 field has several outputs: the CA1 field of the hippocampus, the lateral septum, and the entorhinal cortex (from the ventral hippocampus only). The CA1 field continues the matrix calculations and calculates the inverse (or pseudo-inverse) matrix of the current location. This information is passed to the subiculum, where it is combined with the stored coordinates of the desired locations (goals) to calculate the transform matrix necessary to move to that location. The transform matrix, in turn, is conveyed to the motor programming circuits in the posterior hypothalamus (particularly the mamillary bodies) via the fornix. In addition, it is sent to the deeper layers (4) of the entorhinal cortex and thence to the caudate nucleus, where it can also influence motor circuitry. The second major output of the CA3 field is directed to the lateral septum via the fimbria. The lateral septum, according to the present theory, acts as a control system that modulates the theta generating and synchronizing mechanism in the medial septum as a function of the state of the current location matrix in the CA3 field. I imagine that the current location matrix can be characterized both by its ability to match the incoming sensory stimuli and predict the ensuing inputs on the basis of present configuration and by some internal consistency parameters (such as the absolute global level of overall firing rates, or the changes in these levels from one moment to the next or from one part of the CA3 field

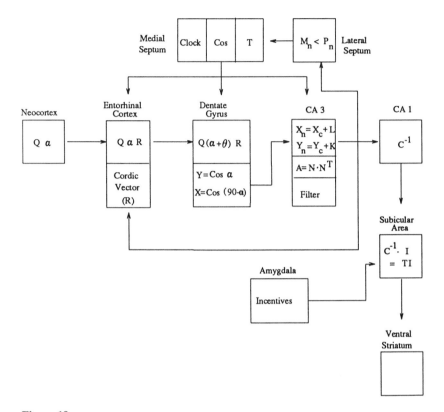

Figure 19
Block diagram of the computational model of the hippocampal system. The main
direction of information flow is from left to right, but there is a feedback of the
calculated distance R from the CA3 field to the entorhinal cortex. The qualities (Q)
and egocentric angles (α) of the stimuli enter the entorhinal cortex from the neocortex and there are combined with the calculated distances (R) fed back from the hippocampus. This information is sent (via the perforant path) to the dentate, where it is
rotated by the angle required to bring it into correspondence with the stored representation of the environment and where the x and y values are calculated. These, in
turn, are sent (via the mossy fibers) to the CA3 field, where they are shifted as a
function of the forward (K) and lateral (L) displacements of the movement. The CA3
field also calculates the autocorrelation (A) of the new location (N) by multiplying it
by its transpose (N'). In addition, the varying ratios of the granule to CA3 pyramidal
cells may act as a filter. The CA3 neurons project to several areas. The projection to
the lateral septum is used to assess the state of some global parameter (M_n) such as
the total amount of neural activity. If this exceeds some level (P_n), a signal is sent to
the medial septum to alter the theta control system. The medial septum has several
functions. It acts as a clock to synchronize the computations in the hippocampus, as
a cosine generator, and as the source of the transform matrices (both those associated
with movement and those that are movement-independent). A second output of the

to the next). It is in the lateral septum that these parameters are calculated and compared with stored values, and it is the lateral septum that, when it detects deviations from these stored values, triggers changes in the medial septal theta mechanism. Thus, the lateral septum is viewed as a part of the behavioral exploration circuitry which is designed to construct maps, to monitor them, and to modify them when they deviate from specific global criteria. These criteria are not fixed but can be altered by signals ascending from the hypothalamus and the brain stem via the medial forebrain bundle. Another part of the behavioral exploration circuitry is the nucleus accumbens, a part of the basal ganglia ventral to the septum, which also receives a large input from the CA3 field and which, on the present view, is involved in the control of the motor patterns (for example, myostatial sniffing or whiskering) involved in exploration in the rat.

In order for the inverse matrix of the current location to guide behavior to a particular location in an environment, it must be multiplied by the matrix representing that location. Many of these desired locations will contain food or water or will be associated with safety, and I will therefore call them *incentive locations*. The information about incentives probably derives from the amygdala and the frontal cortex. The incentive-location matrices and the transform matrices (which result from their matrix multiplication by the inverse of the current location matrix) are placed in the subicular area lying between the CA1 field and the entorhinal cortex. These include the subiculum, the presubiculum, the parasubiculum, and retrosplenial area E. In these areas, incentive-location matrices stored during exploration and routine patrolling can be activated under the appropriate motivational circumstances. If a rat finds itself in a familiar environment at dinnertime or when it feels thirsty, it can activate the set of appropriate incentive-location matrices for that motivation in the subicular region, where they are multiplied by the inverse of the current location matrix coming from the CA1 subfield in order to compute the transform matrix. As was stated above, on this reading the subiculum is probably the area that computes the transform matrix required to take the animal from its present location to the location of the incentive.

An alternate candidate for the storage of the incentive-location matrices is

---

CA3 field goes to the CA1 field via the Schaffer collaterals. It is in the CA1 field that the inverse matrices (C^{-1}) are computed. These, in turn, are sent to the subiculum, where they are multiplied by the incentive matrix (I) activated from the amygdala to give the incentive transform (TI) necessary to move from the present location to the incentive location. The final output of the CA3 field is the feedback loop to the medial entorhinal cortex.

the lateral entorhinal cortex itself. This area also receives inputs from the amygdala and the lateral hypothalamus in addition to inputs from neocortical areas via the perirhinal cortex. The argument against this is that the cells in the CA3 and CA1 fields of the hippocampus do not show any preference for areas where incentives are located.

6.1 The Entorhinal Cortex as the Interface between the Egocentric Vectors of the Neocortical Taxon Systems and the Hippocampal Mapping System

Layers 2 and 3 of the entorhinal cortex are the major source of inputs to the hippocampus proper, synapsing on the apical dendrites of the dentate granule cells and the distal apical dendrites of the CA3 and CA1 pyramids (stratum moleculare). On the present model, the lateral cortex supplies the stimulus qualities Q and the head-centered reference coordinates α derived from the stimulus information contained in the neocortex and the medial entorhinal cortex supplies the distances R derived from the CA3 or CA1 fields of the hippocampus proper or from the subicular region (including the subiculum, the presubiculum, and the parasubiculum), all of which project to it.

The hippocampus and the subicular areas appear to constitute a major source of inputs to the medial entorhinal area, but these are only sparsely connected to the lateral entorhinal area (LEA). The LEA receives much of its input from the perirhinal cortex situated around the rhinal fissure, from the amygdala, and from the olfactory system. The perirhinal cortex is a transition cortex which receives inputs from widespread areas of the neocortex (Deacon et al. 1983).

The sparse input from the subiculum to the lateral entorhinal area (Kohler 1985) and the connections from the medial entorhinal area to the lateral entorhinal area (Kohler 1986) would provide the substrate for associations between the distances of objects and their qualities in the entorhinal cortex itself. That is, it might be possible to use this information to assign an R to a particular size of an object in a particular environment. Over repeated exposures to an environment, the entorhinal cortex might come to contain all the information necessary for operation in a restricted set of familiar environments, although it could not cope with novel environments, changes in a familiar environment, or a large number of similar environments.

The medial entorhinal cortex receives its primary inputs from the hippocampus and the subicular area. This "feedback" connection may be partly responsible for the movement-related theta input, which has been identified as atropine-insensitive and which depends on the integrity of the entorhinal cortex (Vanderwolf and Leung 1983). Unlike the lateral entorhinal input, the medial input has a restricted lamellar pattern of projection where a small patch of the medial entorhinal cortex projects to a restricted patch of the hippocampus. The inputs from the hippocampal and retrohippocampal structures to the medial entorhinal area serve several functions. One conveys the computed distances for the different stimuli and stimulus configurations. Another (from the postsubiculum; see Ranck et al. 1987) provides information about the direction in which the animal is facing in an environment. It is not clear how the latter is computed. One possibility is that the information from the lateral entorhinal cortex is filtered (as I suggested in section 3) into stimuli that are very far away (infinite R's) and therefore useful for calculating direction and stimuli that have finite distances and are therefore useful for constructing a map. The former are analyzed in the postsubiculum and the latter in the hippocampus.

The input from layer II of the entorhinal cortex to the dentate granule cells, then, conveys two types of information: R and the α of the environmental stimuli (Q). I assume that the Q's are represented by the location of the activity within the lateral entorhinal cortex in the same way as in the perirhinal cortex: labeled line coding (Deacon et al. 1983). The projection of the lateral entorhinal cortical information onto the granule cells is many-to-many. This multiplexing of the input information means that each lamella of the dentate has most of the sensory information available to it. Within each lamella, any particular granule cell will be sensitive to combinations of stimuli with particular egocentric angles (see O'Keefe and Nadel 1978).

The projection of the medial entorhinal area onto the same granule cells is a one-to-one lamella projection. It is thus reasonable to assume that each of these sets of distances enters into computations with the stimulus configurations in their lamella.

6.2   The Dentate Gyrus Rotates the Current Location Matrix

The putative granule cells of the dentate fire like the interneuronal theta cells (Rose 1983); however, unlike the theta cells, they are relatively silent during nonmovement or LIA periods. It is clear that some of them, at least, are place-coded. I interpret this to mean that they are primarily responsible for encoding part or all of the transform matrix representing the translocation resulting from the intended movements of the animal. When this matrix is multiplied together with the current location matrix in the CA3 field, the result is a matrix representing the new or intended location. One possibility is that the rotation and translation components of the transform matrix are separated. On this view, the role of the dentate gyrus is to rotate the current input matrix whereas that of the CA3 is to multiply the rotated matrix by the translation matrix. As we saw in section 3, the transform matrix that rotates the coordinate frame involves multiplication of the current stimulus location matrix by cosα and sinα (or cos (90 − α)). Since the theta mechanism approximates to a cosine wave and the excitability of the dentate cells varies as a function of the theta phase (Rudell et al. 1980), it seems reasonable to suggest that the computation is carried out by delaying the R input by a period equal to the egocentric taxon angle α. On this reading, the role of the lateral entorhinal input is to produce this delay relative to the medial entorhinal R inputs. For example, if stimulus B occurs at $R45°$ (in taxon space) (see figure 7) and the animal rotates 90° anticlockwise, the stimulus will rotate 90° clockwise to $R135°$. This can be accomplished by adding the rotation (90°) to the angle of the original vector (45°) to obtain the new vector angle (135°). This Q angle results in a uniform shift in the polar vector representations in the dentate by adding that angle to the preexisting delay to obtain the new delay. Note that the delay need only range over the angles 0°–180°. The R input is multiplied by the angle α because it strikes the granule cells at the appropriate part of the theta cycle. The outputs of the granule cells are the Y coordinates of the stimulus array in rectangular space. It is not clear to me how the X coordinates are calculated. Perhaps this is done in the second blade of the dentate; in that case one might expect the theta wave to be 180° out of phase in the two blades (see Buzsaki et al. 1986) or the input to one blade to be (90 − α) rather than α itself. The x and y outputs might be segregated in the infra- and suprapyramidal bundles of the mossy-fiber pathway, which make contact with the basal and apical dendrites respectively. In any case, the x coordinate will vary little (unless the animal moves sideways) and may need little alteration.

Within the present model, the CA3 field has several roles; these will be reviewed in the next subsection.

6.3   The CA3 Field Finishes the Transformation Calculation, Stores an Autoassociation Matrix, and Acts as a Search Funnel during Map Retrieval

Place cells in the CA3 field represent an environment in a distributed fashion and maintain their place fields in the memory phase of the cue-controlled-environment spatial-working-memory experiment (see section 2). The roles proposed for this field are (1) to complete the computation that predicts the outcome of the current movement by applying the second part of the transform matrix (the part that translates the coordinate reference frame in rectangular coordinate space), (2) to provide the substrate where the current location matrix is multiplied by itself, creating an autoassociation matrix that enables parts of the input pattern or distortions of the input pattern to retrieve the entire representation of an environment, and (3) to act as a memory-retrieval funnel which progressively narrows the possible set of stored representations corresponding to the current sensory input.

After the matrix representing the stimulus vectors has been rotated and transformed into x and y coordinates in the dentate, it only needs to be translated in order to bring it into correspondence with the position at the end of the intended movement. This is done in the CA3 field, so this field is the first within the hippocampus to contain the expected location matrix. In common with the transformation that takes place in the dentate, the translation matrix is carried into the hippocampus on the theta system, indirectly from the medial entorhinal cortex and directly from the medial septum. In work begun with the late Abe Black, Richard Morris and I and our colleagues have replicated and extended a finding of Whishaw and Vanderwolf (1973) that the frequency of theta in the hippocampal EEG during jumping is a function of the distance jumped (O'Keefe and Nadel 1978, pp. 180–182; Morris and Hagan 1983). Although the theta wave is not easily recorded from the CA3 EEG, I will assume that cells in the CA3 field burst in phase with the dentate EEG, as do most cells in the hippocampus. The computation might be done using principles similar to those of systolic architecture or wavefront array processors (see section 4 above). With each theta wave the translation matrix is systoled across the CA3 dendrites in one direction, while the slowly conducting mossy fibers traverse them at a slower speed and perhaps in a different direction. The partial sums are accumulated in each pyramidal cell and passed to neighboring pyramidal cells via the axon collaterals of the CA3 pyramids, where they accumulate the summed and shifted results. This axon collateral plexus supports a considerable amount of excitatory interconnection between CA3 neurones. In the CA3 field, Ishizuka et al. (1986) report that each pyramidal cell makes connection with 2,300 other CA3 pyramids within a slice 400μm thick. This is about 4 percent of the length of the hippocampus. Since there are approximately 1.43×10^5 neurons in the CA3 field of the rat (Gaarskjaer 1978a), this means that each CA3 pyramidal neuron may contact up to 30 percent of the total. Braitenberg and Schuz (1983) have estimated that mossy fibers contribute only a small proportion to the total synaptic input to the CA3 pyramids, the inference being that many of the remainder are internal connections between CA3 neurons. It should be noted, however, that direct attempts to test the degree of excitatory coupling between CA3 pyramids using intracellular recording have led to a much lower estimate of functional connectivity (Miles and Wong 1987).

The matrix of firing patterns in the CA3 field that results from these transformations represents the predicted location matrix.

The second computation carried out in the CA3 field changes the matrix
representation of an environment into a form that enables part/whole retrieval
or retrieval of the best representation for corrupted or changed input data. As
we saw in section 2, activating part of the map of an environment activates
all of it. The most often suggested method for accomplishing this is to construct an autoassociation matrix in which a vector or matrix is multiplied by
itself (Kohonen 1984). Several other authors have pointed to the collateral
afferent plexus within the CA3 field as a possible substrate of an autoassociation matrix (see, e.g., McNaughton and Morris 1987). Another possibility is
the interesting anatomical arrangement in CA3a in which the mossy-fiber
axons from the dentate granule cells at one level cross at right angles to those
at another level. Although the mossy fibers remain within their lamella of
origin as they course through subfields CA3c and CA3b, when they reach
CA3a they turn sharply at right angles to the lamella and course in the direction of the longitudinal axis primarily in a temporal direction. The amount of
descent of a particular mossy fiber in the temporal direction depends on its
origin within the granule-cell lamella. Fibers originating at the tip of the
lateral (buried) blade of the dentate descend for distances up to 1,600 μm,
whereas those originating at the tip of the medial (exposed) blade appear not
to descend at all. As one moves between these two extremes, there is a graded
amount of descent (Gaarskjaer 1978b). The effect of this pattern is to provide
a rectangular grid of granule inputs to the CA3a pyramids where the pattern
of activity within each lamella of the dentate is associated with itself in the
CA3a field (see figure 20). This autoassociation is accompanied by synaptic
changes in the synapses activated, and the result will be the storage of the
autoassociation pattern in the CA3a field. The grain of the autoassociation
would appear to vary with the septo-temporal location within the CA3a field
of the hippocampus. Gaarskjaer's (1978a) quantitative estimates of the ratio
of granule cells to CA3 pyramidal cells indicates that this ratio is not constant
along the long axis of the hippocampus. Overall there are 9.9×10^5 neurones in the granule-cell layer of the dentate and 1.4×10^5 pyramids in the
CA3 layer. Although the CA3 layer was not divided into subfields, it is reasonable to assume that the data apply to CA3a as well as to the others. The
ratio of granules to CA3 pyramids varied from about ten granules for each
pyramid in the septal region to about one granule for each pyramid in the
most temporal regions. This change is due mostly to changes in the absolute
number of pyramidal cells. Recall that one of the functions postulated for the
dentate is that of a multiplexer; this means that each section of the dentate

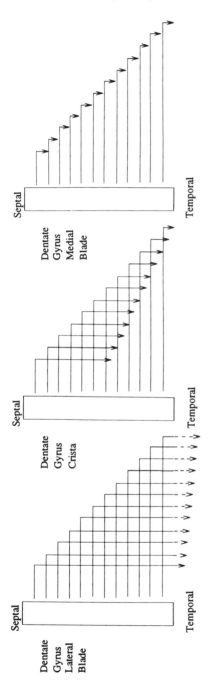

Figure 20
Presumed pattern of innervation of the CA3 field by the mossy fibers from the dentate gyrus. The fibers originating in different parts of the dentate spread over greater areas of the CA3a field. Those from the lateral blade spread widely (top panel), and the resulting pattern of crossing fibers may form the basis for the association of a unit firing pattern with the transpose of itself. The fibers from the central bend or crista of the dentate spread less (center panel), and those from the medial blade spread least of all (bottom panel). Varying the location of unit firing along the medio-lateral axis of the dentate may vary the amount of autoassociation of the pattern in the CA3 field.

contains the pattern for representing the environment. As a consequence of these anatomical features, the matrix at the septal end of CA3 which stores the environmental representation is much grosser than that at the temporal end. It is possible that the search for the appropriate matrix for a set of environmental inputs proceeds from the septal to the temporal end of the hippocampus. The activation of a crude representation in the septal end might assist in the activation of a more precise representation at the next lamella via the interconnecting CA3 collaterals. In this way, a wave of activation would spread from the septal end of the CA3 field to the temporal end during each theta cycle, increasing the grain of the representation (and decreasing the number of possible representations) from the septal to temporal end (see figure 21). The system would work as a progressively narrowing filter with a wide band at the septal end, gradually tapering toward the temporal end. Recall that the output to the medial entorhinal cortex (primarily layer IV; see Hjorth-Simonsen 1971) arises only in the temporal CA3 field. Thus, this

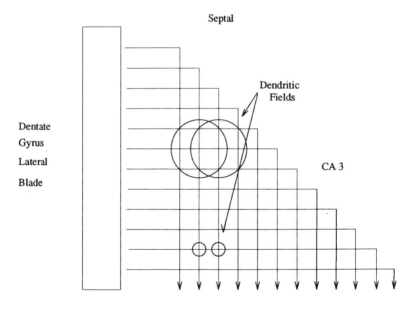

Figure 21
The lateral dentate pattern of termination in CA3a, with circles representing the relative sizes of dendritic fields. The different sizes of the circles reflect the fact that the dendritic fields of the CA3 cells in the more septal part of the hippocampus may be larger than those in the ventral part. Not to scale.

output at least would convey fine-grain representations of an environment. This projection is one of the feedbacks from the hippocampal and subicular areas which carry the estimates of the distances of the stimuli represented in the upper layers of the lateral entorhinal cortex. The information, however, is in rectangular coordinates and needs to be transformed back into polar coordinates. This is done by a method like the vectoring one used in the Cordic vector-rotation system. I assume this calculation is carried out in layer IV of the entorhinal cortex and then projected to layers II and III via the extensive short axonal intracortical system described by Kohler (1985).

6.4 The Role of the CA1 Field as a Matrix Inverter

No one has yet found any differences between the place fields of complex spike cells in the CA3 and CA1 fields. This suggests that the difference may be in the pattern across cells. In order for the map to be useful in guiding the animal to locations associated with reward, it is necessary to have the inverse matrix of the current location so that it can be multiplied by the matrix representing the "goal" location to yield the required transform matrix. Zipser (1986) has also suggested that goals could be located using the inverse matrix, although as part of a different model from the one described here. I suggest that CA1 is the subfield where the inverse matrix is computed. The major input to this field is from the CA3 field via the Shaffer collateral system. Unlike the lamellar bounded projections of the granule cells to CA3b and CA3c, this projection enjoys quite a wide spread along the septotemporal extent of the CA1 field. In addition there is a direct projection of the layer III cells of the lateral and medial entorhinal cortex into the tips of the apical dendrites of the CA1 pyramids (Steward and Scoville 1978). The termination pattern of this projection is different from that seen in the dentate or CA3 field. The fibers end in a small patch of CA1 whose location varies from the CA3 to the subicular end of the CA1 field as a function of the fibers' origin in the entorhinal cortex. Fibers from the lateral entorhinal cortex terminate in the part of the CA1 field close to the subiculum, whereas those from the medial entorhinal cortex terminate close to the CA3 field. The spread of the termination along the septotemporal axis of the hippocampus is the same as the layer III projection from the entorhinal cortex to the dentate.

One of the most interesting aspects of the physiology of CA1 neurons in the rat is the presence of a gradual shift in the theta phase from the pyramidal-cell layer to the molecular layer (Winson 1976a,b). Work by Buszaki, Leung, and Vanderwolf (1983) has suggested that theta is the result of several generators and at least two dipoles in each of CA1 and the dentate. On the basis of depth mapping of the voltages during different behaviors, the relationship

of the theta units and the complex spike units to different phases of the theta
cycles, and the effect of anticholinergic drugs (such as atropine) and anaes-
thetics (such as urethane and ether) Buszaki et al. have proposed a model of
the dipoles in which

• one dipole is created by an excitatory drive impinging on the apical dendrites of the CA1 pyramids from the entorhinal cortex (this afferent drive is
not blocked by cholinergic antagonists such as atropine or scopolamine),
• the other dipole is created by the inhibitory drive generated by the basket-
cell plexus impinging on the soma of the pyramidal cells in the stratum pyr-
amidale (a vital synapse in this part of the circuit is cholinergic, and thus
this dipole is atropine-sensitive), and
• these two dipoles are approximately 45° out of phase with each other (this
phase shift between the two generators is responsible for the slow phase
shift recorded by an extracellular electrode as it moves from the pyramidal
layer to the hippocampal fissure).

Neural modeling by Leung (1984) has suggested that these extracellular voltage gradients are reflected by intracellular voltages. This means that during
the theta period the intracellular voltages are changing in a quasi-sinusoidal
fashion and this wave is moving up and down the dendrites, changing its
excitability to inputs with a period equal to the theta cycle. If this is the case,
then a set of Schaffer collateral inputs, impinging on different parts of the
dendrites of a CA1 pyramidal cell at the same time will find the different
patches in a different state of receptivity and will be multiplied by different
values of $\cos\theta$. In addition there appears to be a shift in the phase of the theta
wave from the CA3 end of the CA1 field to the subicular end of approximately 55° (subiculum leading CA3) (Green and Rawlins 1979; see also Buzsaki et al. 1986). Thus, an input to the CA1 basal dendrites may be sweeping
in the opposite direction to the input from the CA3 Schaffer fibers. The input
from the entorhinal cortex appears to be at right angles to the lamellar axis,
so that the CA1 neuron would sense the intersection of these three "waves"
of information. Although it is not possible to specify the exact computational
mechanism at this time, I propose that the CA1 matrix provides the substrate
for computing the inverse of the CA3 matrix using a recursive algorithm akin
to the techniques for computing the pseudo-inverse of a matrix proposed by
Greville and Hestenes (see Boullion and Odell 1971, pp. 71–75). In the Greville algorithm the matrix to be inverted is partitioned and operated on a
column at a time. As each column of the matrix is run through the algorithm,
another row is added to the inverse matrix and the existing inverse matrix is
modified. The calculations for computing these are not important except that

they include multiplication of the transpose of each vector column by the column itself as well as multiplication of the existing matrix by a vector. This type of algorithm would appear suited to computation on a wavefront processor in which each vector comprises a wave and the resulting inverse matrix resides in the array of CA1 neurons at the end of the successive waves.

An alternative technique (proposed by Hestenes) operates directly on the entire matrix to be inverted. First the matrix is transposed and expanded by the addition of orthogonal row vectors to fill out the matrix. Then a set of matrices are generated which, when multiplied with this expanded matrix, progressively transform it into the pseudo-inverse. This type of algorithm might require two layers of circuits: one to store and update the augmented matrix during the calculation and one to calculate the sequence of transform matrices. There are several places in the hippocampal system where the anatomy might lend itself to this type of calculation. Within the present schema, I suggest that the inverse matrix is calculated in the CA1 field, perhaps in conjunction with the subiculum.

6.5   The Subicular Regions Calculate the Transform Matrix Needed to Go from the Current Location to a "Goal" in a Familiar Environment

There is little information available about the subicular cells, but they receive a strong input from the CA1 pyramids, the entorhinal cortex, and the amygdala, and there is a strong theta rhythm which can be recorded from the subiculum. In turn, they project to the entorhinal cortex and via the fornix to the mammillary bodies. One possible function of the subiculum might be to calculate the transform matrix needed to get from the current location to a goal. Experiments (O'Keefe and Speakman 1987b) in which we have retrained the animal to a new goal location while recording from place cells in CA1 indicate that they do not change their place fields as a result of this manipulation. I assume therefore that the information about goal locations in an environment is located outside the hippocampus and probably in the retrohippocampal areas such as the subiculum and parasubiculum. The subiculum calculates the transform matrix needed to change the center of the reference framework to the goal location by multiplying the inverse of the current matrix coming from the CA1 field by the goal-location matrix (see section 3). This information is then relayed to the motor programming centers, where it can be translated into specific instructions to drive the motor system toward that location. This would involve an appropriate rotation and translation. As the animal moves toward the goal, the system continually updates the transform matrix to correct for deviations.

6.6   The Role of the Septum as a Global Clock and a Trigonometric-Function Generator

One way to synchronize parallel processing elements is to provide a global clock (see section 5). The medial septum generates the clock signals, and this keeps all the hippocampal, subicular, and entorhinal cortices in step. It is probable that many other areas of the neocortex are synchronized to this pacemaker as well. One way this might be used is to insert delays at various points in the circuitry. As we have seen, systematic delays can be used to rotate vectors, and this might occur in the dentate. Another possible function of the theta system is to provide a sinusoidal-like input to the different cells in the circuit. If a set of inputs is delayed relative to this wave, then it is possible that the effect is to multiply that input by the cosine of the delayed angle. The two branches of the septal projection—a noncholinergic one to the entorhinal cortex via the cingulum and the dorsal fornix and a cholinergic one to the hippocampus via the fimbria—would provide ample opportunities for all these possible functions.

Conclusion

In this chapter I have tried to put the O'Keefe-Nadel theory of the hippocampus as a cognitive map on a firmer computational basis. Recent lesion and electrophysiological evidence has lent substantial support to the general ideas expressed in the theory and has provided further suggestions about the capabilities of the mapping system for storing and manipulating locale representations. Although it is probably premature, I have attempted to locate different parts of the computational model within the circuitry of the hippocampal system in the hope that this will enable us to make specific testable predictions.

Acknowledgments

I would like to thank Andrew Speakman and Michael Recce for valuable comments on a previous draft, and Michael Recce for help with the figures. This work was supported by the Medical Research Council of Great Britain and the Sloan Foundation.

References

Aggleton, J. P., P. R. Hunt, and J. N. P. Rawlins. 1986. The effects of hippocampal lesions upon spatial and non-spatial tests of working memory. *Behavioral Brain Research* 19: 133–146.

Andersen, P., and P. Hvalby. 1986. Long-term potentiation—Problems and possible mechanisms. In *The Hippocampus,* volume 3, ed. R. L. Isaacson and K. H. Probram (New York: Plenum).

Barnes, C. A. 1988. Spatial learning and memory processes: The search for their neurobiological correlates in the rat. *Trends in Neuroscience* 11: 163–169.

Bliss, T. V. P., and T. Lomo. 1973. Long-lasting potentiation of synaptic transmission in the dentate area of the anaesthetised rabbit following stimulation of the perforant path. *Journal of Physiology (London)* 232: 331–356.

Blomfield, S. 1974. Arithmetical operations performed by nerve cells. *Brain Research* 69: 115–124.

Boullion, T. L., and P. L. Odell. 1971. *Generalized Inverse Matrices.* New York: Wiley-Interscience.

Braitenberg, V., and A. Schuz. 1983. Some anatomical comments on the hippocampus. In *Neurobiology of the Hippocampus,* ed. W. Seifert (London: Academic).

Buzsaki, G., J. Czopf, I. Konadakor, and L. Kelleny. 1986. Laminar distribution of hippocampal rhythmic slow activity (RSA) in the behaving rat: Current-source density analysis, effects of urethane and atropine. *Brain Research* 365: 125–137.

Buzsaki, G., L.-W. S. Leung, and C. H. Vanderwolf. 1983. Cellular bases of hippocampal EEG in the behaving rat. *Brain Research Reviews* 6: 139–171.

Deacon, T. W., H. Eichenbaum, P. Rosenberg, and K. W. Eckmann. 1983. Afferent connections of the perirhinal cortex in the rat. *Journal of Comparative Neurology* 220: 168–190.

Eich, J. M. 1982. A composite holographic associative recall model. *Psychological Review* 89: 627–661.

Eich, J. M. 1985. Levels of processing, encoding specificity elaboration and CHARM. *Psychological Review* 92: 1–38.

Gaarskjaer, F. B. 1978a. Organization of the mossy fiber system of the rat studied in extended hippocampi. I. Terminal area related to number of granule and pyramidal cells. *Journal of Comparative Neurology* 178: 49–72.

Gaarskjaer, F. B. 1978b. Organization of the mossy fiber system of the rat studied in extended hippocampi. II. Experimental analysis of fiber distribution with silver impregnation methods. *Journal of Comparative Neurology* 178: 73–88.

Gasson, P. 1983. *Geometry of Spatial Forms.* Chichester: Ellis Horwood.

Green, K. F., and J. N. P. Rawlins. 1979. Hippocampal theta in rats under urethane: Generators and phase relations. 1979 *Electroencephalography and Clinical Neurophysiology* 47: 420–429.

Grossman, S. I. 1984. *Elementary Linear Algebra.* Second edition. Belmont, Calif.: Wadsworth.

Hjorth-Simonsen, A. 1971. Hippocampal efferents to the ipsilateral entorhinal area: An experimental study in the rat. *Journal of Comparative Neurology* 142: 417–438.

Ishizuka, N., K. Krzemieniewska, and D. Amaral. 1986. Organization of pyramidal cell axonal collaterals in field CA3 of the rat hippocampus. *Society for Neuroscience Abstracts* 12: 1234.

Kesner, R. P., and J. M. Novak. 1981. Memory for lists of items in rats: Role of the hippocampus. *Society for Neuroscience Abstracts* 7: 237.

Kohler, C. 1985. Intrinsic projections of the retrohippocampal region in the rat brain. I. The subicular complex. *Journal of Comparative Neurology* 236: 504–522.

Kohler, C. 1986. Intrinsic connections of the retrohippocampal region in the rat brain. II. The medial entorhinal area. *Journal of Comparative Neurology* 246: 149–169.

Kohonen, T. 1984. *Self-Organization and Associative Memory.* Berlin: Springer-Verlag.

Kubie, J. L., and J. B. Ranck. 1983. Sensory-behavioural correlates in individual hippocampus neurons in three situations: Space and context. In *Neurobiology of the Hippocampus,* ed. W. Seifert (London: Academic).

Kung, H. T. 1982. Why systolic architectures? *IEEE Computer* 15: 37–46.

Kung, H. T., B. Sproull, and G. Steele, eds. 1981. *VLSI Systems and Computations.* Rockville, Md.: Computer Science Press.

Kung, S.-Y., K. S. Arun, R. J. Gal-ezer, and D. V. Bhaskar Rao. 1982. Wavefront array processor: Language, architecture, and applications. *IEEE Transactions on Computers* C-31: 1054–1066.

Langmoen, I. A., and P. Andersen. 1983. Summation of excitatory post-synaptic potentials in hippocampal pyramidal cells. *Journal of Neurophysiology* 50: 1320–1329.

Leung, L.-W. S. 1984. Model of gradual phase shift of theta rhythm in the rat. *Journal of Neurophysiology* 521: 1051–1065.

McNaughton, B. L. 1983. Activity dependent modulation of hippocampal synaptic efficacy: Some implications for memory processes. In *Neurobiology of the Hippocampus,* ed. W. Seifert (London: Academic).

McNaughton, B. L., and R. G. M. Morris. 1987. Hippocampal synaptic enhancement and information storage within a distributed memory system. *Trends in Neurosciences* 10: 408–415.

McNaughton, B. L., C. A. Barnes, and J. O'Keefe. 1983. The contributions of position, direction and velocity to single unit activity in the hippocampus of freely moving rats. *Experimental Brain Research* 52: 41–49.

Miles, R., and R. K. S. Wong. 1987. Excitatory synaptic interactions between CA3 neurones in the guinea-pig hippocampus. *Journal of Physiology* 373: 397–418.

Morris, R. G. M., and J. J. Hagan. 1983. Hippocampal electrical activity and ballistic movement. In *Neurobiology of the Hippocampus,* ed. W. Seifert (London: Academic).

Morris, R. G. M., A. H. Black, and J. O'Keefe. 1976. Hippocampal EEG during a ballistic movement (abstract). *Neuroscience Letters* 3: 102.

Morris, R. G. M., P. Garrard, J. N. P. Rawlins, and J. O'Keefe. 1982. Place navigation impaired in rats with hippocampal lesions. *Nature* 297: 681–683.

Muller, R. U., and J. L. Kubie. 1987. The effects of changes in the environment on the spatial firing of hippocampal complex-spike cells. *Journal of Neuroscience* 7: 1951–1968.

Muller, R. U., J. L. Kubie, and J. B. Ranck. 1987. Spatial firing patterns of hippocampus complex-spike cells in a fixed environment. *Journal of Neuroscience* 7: 1935–1950.

Murdock, B. B. 1982. A theory for the storage and retrieval of item and associative information. *Psychological Review* 89: 609–626.

Nadel, L., and L. MacDonald. 1979. Hippocampus: Cognitive map or working memory? *Behavioral and Neural Biology* 29: 405–409.

O'Keefe, J. 1976. Place units in the hippocampus of the freely moving rat. *Experimental Neurology* 51: 78–109.

O'Keefe, J. 1983. Spatial memory within and without the hippocampal system. In *Neurobiology of the Hippocampus*, ed. W. Seifert (London: Academic).

O'Keefe, J. 1985. Is consciousness the gateway to the hippocampal cognitive map? A speculative essay on the neural basis of mind. In *Brain and Mind*, D. A. Oakley (London: Methuen).

O'Keefe, J., and D. H. Conway. 1980. On the trail of the hippocampal engram. *Physiological Psychology* 8: 229–238.

O'Keefe, J., and L. Nadel. 1978. *The Hippocampus as a Cognitive Map*. Oxford University Press.

O'Keefe, J., and A. Speakman. 1987a. Single unit activity in the rat hippocampus during a spatial memory task. *Experimental Brain Research* 68: 1–27.

O'Keefe, J., and A. Speakman. 1987b. Hippocampal place field activity is not related to the location of the goal or the intended response in the cue-controlled environment. *Neuroscience Letters* 29: S96.

O'Keefe, J., L. Nadel, S. Keightley, and D. Kill. 1975. Fornix lesions selectively abolish place learning in the rat. *Experimental Neurology* 48: 152–166.

Olton, D. S., J. A. Walker, and F. H. Gage. 1978. Hippocampal connections and spatial discrimination. *Brain Research* 139: 295–308.

Ranck, J. B., R. U. Muller, and J. S. Taube. 1987. Head direction cells recorded from past subiculum in freely moving rats. *Neuroscience* 22 (suppl. 528P): S177.

Rose, G. 1983. Physiological and behavioural characteristics of dentate granule cells. In *Neurobiology of the Hippocampus*, ed. W. Seifert (London: Academic).

Rudell, A. P., S. E. Fox, and J. B. Ranck. 1980. Hippocampal excitability phase-locked to the theta rhythm in walking rats. *Experimental Neurology* 68: 87–96.

Scoville, W. B., and B. Milner. 1957. Loss of recent memory after bilateral hippocampal lesions. *Journal of Neurology, Neurosurgery, and Psychiatry* 20: 11–21.

Shepherd, G. M., and R. K. Brayton. 1987. Logic operators are properties of computer-simulated interactions between excitable dendritic spikes. *Neuroscience* 21: 151–166.

Steward, O., and S. A. Scoville. 1978. Cells of origin of entorhinal cortical afferents to the hippocampus and fascia dentata of the rat. *Journal of Comparative Neurology* 169: 347–370.

Sutherland, R. J., B. Kolb, and I. Q. Whishaw. 1982. Spatial mapping: Definitive disruption by hippocampal or medial frontal cortical damage in the rat. *Neuroscience Letters* 31: 271–276.

Vanderwolf, C. H., and L.-W. S. Leung. 1983. Hippocampal rhythmical slow activity: A brief history and the effects of entorhinal lesions and phencyclidine. In *Neurobiology of the Hippocampus,* ed. W. Seifert (London: Academic).

Volder, J. E. 1959. The CORDIC trigonometric computing technique. *IRE Transactions in Electronic Computing* 8: 330–334.

Weiser, U., and A. Davis. 1981. A wavefront notation tool for VSLI array design. In *VLSI Systems and Computations,* ed. H. T. Kung et al. (Rockville, Md.: Computer Science Press).

Winson, J. 1976a. Hippocampal theta rhythm. I. Depth profiles in the curarized rat. *Brain Research* 103: 57–70.

Winson, J. 1976b. Hippocampal theta rhythm. II. Depth profiles in the freely moving rabbit. *Brain Research* 103: 71–80.

Whishaw, I. Q., and C. H. Vanderwolf. 1973. Hippocampal EEG and Behaviour: Changes in amplitude and frequency of RSA (theta rhythm) associated with spontaneous and learned movement patterns in rats and cats. *Behavioural Biology* 8: 461–484.

Zipser, D. 1986. Biologically plausible models of place recognition and goal location. In *Parallel Distributed Processing: Explorations in the Microstructure of Cognition, volume 2: Psychological and Biological Models,* ed. J. L. McClelland, D. E. Rumelhart, and the PDP Research Group (Cambridge, Mass.: MIT Press).

Chapter 9

| Neuronal Mechanisms for Spatial Computation and Information Storage | B. L. McNaughton |

In recent years, there has been a flurry of excitement in cognitive science created by the growing awareness that "brainlike" models can be constructed which are capable of providing more accurate accounts of higher cognitive processes than earlier "computerlike" models. While such statements have a tendency to raise eyebrows among neuroscientists, who have traditionally held this principle to be self-evident, neuroscience has, in general, been guilty of an equally limiting implicit assumption: that a sufficiently detailed description of the properties and connections of neurons will lead, of itself, to an understanding of brain function. The present volume, and the meeting that inspired it, can be taken as an indication of an increasing effort by neural and cognitive scientists to establish some common language by which the conceptual and empirical advances made in one area may lead to useful predictions and explanations in the other. There are clearly some serious obstacles to be overcome. On one hand, knowledge in the neurosciences is rather erratic. Whereas certain aspects of neural function are known and expressed in far more detail and complexity than can be practically incorporated into computational models, many equally important aspects are understood poorly, if at all. On the other hand, many "connectionist" or "parallel distributed processing" models invoke processes or relations that are demonstrably uncharacteristic of neural systems while ignoring much of the known computational richness of those systems. Although this practice is sometimes justified by the claim that the connectionist "units" are not necessarily neurons but may represent collections of neurons, this makes it difficult to conceive of empirical tests of some of these models at the neural level. Admittedly, the problems of the computational expense of any realistic brain model, coupled with the difficulty of knowing *a priori* which parameters may be simplified or excluded, present serious difficulties.

Another obstacle is related to the classes of problems that the two fields have traditionally addressed. Brain science has generally concentrated its efforts at the sensory-input or the motor-output end of the system, or at simple forms of adaptive modification of behavior, where the problems, if somewhat low-level from the cognitive viewpoint, have at least been experimentally tractable. Cognitive science has typically addressed the higher levels of human behavior, such as language and skilled performance, which are the levels least accessible to physiological investigation. A useful way to start would be to address some aspect of animal cognition that is sufficiently complex and analogous to human performance to be of interest to cognitive scientists, but yet is sufficiently well understood at the neural level to make feasible the development of models that are both "neurally inspired" and empirically testable with current physiological and behavioral techniques. One such problem is the internal representation and storage of knowledge about spatial relationships in the environment. My goal in this chapter is to outline the extent to which the neural substrates of this process, as they are currently understood, conform to and might supplement some of the fundamental tenets of "connectionist" (see, e.g., Feldman and Ballard 1982; Sutton and Barto 1981) or "parallel-distributed processing" (see, e.g., Rumelhart and McClelland 1986) models of cognitive processing and information storage.

This chapter is directed primarily to cognitive scientists, rather than to neuroscientists. Accordingly, I shall attempt to reduce the experimental literature to a few findings that might be useful in terms of increasing the "neural plausibility" of PDP models, and to communicate these in a language that will be at least partly familiar to followers of the PDP literature. In attempting to find a balance between pragmatism and reality I will resort to numerous "useful simplifications," which may appall both physiologists and mathematicians. Hopefully these will at least serve to stimulate debate.

Most of what is known about the neural basis for the internal representation of spatially extended environments has come from behavioral and neurophysiological studies on rats. These relatively "simple" animals show a remarkable capacity to store and use information about the spatial relationships of distal sensory cues in the environment (see, e.g., O'Keefe and Nadel 1978), a fact which has come as somewhat of a surprise to many traditional S-R psychologists. Examples of this skill are found in the rat's ability to keep an accurate record of more than a dozen recently visited locations (Olton, Collison, and Werz 1977) and to learn rapidly to associate particular locations in an environment with either food or safety. This can be done in the complete absence of any specific direct cue indicating the presence of these features from a distance. In addition, O'Keefe and Conway (1978) have demonstrated that rats must construct some form of internal representation of the environment which they are able to recall and use in a navigational problem in which they are given information about starting location only. O'Keefe and Nadel (1978) proposed, largely on the basis of experiments involving either selective brain lesions or physiological recordings from single neurons in rats performing "spatial" tasks, that rats are capable of forming and using "cognitive maps" of their environments, and that the neural structure most centrally involved in this capacity is the hippocampal formation.

The main themes of this chapter will be how the physiology and connectivity pattern of the hippocampus and some of its related structures might be translated into the framework of some simple "connectionist" models for associative memory, and how insights derived from such models can be used to guide our investigations into the relationship between neural activity and complex spatial behavior. I will end with the outline of a distributed, "neurally inspired" model, which attempts to explain, in part, how neuronal representations of particular locations might be integrated into a computational structure that would have at least the outward appearance of a cognitive map.

1 Some Simple Tools for Thought About Neural Networks

The basic principles underlying distributed information storage in brains or "brainlike" model systems appear (with hindsight) remarkably simple. There are three fundamental ones. The first is that information is represented as a pattern of activity (state vector) within a population of (more or less) simple interacting integrator elements (neurons), wherein any given element is involved, at different times, in the representation of many different events. Associative memory then becomes an expression of the ability either to reinstate one pattern given a related one or, more generally, to reinstate a previously active pattern given only a fragment or a facsimile of the original (pattern completion, feature detection). The second notion is that this information is stored as a specific distribution of connection weights (synaptic strengths) among elements of the population. Finally, the rules governing the modification of connections used to store information must somehow capture the temporal association of activity of two or more elements.

These principles, first clearly expressed by Hebb (1949), were made explicit and considerably refined by several theorists, including Steinbuch (1961), Marr (1969,1970,1971), Willshaw and von der Malsburg (1976), Nass and Cooper (1975), and Kohonen (1978). A number of very powerful models of parallel computation have appeared more recently. However, the translation of these models into explicitly neural terms is still somewhat unclear. This, as was suggested above, reflects both the reticence with which the brain gives up its secrets and a corresponding unwillingness on the part of many theorists (particularly those based primarily in cognitive science, artificial intelligence, and applied mathematics) to be bound by the limited base of empirical data in the neurosciences. Although at least some of these currently unconstrained ideas are generating surprising new insights into neural function, at present the earlier models appear to give the best fit to the neural data.

The starting point for most of these models is the "linear correlation matrix" or "learning matrix" (Steinbach 1961). Let us take, for example, a square matrix through which six binary-state channels running horizontally interact with six similar channels running vertically. Assume that the junctions themselves are also binary, and that they are controlled by a simple conjunction rule (Hebb 1949) such that a junction undergoes an irreversible transition from 0 to 1 if and only if both of its inputs are 1 at the same time. It is possible to store associations between pairs of patterns on the X and Y inputs of such a matrix so that a more or less faithful copy of one stored pattern can be reconstructed by presenting the alternate channel with the corresponding paired associate. This is illustrated in figure 1A, in which the X,Y pair (000111,110100) has been presented to the system and has resulted in a specific pattern of modified junctions.

Recall requires the formation of the inner product of the input vector with the connection matrix and then carrying out an integer division on the result by the sum of the elements of the input vector. The process can be made obvious by working through the example of figure 1A. Multiply every row element of the matrix by the corresponding element of the horizontal input vector and then sum the columns. The result is 330300. Dividing this by the sum of the active elements in the input results in the correct Y associate: 110100.

There are two particularly striking features of these sorts of devices. One is that more than one pair of input patterns can be stored in the same matrix without confusion, even if the patterns overlap to some degree. The other is that the entire input pattern need not be presented in order for accurate recall of the complete output to be achieved; as a result of the division operation, any unique subset of the input in question will do. Figure 1B shows the same matrix after two additional patterns have been stored. Those unfamiliar with this phenomenon might benefit from verifying that each input vector can be recalled without error by presenting the system either with its corresponding paired associate or with a unique fragment thereof and performing the recall operation just defined.

Obviously, the storage capacity of such systems is not unlimited, as can

A

	X1	Y INPUTS (Y1: 1 1 0 1 0 0)
X	0	0 0 0 0 0 0
I	0	0 0 0 0 0 0
N	0	0 0 0 0 0 0
P	1	1 1 0 1 0 0
U	1	1 1 0 1 0 0
T	1	1 1 0 1 0 0
S		

(left axis: X INPUTS; bottom label: X1)

B

Y INPUTS — Y3: 1 0 0 1 1 0 / Y2: 0 0 1 0 1 1 / Y1: 1 1 0 1 0 0
X INPUTS columns: X3 X2 X1 (bottom labels)

C

Y INPUTS — Y4: 1 1 0 0 0 1 / Y3: 1 0 0 1 1 0 / Y2: 0 0 1 0 1 1 / Y1: 1 1 0 1 0 0
X INPUTS columns: X4 X3 X2 X1 (bottom labels)

Figure 1

A: Correlation matrix after storage of one paired associate (X_1: 000111, Y_1: 110100) using the "Hebb" principle. Recall of Y_1 given X_1 is achieved by multiplying each row element by the corresponding input, summing the columns, and then performing an integer division of the result by the sum of the elements of the input (i.e., 330300/3 = 110100). **B:** The same matrix as in A after the associative storage of two more pairs of inputs. Even though these patterns are nonorthogonal (i.e., they share some active elements, and hence are somewhat correlated), associative recall is still possible because of the normalization operation. For example, multiplication by the input vector X_1 yields 332311. Integer division by 3 yields the correct result, Y_1: 110100. The correct result can also be recalled from partially obscured input. The subset of X_1:000110 is unique. Thus, multiplication yields 221210, which after division by 2 results in the complete Y_1 pattern. This pattern-completion effect is the essence of associative memory, whether it involves recall of one event given another (heteroassociation) or recall of a whole event given a unique part of it (autoassociation). **C:** Illustration of the problem of saturation, common to any distributed association device in which connection strengths are irreversibly modified. Storage of the fourth paired associate has caused interference with the ability to recall Y_3 given X_3.

readily be inferred by considering what the output pattern looks like after all the junctions have been modified. Figure 1C illustrates an intermediate case in which some input patterns are subject to "interference." Although the storage capacity of such matrices goes up impressively with the dimensionality of the input channels, this ultimate limit on capacity may nevertheless pose problems for actual neural systems. There are ways of alleviating this storage limitation; I shall return to this subject after reviewing several simple ways in which the correlation matrix notion may be translated into networks resembling neuronal circuits.

The most direct transformation of the correlation matrix into something resembling a neural circuit is shown in figure 2A. There are six "principal" neurons, which receive connections from axons corresponding to the X and Y channels of figure 1. The X and Y pathways, however, make different kinds of synapses. X connections resemble the modifiable junctions of the correlation matrix. X axons make contacts exhaustively with the principal cells (i.e., nonspecific connections). These synapses have strengths (or weights) equal to 0 unless activity on the parent fiber is correlated with output from the principal neuron (postsynaptic element), in which case the strength is permanently changed to 1. The Y input fibers make strong one-to-one (i.e., specific) connections with the principal cells. We refer to these strong specific inputs as "detonator" synapses, because their activity leads to unconditional discharge from the corresponding principal neuron. This simplifying assumption need not be taken too literally, however. In situations where all that is required is some unique representation of an input, rather than an exact copy, cooperation of multiple "detonators" will suffice. The state of the weight matrix in figure 2A is exactly the same as that in figure 1B, and the same accurate recall of Y patterns can be elicited by presentation of their associated X inputs. The obvious question arises, however, as to how the division and truncation operations—needed to achieve accurate recall in the correlation matrix—might be implemented in neural nets.

The solution, which was in fact suggested by Marr (1969, 1971), involves the use of "feedforward" inhibition from the nonspecific inputs. This inhibitory signal is presumed to implement the division of the excitation in the principal cells by an amount proportional to the number of fibers active in the input set, thus ensuring that only those elements respond to a given input for which the number of modified (enhanced) connections in the input set is maximal. The elaboration of this hypothesis will require some digression into the biophysics of neuronal interactions. The reader should be aware that the treatment that follows is neither mathematically nor physiologically rigorous.

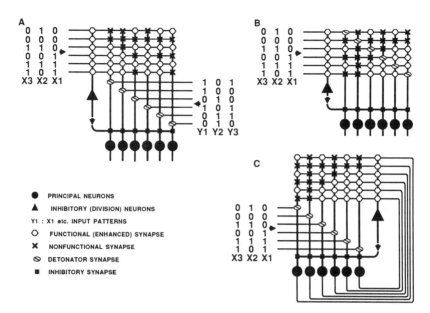

Figure 2

A: Implementation of the heteroassociative correlation matrix using "neuronlike" elements. In the simplified case, the Y input patterns are imposed on the population of principal neurons by means of "detonator" synapses, which unconditionally discharge the principal neurons they connect to and also set up the conditions for enhancement of converging inputs on the X_1 inputs (which are densely connected to the principal cells by modifiable synapses). The normalization operation during recall is accomplished by an inhibitory interneuron that samples the density of activity on the X pathway and feeds forward a proportional conductance shunt to the principal cells. **B:** A realization of autoassociation that is logically equivalent to making the X and Y input patterns to the network in A identical to each other. Each fiber of the input pathway makes many weak but modifiable connections and one detonator synapse (or a few). This might be achieved, for example, by having a parallel fiber make mostly weak but modifiable synapses on dendritic spines, but a few shaft synapses as well. This network can complete a given input pattern from any unique fragment of that pattern. **C:** A different realization of autoassociation that makes use of what Marr (1971) called a collateral effect. By use of feedback from the output of the principal cells back into their own dendrites via modifiable connections, and by holding the input constant long enough for the feedback to coincide with the input, each element of a pattern becomes associated with each other element, allowing subsequent pattern completion. Although this indirect method may seem more complex than that of B, it does have several interesting additional properties, one of which is the ability to hold a pattern in an active state by reverberation. It is also useful for pattern completion by *progressive* recall in networks in which the feedback is more sparsely distributed than illustrated here. Source: McNaughton and Morris 1987.

Rather, it is an attempt to express these interactions in terms of the sort of framework commonly used for PDP modeling (see, e.g., Rumelhart and McClelland 1986), in the hope of aiding in the construction of more neurally plausible models without undue computational expense.

Many such models begin with a set of processing units U, which, if we ignore the spatial distribution of synapses on dendrites, can be equated with neurons, and a matrix of connection strengths or "weights," which can be related to the concept of synaptic efficacy. The set of units is associated with an activation vector $A(t)$, which is easily translated into membrane voltage $V(t)$ associated with synaptic input and an output vector $O(t)$ whose components, in a neural model, might take on the value 0 or 1 depending on whether an action potential is elicited. Note that the binary nature of the output function accounts for the decimal truncation in the division operation alluded to above. The functional relation between $A(t)$ and $O(t)$ can be quite complicated. However, a common and useful simplification is to begin with a probabilistic threshold function (figure 3A) of the form

$$\pi(o_i(t) = 1) = \frac{1}{1 + \exp[-(v_i - q_i)/k_i]}, \tag{1}$$

where π denotes probability, q_i is the value of v_i at which the ith neuron fires 50 percent of the time, and k_i can be thought of as a noise term controlling the steepness of the threshold step. The k term might be considered as resulting from thermal noise, or from the random effects of inputs not explicitly accounted for in the particular model under consideration. The π value corresponding to a fixed membrane voltage could be assumed to translate into a particular average frequency of output of the unit in question, if q_i is assumed constant. For most neurons, however, q is not constant. First, there is the so-called refractory period, during which the threshold is, in effect, infinite. This period is on the order of a millisecond (which is thus a useful value of Δt in discrete-time simulations, because refractoriness can then be ignored). Alternatively, an exponential recovery of resting threshold can also be employed. Threshold is also controlled by a slower process known as accommodation, which results in firing rates that vary in time after a change in v_i (figure 3B). This process is not completely understood, but a simple model for it which fits well for many neurons was given by MacGregor and Oliver (1974). In difference form,

$$\Delta q_i = [-q_i + q_i^r + b_i (v_i - e_i^r)]/d_i, \tag{2}$$

where $b_i \geq 0$ and $0 < d_i < 1$. The parameter d controls the rate at which q changes, e^r represents the resting value of v in the absence of input, and b

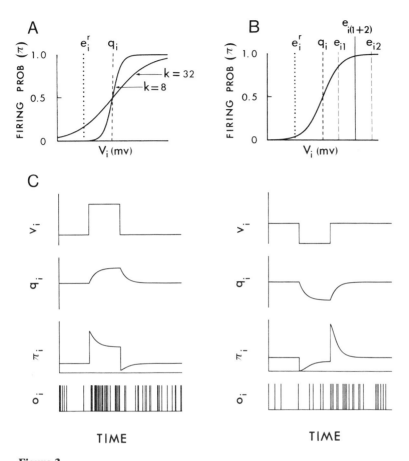

Figure 3
A: Threshold behavior of neuronal output can be *roughly* approximated by a simple
sigmoid curve relating probability of output (π) to membrane potential (v_i). **B:** In
real neural systems, *inhibition* is a relative term. Assume that there are two synapses, both of which are "excitatory" in the sense that, although they have different
e_{ij} values ($e_{i1} < e_{i2}$), both values lie above the resting potential of the cell and hence
tend to increase the probability of discharge. If all other parameters are the same, the
combined effect of the two synapses active together will be a smaller increase in
firing probability than if synapse 2 were active alone. **C:** For most neurons, the
threshold point is not constant but is a function of the recent history of v_i. For a brief
period immediately after an output event (action potential), the threshold is effectively infinite. A slower process, known as accommodation, results in an accentua-
tion of neuronal responses to *changes* in the input. This is illustrated for step
increases (left) or step decreases (right) in the activation parameter v_{ij}.

controls the steady-state value q attains at a given v. The general consequence of this function is that a rapid increase in activation produces an initial large increase in firing rate, which settles down to a somewhat smaller increase in rate after about d cycles. Conversely, a rapid decrease in activation leads to an initial large suppression of firing, which approaches a smaller steady-state suppression exponentially. These effects tend to accentuate *changes* in activation state.

For "point" neurons (i.e., those for which the spatial distribution of input over the dendritic surface is relatively unimportant), the "activation" rule of PDP formalism would be somewhat different from those typically assumed in PDP models. The difference has important logical consequences for computation in neural nets. In a neural model, the synaptic-weight matrix W would have to be represented by two matrices. The matrix G represents the conductance induced in the membrane of unit i by a synapse from unit j if the output state (o_j) of that unit is equal to 1 (i.e., neuron j emits an action potential). The matrix E represents the equilibrium values of v_i toward which the g_{ij} drive the activation state. Thus, the terms $(v_i - e_{ij})$ take on the aspect of driving forces which can be positive or negative depending on the current value of v_i. For this reason, the concepts of excitatory and inhibitory connections are only *relative* ones, and summation of inputs is not necessarily either linear or monotonic. The possibility exists, for example, that an "excitatory" synapse whose e value is just above the 50-percent firing threshold may actually suppress the high rates of discharge that would normally result from activation of a different class of "excitatory" synapse whose e value was far above threshold. It should also be mentioned that there exist certain synapses whose associated conductance channels are normally in an open state. In these cases, synaptic transmission involves a decrease in conductance.

Neurons come in a wide but not unlimited variety of types, and the values of e_{ij} are physically determined by factors contributed by the interaction of the ith and jth types. However, there is a strong tendency for the e_{ij} to be *matched* with the type of the presynaptic unit u_j. This is why most neurobiologists object to the use of positive and negative synaptic weights from the same unit in some PDP models. Although mixed weights are not biologically implausible, they represent relatively special cases. Each unit is also associated with resting values of conductance g_i^r and equilibrium potentials e_i^r to which the activation states tend in the absence of external input. Each connection drives the activation toward its own equilibrium point in proportion to the contribution of its conductance to the total conductance of the "postsynaptic" element. This change in activation state can be approximated by

$$\Delta v_i = \frac{g_i^r (e_i^r - v_i) + \Sigma_j o_j g_{ij}(e_{ij} - v_i)}{g_i^r + \Sigma_j o_j g_{ij}}, \qquad (3)$$

where o_j is the output state (0 or 1) of the jth neuron.

A number of studies have shown that most central "inhibitory" synapses are associated with e_{ij} values very close to e_i^r while "excitatory" synapses have values of e_{ij} which are positive to e_i^r. For simplicity let us suppose that synapse j is inhibitory while synapse k is excitatory: $e_{ij} = e_i^r = 0$ and $e_{ik} = 1$. Then equation 3 reduces to

$$\Delta v_i = \frac{o_k g_{ik}}{g_i^r + o_k g_{ik} + o_i g_{ij}}. \qquad (4)$$

Clearly, the excitatory effect is essentially *divided* by the sum of the inhibitory effects. The threshold function then takes care of the decimal truncation. This division effect becomes even more pronounced in situations where the excitation is applied to a dendrite and the inhibition is applied to the site of output initiation at the soma, a common configuration in many parts of the nervous system.

There are several other consequences of this particular form of activation function. First, the effects of synapses with the same values of e_{ij} will summate in a nonlinear fashion, since their combined effect will be to drive v_i asymptotically closer to e_{ij}. Second, the combined effect of two synapses which are both excitatory but which differ with respect to their e_{ij} will be an activation which is *less* than that of the synapse with the greater e_{ij} alone. Finally, because neuronal membranes have the properties of electrical capacitors, v_i cannot change instantaneously. In general, while synapses are active, v_i changes rapidly, with a time constant of $c_i/(g_i^r + \Sigma_j o_j g_{ij})$, where c_i is the membrane capacitance. When no synapses are active, v_i returns to e_i^r more slowly, with a time constant equal to c_i/g_i^r. This property allows for the temporal summation of inputs over times on the order of c_i/g_i^r. For hippocampal neurons, this time is about 10 msec. For point neurons, the temporal integration property may be included by multiplying equation 3 by a factor σ, where

$$\sigma = 1 - \exp\{[-(g_i^r + \Sigma_j o_j g_{ij})\Delta t]/c_i\}. \qquad (5)$$

From equation 4 we saw that certain types of synapses have the effect of performing a division operation on the activation caused by others. The way in which Marr proposed that inhibition could be used to sharpen up recall is illustrated in figure 2A. By making use of a set of inhibitory neurons that sampled the excitatory input from the afferent pathways and supplied inhibition to the cells where memory was stored, the activation of the memory cells would be divided by a term which was proportional to the total number of afferents active at a given time. In this way, only those cells with the correct number of active modified synapses would fire.

In the usual discrete-time PDP formalism, in which there is a constant delay across all units between output and the increment of the activation function, this inhibitory scheme will fail. This is because the inhibition will arrive one cycle after the excitation—too late to prevent the spurious output. If one is interested only in the average output of the network over numerous cycles during which the input is held constant, this may not matter very much because the necessary inhibition will be performed on the second and succeeding cycles. If the behavior of the system from cycle to cycle is deemed important, however, then the usual PDP formalism will require the introduction of special-purpose (and conceptually awkward) delay units to accommodate this effect. As will be shown below, there is clear evidence from hippocampal anatomy and physiology for a class of inhibitory interneurons with exactly the properties required by the division hypothesis. These neurons are few in number, receive input from the principal afferents, and distribute inhibition over a wide area. Their discharge trains carry relatively little specific information. They also respond significantly more quickly to afferent stimulation than the principal cells, so that the inhibitory division is effected quickly enough to limit the activation produced by the same input event. The inhibitory synapses made by these cells have e_{ij} values very close to e_i^r, as is necessary for a division operation.

Having established that the required recall operations are at least neurally plausible, let us return to a consideration of several interesting properties of this neuronal matrix memory scheme and some of its possible variants. The system shown in figure 2A is one example of what has been called hetero-association. That is, the pattern of output generated by input on the Y pathway is encoded in the weights of synapses on the X pathway in such a way that it can be recreated at some future time by presenting the corresponding X input alone. One interesting property of such storage, emphasized in PDP models of this nature, is that recall is resistant to the effects of incomplete input information. Any unique subset of a stored X pattern will elicit complete recall of the appropriate Y pattern. This pattern-completion effect can be exploited in arrangements known as autoassociation, which provide the capability of recalling a complete representation of a learned event from a reduced subset of the original. We shall consider two possible neuronal implementations. The direct version is shown in figure 2B. Let us assume that there is only one input pathway, and that it is exhaustively connected with the principle cells. A small proportion of these synapses are particularly strong and distribute to only a few principal cells (in this case, only one). The rest of the synapses are initially weak. The strong synapses control both the output pattern of the net and the modification of the weak synapses. The network shown has stored three events of size 3, which can all be recalled by presentation of any size-2 subevent not shared by some other event. Events X_1 and X_2 can even be recalled by size-1 subevents on the third and sixth fibers, respectively.

An indirect or reentrant version of an autoassociative net is shown in figure 2C. Here we have the input pathway making specific detonator synapses with the principal cells, which project exhaustively back upon themselves via weak but modifiable synapses. This device was called a "collateral effect" by Marr (1971). The system behaves in much the same way as direct autoassociation, with some interesting possible variations. First, once activated, the input can be silenced and the network will recycle the same pattern indefinitely unless it is explicitly turned off by some inhibitory process. In this respect the system can be used to implement Hebb's notion of reverberatory activity for short-term pattern storage. Second, for normal pattern storage, the input must be held constant for at least one cycle so that the output pattern becomes correlated with the input pattern. By making the input pattern change from cycle to cycle, the system can be used to store and recall sequences of patterns, because the input at time $t + \Delta$ becomes associated with the system state at time t. This bears some resemblance to Hebb's notion of a "phase sequence." Finally, a recurrent configuration can accomplish autoassociative pattern completion in systems that are more sparsely connected than that of figure 2C (i.e., systems for which the number of principal neurons exceeds the number of connections per neuron). In this case, although correct recall cannot be accomplished by a single pass through the system (because of the lack of appropriate direct connections), a progressive recall procedure can be employed in which the output of each cycle of recurrent excitatory activity more closely approximates the complete desired output (Marr 1971; Gardner-Medwin 1976; E. T. Rolls, personal communication).

As was mentioned above, all distributed information-storage systems of the kind outlined here are subject to degradation of stored information through saturation of their modifiable connections. There is a limit above which stored information is disrupted and no further storage is possible. There are several ways of alleviating this problem to some extent. The first is to keep the number of fibers active in any one event as small as possible, and to keep the input events as orthogonal to one another as possible (i.e., by minimizing the degree of overlap of active elements across events). It is generally recognized that this can be accomplished by efficient coding strategies, such as expressing visual images as sets of lines and edges or otherwise reducing sensory experience to compact feature descriptors. Where the inputs cannot be kept orthogonal, use can be made of a kind of orthogonalizing filter first suggested by Marr (1969), who used the term "codon representation." The basic idea is very simple. Suppose the activity of a set of n_1 units is projected onto a larger set of n_2 units in such a way that the total number (α) of active units in each population is held constant. For two randomly selected patterns each using α active inputs, the probability that any given fiber in population 1 is active in both is α^2/n_1^2, whereas in population 2 this is reduced to α^2/n_2^2. An example of codon representation is illustrated in figure 4. Finally, when all else fails, the memory limitation of a system can be overcome by either allowing information to decay or allowing competitive processes to occur whereby connections are increased only at the expense of decrease in the strength of other connections. The latter method may be undesirable for event storage, because previously stored events are subjected to random degradation. However, competitive learning may be quite useful for the development of detectors for regularly occurring classes of stimulus features (Rumelhart and Zipser 1986).

2 The Hippocampal Formation as a Connectionist Model

In this section I will try to summarize the organization of the hippocampal connectivity matrix, and the current understanding of the rules governing the synaptic weights and their modification, in the context of the foregoing simple theoretical considerations.

The hippocampus can be thought of as consisting of two sheets of cells folded around each other as illustrated in figure 5. It is actually topologically equivalent to the extreme margin of the cortical mantle, and it constitutes what many anatomists would consider the highest level of association cortex by virtue of its reciprocal connections with other (polymodal) cortical association areas and its lack of direct interaction with primary sensory areas. At the transition from neocortex to hippocampus, the cellular architecture simplifies from the characteristic six-layer cortical structure to essentially a single layer of cells, whose dendrites are all oriented more or less parallel to one another. Anatomists typically refer to two coordinate axes within this system: a transverse ("lamellar") axis and a longitudinal ("septo-temporal") axis. To a first approximation, the hippocampal formation is subdivided into longitudinal subregions which differ with respect to their principal cell types and/or connection patterns. An exception to this overall scheme is the so-called hilar region in the fold of the dentate gyrus; this might more properly be considered a sublayer of the latter.

The pattern of excitatory connectivity is highly directional (Lorente de No 1934) with respect to the transverse axis (figure 5). Information from neocor-

A

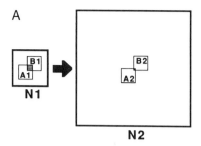

B

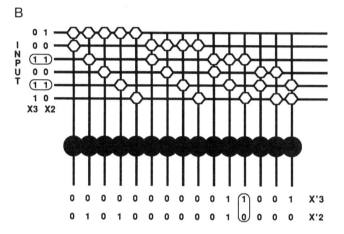

Figure 4

A: The general principal involved in Marr's "codon" idea can be illustrated by considering two sets of neurons. Let set N_1 contain 100 units, and let set N_2 contain 1,000. Assume that N_1 is randomly connected to N_2 by converging and diverging excitatory fibers. Assume also that the threshold for discharge in N_2 is adjusted such that, on average, the same absolute number (α) of units in each population are active in any given event. Then for two events A_1 and B_1 in N_1 and their transforms A_2 and B_2 in N_2, the probability that a given unit in N_1 is active in both events is simply the square of $\alpha/100$, whereas in N_2 the corresponding probability is $(\alpha/1,000)^2$. Thus, for any given pair of events, the representations in N_2 are more different from each other than the corresponding representations in N_1, because fewer units are common to both events. The same principle applies if N_1 and N_2 are the same size but the absolute activity level in N_2 is made much less than that of N_1. B: A specific example of pattern separation by expansion of the input pathway. In this case, each size-2 subset of input fibers from N_1 drives a single unit in N_2. Units in N_2 have thresholds equal to 2. It can be seen that although the two input patterns overlap by two units, their representations in N_2 overlap by only one unit and hence are more *orthogonal*. In general, these principals can be used by neuronal networks to minimize the degree of confusion between stored patterns and to increase the number of patterns that can be stored without interference.

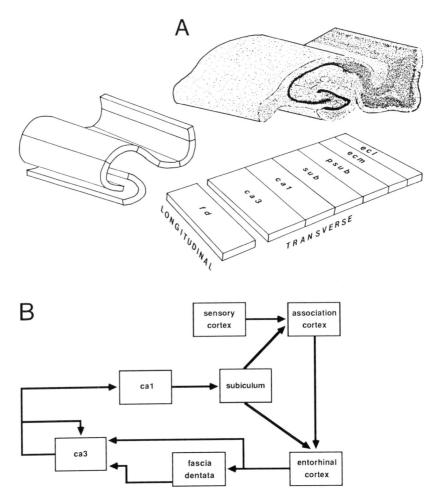

Figure 5
A: Illustration of the way in which the hippocampal formation can be conceptually unfolded along its longitudinal axis. (ecl—lateral entorhinal cortex; ecm—medial entorhinal cortex; psub—pre- and parasubiculum; sub—subiculum; CA1—regio superior; CA3—regio inferior; fd—fascia dentata). **B:** Illustration of the principal flow of excitatory connections between hippocampal subfields. Some of these connections are highly restricted in the longitudinal axis, giving rise to the notion of a predominantly transverse or "lamellar" organization of hippocampal circuitry. Extensive longitudinal excitatory connections exist, however (especially in CA3 and the hilar portion of the fascia dentata), and the degree of longitudinal spread varies among different projections, with the "mossy"-fiber system from fd to CA3 being the most restricted and the CA3 to CA3 intrinsic excitatory connections perhaps the least restricted. The intrinsic inhibitory circuits also have considerable longitudinal spread.

tical association areas collects in a temporal zone known as entorhinal cortex, which is actually subdivided into two distinct parts. From entorhinal cortex, a massive fiber system known as the "perforant" path projects to the fascia dentata (also called dentate gyrus), where it gives rise to over 80 percent (Matthews, Cotman, and Lynch 1976) of the excitatory connections onto the principal cells of that zone, the granule cells. Collaterals of these input fibers also pass forward to the pyramidal cells of CA3 (also known as regio inferior), where the information carried by them converges with its own transform via the axons of the dentate gyrus granule cells. The CA3 pyramidal cells are extensively interconnected (Swanson, Wyss, and Cowan 1978) by a system of excitatory collaterals of their main axon (the longitudinal association system), which also project to the pyramidal cells of CA1 via the Schaffer collateral system. CA1 pyramidal cells transmit to the subicular complex, which is the major return pathway for hippocampally processed information to the neocortex and which also feeds back into the circuit at the entorhinal cortex (Swanson and Cowan 1977).

The perforant path projection from entorhinal cortex has some interesting topographical and physiological properties. First, the terminal fields from entorhinal cells to fascia dentata and CA3 show a gradation of anatomical specificity according to their location along the transverse axis (Wyss 1981). Cells in the "medial" entorhinal cortex terminate in relatively narrow transverse strips. The width of these strips increases as the location of the parent unit moves toward the "lateral" entorhinal cortex to the point that cells located most laterally in entorhinal cortex project to almost the entire longitudinal extent of the dentate gyrus and CA3.

Superimposed on this gradation from specific to nonspecific topography is another topography with respect to the location of the terminal fields along the dendritic axis, normal to the plane of the cell layers (Hjorth-Simonsen 1972; Steward 1976). There is a rather precise relation between the location in the transverse axis of an entorhinal afferent (and hence its specificity) and the distance of its terminal field from the cell body of the target neuron along the dendritic axis. The more specific afferents terminate closer to the cell bodies. This gradient of input location gives rise to a gradient of effective synaptic weight (assuming that the other synaptic variables are the same), because currents generated at remote synapses leak out of the dendrite on their way to the cell body (the "spike generator zone"), where the neuronal activation function typically is translated into output (Jefferys 1979). The more remote the synapse, the greater the loss of effective activation (Rall 1962). In the case of the granule cells, this leakage factor would be expected to result in about a twofold reduction in synaptic weight 'between the most specific (proximal) synapses and the most nonspecific (distal) synapses.

Other factors conspire to create an even larger difference in effective synaptic weight between the proximal and distal synapses of this system. It turns out that the distinction between medial and lateral entorhinal projections is more than just an anatomical one. The synapses of these projections have been found to stain differentially with a histological procedure (Timm staining) which reveals certain differences in synaptic biochemistry (Haug 1973). This stain creates a sharp line of demarcation between the middle third of the dendritic layer of the dentate gyrus and the outer third. These two zones correspond to the terminal fields of the medial and lateral perforant paths, respectively. There are also some discrete differences in the termination patterns of other cortical and subcortical afferent systems in the two subdivisions of the entorhinal area, as well as clear morphological differences (Steward and Scoville 1976) in the cells of origin of the two components of the perforant path. These two components differ with respect to certain other parameters which determine synaptic weight, irrespective of dendritic location. In order to explain this we must diverge somewhat into a brief discussion of the neurophysiological techniques and findings related to the analysis of synaptic transmission.

Synaptic transmission is generally studied in experiments in which one unit or (usually) a group of units is stimulated with a very brief electrical current which sets the output function to 1. The "response" recorded at a different unit or group of units is a measure related to either their activation or their output functions (or both) in ways which depend upon the particular recording technique employed. In this chapter I will be referring to three different techniques: extracellular single-unit recording, intracellular recording, and extracellular field potential recording. Extracellular single-unit recording typically involves placing a fine-tipped metal electrode very close to an individual unit, and gives information only about the output state of that unit. This technique can be usefully applied to freely behaving animals. Intracellular recording involves penetrating the membrane of single units with a very fine-tipped (< 1 μm) glass capillary filled with some conductive solution. This technique typically measures the activation state (v_i) and the output state (o_i) of a single unit. This method is rather difficult, and it can generally only be applied either to deeply anesthetized animals or to thin slices of brain tissue maintained in an artificial medium. Neither of these preparations can reveal much in the way of behavioral correlates of neuronal activity. The third method, extracellular field potential recording, can also be applied to freely behaving animals. However, it is clearly interpretable only in parts of the brain (such as the hippocampus) where the structural regularity allows both the synchronous activation of a major input system and the linear superposition of a large number of minute dipole-like electric fields generated by individual elements. Extracellular field potential recording is able to provide a measure proportional to the number of units in the afferent population from which the electrical stimulus elicited output, a second measure related to the average membrane electrical current in the population of receiving cells which results from the evoked input (this measure, known as the population field epsp, is related only indirectly to the activation parameter v), and a measure of the proportion of units in the receiving population whose output states become 1 as a result of stimulation (the "population spike"). It is the measures relating to evoked changes in activation state that can tell us something about the synaptic weights. In the case of intracellular recording, one can obtain a measure directly proportional to

$$\sum_j (o_j w_{ij}). \tag{6}$$

In the case of the extracellular field epsp, the signal is related approximately to the average change in activation state in the population. If $v_i(t)$ prior to stimulation is assumed to be constant, then it is possible to draw inferences about changes in the average synaptic weights in the population from changes in the extracellularly recorded synaptic response evoked by synchronous electrical activation of a fixed population of afferent fibers. Given small inputs and a constant baseline activation state, the extracellular record provides a useful approximate measure of the average synaptic conductance ($\sum_i g_{ij}/n$) of the population.

The story becomes more complex, however, because these g_{ij} terms are actually functions of several other variables which change in interesting ways depending on the experience of the network. One can decompose g_{ij} conceptually into a "presynaptic" function m_{ij} (which represents the average amount of a chemical neurotransmitter substance released from synaptic terminals during an output pulse) and a "postsynaptic" function b_{ij} (which is related to the amount of conductance due to the release of a unit of transmitter). Both of these can be further decomposed into physically significant components. We shall see later that the function b has a linear and a nonlinear component, and that the latter is crucially involved in regulating long-term changes in synaptic weights. For the time being, however, we are interested only in the linear part of b. The function m, on the other hand, is decomposable into a stochastic equation:

$$m_{ij}(t) = o_j(t)n_{ij}(t)p_{ij}(t), \tag{7}$$

where $n_{ij}(t)$ is the number of "quanta" of transmitter in a potentially releasable state (sometimes also thought of as the number of "loaded" release sites) and $p_{ij}(t)$ is the probability of release of one quantum. It turns out that both p_{ij} and n_{ij} are dynamic functions of the recent output history of their parent unit, u_j. Whenever $o_j = 1$, n_{ij} is reduced by a factor $(1 - p_{ij}(t))$. The function $n_{ij}(t)$ recovers its rest value approximately exponentially with a time constant of about 2 or 3 seconds. This can also be thought of as resulting from the stochastic "reloading" of individual sites emptied during the preceding release event. The probability term $p_{ij}(t)$, on the other hand, is subject to three apparently separate physical effects which tend to increase p_{ij} each time $o_j = 1$. As will be elaborated below, these three components to Δp_{ij} accumulate with different increments and decay with different time constants. With a system at rest, a single output event causes a significant increment in only the fastest of these processes, which is known as facilitation. Under these circumstances, the transmitter released during a second output event occurring t seconds after an earlier event is approximated by

$$m_{ij}(t) = p_{ij}^r + \Delta p_{ij}^f \exp(-t/\tau_f)(n_{ij}^r \{1 - [p_{ij}^r \exp(-t/\tau_n)]\}), \qquad (8)$$

where Δp_{ij}^f is an increment of p_{ij} and where $1/\tau_f$ and $1/\tau_n$ are the rates at which p_{ij} and n_{ij} recover their resting values. Because τ_f is much smaller than τ_n (0.1 sec versus 4 sec), the resting probabilities of transmitter release can be estimated by determining what is known as a paired pulse response curve, in which the change in response size due to a preceding response is plotted as a function of stimulus interval. Extrapolation of the slow exponential recovery to zero interval gives a measure of p_{ij}^r. Curves illustrating this function for the medial and lateral perforant paths are shown in figure 6. The extrapolation operation leads to the conclusion that p_{ij}^r is about 0.3 in the medial pathway and only about 0.05 in the lateral pathway. This difference in resting probability of transmitter release is thus another factor that makes lateral-path synapses intrinsically somewhat weaker than those of the medial path (McNaughton 1980).

To summarize up to this point, then: The principal cortical inputs to the dentate gyrus are organized according to a plan resembling the heteroassociative model of figure 2A, with a set of relatively weak nonspecific inputs converging with a different set of stronger and more anatomically specific inputs.

Hidden within this structure may also be found an organization resembling the linear autoassociative model of figure 2B. Studies of the microphysiology of individual medial perforant path connections to the dentate gyrus have revealed that the majority of these synapses are extremely weak. About 2 or

3 percent, however, appear to generate activations that are greater than the rest by a factor of from 10 to 20 (McNaughton, Barnes, and Andersen 1981). The distribution is clearly bimodal. These synapses could thus act like "detonators" by exerting a disproportionate influence on the output state of their targets and, as we shall see below, on the control of synaptic modification in the weaker elements. What these strong synapses represent is still a matter of conjecture. One possibility is that they are synapses on dendritic shafts rather than dendritic spines. Shaft synapses make up only a few percent of the total excitatory input (Laatsch and Cowan 1966). Theoretical studies (e.g. Koch and Poggio 1982; Miller, Rall, and Rinzel 1985) have indicated that the arrangement of synapses on spines could lead to a large (5- to 10-fold) attenuation of the synaptic signal as seen from the cell-body trigger zone. Thus, there is some suggestive evidence from both anatomy and physiology for the implementation of a heteroassociative mechanism, a linear autoassociative mechanism, or both within the dentate gyrus.

Finally, some attention must be given to the numerical relations of this projection. The granule cells are rather numerous; estimates for the rat are about 10^6 (Gaarskjaer 1978), versus about 10^5 entorhinal projection cells. Each granule cell receives about 6×10^3 perforant path terminals (West and Andersen 1980), which means that the average divergence of the entorhinal projection cells must be about 6×10^4. In other words, there is about a tenfold increase in cell numbers from entorhinal cortex to dentate gyrus, and *on average* each entorhinal cell connects to about 6 percent of the granule-cell population. This expansion in cell numbers could be acting as the sort of pattern separator suggested by Marr's (1971) codon idea (see figure 4) if the absolute number of entorhinal and dentate units active at one time were held constant. Unfortunately, however, the limited available data indicate that dentate granule cells have among the highest activity rates in the hippocampal formation (Rose, Diamond, and Lynch 1983; McNaughton 1985). This does not appear to be consistent with a pattern-separation function.

Next, let us consider the output of the granule cells, first with respect to their connections within the dentate gyrus and then with respect to their projection to CA3. The granule cells definitely do not make connections with one another. They do, however, make at least two kinds of connections within the hilar region (Claiborne, Amaral, and Cowan 1986). The first is onto an inhibitory interneuron: the basket cell discussed above (see figure 2). Basket cells are rather sparse in number, usual estimates being on the order of one per 100–200 granule cells. Their inhibitory influence, however, is powerful and widespread. Basket-cell axons travel for 30 percent or more of the longitudinal and transverse ranges (Struble, Desmond, and Levy 1978) of the

A

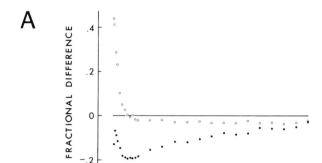

B

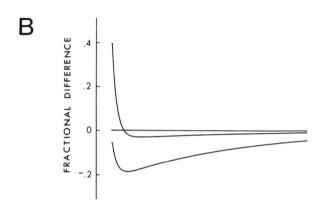

C

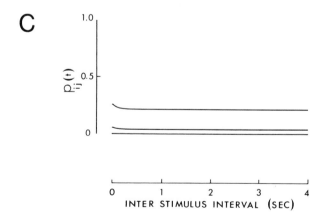

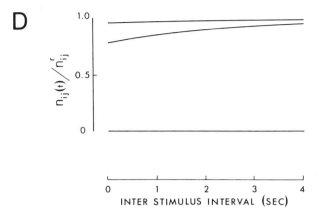

Figure 6
If a resting synapse is activated at time zero and again at a variable time later, the synaptic strength can be seen to fluctuate as a function of the interval between the two output events. The fluctuation is influenced by at least two processes, one involving a transient increase in the probability of quantal release of transmitter (p_{ij} of equation 7) and one involving a reduction in the number of quanta available for release (n_{ij} of equation 7) due to the fact that a certain number were used on the first response and these are replaced only relatively slowly. An estimate of the proportion of n_{ij} used on the first response can be made by extrapolating the slow recovery curve to zero interval (ignoring the early transient increase in p_{ij}, a process referred to as "facilitation"). This estimate reflects the resting probability of release. The data curves presented in part A are for the medial (closed circles) and lateral (open circles) perforant-path projections to the granule cells of fascia dentata. The data are represented as fractional difference of a test response delivered at various intervals after a control response elicited from the system at rest ($[m_{ij}(t) - m_{ij}^r]/m_{ij}^r$). These different responses to varied activations are simulated in part B by a simple model based on the assumption that the release probability is related to fourth power of the concentration of calcium ion in the synapse and that this concentration is slightly and transiently raised after each impulse. The underlying changes in p_{ij} and n_{ij} are shown in parts C and D, respectively. The only parameter manipulated was the resting release probability (via the resting level of internal calcium). These simulations thus suggest that medial perforant-path synapses have a considerably higher resting probability of release than those of the lateral perforant path.

dentate layer, giving off multiple terminal baskets which surround granule-cell bodies. There are no quantitative data on the convergence and divergence of these axons; however, a very rough guess would be that each basket cell contacts about 1,000 granule cells and that each granule cell receives only about ten basket-cell contacts. The latter guess is guided by the fact that a single basket terminal covers a considerable proportion of the cell body, making multiple contact sites for transmitter release.

The typical basket cell is located near the bottom of the granule-cell-body layer, and gives rise to both ascending and descending dendrites. There is clear evidence that the ascending dendrite, which can run to the top of the molecular layer, receives excitatory connections from the perforant pathways, as well as from another axon system which arises from the second main hilar recipient of granule-cell connections (see below). The descending dendrite, on the other hand, receives excitatory connections from the granule-cell axons and inhibitory influences from several subcortical regions. Again, numerical data are lacking, but a coarse guess would be that each basket cell receives several thousand contacts of all types. These are exclusively on dendritic shafts rather than spines, which makes it likely that they are generally quite powerful and fast. The physiological support for this conjecture will be discussed presently. In view of the configuration of basket-cell basilar dendrites and the organization of the granule-cell axonal plexus in the hilus, each basket cell could receive contacts from any granule cell within a transverse strip of dentate gyrus roughly 0.5–1 mm in width (i.e., about 10 percent of the population). The granule-cell-to-basket-cell divergence is not known; however, the upper limit is probably less than about 50, and the true number could be considerably lower if the granule-cell axon makes multiple contacts with the basket cell, as seems likely from the data of Amaral (1978). The general connectivity pattern of the basket cell is consistent with the notion that it takes samples of activity *density* in both the afferent fiber systems and the granule cells themselves and divides the net excitation of the granule cells by some weighted proportion of these.

The granule cells contact at least one other cell type in the hilus: the large multipolar cells that have been called "mossy cells." (This term may lead to some confusion because the axons of the *granule* cells are called "mossy fibers"; therefore, the term multipolar cell will be used here.) The axon of the hilar multipolar neuron travels extensively up and down the long axis of the dentate gyrus, making excitatory contacts in the inner portion of the dentate molecular layer on the dendrites of *both the granule cells and the basket cells*. The number of multipolar cells is about 2×10^4, and each granule cell probably receives about 2×10^3 such contacts, which means that each multipolar cell contacts about one in ten granule cells. The multipolar-cell connection with the granule cell is apparently considerably weaker than perforant-path connections. The connection to the basket cell, however, is probably rather strong (Buzsaki and Eidelberg 1981; Douglas, McNaughton, and Goddard 1983).

After extensive ramification immediately below its cell body, the granule-cell axon sends off a collateral known as the "mossy fiber," which makes synaptic connections in CA3 within a narrow (0.3–0.5 mm) transverse strip (Blackstad, Brink, Hem, and Jeune 1970). Judging from their morphology, these mossy-fiber synapses may be good candidates for "detonator" synapses. The synaptic "bouton" is among the largest in the brain, and is located very close to the pyramidal cell body and makes multiple contacts with both short spines and dendritic shafts. Each granule cell probably contacts only about 15 out of about 1.5×10^5 CA1 pyramidal cells, and each pyramidal cell receives input from about 100 granule cells (based on quantitative studies by Claiborne, Amaral, and Cowan [1986]). Only a few of these connections probably need to be active to fire the pyramidal cell (Brown and Johnston 1983). The granule-cell axon also makes excitatory connections with the CA3 basket cells (Frotscher 1985), which are similar in their distribution, connectivity, and physiology to dentate basket cells.

The CA3 pyramidal cell has a unique arrangement of connections. We have already seen that it receives a highly specific and powerful input from the granule cells. In addition, the pyramidal cell receives weak excitatory inputs from the same set of perforant-path axons that drive the granule-cell input. This set of connections therefore resembles a heteroassociative version of autoassociation. The principal inputs make weak direct connections, and strong indirect connections via an intermediate set of units. In addition, the CA3 pyramidal cells are the only cells in the hippocampus that are extensively interconnected (in a manner analogous to the reentrant autoassociative network of figure 2C). The CA3 axon also makes extensive connections with the pyramidal cells of CA1 (via a branch known as the Schaffer collateral), and with pyramidal cells of both CA3 and CA1 of the opposite hemisphere. Yet another branch leaves the hippocampus via its anterior end, to terminate in the lateral septal nucleus (Swanson and Cowan 1979) as part of a system that generates rhythmic excitability oscillations throughout the hippocampus.

3 Modulation and Modification of Synaptic Weights

In most PDP models, at least some of the synaptic weights are considered modifiable. The modification rules used vary considerably from model to model, but they all have in common some variant of the principle, generally attributed to Hebb (1949), that the modification of one connection is some joint function of the activation states of both the sending and the receiving units. As we shall see, this general principle has been verified with respect to changes in synaptic weights acting over quite long time periods. Over short times, however, an additional set of rules seem to apply—rules with very different logical consequences. These rules govern the dynamics of m, the presynaptic component of the weight function which reflects the mean number of transmitter quanta released per impulse (equation 7). This function is solely concerned with the recent history of activity of the sending unit.

The medial and lateral perforant paths (which, as we have already seen, differ with respect to the parameter p_{ij}^r, the resting probability of release) provide a good example of the dynamic range of effects of presynaptic activity in different types of synapses. When tested with pairs of impulses from rest, the medial path exhibits considerable synaptic depression, whereas the lateral-path responses are facilitated at short intervals. The relative depression of the medial-path synapses can be converted to relative facilitation by lowering the external calcium-ion concentration, a treatment that lowers the resting release probability p_{ij}^r. During repetitive activity at frequencies up to 20 Hz, the medial-path responses are driven down to steady-state values well below their resting level. The lateral responses show an initial facilitation, which appears to fall off to a steady-state value near the resting level. At still higher frequencies, both responses are depressed (McNaughton 1980). For neither path, however, is the response depression as severe as would be predicted from a constant p_{ij}^r and a 2- or 3-second recovery time constant for n. This discrepancy might be accounted for by assuming that the recovery of n is faster than a single exponential during the very early phase.

In the cases discussed so far, we have considered the response of groups of synapses comprising a small percentage of the total population but nevertheless consisting of thousands of individual synapses. Thus, the n term has actually referred to the sum of n in the group, and so has behaved like a continuous variable. In order to see how the equation for m translates into individual synaptic weights, it is necessary to examine the behavior of individual or very small groups of synapses, and to discuss some recent findings concerning the physical basis of the n term.

The probabilistic expression of presynaptic transmitter release implies that if n is actually rather small, there will be a measurable number of occasions on which the actual number of transmitter quanta released from a terminal is zero. Figure 7C illustrates a set of synaptic responses recorded intracellularly from a single granule cell after stimulation of just a few medial perforant-

A   B

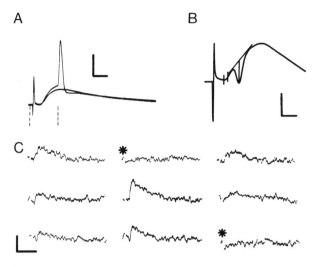

Figure 7
A: Superimposed examples of an intracellular record of v_i of a granule cell of the
fascia dentata after stimulation of a considerable number of inputs (approximately
400). One stimulus is just below the output threshold and one just above. The early
spike is an electrical artifact from the stimulus pulse; the later spike is the output
event (action potential). **B:** Extracellularly recorded field potentials recorded from
the fascia dentata after stimulation of the excitatory afferents at low or high intensity.
The slow potential is an indirect measure of the net synaptic current flow in the
granule-cell population. The negative spike potential reflects the summed output
from the population. **C:** The essential unreliability of unitary synaptic transmission
at many central synapses is illustrated in this series of v_i transients (epsps) recorded
intracellularly from a single granule cell of the dentate gyrus in response to stimulation of at most several perforant-path axons. Responses marked with asterisks represent occasions on which apparently no neurotransmitter was released. These
response failures occur on about one-third of all output events (action potentials) on
the afferent fibers.

path fibers. The response amplitude fluctuates, and on some trials it is indistinguishable from zero. Analysis of the mean amplitude of responses of single
medial fibers and the statistical distribution of response strength leads to the
conclusion that these fibers fail to release *any* transmitter on about 37 percent
of trials and, on the average, release only a single quantum per event. This
means that n must be rather small—certainly less than 3 or 4. In the limiting
case of $n = 1$, the expression for the rate of recovery of n reduces to an
expression for the exponential distribution, over many trials, of waiting times
for the all-or-none recovery of n, where the probability of recovery is constant
in time. There are several interesting consequences of these sorts of findings.

One is that, for synapses at which both p and n are rather small, high rates of presynaptic discharge may be required to ensure that *any* transmitter at all is released over the integration time of the receiving neuron. This has important implications for the mechanisms of persistent synaptic modification (to be discussed presently). Another interesting result of the presynaptic dynamics as discussed to this point is that the *stability* of the presynaptic function can be manipulated by varying both n and p. In general, if n is large and p small, the response might be stable or might increase. On the other hand, a large p and small n will produce responses that depress rapidly.

So far we have considered the effects of rapidly decaying increments in p following single or a few impulses, and we have seen generally that, as p increases, the *maintained* response to inputs at fixed frequencies falls as a function of frequency, because of a net depletion of n. There exist, in addition, at least two apparently different processes that contribute small increments to p with each impulse, and that decay rather slowly. The result is that, after periods of elevated activity, the response to lower frequencies does not merely recover but exhibits a significant overshoot. This is illustrated in figure 8, where the response to stimuli at ⅓ Hz is shown over the course of several minutes following a brief episode of high-frequency activity (250 Hz, for 0.2 sec).

The increase in p during repetitive activity and its return to p^r after the activity is terminated can be adequately described by a three-component model in which the three components each increase toward their own asymptotes with succeeding stimuli and decrease afterward with their own time constants. The total increase is of course limited by the difference between p^r and 1. The decay can be approximated very closely by

$$p(t) = p^r + \Delta p^f \exp(-t/\tau^f) + \Delta p^a \exp(-t/\tau^a) + \Delta p^p \exp(-t/\tau^p), \qquad (9)$$

where Δp^f, Δp^a, and Δp^p are the partial increments to p^r immediately after the last stimulus and where τ^f, τ^a, and τ^p are the corresponding time constants. In the synaptic-physiology literature, these components are generally referred to as facilitation, augmentation, and potentiation, respectively (Magleby and Zengel 1976a,b). The corresponding time constants are remarkably similar across different synaptic types (Zengel and Magleby 1982; McNaughton 1982), being approximately 0.1, 5, and 60 seconds. These differing time constants may simply reflect the relative rate constants for release of calcium ion from different intraterminal buffers where the calcium that enters the terminal after an impulse is temporarily sequestered.

It is important to note that, provided the number of coactive fibers is kept small, this transient increase in p can be elicited over and over without any

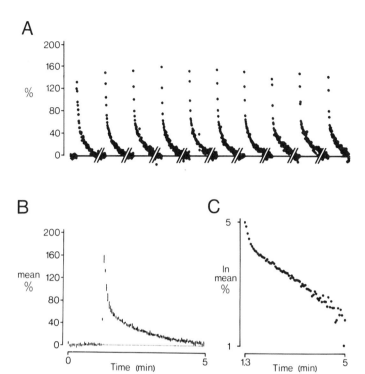

Figure 8

Transient increases in transmitter release probability can be elicited repetitively without any long-term effect on synaptic efficacy. In the experiment illustrated here, the lateral perforant path was stimulated with a brief burst of pulses at high frequency, once every 10 minutes, for ten trials. The resulting increase in synaptic strength was assessed using low-frequency stimulation (⅓ Hz) and is expressed here as a percent increase above the resting response. The average of the data in A is shown in linear coordinates in part B and in semilogarithmic coordinates in part C. The latter plot illustrates the two slower exponential components of the recovery time course (equation 9). The faster component is not seen on this time scale.

change in its relative magnitude and with *no tendency toward increased persistence*. This is illustrated in figure 8.

A final word needs to be said about the physical basis of the parameter n. The statistical nature of quantal release of neurotransmitter was discovered at about the same time as the first electronmicrographs of nerve terminals began to reveal the presence of small membrane sacs or "vesicles" within the nerve terminal. These were subsequently shown to contain neurotransmitter in amounts comparable to the quanta released during transmission. It was naturally assumed at first that the n parameter could be equated with the number of these vesicles seen in electronmicrographs. However, statistical analysis of synaptic-response fluctuation at a number of different types of synapse in the nervous system has generally led to values of n which are far smaller than the number of synaptic vesicles in the terminal. More recent work has established reasonably clearly that n is equivalent to the number of distinct specialized contact sites between a terminal and its postsynaptic target (Korn, Mallet, Triller, and Faber 1982; Redman and Walmsley 1983). These sites—which, at most excitatory synapses, show up under the electron microscope as asymmetric dense zones of apposition (Gray 1959; type 1)—appear to represent discrete sites for release of a single transmitter quantum. The release from a site is an all-or-none event that occurs with probability p. The site presumably is then reloaded from the pool of transmitter vesicles in the terminal. On the assumption that reloading occurs when a vesicle contacts a site and that vesicles are in random motion, the distribution of reloading latencies for a single site would be exponential with a mean equal to the observed time constant for the ensemble (2–3 sec).

The importance of these findings is that they provide a means of interpreting the morphology of connections. Synapses that have multiple contact sites will be either very powerful or much less subject to depression at steady activation rates, depending on the resting value of p. Most perforant-path synapses have only one or two contact zones per postsynaptic cell. The mossy-fiber terminals of the granule cells and a number of terminals within the hilus, on the other hand, may have half a dozen contact zones or more. Much more needs to be learned about the relative tendencies of other hippocampal connections toward facilitation or depression under maintained activity before an accurate model of the system dynamics can be developed.

The synaptic-weight changes we have considered so far are determined solely by the pattern of activity of the presynaptic fibers, and are of relatively short duration. Both of these properties are generally inconsistent with the weight-change rules of most or all PDP models, although they clearly must play a role in the dynamic pattern of activation of the system. We now turn to a phenomenon that appears to have much in common with such models and is clearly the best candidate for an associative-learning mechanism yet revealed by neurophysiology. The basic phenomenon is illustrated in figure 9. In this experiment, a small set of fibers was stimulated at ⅓ Hz and the corresponding synaptic responses were recorded. A brief (0.5 sec) episode of high-frequency (200 Hz) activity was inserted at L. This resulted in the transient elevation of synaptic strength that was just discussed. After recovery of baseline, a second episode of high-frequency stimulation was introduced (H). This stimulation was of exactly the same frequency and duration as the original. The difference was that during the second high-frequency episode the stimulus *intensity* was increased so that a much larger population of afferents was brought into coactivity at high frequency. After this event, the stimulus intensity was returned to its original low level. As figure 9 shows, there was initially the same transient growth of the response. Superimposed on this, however, was a much more enduring change in synaptic efficacy. This phenomenon was originally called long-lasting *potentiation* by its discoverers (Bliss and Lomo 1973; Bliss and Gardner-Medwin 1973), who at the time had no grounds to differentiate it from the "potentiation" discussed above (which contributes to an increase in p, the probability of transmitter disease). Although the name long-term potentiation or LTP is still in common usage, I will refer to the phenomenon as *long-term enhancement* (LTE) to keep the distinction clear. That LTE is not just an enduring form of potentiation is illustrated in figure 10, which demonstrates that, although p does indeed increase transiently after the stimulation used to induce LTE, this increase returns to the baseline level with the same time course as when no LTE is induced. Thus, there is a persistent increase in the synaptic-weight function that does not involve increased p as we have defined it.

The fact that it was necessary to coactivate many fibers during a high-frequency input event in order to elicit LTE suggests immediately that the control of this change involves something more than merely the state of the sending fiber. This was made more clear in experiments employing stimulation of both the medial and lateral perforant paths simultaneously or separately (figure 11). The results of such experiments show clearly that LTE is an associative phenomenon (McNaughton, Douglas, and Goddard 1978). Low-intensity input to either pathway that fails to elicit LTE when delivered independently can elicit robust LTE when delivered conjointly. The same sort of cooperativity among coactive afferents has also been demonstrated in the CA3 projection to CA1 (Lee 1983).

There is now a considerable body of experimental data on the mechanisms regulating the expression of LTE. It will be recalled that the conductance term

A

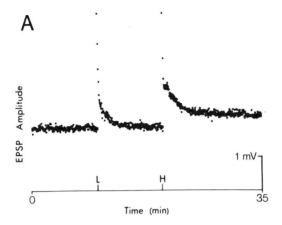

B

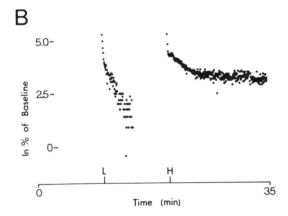

Figure 9

Long-term enhancement (LTE) of hippocampal synapses requires convergence of multiple coactive afferents. In the experiment illustrated here, the efficacy of synaptic transmission in a small group of perforant-path fibers to the fascia dentata was assessed by applying weak electric shocks once every 3 seconds and recording the extracellular-field epsp generated in the granule cells. High-frequency stimulus bursts (100 stimuli at 200 Hz) were applied at *L* and *H*. The burst at *L* was delivered at the same low stimulus intensity as the test shocks. The burst at *H* was delivered at about 10 times the test stimulus intensity. This activated a large number of afferent fibers. Short-term augmentation and potentiation followed both the *L* and *H* bursts. In addition, however, LTE developed after the *H* burst. The data in part A are replotted in part B on a semilogarithmic axis in order to illustrate the differences in decay rate between "potentiation" and "enhancement." Experiments of this sort were the first indication that LTE possessed the conjunctive characteristics necessary for associative memory.

g_{ij} of the synaptic-weight function must be decomposed into a presynaptic component m_{ij} (the amount of transmitter released) and a postsynaptic component b_{ij} (the conductance per unit transmitter released). At perforant-path and other hippocampal synapses exhibiting LTE, however, there are two components to b_{ij}, one of which has an unusual property. This component is dependent both on the activation state already present on the postsynaptic cell at the time of arrival of the transmitter and on the amount of transmitter released (see Collingridge 1985). Below a certain level of v_i this component is inactive. A rough approximation would be to describe g_{ij} as follows:

$$g_{ij} = m_{ij}\left(z_{ij} + \frac{h_{ij}}{1 + \exp[-(v_i - f)/w]}\right), \tag{10}$$

where z_{ij} represents the classical (linear) conductance, f is the membrane potential at which the second component is equal to $h_{ij}/2$, and w controls the slope of the transition from 0 to h_{ij}. This slope is probably rather steep, and the value of f is significantly in excess of the corresponding threshold for the output function (equation 1). A slight complication results from the fact that the z and h terms may each be associated with different equilibrium values e_{ij}^z and e_{ij}^h, where the latter term is relatively more activating than the former.

One result of all this is that for transient inputs the relation between probability of output and number of active inputs will be upwardly inflected for large inputs. This will tend to make activity "bursty." The major result of interest, however, is that the control of LTE is exerted by the second component. By mechanisms not yet understood completely, the opening of the conductance channel underlying the voltage-dependent component of g_{ij} results in the induction of LTE (Collingridge, Kehl, and McLennan 1983; Harris, Ganong, and Cotman 1984).

The dependency of the LTE induction mechanism on the postsynaptic voltage confers several interesting properties on LTE. First, it explains the cooperativity effect. No synapses are modified unless the postsynaptic cell is rather strongly depolarized—the essence of the Hebb synapse. Second, it accounts for the presynaptic and postsynaptic specificity of LTE. Several studies have demonstrated that only the connections of the units that were coactive are modified (McNaughton and Barnes 1977; Andersen, Sundberg, Sveen, and Wigstrom 1977), and then only those that converged in sufficient numbers on common postsynaptic elements (Levy and Steward 1979). The receiving unit emerges as the integrator which, given activity on a set of units, exercises the ultimate control over which connections will be enhanced. This is a common element of virtually all theoretical models for the associative modification of connection weights.

A

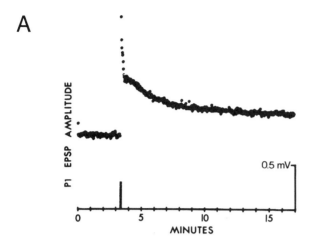

B

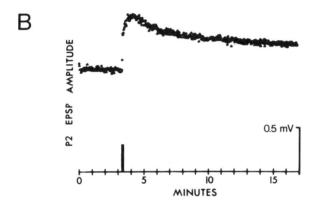

C

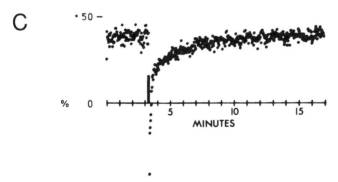

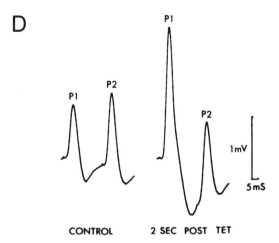

Figure 10
Evidence that LTE is not just a long-term form of potentiation was provided by the
demonstration that, whereas both augmentation and potentiation involve an increase
in the parameter P_{ij} (equation 7), no such increase is observed in the presence of LTE
once the accompanying transient augmentation and potentiation have decayed. The
dissociation of these processes was demonstrated by the use of a double shock paradigm on the lateral perforant path. Stimulus pairs with a short interstimulus interval
were presented once every 3 seconds. The relative amplitudes of the two responses
in each pair were compared (see figure 6) before high-frequency stimulation and
after a stimulus train that generated augmentation, potentiation, and LTE. As is evident from equation 7, n_{ij} will be depleted in proportion to the initial value of p_{ij},
resulting in a reduction of the product m_{ij}, the amount of transmitter released during
the second response. This depletion was greatly increased in the presence of augmentation and potentiation, indicating that these processes involved an increase in
p_{ij}. However, the increased depletion decayed with the decay of augmentation and
potentiation, even though the absolute magnitude of the synaptic response remained
elevated because of the presence of LTE. The magnitudes of the first and second
synaptic responses in each pair are shown in parts A and B, respectively; the relative
difference between them is shown in part C. The time of application of a high-
frequency pulse train is indicated by the vertical bar. Response pairs measured before and shortly after the stimulus burst are shown in part D.

A

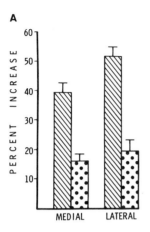

B

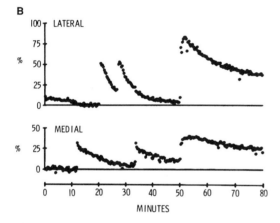

Figure 11

Cooperativity of inputs in the generation of long-term enhancement of synaptic transmission applies not only within a particular pathway but also between functionally different excitatory inputs. In the experiment illustrated in part A, the medial and lateral perforant paths were stimulated either separately (dots) or conjunctively (stripes). Much more LTE was generated when the inputs were synchronous. Data from a similar experiment are shown in part B. Field epsp amplitude changes are plotted as a function of time using low-frequency test stimuli. Each transient is a result of a brief high-frequency input. Asynchronous inputs generated only short-term changes, whereas LTE was induced by the temporal association of the inputs.

The voltage dependency also accounts for the modulatory role played by other inputs, and for certain temporal constraints on the LTE mechanism. It has been found, for example, that coactivation of certain inputs from the midbrain and septal areas increase LTE of perforant-path connections without themselves undergoing enhancement (Laroche and Bloch 1983; Robinson 1986). Conversely, coactivation of the commissural/associational system (the axons of the hilar multipolar neurons) reduces or blocks perforant-path LTE, but does not alter the multipolar cell connection strengths themselves (Douglas, Goddard, and Riives 1982). Pharmacological studies have shown that antagonists of the inhibitory inputs from basket cells increase LTE in CA1, whereas application of the inhibitory transmitter itself reduces LTE (Scharfman and Sarvey 1985; Wigstrom and Gustafsson 1983). Recently it has been shown that—although activation of one afferent fiber set with a single stimulus does not itself induce LTE—if a convergent set is driven at high frequency at the same time, LTE of the first set is induced (Gustafsson and Wigstrom 1986). There is a narrow temporal window over which this and other "heterosynaptic" effects are observed. This window is on the order of the time constant of the membrane (see, e.g., equation 5). The temporal constraint is relaxed somewhat under certain conditions where multisynaptic or other processes extend the influence of the first input well beyond the membrane time constant. For example, recent studies have found that greater LTE of a set of inputs occurs if they are stimulated about 200 msec *after* a different set than if the two sets are stimulated together (Larsen, Wong, and Lynch 1986; Rose and Dunwiddie 1986). The explanation for this effect appears to be that feedforward inhibitory effects limit the voltage change when the two inputs are simultaneous. The inhibitory effect itself wears off within about 200 msec. However, the inhibitory synapses themselves may undergo synaptic depression so that they are less effective at limiting the voltage change due to an excitatory input following 200 msec after an earlier one. This later input is then more able to induce LTE. Some caution needs to be exercised in extrapolating these results, which are based on massed synchronous activation of the system, to the quasi-random activity pattern observed during normal function.

Most of what has been said so far is consistent with the notion that LTE behaves in much the same manner as predicted by Hebb. That is, there may be some relation between LTE and postsynaptic output. Note that if the threshold function for the opening of the voltage-dependent component of g_{ij} has the same parameter values as the output threshold function, the system would behave exactly like a Hebb synapse. It turns out, however, that there is no direct physical coupling between postsynaptic output and the modification process. This has been demonstrated in several studies that have prevented postsynaptic discharge during a high-frequency input event by either inducing inhibition or by preventing the soma membrane from reaching threshold by passing current with a microelectrode (McNaughton et al. 1978; Wigstrom et al. 1982). Thus, a reasonable approximation for the rule governing LTE is that it occurs only at activation levels somewhat above the output threshold, i.e., when the cell is sufficiently activated that it would fire repetitively in the absence of strong inhibition.

The time course of LTE has several interesting properties, the first of which is that it does not appear to be permanent in the structures in which it has been studied (primarily the hippocampus). The factors governing LTE decay are poorly understood. There appears to be some stabilizing effect of repetition of the high-frequency stimulus. For example, in unanesthetized animals with permanently implanted electrodes, LTE after a single high-frequency input decays approximately exponentially, with a time constant of several days. Daily repetition of the same stimulus results in both a cumulative growth of LTE, up to a saturation point, and an accompanying increase in the apparent decay time constant up to about five weeks (Barnes 1979; Barnes and McNaughton 1980). With one caveat, this seems to be the limit on the decay-time constant. The caveat is that the decay may not be precisely exponential, and it is possible that a small component of LTE may persist for much longer. There are technical difficulties in demonstrating this, however.

There are currently two different but not necessarily exclusive views as to how the decay of LTE is regulated. The most common hypothesis is that the decay is spontaneous, in the sense that it is due to factors that are intrinsic to the enhanced synapse, and independent of other influences. The alternative view is that some form of competition is involved. There is indeed some evidence that when LTE is induced on one population of afferents, the weights of synapses that were inactive at the time are decremented (Abraham and Goddard 1983; Levy and Steward 1979). These decremental effects have generally been small, and they are not always demonstrable. It is worthwhile, however, to consider several hypothetical mechanisms for how competition *might* operate, and to assess the available evidence in this light.

One model for competition that has been entertained in both the PDP and neurophysiological literature could be called the "competitive redistribution model." This model assumes that each unit has a fixed amount of input weight, distributed among its afferents. If an input event exceeds the modification threshold, all connections give up some proportion of their weight. The released weight is then redistributed equally among the active inputs. This algorithm can lead to the development of units that respond selectively to certain classes or "features" of the input set (Rumelhart and Zipser 1986). The existing hippocampal data, however, argue strongly against this version of competition, because the redistribution rule carries the implication that, as the number of active fibers in an event increases, the percent change in the response of the active population decreases. This is more or less the opposite of what is seen experimentally. A variant of this rule might increase activated synapses in proportion to the difference between their current and some maximum state and decrease inactive ones in proportion to the difference between their current and some minimum state (assuming, of course, that some modification threshold had been reached). With suitable parameter adjustment, some of the experimental data is consistent with such a scheme.

The discussion of LTE physiology must end with a major question. While there is reasonably good understanding of the mechanisms governing the initiation of LTE, we are still rather ignorant of precisely how this phenomenon is expressed in the network. LTE has so far been studied only in *populations* of afferent fibers. We do not yet know whether it is expressed as relatively small changes throughout the population or as large changes in a few elements. Data have been marshaled in support of all the following classes of mechanisms: increase in postsynaptic sensitivity (parameter z_{ij} of equation 10) (Lynch, Halpain, and Baudry 1982), increase in sites for transmitter release (n_{ij} of equation 7) (Dolphin, Errington, and Bliss 1982), and decrease in the attenuation factor introduced by the dendritic spine (Van Harreveld and Fifkova 1975). It is also not yet clear whether LTE occurs at connections from the afferent fibers onto inhibitory interneurons (Buzsaki and Eidelberg 1982; Haas 1985). Finally, an increased n_{ij}, as alluded to above, could represent formation of a new connection if n_{ij} was initially zero. This would be logically equivalent to the binary state transition of the synapses of the simple models presented above. There is some evidence for such formation of new synapses (Chang and Greenough 1984).

Let us turn now to a consideration of whether the phenomenon of LTE in hippocampal circuits has, in fact, anything to do with memory. To begin with, the enormous literature on the effects of hippocampal damage clearly indicates that the hippocampal formation is crucially involved in establishing enduring memories of certain types. The precise nature of this involvement has been, and will no doubt continue to be, a subject of debate. No single characterization of it is likely to satisfy everyone interested in the subject at the present time. There is considerable agreement, however, that one of the results of hippocampal damage in both animals and humans is an inability to store information about spatial relationships in the environment in such a way that it can be subsequently used to guide navigation. At the same time, the ability to learn simple (unconditional) discriminations among objects or among appropriate motor responses remains intact. In the following, I shall review briefly the evidence suggesting that hippocampal LTE plays a role in laying down memories of spatial relationships.

The first evidence for such a relationship was provided by a study of the effects of aging on LTE and spatial memory (Barnes 1979). Rats have a natural aversion to open, brightly illuminated spaces, and when placed in such a situation they will reliably seek and enter a dark enclosure if one is available. The experiment was conducted on a brightly illuminated circular platform with eighteen equally spaced holes around the perimeter. Below one hole was an escape tunnel that could not be detected by a rat from a distance on the maze surface. Once a day, the rats were placed in a random orientation in the center of the platform. Over the course of about two weeks, the animals learned to locate the tunnel with respect to the distal sensory stimuli. (The use of local cues such as olfactory gradients or small surface features was ruled out.) The old animals learned more slowly and forgot what they had learned more rapidly. The same animals then underwent surgical implantation of electrodes for chronic recording and stimulation, and were examined for their ability to express and to maintain LTE in the unanesthetized state. Both age groups exhibited the same degree of LTE after perforant-path stimulation; however, the LTE decayed almost twice as quickly in the old animals. In addition, there was a statistically significant correlation within animals of a given age group between performance on the task and persistence of LTE. Subsequent studies (Barnes and McNaughton 1985) showed that the ratio of LTE decay rates between young and old animals agreed to within a few percent with the corresponding ratio of forgetting rates.

Earlier in this chapter, where the issue of saturation of distributed memory systems was raised, it was pointed out that as the number of modified connections approached its limit there would be a disruption of previously stored information and an inability to acquire new information. These predictions have been applied to the hypothesis that LTE, as observed experimentally, represents the process that normally is used to store spatial information in the hippocampus (McNaughton, Barnes, Rao, Baldwin, and Rasmussen 1986). The experiments were conducted using the circular-platform spatial problem just described. In one experiment, the animals were first trained to asymptotic performance on the task, with the tunnel remaining fixed relative to the distal spatial cues. Half of the animals then received high-frequency stimulation bilaterally. This was repeated over several days until the LTE mechanism was saturated. The other half of the animals received only low-frequency stimulation, which did not induce LTE. The animals were then reintroduced to the problem and required to learn a new tunnel location 135° away from the original. The control animals had no difficulty learning the new problem. The LTE group failed to show any learning at all over a five-day period. A second experiment, in which the animals were trained in one room, subjected to LTE induction, and then retrained in another room, produced the same severe learning deficit. Finally, an experiment was conducted in which LTE was induced immediately *after* exposure of animals to novel spatial information. This produced a significant memory impairment. There was one pattern of results, however, that was not consistent with the general hypothesis. It was found that—although the acquisition of new spatial information was impaired and the memory for recently acquired information was disrupted—well-established, older spatial memories were left intact. This finding is similar to the retrograde gradient of memory loss often seen with hippocampal damage (Squire 1982) and is consistent with the hypothesis that there is a second memory system—perhaps elsewhere in the cortex—which acquires information much more slowly than the hippocampus and which, in addition, requires a normally functioning hippocampus to do so. A variant of this hypothesis, originally put forward by Marr (1971), is that the hippocampus functions as a high-capacity temporary memory involved in the formation of efficient recoding schemes for entering information in more compact form into permanent memory. In the context of spatial learning, this hypothesis would have the hippocampus store the raw data of experience as it occurred. Once experience had established which features of an environment were reasonably stable and how they might best fit in with existing classification schemes, these features might be encoded in permanent memory. This would keep the number of permanent storage elements used to a minimum and would also prevent the immediate storage of information that was likely to be unreliable. This storage of experiences is what Marr referred to as "simple" memory, in contrast to the orthogonalized (classified) memory of the cortex to which the hippocampal simple representations were presumably directed during "consolidation." This idea has much in common with the notions of event or "episodic" (Tulving 1983) or "declarative" (Squire and Cohen 1984) memory.

The obvious converse to the experiments just described is that, if it were possible selectively to block LTE, then the acquisition of spatial information should likewise be prevented. As it happens, neuropharmacologists (Watkins and Evans 1981) have discovered a drug that selectively blocks the voltage-dependent component of the synaptic conductance (parameter h_{ij} of equation 10) underlying LTE initiation. This drug has little or no effect on normal synaptic responses to stimulation of the perforant path at low frequency, but prevents the booster effect seen when high-frequency input of enough fibers results in activation of the voltage-dependent channels. As a result, LTE is prevented. In an experiment testing the effects of this drug on spatial memory, small devices were implanted in rats which expelled extremely minute amounts of the drug into the hippocampal region continuously over a two-week period (Morris, Anderson, Lynch, and Baudry 1986). The behavioral task was similar to the circular platform in principle, but differed in detail. Rats were released into a large circular tank of water made opaque by the addition of a small amount of milk. In one quadrant of the tank was an escape platform, submerged just below the water surface. The only available solution to the task was to learn the spatial relation between the hidden platform and the distal sensory cues. Rats are good swimmers and learn this problem readily. Two tests of learning were employed. One was the average escape latency; the other involved the use of probe trials in which the platform was removed. In this case, the measure of learning was the amount of time spent by the animal in the appropriate quadrant of the pool. Control animals minimized their escape latencies and maximized their search in the correct quadrant on probe trials. Animals in which LTE had been blocked were greatly impaired on both measures.

Of course, neither experiment is sufficient to prove that LTE in the hippocampus is the storage mechanism for spatial information, but the convergent results of prevention and saturation of LTE do provide a strong case in favor of the hypothesis.

4   Evidence from Studies of Single Hippocampal Neurons

The foregoing discussion has suggested that hippocampal synapses have the necessary modification properties to implement some form of distributed memory of the sort outlined in figure 2, and that it is possible, without too great a stretch of the imagination, to observe the necessary anatomical organization within hippocampal circuitry. The models, however, also make rather strong predictions about the properties of single units within the hippocampus in relation to afferent input and information transfer.

In general, there should be (at least) two classes of cells: a principal neuron type and an inhibitory interneuron. Let us consider the interneuron first. The distributed-memory model makes at least five predictions concerning the properties of these cells.

First, they need not be nearly as numerous as the principal cells. We have already seen that the hippocampal basket cells number less than 1 percent of the principal cells.

Second, the interneurons must receive excitation from the same sources as the principal cells, in order that they may compute a measure of how many of these afferents are currently active. There is strong anatomical (Amaral 1978; Frotscher, 1985) and physiological (Alger and Nicoll 1982; Buzsaki and Eidelberg 1981; Douglas et al. 1983) support for this assertion.

Third, the interneurons must respond to changes in the number of afferents active considerably more quickly than the principal neurons, in order that the division operation be in effect by the time the excitation of the principal cells reaches the somatic integration site. A possible anatomical basis for this faster response can be found in the fact that, whereas excitatory afferents to principal cells terminate almost exclusively on dendritic spines, such spines are completely absent from the dendrites of the inhibitory basket cells. Some theoretical studies have suggested that the dendritic spine may both attenuate and slow the transfer of synaptic excitation to the soma. More direct evidence for this assertion, however, comes from recordings made from putative inter-neurons, both *in vitro* and in the awake animal, after electrical stimulation of the afferent pathways.

A frequent observation during intracellular-recording studies is that afferent stimulation results in a complex response involving an inhibitory postsynaptic potential (ipsp) superimposed on an excitatory one (epsp). The ipsp begins well before the peak of the epsp, prior to the generation of any spikes by the principal cell. Because the afferent pathways themselves do not contain inhibitory fibers, the most plausible interpretation is that the interneuron activation must have reached its output threshold more rapidly than the principal cells. This is confirmed by direct recordings from the interneurons themselves (Ashwood, Lancaster, and Wheal 1984; Fox, Wolfson, and Ranck 1986). These authors recorded from hippocampal interneurons (which are also called "theta" cells, on the basis of the electrophysiological criterion that they are active whenever the so-called theta rhythm is present in the EEG) in awake animals with chronically implanted stimulation electrodes which could activate afferent fibers to CA1. Stimulation at low intensity elicited one or a few spikes from such cells without any evidence of discharge from principal (pyramidal) cells. With increasing stimulus intensity, the interneurons responded earlier and with increasing numbers of spikes. This response always occurred well before the appearance of a population spike in the record, reflecting the discharge of pyramidal cells. Thus, whereas the pyramidal cells respond to afferent stimulation in a discrete fashion (either there is one spike or there is none), the inhibitory interneurons respond in a graded fashion (the more afferents active, the more spikes are emitted) and at considerably shorter latency than the pyramidal cells. The latency reduction would help to keep the inhibitory signal proportional to the afferent input, because it would position the ipsp closer to the origin of the epsp, thus providing a more effective current shunt at the time of peak excitatory current at the soma.

The correct anatomy and response properties would be of little help if the interneurons were not able to implement something analogous to a division operation (the fourth prediction of the model under consideration). As discussed above, this requires that the equilibrium point for the inhibitory synapse be near the resting potential. It is well established that hippocampal interneurons employ the neurotransmitter GABA, which is associated with a selective conductance to chloride ion. In most mammalian neurons, including hippocampal cells, chloride ion is at equilibrium at or near the resting potential. Although the proximity of the ipsp equilibrium to rest has been confirmed in several *in vitro* studies (see, e.g., Eccles, Nicoll, Oshima, and Rubia 1977), evidence that this assertion also holds in the intact animal can be obtained indirectly through analysis of evoked field potentials. In the dentate gyrus, it is possible to stimulate the axons of the granule cells directly, so that the action potential travels back toward the soma (antidromic activation). Since these axons branch to excite basket interneurons, which then terminate on granule cells, it is possible to use antidromic activation to set up strong inhibition well before a second electrical stimulus to the excitatory afferents of the perforant pathway. The perforant path evoked population field epsp is a measure of how much synaptic current is generated, and this depends on the synaptic conductance (g_{ij}) and on the difference between the actual membrane potential and the excitatory equilibrium (see equation 3). If the inhibition results in any significant shift in the membrane potential from rest, this shift will affect the measured field epsp. A hyperpolarization would increase the field epsp, whereas a depolarization would decrease it. Figure 12 shows the result of such an experiment (Rao and McNaughton, unpublished). In the presence of inhibition set up by an antidromic stimulus, the perforant path evoked population spike is completely blocked without any change in the field epsp component of the response. Thus, the inhibitory conductance must have blocked output by short-circuiting the granule-cell membrane, rather than by shifting the membrane potential appreciably. This short-circuiting is formally equivalent to a division, as can be seen in equation 4.

The fifth major prediction of the model with respect to the inhibitory interneurons relates to the information content of their spontaneous activity during normal behavior. According to the model, these cells should be transmitting information not about which afferents are active, but only about how many are active. The consequence is that the interneurons should appear nonselective over whatever information domain the principal cells appear to code for.

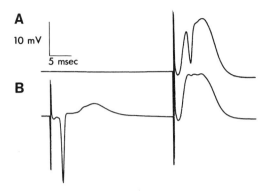

Figure 12
Illustration of an experiment providing one line of evidence that inhibition in the intact hippocampus operates primarily through a conductance shunt mechanism and, hence, implements a division operation. Extracellular field potential records were taken from granule cells of the dentate gyrus in response to stimuli either of the perforant path alone (A) or of the perforant path preceded by stimulation (B) of the axons of the granule cells themselves (referred to as antidromic activation because the output travels backward along the axon). The antidromic spike activates inhibitory basket cells (too few in number for their extracellular fields to contribute to this record), which block the output from the granule cells that should normally have been superimposed on the synaptic field potential. The fact that the synaptic field potential is itself unchanged indicates that the same net membrane current is induced in response to the excitatory input with or without the inhibition. This can occur only if the term $(e_{ij} - v_i)$ of equation 3 is unchanged. Therefore, it must have been a membrane conductance shunt (i.e., the increased inhibitory conductance), rather than a subtractive hyperpolarization, that prevented the granule cells from reaching their threshold voltage.

In the case of the rat hippocampus, the major determinant of activity for the principal cells is the location of the animal within a particular environment (see below). A given pyramidal cell is almost silent except when the animal is within that cell's "place field" (O'Keefe and Dostrovsky 1971; O'Keefe 1976). The interneurons behave very differently. They increase their rates whenever the animal is engaged in behavior that is likely to change the constellation of sensory input (Ranck 1973). These behaviors include all translational behaviors, as well as certain forms of sensory scanning (i.e. sniffing) not associated with overt translational movement. Because most sensory cells and many central cells exhibit accommodation (see equation 2) and are therefore most sensitive to *changes* in the input, the periods of translational movement are likely also to be the periods in which there is the highest density of afferent input. Examples of the spatial distributions of typical hippocampal pyramidal and interneuronal activity during a commonly used spatial behavioral task are shown in figure 13. Although intensive application of statistics can sometimes reveal a small degree of spatial selectivity in these interneurons (McNaughton, Barnes, and O'Keefe 1983; Kubie, Kramer, and Muller 1985), this selectivity is manyfold less than for the principal cells.

One final observation about inhibition, which is not a strong prediction of the model but which can at least be interpreted in the same framework, relates to the "theta" cycle of the hippocampal gross electrical activity (EEG). The entire hippocampal formation undergoes a rhythmic (7 Hz) cycle of excitation and inhibition whenever the animal is engaged in translational behavior or sensory scanning (figure 14). Both basket interneurons and pyramidal cells are most active during the excitatory phase of the cycle, the difference being that the presence of theta appears to be a necessary but not a sufficient condition in the case of the pyramidal cells (Bland, Andersen, Ganes, and Sveen 1980; Fox et al. 1986). There has been extensive speculation over the years as to the significance of this rhythmic activity. The autoassociative model of figure 2C leads to a new interpretation. In distributed systems with feedback, the most efficient recall is achieved if the network is explicitly shut off before the arrival of updated external information. Where this information is only transiently available, such preinactivation is absolutely necessary to prevent the indeterminate interaction of the input with activity already going on in the system. Of course, if the input can be held constant, and if enough time is allowed for the sort of "thermal equilibration" called for by several recent PDP models (see, e.g., Hopfield 1982; Smolensky 1986), then preinactivation is unnecessary. However, the fastest, most accurate recall is achieved if information is always presented to a quiet network. This permits pattern completion within a single cycle if the network is densely connected, and within a small number of cycles otherwise. Such inactivation may be provided by the theta rhythm.

The distributed-processing model also makes several predictions about the properties of the principal neurons of the net, i.e., the hippocampal pyramidal cells.

One of these relates to one solution to the saturation problem, namely that the activity density of the population must be kept as low as possible. Hippocampal pyramidal neurons in the freely moving rat are, on average, among the quietest neurons in the nervous system, with mean discharge rates of less than 1 Hz (as compared with peak rates well in excess of 100 Hz while the animal is in the appropriate location in space). Again, this is more consistent with the single-cycle recall model considered here, than with the relaxation

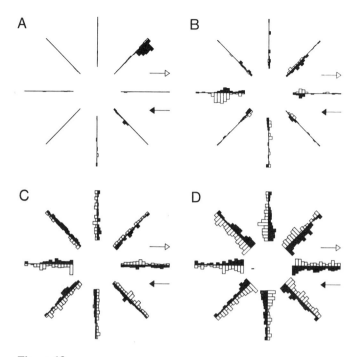

Figure 13
Typical examples of the sorts of neuronal activity recorded from the two principal cell types of region CA3 of the hippocampus while a rat moved freely over the surface of a maze consisting of eight radial runways (arms). During these experiments, the animals were being reinforced for entering each arm by the delivery of a small quantity of chocolate milk at each arm end. Extracellular single-unit recording methods were applied to monitor the output events of the neurons; at the same time, the animal's head position was tracked automatically at 20 points per second. The data were analyzed by first dividing the maze surface into segments and then subdividing the segments according to the radial direction the animal was moving if it passed through a given segment. The histograms represent the average number of output events emitted per bin, divided by the total time spent in the corresponding position/ direction. This provides a measure of the positional and directional selectivity of neuronal activity. The principal cell type, the pyramidal cell (examples A and B) is highly specific for position and direction; this suggests that something about a particular "local view" may be represented in its output. The inhibitory interneurons (examples B and C) show little or no such selectivity, but are most active whenever the position/direction is changing. This lack of specific information is consistent with the idea that these cells signal not *which* inputs to the system are active but only *how many*.

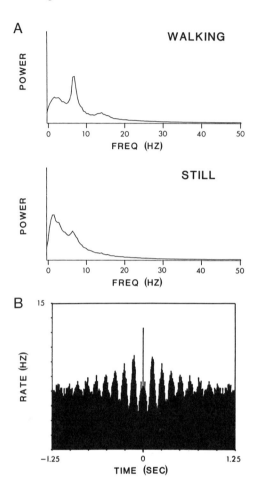

Figure 14
Whenever a rat makes translational movements, the entire hippocampal formation undergoes a rythmic excitability cycle at about 7 Hz. This cycle can be observed in the power spectrum of the gross electrical activity of the hippocampus (A) and in the autocorrelation function of most individual hippocampal neurons (B). The latter analysis provides a measure of the frequency with which output events are followed or preceded by other outputs from the same unit as a function of interval. All hippocampal neurons exhibit such periodicity; however, it is most pronounced in inhibitory interneurons, such as the one illustrated here, because they are active on each cycle. Pyramidal cells are only active on cycles in which particular information is provided to the system. (Part A courtesy of E. J. Green.)

models (referred to above) in which recall is a process of "cooling" the system from a state of high population activity down to the low-activity state most consistent with the current input.

A second strong prediction of the distributed paradigm is that each principal cell should participate in a number of different representations. Certain earlier attempts to simulate associative learning in neural nets were able to store only orthogonal vectors, because the models lacked the critical normalization operation effected by the inhibitory division. As a result, each unit could be involved in only one stored representation, and the storage capacity was correspondingly severely limited. Hippocampal pyramidal cells conform to the full distributed model in that, for any given "environment" (the precise definition of which is still rather fuzzy), a given pyramidal cell has about a 70 percent chance of having a discrete preferred firing location. So, for example, one cell has about a 49 percent chance of being involved in each of two given environmental representations (Kubie and Ranck 1983). In the absence of such a discrete field, the cell is virtually silent during exploratory activity.

An important question still remains: Why does a given cell have a high probability of having one field in each of two environments, whereas there appears to be a relatively low probability of having two fields in the same environment? This would suggest that the cell was influenced by information contained within the system about the environment as a whole, and not just by local cues. Split fields do occur, and the question will require considerably more quantitative study before such a conclusion can be firmly drawn. Nevertheless, the spatial selectivity can be rather strikingly precise; this, no doubt, is what led O'Keefe and Dostrovsky (1971) to the notion that pyramidal-cell discharge represents a point in a maplike internal representation. At this point we enter into the final theme of the chapter: the question whether the computational structure of the spatial representation is isomorphic with the concept of a map as a global representation of spatial relationships or whether there is a simpler structure that, while having much of the outward appearance of a map, would be easier to implement using the simple notions about distributed processing outlined so far.

5 What Is a Cognitive Map?

Most people's concept of a spatial map encompasses the idea of a set of points in some way topologically ordered in relation to some geographical distribution of objects (or at least sensory features). A (perhaps simple-minded) corollary is that if neurons represent points in such a space, then neighboring neurons should code for neighboring locations. Part of the basis for such a conjecture comes from the precise topological mapping of sensory receptive surfaces on the corresponding primary neocortical areas. A similar topological relation has been explicitly sought in several studies of hippocampal spatial units, and there is general agreement that the likelihood of finding neighboring cells coding for neighboring points is no greater than chance. Even with newer recording techniques that permit isolation of several hippocampal cells simultaneously (McNaughton, O'Keefe, and Barnes 1983), the observation of adjacent cells active in adjacent places is the exception rather than the rule.

A more sophisticated formulation of the same notion is that it is not the topography of the neurons themselves that codes anything but the topological relations implied by their pattern of interconnections. Such a notion implies that, although neighboring cells encode different places, a given set of cells will maintain a constant geometrical relation among the places represented in different environments. In addressing this question, Kubie and Ranck (1983) examined the relation among firing fields of different cells across three environments: the animal's home cage, a second box, and an elevated open maze in a large room. The results were again negative; there was no preservation of geometrical relationships across environments.

Implicit in the original coining of the term "place cells" was the notion of coding for a directionless point in some Cartesian reference frame. This notion has had to be abandoned, or at least radically altered, because of the finding that the direction that an animal was facing in a particular cell's preferred location accounted for virtually all the location specificity (McNaughton et al. 1983). Examples of such directional specificity are shown in figure 13. There are two possible interpretations of this finding, a simple one and a complex one. The latter is, obviously, that the brain contains both a map and a compass, and each cell represents a location point and a direction. The former is that place cells are merely responding to the particular constellation of sensory features present at a given location while facing a particular direction—in other words, they represent nothing more sophisticated than the *local view* of the world. Such an explanation carries little or no excess computational baggage other than the assumption of a diversity of connectivity, for which the evidence has already been presented.

In a masterful stroke for the side of complexity, O'Keefe (1983) demonstrated that, so long as the animal "knows" where it is, as inferred from its behavior, virtually the entire set of sensory cues available at any particular location can be removed without disruption of the normal place specificity. This experiment is described more completely in O'Keefe's chapter in the present volume. Briefly, animals were trained to obtain reward in relation to a particular location defined by a set of controlled stimulus cues within a curtained-off enclosure. These cues were rotated with respect to the laboratory from trial to trial; not surprisingly, the location specificity rotated with the controlled cues. Animals were then presented briefly with a view of the cues from one location, the cues were removed, and after some delay the animals were permitted to run to the reward location. So long as the animals demonstrated knowledge of the reward location relative to the last-seen cue orientation, place-specific neuronal activity was preserved. If the animal made errors, the firing shifted according to where the animal "thought" it was as inferred from its behavior.

These conclusions were confirmed independently (Jones Leonard, McNaughton, and Barnes 1985) in a study in which several hippocampal neurons were monitored simultaneously each day over a period of about three weeks. Place-by-direction-specific activity was plotted daily as the animals performed forced-choice running on a radical maze, and was found to be very reproducible from day to day. On the next day, the lights in the recording room were extinguished and the animal was brought into the room in an enclosed box, which was rotated several times to produce disorientation. The animal was then released onto the maze and allowed to run the task in the dark. The animal had no difficulty in doing so—presumably because, although it did not possess information about its angular coordinate, its other senses provided adequate information about its radial coordinate on the maze. Interestingly, this was reflected in the way in which the units were disrupted. The cells continued to fire at the same radial position and while the animal faced the same radial direction on the maze, but were disrupted with respect to which arm they were active on. The second phase of the experiment involved merely turning on the room lights again. This completely restored the normal firing pattern. In the final phase, the room lights were again turned off—this time, however, in the animal's presence. The difference between the two dark phases was thus that only in the second one did the animal know its starting orientation. With this information, the normal firing pattern was maintained in darkness.

If nothing else, these observations conform to the major prediction of the distributed-memory paradigm: the ability to complete a representation on the basis of fragmentary input. They also indicate that the place-by-direction specific firing can be driven by the internal representation of an environment in the absence of the actual sensory information defining that space. The issue concerns the nature of the structure of this representation.

In attempting to preserve the map analogy, O'Keefe (personal communication) has argued that in his experiment the animal actually has two sets of cues: the salient controlled cues, which rotate from trial to trial and constitute the principal components of a map, and a set of uncontrolled laboratory-frame cues. O'Keefe argues that on each trial the animal forms a new association between the rotated map and the uncontrolled cues during the few seconds of cue exposure (see O'Keefe's chapter in this volume for an updated version of this hypothesis). The uncontrolled cues would then serve as recall cues during the experiment to complete the representation of the map in its current orientation. This explanation is not implausible, particularly as a certain percentage of cells in O'Keefe and Speakman's study responded either to the fixed reference frame or to some interaction of the frames. However, what must really be demanded is that there are two maps that can be globally rotated relative to each other and *transiently* linked in a particular orientation for one trial only. This must follow, since the animal does not have the opportunity to observe the conjunction of controlled and uncontrolled cues from all orientations at the start of a trial. The experimental test of this interpretation would be relatively straightforward; it would involve two sets of controlled cues, both of which would be made considerably more salient than the laboratory cues. Introducing a rotation of the background cues after the foreground cues are removed should rotate the animal's foreground map and shift its place-cell activity accordingly.

An alternative explanation suggested by these studies dispenses altogether with the notion of a map as an active global representation, and requires little more than local associations. The hypothesis is that during exploration of the maze, the animal forms a linked set of conditional associations between local views of the environment and specific movements. Given a starting location and orientation and information about a movement, it may recall a representation of the appropriate resulting local view. This, in turn, would serve as the new start location, so that accurate spatial localization could be preserved over long movement sequences, as was observed in the experiments described above. Such a memory would take the form of a transition matrix linking local views with movements. This is illustrated in figure 15. The one difficulty with this hypothesis is that it appears at first to require that the animal actually experience every possible transition. In the case of the maze situation, this is probably very nearly true by the time recordings are actually made. However, in its simple form, the hypothesis would not account for how novel trajectories to a particular target are generated. There would appear to be at least three possible solutions. An obvious one would be to make use of spatially invariant landmarks (Zipser 1985) and learn associations between goal objects and these landmarks. Rats with hippocampal damage can,

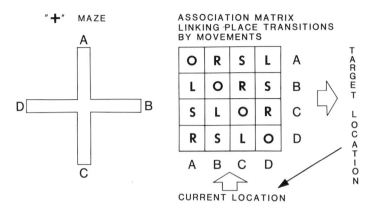

Figure 15
Illustration of the transition-matrix concept of place learning. Imagine that a rat runs
on a cross-shaped maze with locations specified by four sets of stimulus features
(*A,B,C,D*). Ignoring for the moment that the animal must make 180° turns at the
arm ends, the exploration of this environment involves filling in a square matrix
whose axes correspond to locations, with the specific movements, (*L*eft, *R*ight,
*S*traight) linking these locations. The location information need not be anything more
complicated than a representation of the "local view" of the environment.

in fact, still accomplish this readily. This solution, however, is not much help
if the route to be followed does not have such invariant landmarks visible
throughout. Notice, though, that if any two trajectories through a spatial transition matrix overlap, then a new trajectory can be computed at the point of
overlap (e.g., in figure 15 the trajectory *ABCDA* could be computed if the
animal had experienced on different occasions *ABCBA*. and *ADCDA*). A third
solution would be to provide the system with the ability to compute *movement
equivalences* (such as that a 270° left turn is equivalent to a 90° right), or
even more complex sequence equivalences. The point is that if there is *any*
path in the transition matrix connecting two locations, the computation of
other routes by means of spatially equivalent movement sequences should not
be particularly difficult.

6   Movement Representation

A minimum requirement of the spatial transition matrix hypothesis is that a
robust representation of the specific state of movement of the animal be available. At the very least, this representation must contain units that discriminate
among left turns, right turns, and forward motion. It turns out that there are

at least two regions within the rat parietal neocortex where such cells can readily be observed. One of these is the primary sensory-motor area representing the hindlimb and trunk regions (in the rat, the sensory and motor cortical areas overlap for this part of the body). The second region is the rat analogue of the posterior parietal region (area 7). In both humans and sub-human primates, lesions of this area are associated with severe deficits in orientation, egocentric localization, and spatial perception. In the freely moving rat, a significant proportion of cells recorded in these areas (about 40 percent) are clearly selective for the animal's state of motion (McNaughton, Green, and Mizumori 1986). These cells fall into one of three broad categories of response type: left turns, right turns, and forward motion. Examples of these are illustrated in figure 16. Within these categories there are some interesting variations. Some cells predict their associated movement by hundreds of milliseconds, and are therefore probably linked to the movement-generating systems. Other cells are clearly somatosensory, responding to passive bending of the trunk or the neck in the appropriate direction, or to flexion of one ankle as in walking. Other cells respond to passive rotation in one direction, even in darkness, and hence are probably driven by the vestibular system. Still others appear to be responding to visual input. Apparent combinations of modalities also occur. It appears, therefore, that the rat nervous system constructs a highly robust and redundant global representation of its state of motion through space. There is even some suggestion that the system is capable of computing the spatial equivalence of certain simple movements (figure 17). One parietal-cortex neuron was activated whenever the rat made a left turn on the maze. This cell was inactive during all right turns of less than 180°. If a right turn exceeded 180°, so that the animal entered what had recently been its left egocentric space, the cell was intensely activated. In order for this effect to be observed, the animal had to remain motionless for several seconds prior to the onset of the turn. The effect was not seen if the animal circled continuously to the right, although continuous left circling resulted in maintained activity. Apparently, the few seconds of immobility were necessary to reset some sort of egocentric reference frame, from which the spatial equivalence of 90° left and 270° right was computed.

7   The Neural Implementation of the Spatial Transition Matrix Hypothesis

In summary of the main arguments presented up to this point: Neurally plausible implementations of heteroassociative and autoassociative memory can be developed using circuitry and physiology closely resembling that observed in (but not necessarily restricted to) the mammalian hippocampus, internal representations of local views of familiar environments can be completed from minimal sensory cues and possibly from movement information alone given a starting location, and a substantial part of the cortical circuitry may be involved in the representation of the state of motion of the animal. The question is: Can these ideas be integrated into a model that captures the idea that spatial relations are represented as a linkable set of *conditional* associations with the property that, given a representation of a particular local view and a representation of a specific movement, a representation of the *resulting* local view can be recalled from memory in the complete absence of the corresponding sensory input? Such a model might also be appropriate for the more general problem of learning conditional associations between actions and their consequences.

One solution would be to distribute the outputs of the spatial and movement representations randomly over a third set of neurons in such a way that each possible combination of local view and movement leads to a unique output state of this population (figure 18). Using this output as the modifiable input to a heteroassociative net, whose detonator input carries information about the local view, would produce a system whose current local representation would become associated with the compound event representing the conjunction of the preceding local view and the preceding movement. In a familiar environment, sensory information would only be required to establish the starting location. Subsequent local representations could be recalled solely from the movement subset of the compound view-movement event leading to the particular target view in question.

It is interesting to note that the memory for the conjunction of local views and movements is a specific case of the broader notion of episodic or declarative memory, which is so severely disrupted by damage to the hippocampal system in humans. Moreover, the foregoing model may also serve as a framework for understanding the general problem of concept formation—a problem that is to some extent reduceable to conditional relations between actions and their consequences.

Acknowledgments

This work was supported by grants from NINCDS and the A. P. Sloan Foundation. I am also grateful to C. A. Barnes, E. J. Green, S. J. Y. Mizumori, and P. Smolensky for helpful comments on the manuscript, to G. Rao and S. Scott for assistance with the figures, and to B. Petersen for secretarial assistance.

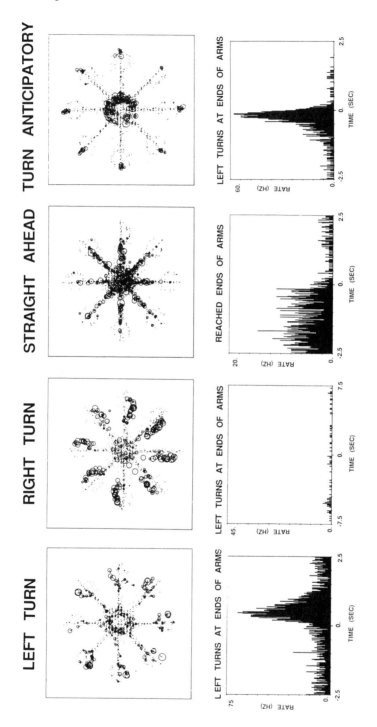

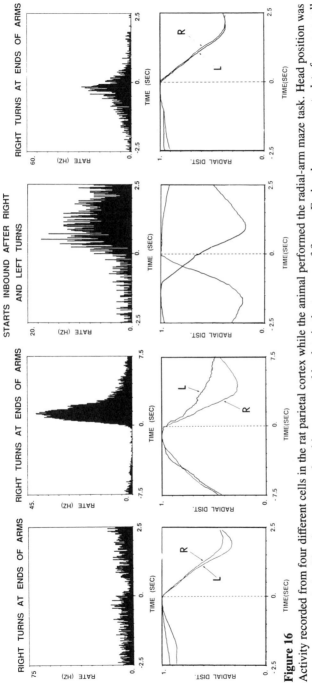

Figure 16

Activity recorded from four different cells in the rat parietal cortex while the animal performed the radial-arm maze task. Head position was tracked and recorded at 20 points per second and is represented by dots in the top row of figures. Each column represents data from one cell. In the top row, neuronal activity is represented by circles whose diameters are proportional to the locally computed firing rate. The middle two rows are perievent-time histograms centered at the onset of behavioral events of interest and representing the average response over a number of such events. The final row represents the average radial coordinate on the maze for the behavioral events for which the event histograms were constructed. For example, while the animal is approaching an arm end, the radial coordinate is increasing. While the animal eats at the end of an arm, the radial coordinate is relatively constant. At the onset of an about turn, the coordinate begins to decrease. The high proportion of cells that can be classified into "left turn," "right turn," or "straight ahead" categories suggests that a global representation of the animal's motion state must be of considerable importance.

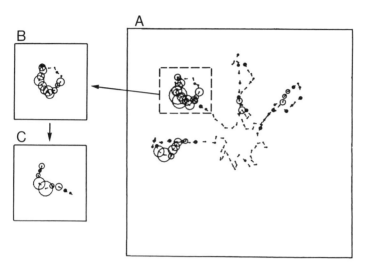

Figure 17

Evidence that spatial equivalences among different movements may be computed in the rat cortex was provided by one neuron that responded either during left turns, or on right turns if the turn angle exceeded 180° relative to a recent rest location. An excerpt from a larger data set is illustrated in part A. Local firing rates on the eight-arm maze are represented by the diameter of the circles centered on position coordinates. The direction of movement is indicated by the dashes. The sequence on the northwest arm has been further subdivided. It begins with a right turn at the arm end associated with low firing. In this unusual case, the animal continued its turn through 360°. The firing rate increased dramatically at about 180° (B). The animal then turned back to its left (C), which was also associated with a high firing rate. Two simple right turns and one simple left turn are shown on the other three arms. Further observations (see text) suggest that this cell's spatial-reference frame was re-initialized by brief periods of immobility.

References

Abraham, W. C., and G. V. Goddard. 1983. Asymmetric relationships between homosynaptic long-term potentiation and heterosynaptic long-term depression. *Nature* 305: 717–719.

Alger, B. E., and R. A. Nicoll. 1982. Feed-forward dendritic inhibition in rat hippocampal pyramidal cells studied *in vitro*. *Journal of Physiology* 328: 105–123.

Amaral, D. G. 1978. A Golgi study of cell types in the hilar region of the hippocampus in the rat. *Journal of Comparative Neurology* 182: 851–914.

Andersen, P., S. H. Sundberg, O. Sveen, and H. Wigstrom. 1977. Specific long-lasting potentiation of synaptic transmission in hippocampal slices. *Nature* 266: 737.

Ashwood, T. J., B. Lancaster, and H. V. Wheal. 1984. *In vivo* and *in vitro* studies on

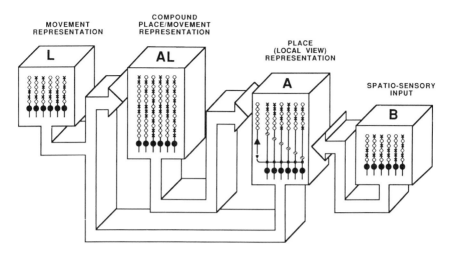

Figure 18
One possible solution to the problem of implementing the transition-matrix model
for conditional association of local view representations with movements is to generate a compound representation for specific combinations of locations and movements. These event representations can be easily produced by projecting the output
of a heteroassociative matrix representing the local view with the output of the
movement representation system onto a third set of neurons via random excitatory
connections. This could produce a system whose output vector is unique for each
combination of local view and movement. Projecting this information back into the
heteroassociative network via modifiable synapses would permit the current local
view representation to be associated with whatever combinations of view and movement that preceded it. Subsequently, that representation could be recalled whenever
an appropriate compound place/movement representation was presented (e.g., in the
present case, the compound *AL* should be sufficient to recall a representation of arm
B of figure 15). Note that only the starting place representation needs to be specified.
The system would then be capable of internally generating representations of sequences of location representations on the basis of movement input alone. It should
also be noted that unique trajectories could be computed at points of overlap or previously experienced trajectories, thus providing the system with the outward appearance of a cognitive map.

putative interneurons in the rat hippocampus: Possible mediators of feed-forward inhibition. *Brain Research* 293: 279–291.

Barnes, C. A. 1979. Memory deficits associated with senescence: A behavioral and neurophysiological study in the rat. *Journal of Comparative and Physiological Psychology* 93: 74–104.

Barnes, C. A., and B. L. McNaughton. 1980. Spatial memory and hippocampal synaptic plasticity in middle-aged and senescent rats. In *The Psychobiology of Aging: Problems and Perspectives*, ed. D. Stein (Amsterdam: Elsevier North-Holland).

Barnes, C. A., and B. L. McNaughton. 1985. An age comparison of the rates of acquisition and forgetting of spatial information in relation to long-term enhancement of hippocampal synapses. *Behavioral Neuroscience* 99: 1040–1048.

Blackstad, T. W., K. Brink, J. Hem, and B. Jeune. 1970. Distribution of hippocampal mossy fibers in the rats. An experimental study with silver impregnation methods. *Journal of Comparative Neurology* 138: 433–450.

Bland, B. H., P. Andersen, T. Ganes, and O. Sveen. 1980. Automated analysis of rhythmicity of physiologically identified hippocampal formation neurons. *Experimental Brain Research* 38: 205–219.

Bliss, T. V. P., and A. R. Gardner-Medwin. 1973. Long-lasting potentiation of synaptic transmission in the dentate area of unanaesthetized rabbit following stimulation of the perforant path. *Journal of Physiology* (*London*) 232: 357–374.

Bliss, T. V. P., and T. Lomo. 1973. Long-lasting potentiation of synaptic transmission in the dentate area of the anaesthetized rabbit following stimulation of the perforant path. *Journal of Physiology* (*London*) 232: 331–356.

Brown, T. H., and D. Johnston. 1983. Voltage-clamp analysis of mossy fiber synaptic input to hippocampal neurons. *Journal of Neurophysiology* 50: 487–507.

Buzsaki, G., and E. Eidelberg. 1981. Commissural projection to the dentate gyrus of the rat: Evidence for feedforward inhibition. *Brain Research* 230: 346–350.

Buzsaki, G., and E. Eidelberg. 1982. Direct afferent excitation and long-term potentiation of hippocampal interneurons. *Journal of Neurophysiology* 48: 597–607.

Chang, G.-L., and W. T. Greenough. Transient and enduring morphological correlates of synaptic activity and efficacy change in the rat hippocampal slice. *Brain Research* 309: 35–46.

Claiborne, B. J., D. G. Amaral, and W. M. Cowan. 1986. A light and electron microscopic analysis of the mossy fibers of the rat dentate gyrus. *Journal of Comparative Neurology* 246: 435–458.

Collingridge, G. L. 1985. Long term potentiation in the hippocampus: Mechanism of initiation and modulation by neurotransmitters. *Trends in Pharmacological Sciences* 74: 407–411.

Collingridge, G. L., S. J., Kehl, and H. McLennan. 1983. Excitatory amino acids in synaptic transmission in the Schaffer collateral-commissural pathway of the rat hippocampus. *Journal of Physiology* (*London*) 334: 33–46.

Dolphin, A. C., M. L. Errington, and T. V. P. Bliss. 1982. Long-term potentiation of the perforant path *in vivo* is associated with increased glutamate release. *Nature* 297: 496–498.

Douglas, R. M., G. V. Goddard, and M. Riives. 1982. Inhibitory modulation of long-term potentiation: Evidence for a postsynaptic locus of control. *Brain Research* 240: 259–272.

Douglas, R. M., B. L. McNaughton, G. V. Goddard. 1983. Commissural inhibition and facilitation of granule cell discharge in fascia dentata. *Journal of Comparative Neurology* 219: 285–294.

Eccles, J. C., R. A. Nicoll, T. Oshima, and F. J. Rubia. 1977. The anionic permeability of the inhibitory postsynaptic membrane of hippocampal pyramidal cells. *Proceedings of the Royal Society of London* B 198: 345–361.

Feldman, J. A., and D. H. Ballard. 1982. Connectionist models and their properties. *Cognitive Science* 6: 205–254.

Fox, S. E., S. Wolfson, and J. B. Ranck, Jr. 1986. Hippocampal theta rhythm and the firing of neurons in walking and urethane anesthetized rats. *Experimental Brain Research* 62: 495–508.

Frotscher, M. 1985. Mossy fibres form synapses with identified pyramidal basket cells in the CA3 region of the guinea-pig hippocampus: A combined Golgi-electron microscope study. *Journal of Neurocytology* 14: 245–259.

Gaarskjaer, F. B. 1978. Organization of the mossy fiber system of the rat studied in extended hippocampi. *Journal of Comparative Neurology* 178: 49–72.

Gardner-Medwin, A. R. 1976. The recall of events through the learning of associations between their parts. *Proceedings of the Royal Society of London* B 194: 375–402.

Gray, E. G. 1959. Axo-somatic and axo-dendritic synapses on the cerebral cortex: An electron microscope study. *Journal of Anatomy* 93: 420–433.

Grossberg, S. 1969. On learning and energy-entropy dependence in recurrent and nonrecurrent signed networks. *Journal of Statistical Physics* 1: 319–350.

Gustafsson, B., and H. Wigstrom. 1986. Hippocampal long-lasting potentiation produced by pairing single volleys and brief conditioning tetani evoked in separate afferents. *Journal of Neuroscience* 6: 1575–1582.

Haas, H. L. 1985. Long-term potentiation and intrinsic disinhibition. In *VII International Neurobiological Symposium, Magdeburg* (New York: Pergamon).

Harris, E. W., A. H. Ganong, and C. W. Cotman. 1984. Long-term potentiation in the hippocampus involves activation of N-methyl-D-aspartate receptors. *Brain Research* 323: 132–137.

Haug, F.-M. S. 1973. Heavy metals in the brain. *Advances in Anatomy, Embryology, and Cell Biology* 47: 1–71.

Hebb, D. O. 1949. *The Organization of Behavior.* New York: Wiley.

Hjorth-Simonsen, A. 1972. Projection of the lateral part of the entorhinal area to the hippocampus and fascia dentata. *Journal of Comparative Neurology* 146: 219–232.

Hopfield, J. J. 1982. Neural networks and physical systems with emergent collective computational abilities. *Proceedings of the National Academy of Science* 79: 2554–2558.

Jefferys, J. G. R. 1979. Initiation and spread of action potentials in granule cells maintained *in vitro* in slices of guinea-pig hippocampus. *Journal of Physiology (London)* 289: 375–388.

Jones Leonard, B., B. L. McNaughton, and C. A. Barnes. 1985. Long-term studies of place field interrelationships in dentate gyrus neurons. *Society for Neuroscience Abstracts* 11: 1108.

Koch, E., and T. Poggio. 1982. A theoretical analysis of electrical properties of spines. *Proceedings of the Royal Society of London* B 218: 455–477.

Kohonen, T. 1978. *Associative Memory: A System-Theoretical Approach.* New York: Springer-Verlag.

Korn, H., A. Mallet, A. Triller, and D. S. Faber. 1982. Transmission at a central synapse. II. Quantal description of release with a physical correlate for binomial *n*. *Journal of Neuroscience* 48: 679–707.

Kubie, J. L., and J. B. Ranck, Jr. 1983. Sensory-behavioral correlates in individual hippocampus neurons in three situations: Space and context. In *The Neurobiology of the Hippocampus,* ed. W. Seifert (New York: Academic).

Kubie, J. L., L. Kramer, and R. U. Muller. 1985. Location-specific firing of hippocampal theta cells. *Society for Neuroscience Abstracts* 11: 1231.

Laatsch, R. H., and W. M. Cowan. 1966. Electron microscopic studies of the dentate gyrus of the rat. I. Normal Structure with special reference to synaptic organization. *Journal of Comparative Neurology* 128: 359–395.

Laroche, S., and V. Bloch. 1983. Conditioning of hippocampal cells and long-term potentiation: An approach to mechanisms of post-trial memory facilitation. In *Neuronal Plasticity and Memory Formation,* ed. C. Ajmone Marsan and H. Matthies (New York: Raven).

Larson, J., D. Wong, and G. Lynch. 1986. Patterned stimulation at the theta frequency is optimal for the induction of hippocampal long-term potentiation. *Brain Research* 368: 347–350.

Lee, K. 1983. Cooperativity among afferents for the induction of long-term potentiation in the CA1 region of the hippocampus. *Journal of Neuroscience* 3: 1369–1372.

Levy, W. B., and O. Steward. 1979. Synapses as associative memory elements in the hippocampal formation. *Brain Research* 175: 233–245.

Lorente de No, R. 1934. Studies on the structure of the cerebral cortex. II. Continuation of the study of the ammonic system. *Journal of Psychological Neurology* 46: 113–177.

Lynch, G., S. Halpain, and M. Baudry. 1982. Effects of high-frequency synaptic stimulation on glutamate binding studied with a modified *in vitro* hippocampal slice preparation. *Brain Research* 244: 101–111.

MacGregor, R. J., and R. M. Oliver. 1974. A model for repetitive firing in neurons. *Kybernetik* 16: 53–64.

Magleby, K. L., and J. E. Zengel. 1976a. Augmentation: A process that acts to increase transmitter release at the frog neuromuscular junction. *Journal of Physiology* 257: 449–470.

Magleby, K. L., and J. E. Zengel. 1976b. Long-term changes in augmentation, potentiation, and depression of transmitter release as a function of repeated synaptic activity at the frog neuromuscular junction. *Journal of Physiology* 257: 471–494.

Marr, D. 1969. A theory of cerebellar cortex. *Journal of Physiology (London)* 202: 437–470.

Marr, D. 1970. A theory for cerebral cortex. *Proceedings of the Royal Society London* B 176: 161–234.

Marr, D. 1971. Simple memory: A theory for archicortex. *Philosophical Transactions of the Royal Society* B 262: 23–81.

Matthews, D. A., C. Cotman, and G. Lynch. 1976. An electron microscopic study of lesion-induced synaptogenesis in the dentate gyrus of the adult rat. I. Magnitude and time course of degeneration. *Brain Research* 115: 1–21.

McNaughton, B. L. 1980. Evidence for two physiologically distinct perforant pathways to the fascia dentata. *Brain Research* 199: 1–19.

McNaughton, B. L. 1982. Long-term synaptic enhancement and short-term potentiation in rat fascia dentata act through different mechanisms. *Journal of Physiology* 324: 249–262.

McNaughton, B. L. 1985. Peak discharge rates of dentate gyrus neurons correspond to choice points on a spatial working memory task. *Society for Neuroscience Abstracts* 11: 1107.

McNaughton, B. L., and C. A. Barnes. 1977. Physiological identification and analysis of dentate granule cell response to stimulation of the medial and lateral perforant pathways in the rat. *Journal of Comparative Neurology* 175: 439–454.

McNaughton, B. L., and R. G. M. Morris. 1987. Hippocampal synaptic enhancement within a distributed memory system. *Trends in Neurosciences* 10: 408–415.

McNaughton, B. L., C. A. Barnes, and P. Andersen. 1981. Synaptic efficacy and EPSP summation in granule cells of rat fascia dentata studied *in vitro*. *Journal of Neurophysiology* 46: 952–966.

McNaughton, B. L., C. A. Barnes, and J. O'Keefe. 1983. The contributions of position, direction, and velocity to single unit activity in the hippocampus of freely moving rats. *Experimental Brain Research* 52: 41–49.

McNaughton, B. L., C. A. Barnes, G. Rao, J. Baldwin, and M. Rasmussen. 1986. Long-term enhancement of hippocampal synaptic transmission and the acquisition of spatial information. *Journal of Neuroscience* 6: 563–571.

McNaughton, B. L., R. M. Douglas, and G. V. Goddard. 1978. Synaptic enhancement in fascia dentata: Cooperativity among coactive afferents. *Brain Research* 157: 277–293.

McNaughton, B. L., E. J. Green, and S. J. Y. Mizumori. 1986. Representation of body-motion trajectory by rat sensory-motor cortex neurons. *Society for Neuroscience Abstracts* 12: 260.

McNaughton, B. L., J. O'Keefe, and C. A. Barnes. 1983. The stereotrode: A new technique for simultaneous isolation of several single units in the central nervous system from multiple unit records. *Journal of Neuroscience Methods* 8: 391–397.

Miller, J. P., W. Rall, and J. Rinzel. 1985. Synaptic amplification by active membrane in dendritic spines. *Brain Research* 325: 325–320.

Morris, R. G. M., E. Anderson, G. S. Lynch, and M. Baudry. 1986. Selective impairment of learning and blockade of long-term potentiation by an N-methyl-D-aspartate receptor antagonist, AP5. *Nature* 319: 774–776.

Nass, M. M., and L. N. Cooper. 1975. A theory for the development of feature detecting cells in visual cortex. *Biological Cybernetics* 19: 1–18.

Nowak, L., P. Bregestovski, P. Ascher, A. Herbert, and A. Prochlantz. 1984. Magnesium gates glutamate-activated channels in mouse central neurones. *Nature* 307: 462–465.

O'Keefe, J. 1976. Place units in the hippocampus of the freely moving rat. *Experimental Neurology* 51: 78–109.

O'Keefe, J. 1983. Spatial memory within and without the hippocampal system. In *Neurobiology of the Hippocampus*, ed. W. Seifert (New York: Academic).

O'Keefe, J., and E. H. Conway. 1978. Hippocampal place units in the freely moving rat: Why they fire where they fire. *Experimental Brain Research* 31: 573–590.

O'Keefe, J., and J. Dostrovsky. 1971. The hippocampus as a spatial map. Preliminary evidence from unit activity in the freely moving rat. *Brain Research* 34: 171–175.

O'Keefe, J., and L. Nadel. 1978. *The Hippocampus as a Cognitive Map*. Oxford: Clarendon.

Olton, D. S., C. Collison, and M. A. Werz. 1977. Spatial memory and radial arm maze performance in rats. *Learning and Motivation* 8: 289–314.

Racine, R. J., N. W. Milgram, and S. Hafner. 1983. Long-term potentiation phenomena in the rat limbic forebrain. *Brain Research* 260: 217–231.

Rall, W. 1962. Electrophysiology of a dendritic neuron model. *Biophysical Journal* 2: 145–167.

Ranck, J. B., Jr. 1973. Studies on single neurons in dorsal hippocampal formation and septum in unrestrained rats. I. Behavioral correlates and firing repertoires. *Experimental Neurology* 41: 461–535.

Redman, S., and B. Walmsley. Amplitude fluctuations in synaptic potentials evoked in cat spinal motoneurons at identified group Ia synapses. *Journal of Physiology* 343: 135–145.

Robinson, G. B. 1986. Enhanced long-term potentiation induced in rat dentate gyrus by coactivation of septal and entorhinal inputs: Temporal constraints. *Brain Research* 379: 56–62.

Rose, G. M., and T. V. Dunwiddie. 1986. Induction of hippocampal long-term potentiation using physiologically patterned stimulation. *Neuroscience Letters* 69: 244–248.

Rose, G., D. Diamond, and G. Lynch. 1983. Dentate granule cells in the rat hippocampal formation have the behavioral characteristics of theta neurons. *Brain Research* 266: 29–37.

Rumelhart, D. E., J. L. McClelland, and the PDP Research Group. 1986. *Parallel Distributed Processing: Explorations in the Microstructure of Cognition. Volume 1: Foundations.* Cambridge, Mass: MIT Press.

Rumelhart, D. E., and D. Zipser. 1986. Feature discovery by competitive learning. In Rumelhart et al. 1986.

Scharfman, H. E., and J. M. Sarvey. 1985. Postsynaptic firing during repetitive stimulation is required for long-term potentiation in hippocampus. *Brain Research* 331: 267–274.

Smolensky, P. 1986. Information processing in dynamical systems: Foundations of harmony theory. In Rumelhart et al. 1986.

Squire, L. R. 1982. The neuropsychology of human memory. *Annual Review of Neuroscience* 5: 241–273.

Squire, L. R., N. J. Cohen, and L. Nadel. 1984. The medial temporal region and memory consolidation: A new hypothesis. In *Memory Consolidation,* ed. H. Weingartner and E. Parker (Hillsdale, N.J.: Erlbaum).

Steinbuch, K. 1961. Die Lernmatrix. *Kybernetik* 1: 36.

Steward, O. 1976. Topographic organization of the projections from the entorhinal area to the hippocampal formation of the rat. *Journal of Comparative Neurology* 167: 285–314.

Steward, O., and A. A. Scoville. 1976. Cells of origin of entorhinal cortical afferents to the hippocampus and fascia dentata of the rat. *Journal of Comparative Neurology* 169: 347–370.

Struble, R. G., N. L. Desmond, and W. B. Levy. 1978. Anatomical evidence for interlamellar inhibition in the fascia dentata. *Brain Research* 152: 580–585.

Sutton, R. S., and A. G. Barto. 1981. Toward a modern theory of adaptive networks. Expectation and prediction. *Psychological Review* 88: 135–171.

Swanson, L. W., and W. M. Cowan. 1977. An autoradiographic study of the organization of the efferent connections of the hippocampal formation in the rat. *Journal of Comparative Neurology* 172: 49–84.

Swanson, L. W., and W. M. Cowan. 1979. The connections of the septal region in the rat. *Journal of Comparative Neurology* 186: 621–656.

Swanson, L. W., J. M. Wyss, and W. M. Cowan. 1978. An autoradiographic study of the organization of intrahippocampal association pathways in the rat. *Journal of Comparative Neurology* 181: 681–716.

Tulving, E. 1983. *Elements of Episodic Memory.* Oxford: Clarendon Press.

Van Harreveld, A., and E. Fifkova. 1975. Swelling of dendritic spines ion the fascia dentata after stimulation of the perforant fibres as a mechanism of post-tetanic potentiation. *Experimental Neurology* 49: 736–749.

Watkins, J. C., and R. H. Evans. 1981. Excitatory amino acid transmitters. *Annual Review of Pharmacology and Toxicology* 21: 165–204.

West, M. J., and A. H. Andersen. 1980. An allometric study of the area dentata in the rat and mouse. *Brain Research Reviews* 2: 317–348.

Wigstrom, H., and B. Gustafsson. 1983. Facilitated induction of hippocampal long-lasting potentiation during blockade of inhibition. *Nature* 301: 603–604.

Wigstrom, H., B. Gustafsson, Y.-Y. Huang, and W. C. Abraham. 1986. Hippocampal long-term potentiation is induced by pairing single afferent volleys with intracellularly injected depolarizing current pulses. *Acta Physiologica Scandinavica* 126: 317–319.

Wigstrom, H., B. L. McNaughton, and C. A. Barnes. 1982. Long-term enhancement in hippocampus is not regulated by postsynaptic membrane potential. *Brain Research* 233: 195–199.

Willshaw, D. J., and C. von der Malsburg. 1976. How patterned neural connections can be set up by self-organization. *Proceedings of the Royal Society of London* B 194: 431–445.

Wyss, J. M. 1981. An autoradiographic study of the efferent connections of the entorhinal cortex in the rat. *Journal of Comparative Neurology* 199: 495–512.

Zengel, J. E., and K. L. Magleby. 1982. Augmentation and facilitation of transmitter release. *Journal of General Physiology* 80: 583–638.

Zipser, D. 1985. A computational model of hippocampal place fields. *Behavioral Neuroscience* 99: 1006–1018.

Contributors

Michel Baudry   Center for the Neurobiology of Learning and Memory, University of California, Irvine

Valentino Braitenberg   Max-Planck-Institut für biologische Kybernetik, Tübingen

Patricia Smith Churchland   Department of Philosophy, University of California, San Diego

Gerald M. Edelman   Rockefeller University

Jerome A. Feldman   Computer Science Department, University of Rochester

Leif H. Finkel   Rockefeller University

Richard Granger   Center for the Neurobiology of Learning and Memory, University of California, Irvine

John Larson   Center for the Neurobiology of Learning and Memory, University of California, Irvine

Gary Lynch   Center for the Neurobiology of Learning and Memory, University of California, Irvine

B. L. McNaughton   Department of Psychology, University of Colorado, Boulder

John O'Keefe   Department of Anatomy and Developmental Biology, University College London

George N. Reeke, Jr.   Rockefeller University

Terrence J. Sejnowski Biophysics Department, Johns Hopkins University

Roger N. Shepard Stanford University

Paul Smolensky Department of Computer Science and Institute of Cognitive Science, University of Colorado, Boulder

Index